D1028249

## Books by Otto J. Scott

THE CREATIVE ORDEAL: THE STORY OF RAYTHEON (*1974*)

ROBESPIERRE: THE VOICE OF VIRTUE (*1974*)

THE EXCEPTION: THE HISTORY OF ASHLAND OIL (*1968*)

# THE CREATIVE ORDEAL

*This Lexington, Massachusetts, location has been Raytheon's headquarters since 1961.*

OTTO J. SCOTT

# THE CREATIVE ORDEAL

## THE STORY OF RAYTHEON

*New York* ATHENEUM 1974

ILLUSTRATIONS CREDITS: page 5, top and lower right, page 6, top, page 9, center, and page 12, top: Barrett Gallagher for *Fortune* magazine, October, 1946; page 7, top: Waltham (Massachusetts) Historical Society, Inc.; page 7, bottom, Massachusetts Institute of Technology Historical Collection; page 8, bottom, *American Machinist* magazine; page 24, top, reprinted by permission from *Time*, The Weekly Newsmagazine, Copyright Time Inc., 1962; page 32, top, *Business Week*, July 9, 1966.

*'Tis wise to learn; 'tis God-like to create.*

JOHN GODFREY SAXE

# CONTENTS

# ILLUSTRATIONS

# THE CREATIVE ORDEAL

# *Chapter* 1 THE PRESENT

ROUTE 128, tracing a great semicircle around the city of Boston, is known as Electronics Highway. Harvard and MIT are enclosed inside its huge loop; so are sixty other colleges and universities, government research laboratories, and hundreds of technology-based companies.

A visitor driving along Route 128, however, sees mainly trees and open fields. Along the way his peripheral vision catches glimpses of glass-hung, often cantilevered buildings, each set proudly back, isolated from its neighbors, accessible only over private winding roads. The names, vaguely familiar and scientific in tone, flick past.

Route 2, one of Boston's major radial highways, cuts across Route 128 northwest of the city in the historic town of Lexington. At that conjunction stands a sign that reads RAYTHEON COMPANY EXECUTIVE HEADQUARTERS. It is a *noiseless* sign, easy to miss.

The building is plain modern, with not a scrap of ornamentation to mar the abstract simplicity of its lines. Inside, the offices are models of hidden engineering: panels can be moved, added, subtracted. The only relief to the senses is a patio heavy with trees where a fountain, visible from inside windows, plays idly. A sense of cloisters arises: a reminder of the earth and its continuity.

That is not inappropriate, for Raytheon was one of the great seedbeds of the electronics industry. It emerged as a national force during World War II and has remained a great national resource ever since.

A few years back, when Raytheon was smaller than it is today but still loomed large on the landscape, it attracted some special at-

*3*

tention in Europe. Articles were written about Raytheon's size and importance. Somehow the tone of the comments made it seem as though the firm enjoyed possessions and properties inherited from others.

That assumption, though implicit, often underlies assessments not only about Raytheon, but about the sort of international high-technology American firm it represents.

Raytheon is, after all, an important corporation. It is not enormous, but it is big even by American industrial standards. It employs over fifty thousand people. Its sales in 1973 amounted to $1,590 million dollars: nearly $1.6 billion. Its earnings after taxes were $46 million.

Its activities are diverse, but their underlying theme remains technology. In air terminals around the world, its electronic equipment makes reservations, prints tickets and boarding passes for airline passengers; its giant radars track streaming aircraft coast-to-coast, and controllers monitor their positions on electronic displays. In a Los Angeles department store customers consider a Raytheon microwave oven, a stove that cooks by radio waves. In Germany, a new nonpolluting refinery pushes skyward, created by a Raytheon subsidiary.

Around the world other activities take place that reflect Raytheon activities and interests. Men lay underground cables in England, search for oil over the Java Sea using acoustic beams, build nuclear power plants. The NATO radars in West Germany and the Hawk missiles alongside were created by Raytheon; U.S. Army and Air Force phased array radar systems, whose electronic eyes see in all directions simultaneously, are also made by Raytheon.

Such far-flung, diverse activities evoke curiosity. How do private citizens manage to engage in so many activities, collect so many dreams and skills under one roof?

Obviously a description of physical parts and activities alone cannot answer such a question. Corporations, after all, are not pure abstractions, for their members are living human beings. Perhaps the difficulties involved in many corporate descriptions lie in too mechanical an approach. Physicians know, for example, that a single human being is too complex to be described in minute detail—that somehow the details of such descriptions do not add together into a recognizable person.

We describe an individual in terms of his activity in the world and along the lines of his thought, his reactions, and his attitudes. We look at his background, at his formative experiences, at his traumas, his infatuations, his efforts, his errors, and triumphs.

In Pope's time, the proper study of mankind might have been man, as he said. In our time, it is what man can do with other men not as managers—but as associates.

To understand what this means, we will have to look at how this firm started and developed—why it attracted some men for the better part of their lives, and lost others; why it succeeded; where it faltered; and what it means as a living part of society today.

To do that, we shall have to start at its beginning.

# *Chapter 2* ORIGINS

INCANTATIONS are no longer in vogue, but many schools of management flourish, and hundreds of books are written and sold each year, on the almost equally unlikely assumption that business success can be made scientifically inevitable—if only one can devise the right "formula."

If that were true, the American Research and Development Corporation—known more succinctly as AMRAD—could not have failed. After all, its original conception was brilliant. Its founder not only foresaw the spectacular commercial success of radio but persuaded J. P. Morgan the younger to back an entry into this fledgling industry at a time when the House of Morgan stood tall on the landscape.

AMRAD's founder, Harold Power, set about to manufacture and sell radio transmitters and other components, as well as complete sets for amateur radio operators. He was enough of a salesman to create and broadcast programs over station WHIL in Medford Hillside, Massachusetts, to attract attention and customers. He may have been the first to do so, though the claim is generally made by Westinghouse's KDKA.[1]

He was also shrewd enough to employ Dr. Vannevar Bush, of MIT, to head the AMRAD technical and research facilities. Dr. Bush, youthfully energetic, in turn hired a youthful scientist named Dr. Charles G. Smith, who had already made some remarkable explorations into the arcane mysteries of thermionic tubes. Both men plunged into further searches along these promising avenues with considerable zest and were watched with interest by a young mechanic, employed in the lab, named John A. (Al) Spencer.

With research facilities situated on the campus of Tufts College, a promising start, a burgeoning new industry to penetrate and with some of Dr. Bush's bright young graduate students in electrical engineering from nearby MIT to assist in special efforts, AMRAD seemed to have all the proper ingredients for the formula of inevitable success. Yet it not only failed to fly, it dropped like a stone.

The collapse was so complete that Harold Power, the founder, departed from the scene and none of the participants ever again heard from or about him. Mr. Morgan withdrew his attention, some few patents, and his money—and that seemed to be that.

The sequel is equally damaging to the magic-formula theory. The fragments of AMRAD were reassembled. And these bits and pieces, which had failed to work efficiently when first put together, even with the fabled glue of Morgan money, miraculously formed the foundation for not one, but two successful industrial and commercial ventures—the second of which became known as Raytheon.

Furthermore, the major difference that marked the divide between unexpected failure and implausible success was not an abstract element, but a broad-shouldered, beetle-browed young man named Laurence Kennedy Marshall. If he had a formula, it was one so subtle that neither then nor later has anyone been able to define it.


Marshall arrived on the AMRAD scene in the aftermath of the Great War—later known as World War I. He did not come as a stranger. He and Vannevar Bush had been undergraduate roommates at Tufts in 1911. At one point they were the only two students brave enough to take a gruesomely difficult course on theoretical mechanics from Professor William R. Ransom. Later Bush wrote, ". . . I was probably one up on Marshall regarding the mathematics involved. But he was certainly several jumps ahead of me in understanding the kind of world we proposed to enter and challenge." [2]

Whether this assessment, then or later, was accurate is a moot point. It was true Marshall's upbringing had been far less sheltered than Bush's. The elder Marshall had managed a butcher store in the city, and Laurence himself had started to work when he was twelve, tending a stall in the heart of Boston's busy Central Market. That sort of early experience tends to develop at least the appearance of confidence. But to move from that start to the stage of borrowing money to enter Tufts, a school attended mainly by the sons of the well-to-do, required considerable inner drive. It was natural enough, then, that Marshall should impress his college roommate as being unusually sophisticated. But Marshall also had a remarkable intellectual inclination—otherwise he would not have entered, let alone survived, Professor Ransom's esoteric course. And for all that Bush was the son of a minister and had developed the social graces that such an upbringing in that period entailed, he had also, despite a notable academic flair, a shrewd and worldly core. The roommates, therefore, shared a number of attributes and, as time proved, were equally possessed by driving ambition.

After they graduated from Tufts in 1911, their paths diverged. Bush, born for the academic life, continued his studies at MIT, garnering high marks, the approval of his teachers, and the respect of his peers. It was an indication of his glittering abilities and diplomatic personality that he was able to move straight from his doctorate to the faculty of MIT, a school of the first rank among those dedicated to the physical sciences, without a ripple of interruption.

Marshall's path was stonier. He discovered that even his hard-won B.S. degree was not enough: it took the recommendation of his mathematics teacher, Professor George W. Swaine, to land him a job at General Electric paying $16 a week. Later he left to work as an engineer for the famous contractor and tunnel builder Pat McGovern and was assigned to the East River tunnel project in New York. This represented both opportunity and danger.

"We worked under fifty pounds per square inch of atmospheric pressure," he said later, "and were supposed to ascend slowly, at the rate of one pound per minute. But I couldn't afford to tarry. I went up and down more quickly than that." [3]

As a result he endured the excruciating pains of the bends [4] a number of times. But he became night superintendent on the monster project and by the time it was ended was a valued and experienced civil engineer. It was not a profession for which he had been trained. "My major was *physics*," he said. "Engineering was the application of these principles."

From 1913 until 1917 Marshall worked for McGovern, constructing bridges and buildings ranging up and down New England. These tasks were not, at that time, systematized to the point of boredom. On the contrary, every large construction effort then took a toll of human lives from among the workers—a cost that was shrugged away as insignificant by both builders and the public. These projects hardened Marshall, but they also taught him much about dealing with other men. He learned how to drive men cheerfully, how to lift their spirits, how to organize and to enter into the resolution of their problems.

In Rhode Island at the outbreak of war, Marshall enlisted as a second lieutenant of artillery and was sent to France. His fellow officers were mainly from Providence and its environs; his major was William Gammell, Jr., a scion of a noted Rhode Island textile family.

Bush, on the other hand, was part of the nation's World War I scientific effort, and worked on the development of anti-submarine devices. It was not satisfying work; scientists in the First World War were considered so many oddballs. The service chiefs and their subordinates tended to wrap everyone in khaki and forget them. That was one of the reasons World War I took such a frightful toll of lives. But though this toll was fearsomely higher than ever before, it was only part of the immeasurable cost of the conflict. Not since the fall of Rome had a dominant civilization suffered such injuries. But unlike in Rome, these injuries had not taken place slowly over centuries, but had erupted with the sudden force of an earthquake.

Whole empires collapsed and dynasties vanished. A swarm of smaller nations were exhumed from the dustbins of history by the Treaty of Versailles and—unique in the annals of the West—all the nations of Europe were losers. Only the Japanese in Asia and the unspeakable Bolsheviks in Euro-Asia could be said to have improved their lot. Everywhere else that men looked, in the disordered and disheveled aftermath, they saw wrecks and wanderers.

At such a time Marshall and Bush seemed unscathed, but that was an illusion. It was true that Marshall successfully emerged from the dangers of France. It was also true that Bush seemed safely ensconced on the faculty of MIT. But an unemployed civil engineer in his thirtieth year with only modest savings of his own was not a figure to attract envy in 1920, and the situation of a college professor was not much better. A fierce wartime inflation had coursed through the United States and burned away a large part of the prewar middle class. Persons on fixed salaries, pensions, and incomes from mortgages and rents—schoolteachers, professors, civil servants, white collar workers—suddenly lost substance and status.

These "new poor," as Mark Sullivan called them,[5] were balanced by a "new rich" [6] consisting of speculators in the stock and commodity exchanges, industrialists, dealers and salesmen expanding new broad-scale businesses such as automotives, appliances, advertising, insurance, entertainment.

These economic changes had sweeping social consequences, exacerbated by the newly legislated Prohibition amendment and the secret tides of the real revolution, whose new world leaders loomed in the Kremlin. In the United States the revolution was subtle and silent, though 1919 saw many bombings and demonstrations. It was, of course, not complete, not all of a piece, but highly mixed. But it was sweeping enough to erase many long-standing social restraints and to warp the traditional American pattern. On one end it pushed an entire class beneath the surface and brushed away whole congeries of manners and attitudes, modes of leisure, culture and judgment, and on the other it brought forward groups conspicuous for their cynicism and for a mindless, hectic life style. At the very moment it attracted the attention of the rest of the world, the tone of the United States altered and became loud, brassy, and vulgar.

Not only did the nation seem cheapened but its leadership lost intellectual vigor. Democrats who had led the nation into an idealistic war began talking like pacifists and promised new miracles of peace from the League of Nations. Republicans who had once been clear regarding a strong, empire-building America turned into isolationists and rashly promised a nostalgic and resentful nation that they would lead it on an impossible journey to the prewar past. Neither position was reasoned or reasonable; both parties descended to emotional appeals and arguments tainted by ideology. The clamor they raised distracted the nation. Industry had overbuilt during the war, farmers were overmortgaged, and social unrest prevailed. Yet these issues were not examined. The lessons of the recent war were neither reviewed nor clarified. The future course of the country was left obscured in clouds of election-year rhetoric.

In such a time, a time of disorder and disgust, Americans turned away from the problems of mankind: they had too many new troubles of their own. Pressed by circumstances, disillusioned regarding the outcome of the war, Americans turned to their individual situations.

That was the climate when Laurence Marshall returned to Boston and sat down to review possibilities with Vannevar Bush. It is no wonder they quickly agreed to combine forces. Since each was a brilliant and ambitious man, it is no wonder they were able to improve their individual situations. But it is a matter of lasting wonder that in the course of these efforts they constructed a vehicle that not only improved the situation of thousands of other men directly, but that improved the nation and, indirectly, the world.

When Dr. Vannevar Bush and Laurence Marshall sat down to talk in 1920, the conversation centered around the fortunes of AMRAD. Dr. Bush told Marshall that AMRAD had many excellent ingredients and people, but that its business did not seem to prosper. He was worried about it. Marshall nodded understandingly and pulled his chair closer, encouraging further confidences.

Dr. Bush explained that he was not close to Power as far as the finances and operations of sales were concerned, but it seemed to him the founder was floundering. Marshall nodded, and said, "Go on."

Finally Bush discussed the research efforts of the lab and dwelled, with some enthusiasm, on the developments he and Dr. C. G. Smith were making in the creation of a new thermionic tube. Marshall nodded but did not seem greatly impressed. Then, almost as an afterthought, Bush explained a gadget, created by the young mechanic Al Spencer, that had recently been shown to him. Marshall took it, his heavy eyebrows coming closer, and looked at it. To the eye, it was simply a metal disc that Spencer had dotted with a hammer; but it would, because it was thermostatic,[7] snap at a certain temperature.

The two men went into the kitchen and put the disc near the stove. Sure enough, when it was sufficiently heated, it snapped and sprang into the air. The men laughed, and Marshall grew interested. He was even more interested when Bush, satisfied with his reaction, told him that this was information he himself valued. Dr. Bush, who could cover his hole card as well as an expert poker player, had already determined that Spencer's thermostatic disc of metal, which could be snapped "like the bottom of an oilcan"—but which would snap at a temperature change as well—was potentially important. Bush was so convinced of its potential that he had already questioned young Spencer very closely as to whether he had developed this thermostatic metal disc on his own time, working alone, or whether it had emerged from observations or the use of the AMRAD facilities at AMRAD's expense.

Spencer assured him he had developed it all alone, on his own time, in the basement of his home. The genesis was not recent, he explained. While tending a furnace in a clothing mill in northern Maine when he was fifteen, Al Spencer had watched the rounded "clean-out" door alter from convex to concave as the heat of the roaring fire within soared and sank. It was an everyday observation, because thermostatic metals, which consisted of two different types, were often rolled into single sheets that would yield to different temperature changes instead of cracking as might a single metal.

Spencer, however, had taken this everyday observation and industrial fact of life one step further. He had produced a "dished" bimetallic sheet that would click when the temperature changed. Young Spencer had produced, Bush said later, "a really striking invention. The basis for an . . . inexpensive electrical switch." [8]

To the disgust of fanatics and the despair of those obsessed by logic, the world moves in a most indirect way. Young Spencer had never been to school: he was self-taught, self-trained—and self-reliant. His father had been killed in a lumber mill accident when Al was only three years old; he had been raised by relatives and had started work in a lumber camp as soon as he "could see over the top of a stove." [9] The measurement was recalled from childhood; the event was part of a harsh upbringing.

"He was one of the most resourceful and ingenious men I ever knew," said Dr. Bush. "He had a sense of humor that Will Rogers would have cherished." [10]

Spencer's "thermostat," as it was called, placed in other hands, might have had a far different history. It was one of the luckier details of Al Spencer's life that Dr. Bush was, inherently, an educator. Though he was working extra hours at AMRAD and was forced into the considerations of business by the times, he was mainly there as a creature of circumstances: because the real wages of a professor in 1920 were insufficient. Basically he was still a professor, though one who took readily to business.

Dr. Bush was not under many illusions regarding inventions. "They're a dime a dozen," he said. "Any reasonably bright chap can make a patentable invention if he puts his mind to it, and . . . if he attempts to patent all of them, he can go broke." [11] Bush had learned this lesson the hard way. In 1912 he had patented an invention that was practical, even important—and lost his money. The experience convinced him that "an invention is valueless unless it is joined with a number of other accomplishments—promotion, financing, development, engineering, marketing, and so on." [12]

That was why Dr. Bush showed Al Spencer's thermostat to Laurence Marshall. The device could be important: a professor of electrical engineering could determine that. But someone more closely attuned to the world of business would have to take it in hand and develop its potential. Bush, who was early convinced of Laurence Marshall's ability to move about in the world, had no better man to approach at that moment. And in that coincidence he was, in his life, as lucky as Al Spencer.

After the war, the demobilized Major William Gammell, Jr., returned to Providence and the management of his family's old, well-established business, the Lonsdale Textile Company. One day in 1920 he received a visit from one of his former officers, ex-Lieutenant Laurence K. Marshall.

"I remembered him, of course," Gammell said later. "I recalled the lieutenant as one of the officers in my battalion, and that he was very bright. But I was surprised to have him call because we had not been close." [13]

Marshall sat down and discussed the Spencer thermostat, and Gammell listened intently. As he listened, Gammell's regard warmed. The common experience of war discloses men better than any other. Under such pressures, both light and dark qualities shine unmistakably; Marshall had been a good officer and a reliable comrade.

Furthermore, Marshall had matured into an unusually impressive man. Though he was not tall, he radiated an athletic presence. His face was clear, his eyes keen, and his eyebrows formidable. He spoke very sensibly about the commercial possibilities of the thermostat, and the substance of his remarks would have attracted the attention of any highly placed businessman. Though the condition of the economy was mixed, the atmosphere of new ventures—especially stock companies—was, thanks to a bull stock market, unusually good. Furthermore, a device that could be used in the booming electrical appliance industry was fashionably intriguing.

"He was a good salesman," Gammell said, and added, with a touch of characteristic self-deprecation, "and I am weak."

Mr. Gammell was not weak, but he was popular, well placed, and singularly free of affectation. His background had been a secure and happy one, and he had no complexes. He was known affectionately as Billy Gammell, and was highly respected.

That call was not the first that Marshall had made in his search for financial backing. He had, prior to going to Providence, made a number of trips to New York City. On one of these, Herbert Marshall (no relative but an old acquaintance), who operated a restaurant in Boston, sat down in the coach beside him.

"I'm sinking all my money in a new venture," Laurence Marshall said. "If you want to get in on it, you can—for five thousand dollars." [14]

The restaurant owner was tempted but held firm. "I happen to have exactly that much extra money," he said, "but I have promised to lend it to my brother-in-law." Years later he recalled the conversation with retrospective regret and added, "My brother-in-law never repaid me."

That sort of response had created many problems for Marshall and Bush. At one point, with rumors going about that Al Spencer had invented something valuable, the young mechanic was approached by some men who wanted to buy his device. Bush, apprised, was alarmed. He urged Spencer not to sell, and said he would guarantee twice whatever was offered—an indication of his belief both in the gadget and in Laurence Marshall, since he could not have produced the money if Spencer had disbelieved him.

But Laurence Marshall, talking to Billy Gammell, gave no hint of these background difficulties. He talked, he radiated confidence—and Gammell believed.


Billy Gammell talked to his friends and later introduced them to Laurence Marshall and Vannevar Bush. A group was formed whose members included some of the best-placed young men in New England. One was Richard S. Aldrich, whose sister married John D. Rockefeller, Jr. Each agreed, after discussions with Marshall, Bush, and Gammell, to become a founding shareholder in the Spencer Thermostat Company.

In 1921, therefore, Al Spencer was lifted from the post of mechanic in the AMRAD laboratories and obscurity to the status of an important stockholder and senior staff member of an enterprise bearing his name, created to market his invention. That was a long way from the Maine woods, the lumber camps, and the bleak period when he had tended a mill furnace.

But all this took time. While these discussions, negotiations, and plans were moving forward, Dr. Bush remained at his post as a consultant to AMRAD. He worked very closely with young Dr. C. G. Smith, whose efforts in developing a new radio tube had grown more than promising.

It would have been hard to find anyone who more closely fit the classic pattern of a scientist than young Dr. C. G. Smith. Quiet, modest, unassuming, he found his work absorbing and completely satisfying. After receiving his B.A. from the University of Texas, he had enrolled at Harvard Graduate School and studied mathematics and physics. Professor Theodore Lyman, one of his teachers, put graduate student Smith to work on a special project designed either to prove or disprove a significant element in the quantum theory of Niels Bohr. That theory, new at the time, was the subject of intense debate among the world physicists, and the inspiration for many such experiments.

Years later Dr. Smith wrote a brief paper he called "The Prehistory of Raytheon." [15] It began with an explanation of the project to which he had been assigned by Professor Lyman, and it is remarkable for the tinge of poetry and emotion it reveals.

"Near the southern horizon," he wrote, "shines the very hot Wolf-Rayet star Zeta Puppis, emitting the bright lines in the spectrum of helium." Originally, he explained, these lines were attributed to the hydrogen atom by the Harvard astronomer E. C. Pickering, who assumed, on the basis of the prevailing mathematical theories of his time, that he was analyzing hydrogen in a state not attainable on earth. His assumptions were accepted, and the lines, or rays, in question became known as the Pickering Series.

But earthbound researchers, attempting to reproduce the lines, used hydrogen and failed. Later, when Bohr introduced his quantum theory, his calculations were applied to the mystery of Zeta Puppis and indicated that the lines represented ionized helium, which has one electron that revolves around the nucleus very "suggestive"—in Smith's word—of hydrogen.

Professor Lyman was very keen to test this matter. It could, as Smith said, "complicate the issue," at a time when Bohr's theory was new.

The professor obtained some pure helium, which was then very expensive, costing $1,500 a cubic foot, and put young Smith to work. He succeeded in producing the spectrum of ionized helium in an electrodeless discharge. "The ring . . . was produced," he wrote. "The Pickering Series was strong . . . and the ultraviolet lines predicted by Bohr were there . . ."

These experiments could have lifted Smith scientifically, and both he and Professor Lyman were understandably elated. But by one of those coincidences that crop up so often in science that they are, by now, taken quite for granted, another researcher—Anderson, in England—independently made the same series of tests, came to the same conclusion, and published his findings first.

Nevertheless Smith had learned some facts about helium that were, as yet, not widely realized. Even after they have been published, abstract facts can remain abstract for years. But experience in working with such facts is personal and can be influencing. In a way, his experiments and observations under Professor Lyman had been the equivalent, for C. G. Smith, of Al Spencer's furnace door.

He had learned, for example, that pure helium "provided a long electron-free path." That detail, of only academic importance in the Harvard laboratories, was of crucial importance in researching for a better radio tube. Dr. Smith had also learned that helium could be purified with relative ease under laboratory conditions, and that the "sputtering" qualities of ionized helium were mild.

Dr. Bush, who joined Smith in his efforts, made an important contribution by suggesting that coating the inside of the tube with the oxides of barium and strontium could help to keep the helium from escaping. His approach, always, was that of a teacher: interested to the point of suggesting improvements. In that he was, as Edward L. Bowles, then a graduate student putting in some time at the AMRAD labs, said, "Superlative. Bush could always improve."

The completed tube employed the short-path principle, based—as Smith was careful to say—on physics developed by Hittorf some forty years earlier. Later there was so much discussion about this short path that most assumed the S tube, named in reality after Smith, was really named after the short path. Smith had that sort of luck.

The development made only a minor stir. Smith and Bush collaborated on a paper they presented to the Boston Section of the Institute of Radio Engineers that was later printed in the official journal.[16] They submitted another, somewhat more intellectual paper to a more august group—the American Institute of Electrical Engineers—and had the satisfaction of being included among those allowed to present a paper to the annual convention in Niagara Falls, with subsequent publication.[17] These are important recognitions in scientific circles, and no doubt provided C. G. Smith with pleasure.

But Power, the head of AMRAD, was confronted with increased business problems and it is unlikely that he interpreted the scientific kudos that Smith and Bush were collecting as any great help to him in his troubles. Vannevar Bush might have pressed the point, but he did not. He was planning to leave as soon as the Spencer Thermostat Company became tangible enough to provide him another equally valuable consultancy.

That came about shortly after the S tube was born and scientifically introduced. As a result, Bush left AMRAD, taking young Al Spencer with him to higher reaches. C. G. Smith and his S tube were among the people and the properties left behind.

The twenties are often reviewed in a nostalgic glow, as having been a period of parties, speculation, and spending. But 1921 was not a good year in the history of the nation. All through 1920 a depression had been spreading beneath the deceptive facade of inflation. The Federal Reserve Board, which had been granted sweeping powers before the war, sat inert while catastrophe loomed. When it finally moved, it moved too far and too fast by hiking interest rates an abrupt 1½ percent.[18]

By 1920 a slide started that picked up speed in the latter half of the year; by 1921 the slide turned into an avalanche. By mid-year five million people were tramping the streets looking for work—a huge number in a nation whose total population was only 105 million—and a half-million farmers were thrown off their land because they could not pay their mortgages. Prices plummeted on the stock exchanges, and the panic was on.

Ordinarily it would be difficult to conceive of a worse year in which to launch a new business. But depressions can be compared to sea storms, if one inverts the analogy. For the most part storms at sea are caused by gales and typhoons that disturb the surface, but leave the depths relatively unscathed. A depression, if it is brief enough, blows with hurricane force through the bottom reaches of society but leaves the top fairly calm. The backers of Spencer Thermostat, who were not putting large sums into the venture, were not greatly affected.

Furthermore Laurence Marshall put his talents to work on Spencer's device. He could see the importance of it. It was a time when the electrical industries had moved from principle to application. Beginning in the late nineteenth century with Edison's electric light, this industry had worked a series of transformations beginning first with the larger needs of the community for light and power, and then moving into industry to animate machinery and to end the age of steam.

In the early decades of this century, the electrical industry was simultaneously extending power lines across the landscape and bringing telephones to every hamlet and home possible, furnishing power for visual signs and displays that appeared in a profusion never before seen—creating, for example, the Great White Way in New York—and in developing a host of devices for the individual. In 1921 the American home was still largely the scene of female drudgery. Ironing was done with flatirons that had to be heated, and it was customary to use several of these heavy instruments in the course of a single effort, heating and rotating them in order to keep ironing. Washing was still done by hand in washtubs, ice was delivered on the shoulders of the iceman, rugs were swept and beaten by hand, floors were scrubbed by individuals on their knees.

Since the electrical industry had grown in the classic pattern of thousands of small entrepreneurs launching piecemeal efforts, it still comprised a crazy quilt of systems. In one neighborhood there was alternating current, and in another the older direct current. Sizes of electrical parts varied beyond reason; power tools were still known only in industry; standardization had not yet really started.

Direct current would burn the Spencer thermostat, as Bush and Marshall discovered when they carelessly plugged a demonstration model into the wrong socket in a New York hotel. As a result they had to cancel an important demonstration.[19]

*18*

Marshall typically decided the thermostat would have to be improved immediately. The average entrepreneur—even one with a technical background—would have demanded that Al Spencer and Vannevar Bush get busy on that project. But Marshall undertook to solve it himself.

He was, after all, an entrepreneur by accident. In reality he was a free intellectual, capable of arriving at solutions of startling originality in almost any area he surveyed. Only Bush, who believed that "any bright chap can invent," thought of Marshall as a businessman. Billy Gammell and his friends, who were businessmen, regarded Marshall and Bush alike as some sort of geniuses.

Marshall's efforts, at any rate, were impressive. Bush, who examined them with interest, explained that Marshall ". . . used two metals which had widely different expansion coefficients." [20] In ordinary language, that meant Marshall had created a thermostat, or switch, that would keep an electric iron from burning out whether used on direct or alternating current. The value of this improvement is hard to exaggerate. It made Al Spencer's original invention infinitely more practical, usable, and commercially viable. It is typical of Marshall, moreover, that he did not call any great attention to his own hand in this accomplishment: the thermostat remained accredited, both initially and in all its future and innumerable extensions and applications, as the brainchild of Al Spencer.

Nevertheless the improvement elevated a possibly commercial item in limited areas to a product with a dazzling future. Billy Gammell and his friends—who had by now become friends of Marshall and Bush—had patiently increased their investments in Spencer Thermostat as these efforts had proceeded. "We had expected to do that," Billy Gammell said. "Men almost always need more money to start a business than they originally plan."

The Marshall improvements led to a more serious tone in the negotiations with appliance—particularly flatiron—manufacturers. The men in Providence were cheered and began to believe that they had picked a winner.


There was less satisfaction in the offices of J. P. Morgan regarding the prospects of AMRAD. Hearing rumors about Spencer Thermostat and its prime movers, Morgan sent an investigator, according to Marshall,[21] to evaluate the situation. He reported back that AMRAD had lost not only the services of Vannevar Bush, but even those of a bright young man who had made an important invention. The loss of this opportunity seemed evidence enough that AMRAD was not alert, and Mr. Morgan, by withdrawing his support, in effect closed it down. Power vanished, the AMRAD facilities were dismantled, and its remaining assets removed to New York. These included, of course, C. G. Smith's patent on the S tube—and that was that.


By early 1922 the depression of 1921, one of the fiercest and briefest in the history of the nation, mysteriously lifted. The reasons for the recovery remain largely unknown. Certainly the government did nothing memorable to assist this turn of fortune. But industrial momentum was recovered, unemployment was reduced, and a wave of business confidence rolled across the land.

This did not mean all was well: many deeply disturbing underlying problems remained unresolved. The diminution in the number of independent farmers swelled the dispossessed populations of the cities and reduced the influence and number of voters in the farm belts. Prohibition ushered in a wave of lawlessness. Gangsters—a new phenomenon—appeared and even achieved a quasi-respectability. The guerrilla war against traditional attitudes and groups in the country conducted in some sectors of publishing, the press, the arts, and theater mounted. But the economic situation of the average citizen improved.

Internationally the United States returned to the stage as the world's strongest economic power concerned with establishing peace. A great disarmament conference held in 1921 resulted in an agreement to restrict the naval power of the United States and Britain to parity with one another and held Japan to an agreement not to build beyond third place. The rhetoric accompanying this accomplishment was lofty. President Harding's popularity soared to an all-time high, and a potential threat in the Pacific appeared resolved by a move of high statesmanship.

In Germany the Weimar Republic, established in part to meet American standards of democracy, announced emergency rule in order to overcome various dissident groups. In Italy the monarchy and the economy were alike threatened by collisions between Communist and newly organized Fascist groups. The name Mussolini began to appear in the world's newspapers with regularity.

Inside the United States, where people were still largely indifferent to world events, the recovery from the brief but bitter depression was, generally, credited to the Federal Reserve System. Nobody has ever traced the origins of this curious belief, which had little basis in fact. Nevertheless a myth arose to the effect that the Federal Reserve System had finally solved the historic ups and downs of the business cycle. One result was that all sorts of men began to dream of launching new enterprises. The examples of Henry Ford, Harvey Firestone, Thomas A. Edison, and others of the "better mousetrap" variety began to take on heroic proportions.

Among the many attracted by these popular examples was Dr. C. G. Smith, who had toiled so diligently in the AMRAD laboratory. He had once gone into business for himself and failed. But though he had a wife and children, and was in circumstances that were, in the polite word, "modest," he continued to invent, to hope, and to plan.

Finally he turned to Laurence Marshall—a figure almost visibly clothed in an aura of invincibility. Smith made what, for him, was a pitch.

Since the results later proved that this conversation was one of the turning points of his life, his own words—written years later for the benefit of a younger generation at Raytheon—seem impossible to improve. Curiously, in his recollections he wrote about himself in the third person.

"Early on a fine morning in May, 1922," he wrote,[22] "Laurence K. Marshall and C. G. Smith were walking up a hill at Tufts College in Medford. Smith said to Marshall that he had just invented a refrigerator for the home. It had no moving parts and would be a Ford among refrigerators. Marshall replied *that we would have to do something about that.*" (Italics added.)

Naturally enough Marshall wanted to see this marvel immediately, but it was not in existence. Smith explained that he had worked it out on paper. Marshall then insisted that the refrigerator should be built, and built immediately. Smith found himself lifted, as though by a hurricane, and hurled into an effort that disrupted his life, and his household, for weeks to come.

Marshall was busy during the day on matters related to the Spencer Thermostat Company, and Smith—who had a living to make—was also occupied. But they were together each evening, and together they built Smith's refrigerator.

Mrs. Smith and the children "were pushed to another part of the house." Smith's bedroom was turned into a workshop and laboratory. Smith recalled that "there was a Cenco oil pump, a mercury diffusion pump and other laboratory equipment crowded into an unusually small bedroom along with the household furniture." He made no mention, in his later recollections, of Mrs. Smith's reaction. It can only be assumed she was resigned to such enthusiasms since she had married an inventor.

While these moonlight efforts were underway, the tireless Marshall completed his thermostat negotiations with Westinghouse.

The conclusion was spectacular, in a public sense. Westinghouse agreed to manufacture the thermostats as part of a new line of electric irons, and to pay Spencer a royalty. On the signing of the agreement, the Westinghouse publicity and advertising groups went into high gear, and issued releases about the new "Million Dollar Thermostat."

By any yardstick it was one of the most successful publicity campaigns ever launched. Newspapers all over the land pounced upon the story: it was exactly the sort of better-mousetrap, Horatio Alger type of tale they then doted upon.

Vannevar Bush was annoyed by the tone of the publicity. In his autobiography, written years later, he was still grumpy. "They had not paid us anything at the time," he pointed out, "before they got through they paid a great deal more than a million dollars . . ." [23]

But despite Bush's scorn of newspaper embellishments and exaggerations, the Million Dollar Thermostat became an instant part of the American myth. Not only was it printed and described everywhere, but it became a sort of hardy perennial, used to illustrate discussions of instant riches based on simple ideas.

The overall effect undoubtedly enhanced Spencer Thermostat in a more than immediate sense, since it made the nation aware of the device and, in the long run, increased its use in other appliances. At the time it put the firm on a sound footing and endowed Laurence K. Marshall with an aura of success.

"It was a great victory," said Billy Gammell with satisfaction. His judgment had been vindicated and he and his friends were in a position to profit from the risk they had taken.

But high-level negotiations, royalties, wealthy men in other parts, and attention in the newspapers were all matters remote from the efforts of C. G. Smith in his cluttered bedroom. "One night," Smith wrote later, "the device was finished and was shown to operate as expected. Marshall phoned for a Taxi and rushed away." Then he added reflectively, "Up to this point Marshall had spent $720." [24]

To Smith's astonishment, his new partner returned in a few days and announced he had raised $25,000 to go into the refrigerator business.

This sort of speed made Smith dizzy. He had been at home in every sense while thrashing with the stubborn, recalcitrant, and complex details of creating a new refrigerator model—but business was another matter.

"Previous to the association with L. K. Marshall," he wrote, "C. G. Smith and Joseph Slepian had initiated a business and failed after a tremendous struggle." [25] Burned by this experience, he reacted to Marshall's business plans like a man confronted with a sudden fire. Pressed, he did not merely want to see his refrigerator capitalized; he wanted some security for himself and his family during the early pioneering period. He also wanted assurance that somehow his share, his rights of ownership, would not be siphoned away by the machinations of businessmen.

Marshall nodded understandingly.

By the time C. G. Smith met with Marshall, Billy Gammell, Richard S. Aldrich, Vannevar Bush, and others in the Suffolk Building at Kendall Square, Cambridge, on the morning of July 7, 1922,[26] his qualms had been settled and he was proudly aware that he was part of a better organized venture than any he had previously known.

It was incorporated as the American Appliance Company according to the laws of Massachusetts. The original incorporators, for the record, were Aldrich, Gammell, and Bush. Capitalization was for ten thousand shares of common stock at no par value, and a charter was drawn to allow the firm to "engage in the manufacture and design, production and sale of machinery, motors and their components," and to raise money for this purpose.

A five-man board of directors was established, whose members were Aldrich, Gammell, Marshall, C. G. Smith and Vannevar Bush. Laurence K. Marshall signed the original charter and bylaws as Temporary Clerk. His signature was a marvel. It was immense, spectacular and extended over a space of several lines. It would not have taken a trained handwriting analyst to have seen, on this document, the most soaring spirit.

Beneath the intricacies of the legal minuet the venture was formed, quite simply, around the prospects of C. G. Smith's refrigerator. The inventor turned over "certain refrigeration and artificial cooling patents" to the firm and received 9,450 shares of stock. He then returned 9,000 of these shares to the company and received an employment contract at $5,000 a year for five years. That was good money then.

He also had the security of a special understanding with the company which ensured that he and Laurence Marshall would each receive one free share of stock for every five sold. That meant that the founders would continue to have a substantial percentage of the firm no matter how large it grew.

The backers, who were essentially the same men who financed the Spencer Thermostat Company, put up varying sums. Aldrich, Gammell, John S. Ames, and R. H. I. Goddard each paid $5,000 for one hundred shares initially. Bush paid $2,500 for fifty shares and also received an employment contract, though only for one year as a consulting engineer, at $2,500. Evan Kennedy paid $2,500 for fifty shares, Charles H. Caskell paid $1,250 for twenty-five shares, and so did R. H. Swarz.

C. G. Smith, the mild and modest center upon which all this activity revolved, was the subject of some conversation. Now that his life had become a matter of value to them all, someone suggested it would probably be sensible for the new company to insure his life for—say —$100,000. Then if anything untoward happened to him, they would not lose their money.

Somewhat stiffly, Smith replied, "I don't know you men very well. I think we'd better reduce the sum." [27]

There was a roar of laughter, and someone—probably Billy Gammell—quickly suggested $50,000. Smith nodded.

Afterward Smith, writing the account, took the hypothetical value of the stock as actual, and said the firm had been "founded for one million dollars." He had not, it seems, really grasped the business details of the venture.

In fact Marshall had persuaded the others—Billy Gammell and nine of his friends—each to put up $10,000 cash, and had split his own third of the overall venture with C. G. Smith. The money was not all forthcoming in advance: American Appliance started with approximately $25,000 in its treasury and the pledges were called upon as time and circumstances directed. But the structure of the venture was soundly crafted, and its backers were men of substance, experience, and caution. They proved that when they elected Aldrich president, and Billy Gammell vice president.

On another level, Marshall could be said to have gathered, though more by accident than design, almost all the elements that had once made up AMRAD. In the second venture drawn from these elements he was aiming again in a new direction. As yet neither he nor Smith, nor for that matter Vannevar Bush, realized that they had overlooked a key element that would, eventually, unlock far more opportunities than those they had, as yet, sighted.

In July 1922, a few weeks after the incorporation ceremonies, Marshall led C. G. Smith to a vacant third floor of the Suffolk Engraving Co. building on Kendall Square, Cambridge. The leader was carrying a string and a piece of chalk, and the two men marked off the space for a wall enclosing the new laboratory of the American Appliance Company. The Smith bedroom would, finally, be restored to sanity.

Then, Smith wrote, ". . . the two characters then engaged in a game or so of tennis won by L. K. Marshall. They returned to the third floor and enjoyed a shower administered by dashing a bucket of water over the opponent." [28]

They were in business.

During the balance of 1922 and into 1923 the world continued its disorderly pattern. In Italy, Mussolini led a march on Rome, was handed the government, and announced the dissolution of all political parties except his own. In Turkey Kemal Pasha announced a republic. The Irish won their independence and hailed the creation of the Irish Free State. England set up a puppet kingdom in Egypt; the Dempsey-Firpo fight took place in the United States and was a sensation.

Toward the end of 1922 a routine senatorial inquiry led, unexpectedly, to the gradual disclosure of a series of illegal acts surrounding the lease of the Teapot Dome national oil reserve to oil tycoon Harry Sinclair. This scandal swelled during 1923 and began to engulf many of the close associates of President Warren G. Harding. In August, before the public was aware of the mess, President Harding suddenly died from what was at first described as ptomaine poisoning. Later an autopsy established the cause of death as apoplexy.[29] Calvin Coolidge, a man whose face was so dour it approached the dismal, was sworn into office.

This unexpected change engrossed Americans. Events elsewhere seemed far less interesting and important, though in Munich a rebellion had been mounted with the assistance of the former German wartime leader, General Ludendorff. It had, at any rate, failed; and its purported leader, Adolf Hitler, had landed in Landsberg castle-prison.

Industrial and entertainment changes seemed far more immediate and important. More automobiles were made during the year than had been made in the previous fifteen years put together; more than fifteen million cars were registered. Colonel Jacob Schiff received a patent for an electric shaver, and in New York Dr. Lee De Forest produced and showed the first sound movie.[30]

These and many other interesting novelties emerged. One that did not emerge, however, was the American Appliance Company's new refrigerator. It had worked as a pilot model, but its delicate balance proved difficult to maintain in a larger size, though C. G. Smith toiled in tireless fashion.

The backers of American Appliance were reasonable men, accustomed to the delays attendant upon launching a new enterprise, and there is no record that they added to the difficulties of C. G. Smith and Laurence Marshall in any way during 1923. They produced their pledges when called upon.

But by the time the firm's second Annual Meeting took place in January 1924, some subtle shifts occurred. John S. Ames, an original investor, withdrew, and Billy Gammell—whose faith was firm—bought his shares. As if to balance the scales, T. Jefferson Coolidge III, another bearer of a famous New England family name, appeared, invested, and was elected a vice president.[31] W. R. Callender, another new investor, also appeared.

Nevertheless the firm was in an awkward posture. C. G. Smith was still confident that the refrigerator could be perfected, but it is not surprising that some changes were made in the agreement that he and Laurence Marshall had originally made with their backers. Later in the year Richard S. Aldrich—a man with many important interests —withdrew from the presidency and that post was assumed by Billy Gammell.

As the months passed, it was clear that they were nearing a critical decision. Marshall, who had begun to develop some qualms, announced he would take a swing around the country to investigate the market. Later, his admirers claimed that the tour convinced him that the time for home refrigerators had not yet dawned, that the American household was still wedded to the iceman—but that seems highly unlikely.

Marshall might have plunged ahead too rapidly, but events have proven that his basic assumptions were uncannily accurate. When domestic refrigerators were mass marketed, they proved immensely successful. But it is clear that he had entered into the adventure hastily from an engineering, development, design, and manufacturing point of view, and that his assumption that he could successfully compete against such giants as Westinghouse, General Electric, and others was really, as Vannevar Bush would say, "nervy."

When Marshall returned three months later, the situation had not improved. Smith was still struggling, and Marshall himself began to lose patience. "We would have to grow hair on metal to make this work," he growled.[32]

Later he discussed the general situation with Vannevar Bush. After passing from the subject of the refrigerator, the conversation turned to observations Marshall had made on his trip. He mentioned that everyone seemed very keen on radio, an instrument that President Coolidge had used to address Congress earlier in the year, and that sports fans, among others, prized highly.

Bush recalled that he and C. G. Smith, when they had toiled at AMRAD, had developed a significant tube, and Marshall came to attention.

❈     ❈     ❈

Late in 1924 Marshall entered the offices of J. P. Morgan at 23 Wall Street to meet a gentleman named John H. Baker. He shook hands and was given a seat, and noticed that Mr. Morgan, who was in the same office, was sitting with his back turned to him.

The men began to talk; their subject was the S tube patents. Baker started to build a strong position by describing how much money these patents had already cost Mr. Morgan, but Marshall—no man to remain silent—knocked it down with an interruption.

"The question is not what they cost," he said, "but what they're worth." [33]

Mr. Morgan, listening, laughed and swung around. From that moment the conversation became real, and fencing was abandoned. Marshall himself does not recall the specific dialogue, but by the time he emerged he had made a deal. The S tube patents would cost American Appliance $50,000, but only $10,000 of this would be in cash. The balance could be paid in shares in American Appliance.

The autumn air of New York was chill, but Marshall walked back to his hotel in a warm glow. In truth, he had made a wonderful deal. Not only had he obtained the S tube patents, but he could now count J. P. Morgan himself among his shareholders.

He had also—though neither then nor later did the thought cross his mind—finally gathered into his hands all the elements with which another man had once failed in a venture called AMRAD.

# Chapter 3 THE TWENTIES

IN the great spate of books extolling the revolutionaries of this century there are few that include—among the fierce, frowning faces of Lenin, Trotsky, Stalin and their followers—any photographs of the smooth-featured, high-collared American businessmen or engineers of the twenties.

Yet it was the Americans who provided the instrumentation for the deepest, most far-reaching and widespread change in the attitudes of mankind that ever took place in such a brief period. Two of these instruments were, in an intellectual and cultural sense, the most important. One was the movies, and the other was radio.

The scientific principles of both were discovered by Europeans. But both were brought to earth, made practical, manufactured, marketed, and distributed to mankind through the operations of the peculiar American system that allowed men individual initiative in their search for a better life.

Neither Laurence Marshall nor C. G. Smith considered themselves revolutionaries: like most Americans they thought they were, somehow, outside the stream of history. Having little sense of pomp, they took for granted—as did their contemporaries and counterparts—that the world would also accept them as prosaic.

Yet their efforts were not simple. Blending business and technology is an art no other nation has mastered as well as the United States. But there is reason to believe that business, as Americans conduct it, is so complex the average man simply cannot follow it.

One of Marshall's major talents in this area was persuasion. He switched the direction of the American Appliance Company from refrigerators to radio tubes. In order to do this, he had to talk his board and shareholders out of what he had talked them into—and then talk them into radio. In the interim, C. G. Smith and Vannevar Bush had not only picked up their original researches in thermionic tubes, but had improved upon them.

When they restarted this effort, there were about 2.5 million radio sets in use in the United States.[1] They operated upon two batteries, an A battery and a B battery. C. G.'s new tube, known technically as a "gaseous rectifier," could not only eliminate the need for a B battery, but would allow the set to operate directly from a wall socket. Because a tube was much less expensive than a battery, set owners could not only plug it in, turn the switch, and hear their programs, but they could obtain such a set at a price closer to the average pocketbook. This improvement did not make home sets possible—they were already in use. But it brought their price far closer to the public grasp, as well as making them easier to keep in operation. It also meant that C. G. Smith had outstripped the armies of researchers and technicians maintained by the engineers of RCA, Westinghouse, and other giants. He had produced a device that changed an industry.

Radio was changing the world. Such events as the Dempsey-Firpo fight in 1923, for which neighbors had crowded into every home that boasted a radio, and listened breathlessly to a round-by-round, simultaneous description of the fight as it proceeded, proved there was a vast and impatient market for sets that functioned simply and that the average man could afford.

Of course, there are those who will say that C. G. Smith's invention was inevitable. Patent examiners, who are expert in evaluating the expected, disagreed. Actually, the argument that a creative accomplishment is inevitable and springs inevitably from the environment is a jealous fallacy. Nothing creative is expected before it appears. That is why there are always so many people, at all times, who believe the world has reached its limits.

Radios that ran on batteries could have been produced and marketed for decades. Automobiles still use batteries, and very few persons consider that detail odd.

But C. G. Smith's new tube would force the entire radio industry into an extensive and expensive new direction. Like every other new product, it could expect a glad reception from those manufacturers with no particular stake in the costs of these changes and an angry response from all to whom it could prove expensive. For that reason Marshall took the precaution of creating a dummy firm—the S Tube Corporation—under the laws of Delaware. He thought that might divert attention from the real source of the innovation for a time.

Meanwhile the third Annual Meeting took place in January 1925, and two new investors—Colonel Theodore Dillon and Havens Grant —appeared. John Axten, listed as the owner of eight hundred shares, a considerable block then, did not appear. The stock was J. P. Morgan's, listed in John Axten's name: he was an assistant to the financier.

After the meeting the directors reelected Billy Gammell president and Jefferson Coolidge vice president. They increased their own number to seven, and placed Havens Grant on the board, where he was to remain for many years.

The directors, who had also renamed Marshall treasurer, for the first time officially recognized his real role by naming him general manager, at a salary of $3,600 a year. This was less than C. G. Smith was receiving, at $5,000 a year, and even less than Vannevar Bush, who received a three-year contract as a consultant at $5,000 a year, as well as an option to buy one hundred shares at $50. But Marshall owned the largest single block of stock with 895 shares (C. G. Smith was runner-up with 815), and was prospering from Spencer Thermostat Company.

These arrangements, however, were inside the family. Marshall's outside activities had grown very strenuous. He scoured New England to find a manufacturer who would produce the new tube to specification in volume, and none would touch it until he lucked upon the Champion Lamp Works in Peabody, Massachusetts.

"This fellow was one of the most hardheaded fellows in the business," Marshall said. "Wouldn't touch a thing until he could see it work." Marshall, to convince him, had to demonstrate the tube.[2] Only then did Champion accept the order.

The man at Champion Lamp was not exceptional. America was then a nation that teemed with hardheaded people who insisted on a demonstration before they would accept a car, a tool, or any other object. Sweeping statements provoked skepticism; being outspoken was considered an essential attribute of individuality. The time when the ordinary man would blindly accept judgments he could not understand had not yet dawned—but it was coming.

❉   ❉   ❉

The new radio tube had excellent market possibilities. Miles Pennybacker, hired as a sales engineer, submitted a list of possible names for the new product. Among them was Raytheon. Pennybacker thought it came from the Greek, but that was only true of the *theon*, which meant "from the gods." "Ray," according to later researchers, meant "a beam of light" in Old French. At any rate Marshall thought the combination euphonious and was pleased. So was C. G. Smith, who regarded the light from Zeta Puppis as, if not a light from the gods, at least a light from the heavens. Smith had another reason as well: he detested the names, then being coined, that attached the syllable -*tron* [3] to electrical products. Like many engineers he cringed from the jargon that darkened technology.

New products—even those presumably protected by patents—do not emerge uncontested, however. To the surprise of all, the Connecticut Telephone & Telegraph Company came hurriedly out of the background brandishing a rival patent claim that appeared amazingly similar to the S tube or, as it was now dubbed, the Raytheon radio tube. Marshall, after huddling with the lawyers, told the directors it would be best to settle with Connecticut Telephone for $7,500,[4] and this was approved.

Meanwhile orders began to increase to sizable proportions, and even more serious troubles began to gather. The engineers at Westinghouse apparently decided the Raytheon patents were not as strong as they appeared, and they copied the rectifier.

It is doubtful if the Westinghouse technicians informed the firm's patent attorney of this decision; later events make it more likely that they assured management they were operating independently. Perhaps they thought their copy would hold up in court, or their immediate supervisors may have reasoned that Westinghouse could afford the long and costly court process that might ensue while, in the meantime, they could compete.

At any rate Raytheon's C. G. Smith and Vannevar Bush quickly analyzed the Westinghouse tube and discovered it was an imitation.

Shortly afterward Dr. Bush, who had become an imposing presence with a growing reputation, called upon Charles Neave, the Westinghouse patent attorney.

"He showed me the Westinghouse tube," Bush wrote. "The glass was coated so that one could not see inside, but he told me Westinghouse did not use the short path idea and hence did not infringe."

"I said, 'Crack it.' He looked at me a moment and then cracked the tube over the edge of his wastebasket; and here was the short path clearly used. So he smiled and said he would advise the Westinghouse Company to keep off the grass." [5]

Al Spencer had a brother, four years older than he, named Percy. It was an oddly genteel name for a man who had spent his boyhood in Maine in hard-scrabble circumstances, and who was to be eternally associated not only with the specifics of hard science, but with hunting, shooting, trapping, fishing, and the outdoors.

After their father had been killed in a mill accident and their mother left, Al Spencer had been raised by an uncle. Percy was the charge of his Aunt Minnie, an itinerant weaver. For a time she and Percy traveled about New England, leading a pinched existence in terms of money and comfort. But in many ways, it was a childhood unique to the American continent that contained values often observed even by those who knew its rigors.

Percy shot his first deer when he was twelve in order to get food for himself and Aunt Minnie. [6] He never forgot his sensations as he eviscerated that carcass, cut it into sections, and hung it in the barn.

"Hunting develops facilities of thought and perception beyond any other pursuit," says Dr. Edward L. Bowles, who later knew Percy well. "A boy develops the habit of watchfulness; of listening with all his faculties, and of being on his own." [7] Bowles, who himself had spent an outdoor boyhood in the Ozark foothills, believes that such an early experience makes a man far more wary and observant than the average.

Percy, verifying Dr. Bowles's theory, developed a frontier personality. Once he nailed a fish to a plank and let it float on the river. An osprey appeared, saw the catch, and dove straight onto it, killing himself in the effort. Percy walked away, and it was significant that he did not play that trick again. He had a gentle side.

Al Spencer had gone to New York City and become a machinist; Percy went to work in a machine shop in Maine after elementary school. He was introduced to electrical matters by a contractor, who hired him as a hand while electrifying a pulp-and-paper mill. Electricity was as alluring then as space to a later generation, and Percy's interest was increased when young David Sarnoff made a national name as the wireless operator who relayed the news of the sinking of the *Titanic*.[8]

Percy took a poor boy's route to education by enlisting in the navy. Later, discharged, he worked for the Wireless Specialty Apparatus Company making electrical equipment and moved to the status of superintendent. During World War I, he worked for the navy as a civilian and was put on loan to the Submarine Signal Company.

Submarine Signal was a firm in thrall to the U.S. Navy, for which it had developed underwater sound devices of considerable importance. It also installed equipment on lightships and shore stations. Percy's skills improved during this employment.

He read widely and assiduously. He devoured technical articles but also books of all sorts. SubSig, as it was called, did not hold him long: underwater sound and devices seemed far less interesting than electricity, that mysteriously lifelike force evoked from the ether that seemed able to animate the inanimate.

A brief contact with American Radio and Research Corporation introduced him to the fascinating mysteries of gas and vacuum tubes, and these seemed attractive. Although SubSig offered young Percy Spencer the management of its Norfolk office, he rejected that to join American Appliance.

Marshall talked to Percy Spencer mainly at the urging of Al, whose admiration for his older brother was immense. Marshall saw a stocky, square-faced young man, built along his own lines though less obviously athletic, whose manner was pleasing without being ingratiating. Percy had a raconteur's gifts and a very shrewd eye. He was added to the tiny three-man staff and sent to the Champion Lamp Works to supervise the production of the B tube. His assignment was purely mechanical: Marshall did not expect him to be more than an able inspector.

Just as business was well established and the firm launched with a market identity, news arrived from Indiana that a firm known as the American Appliance Company had a prior claim to the name and no intention of allowing itself to be confused.

This was appalling, for it meant that the firm had to decide upon a new name for itself without delay, and then go through the added trouble and expense of establishing a new identity with its creditors,

suppliers, and customers. The name Raytheon had already been selected to describe its radio tubes, and it seemed easiest simply to
extend it to the enterprise as a whole. Accordingly the Raytheon
Manufacturing Company was named at a Special Meeting on October
25, 1925.⁹ Pennybacker was pleased, for he had coined the name.
Marshall and the others were less pleased, because they had to go
through an expensive new exercise.

Then another new threat, more far-reaching than any before,
arose. The engineers at giant RCA had gone into high gear as a result of the industry changes attendant on the introduction of the
Raytheon tube. Their countermove was both cunning and quick. They
switched from their 112A tube, whose plate required only 135 volts,
to a 171A tube, which required a 180-volt plate. In effect, the switch
made the Raytheon rectifier obsolete unless it could, very quickly, be
changed to handle a higher voltage.

At this highly critical, potentially disastrous moment, rescue came
from a most unexpected quarter: Percy Spencer, in Peabody, Massachusetts. "At this plant I became quite familiar with the physics of
the gas rectifier, and by observation determined they could be improved," he wrote later.¹⁰

Knowing that the RCA tube made a change critically necessary,
Spencer experimented on his own, and produced a variation of the
Raytheon tube that could handle 180 volts ". . . by altering its physical
shape and enhancing its tendency to approach a conducting voltage
more nearly to . . . an arc."

Spencer shipped his conical-shaped experimental tube to C. G.
Smith, who was surprised but delighted. He and Bush set about some
efforts on the coating, but the essential problem had been resolved.

It was a surprising and almost miraculous development at the
time, and in retrospect loses none of its luster. In personal terms alone,
it was an extraordinary achievement. Dr. C. G. Smith, after all, not
only had graduated from the University of Texas, but had studied
at Harvard Graduate School under the famous Professor Pierce, whose
name still reverberates in the scientific history of early radio. Dr.
Vannevar Bush had graduated from Tufts and MIT, and even Laurence Marshall was well educated in mathematics and physics. Any
man who studied in isolation, on his own, and reached a level where

he was able to follow the activities of such men in technical areas could be proud of an impressive intellectual achievement.

But Percy Spencer not only understood their efforts, he improved upon them at a moment when they were stalled. His contribution helped the company at a crucial moment. Years later he was to emerge again with some improvements that helped an entire civilization; yet awesome though his later triumphs were, none was more timely to the fortunes of Raytheon than his first.

Laurence Marshall sent for Percy to join them in the lab in Cambridge. Meanwhile, C. G. Smith and Dr. Bush began experimenting with new coatings for the improved, cone-shaped tube, which they tentatively titled the BH.

In Peabody, Percy Spencer received this reaction with satisfaction. He sent a case marked "Instruments" ahead, and made his preparations.

Before he himself arrived in Cambridge, some curious soul opened his case, perhaps just to see what sort of instruments Al Spencer's older brother considered important. The men at the laboratory caught a glimpse of another aspect of the extraordinary personality of Percy Spencer when they discovered that his instrument case actually held a Prohibition treasure: twelve bottles of whiskey.[11]


By early 1926 the new BH tube was in volume production at a two-story building leased by Marshall on Carlton Street in Cambridge. This facility was managed by Al Spencer; Percy became a valuable new man in the laboratory. Orders for the BH tube escalated beyond the most optimistic expectations, and Raytheon moved forward to a notable success.

It was a wonderful year for the company, its men, and, in many respects, for the nation. It was not a perfect year: man does not have any. But it was the year when the twenties—with its musical comedies, lawns, tennis, automobiles and styles, the Charleston, jazz, and Al Capone—settled into the form that has since become a cliché. It was the time of big sports and famous athletes; of Mayor Jimmy Walker in New York; of F. Scott Fitzgerald at his peak; of people still shocked by H. L. Mencken; it was the year Sinclair Lewis produced *Arrowsmith*.

Henry Ford amazed both socialists and capitalists that year by introducing the five-day week and the $5-a-day wage. Business soared to new heights; prices on the stock market moved upward and small investors, attracted by the lure of instant riches, began to speculate in large numbers. Gene Tunney beat Jack Dempsey that year, and as a result of the "long count" Dempsey became a folk hero. The world we know began to assume its familiar outlines.

It was also a time when subterranean forces began to collect. The German Army, restricted by the Versailles Treaty to only 100,000 men, made a secret arrangement with the Soviets, and the two combined to create secret weapons factories inside Russia and to exchange technological information.[12] Meanwhile the Army of the United States sank, under the lax, peacetime supervision of the Administration and Congress, to 118,000 men; its ordnance department's research budget fell to one-half its expenditures of 1910. Some idea of how the U.S. armed forces declined can be gathered from the fact that although radio was transforming the American and world society, the army was poorly equipped with this device.[13]

Despite a ghastly civil war in China and the obvious ambitions of Japan in Asia; despite turbulence in Central America of such violence the United States sent troops to Nicaragua; despite outbreaks in French Morocco and persistent demonstrations, arguments, and angry discord in many other places, most people in the United States in 1926 were convinced that a new, large-scale war was not only unlikely but impossible—unthinkable.

Business boomed at Raytheon. Sales soared to over $1 million in 1926, at a time when "a million-dollar company" was considered Big Business. Even more startling was the fact that Raytheon's profit from these sales amounted to $321,000. Such returns were not unknown in the twenties, though later such a margin of profit—almost a third—would be considered immoral in industry (though not in the entertainment field, in sports, and in other popular sectors).

With Spencer Thermostat doing well and Raytheon established as an outstanding success, both Marshall and Bush expanded. Marshall, intent on new fields to conquer, decided to take a fast trip to Europe; he thought a cross-licensing agreement might be arranged with the huge Philips concern.[14] The Germans were again forging ahead industrially. Before he left, Marshall wondered if Dr. C. G. Smith might not want to take a year off entirely, go to Germany with his family, and study its progress. Smith thought he should stick close to his work; prosperity filled him with caution.[15]

*37*

Marshall went to Europe alone. In retrospect his trip was astoundingly ambitious: Philips was one of the world's largest electrical manufacturers; Raytheon was a tiny company in Cambridge. Yet he wanted to arrange a cross-licensing agreement under which—in exchange for his relatively small, though undoubtedly important products—he would market all Philips products in the United States. Marshall thought big.

He arrived at Eindhoven, and on the morning he was supposed to meet with the executives of Philips, "I picked up the papers and read that they had come to a cross-licensing agreement with General Electric. Well, that killed that." [16]

Returning, Marshall stopped in Paris. "I was walking down the street," he said years later, "when I saw a resistor in the window of a small shop. I was curious, so I went upstairs and found a man—Le André—working away at a table, testing his resistor." Outside of testing equipment Marshall saw the room was bare.

Marshall had lucked upon a man who had made a colloidal rectifier that would, if it worked, eliminate the A radio batteries, as the BH tube had eliminated the B batteries. Marshall, who had visions of doubling or more his initial BH tube success, immediately turned the formidable pressure of his personality on Dr. Le André. He was, of course, successful in talking the Frenchman out of his poverty-stricken quarters and onto a boat and carried him—and his colloidal rectifier—back to the United States.

Their passage back to the States was accompanied by a series of communiqués that Marshall wired ahead. One result was that they were met by the press when the boat landed, and the new Raytheon discovery was hailed by a blaze of publicity. Marshall noted, with surprise, that Dr. Le André had, somewhere in mid-Atlantic, "shaved off his Le." [17] Henceforth he was known simply as Dr. André.

The laboratory plunged eagerly into the mysteries of André's rectifier. Among other ingredients it contained a small quantity of sulphuric acid, a tricky compound difficult to control. "It was placed in production in spite of many heated arguments between the few of us determining Company policy," said C. G. Smith—but he did not say who argued what.[18] Knowing the personalities, we can assume that C. G. Smith wanted to hold back, and that Laurence Marshall wanted to forge ahead.

Marshall, a very busy man, on June 21 of that year, married

Lorna Jean McLean, a student at Radcliffe. Young Miss McLean, whose family home was in Berkeley, California, had returned from China not long before. At the home of a neighbor who had a set, she learned—for the first time and at firsthand—of the impact of radio. She was astonished, thrilled, and made suddenly aware of how civilization—as the world had always known it—had been transformed.

"I felt," she said later, "as though I had actually been outside the world and had just returned."

Her concept of the world would change even more after marrying a man who managed an enterprise in the vanguard of that revolution.

After her marriage she continued to attend Radcliffe to get her degree. But in the evenings she often came to the laboratory in Cambridge to wait for Marshall, who liked to plunge into research work after a day of business details. "It was near MIT and also near the subway," she recalled. "It was like an immense room, on the fourth floor.

"I remember sitting on a high stool reading a book of poetry and from time to time looking up to watch the lab at work. There was a series of tube tests underway, and the tubes were placed in slots on a giant drum that revolved slowly, attended by a turbaned Hindu. He was studying at MIT to become an electrical engineer. The lights in the lab glowed softly; the room was quiet; the Hindu was silent, cautious and watchful. I remember thinking that he was darkly handsome. The entire atmosphere seemed charged with mysterious forces." [19]

Then disaster struck. ". . . little Raytheon had its factory going full blast one week and all its orders canceled the next," said Vannevar Bush.[20]

The "club" had fallen upon them. RCA, Westinghouse, General Electric had gotten together—and, according to Bush, scared American Telephone & Telegraph into joining for fear of the Langmuir patents—and issued an agreement which all those who purchased radio parts and manufactured radio sets had to sign. The agreement was the result of a club decision to pool patents. Those who did not sign an agreement to buy "all their tubes" could not receive any. Raytheon, as well as other small tube manufacturers, was left out in the cold.

Marshall was, understandably, outraged. Sarnoff had a reputation at the time for moving first, on the assumption it would take the courts years to catch up and stop him, and Marshall—reflecting this view—asked the directors for permission to sue RCA for $20 million.

President Billy Gammell and the others agreed. But a lawsuit alone, considering the lethargic, snail-like pace of American justice, would not save them. Marshall issued orders to manufacture tubes of every sort—whether patented by the club or not—and the factory resumed operations. "Of course," Bush said, "Raytheon was sued in return, but, matters being a bit complicated, no cease-and-desist order issued from the court."

After only a brief hiatus, therefore, Raytheon's business resumed its boom. By 1927, the year Lindbergh received the acclaim of the world for flying solo across the Atlantic, matters seemed well in hand. Marshall and Vannevar Bush decided to take their wives and visit the Soviet Union.

Their immediate reasons were commercial, but they undoubtedly itched to see the land of mystery for themselves. Their excuse had arisen out of a visit to MIT by the famous Dr. Abram Joffe, president of the Soviet Academy of Sciences. ". . . he had held that post under Czar Nicholas II, under Kerenski, and under the Bolsheviki," wrote Dr. Bush, "which indicates that he was a scientist who disavowed any interest whatever in political matters, and also that he was fast on his feet." [21] Anyone that fast might, in less kindly eyes, be regarded as peculiarly slippery.

Dr. Bush and Mrs. Bush had Dr. Joffe as their house guest during his visit, and they were both charmed. They had reason to be: topflight Soviet citizens then traveled in the United States surrounded by an aura of great events, with the nimbus of the Russian Revolution hovering over their heads, and Dr. Joffe was a truly topflight scientist.

That revolution had been received in American intellectual circles with a combination of fascination and faith. In the backlash of World War I, when Americans learned that most of the atrocity stories attached to Germany had been propaganda creations, there had been a deep revulsion and an equally deep distrust of official information. For that reason when similar atrocity stories began to seep from the Soviet sector, many Americans simply refused to credit them. Unfortunately, their credulity in the first instance was matched only by their incredulity in the second. Europeans who were closer to the scene were not taken in to a similar extent, in either instance.

Nevertheless, many American intellectuals considered it almost a requirement of intelligence to be sympathetic to the Soviet Revolution, and many ordinary persons, not fully realizing that the Communists had forced themselves into power and maintained their control by terror, assumed the Russian Revolution resembled their own revered example.

One result was that a stream of American engineers, technicians, and businessmen poured into the Soviet Union in the middle to late twenties, lured by generous contracts from the Soviet government. Ironically, it was their efforts that were largely responsible for the widely touted industrial accomplishments of the Revolution.

Dr. Bush was not, of course, naïve regarding some of these realities, but he was less interested in politics than in science. In his MIT lecture, Dr. Joffe had discussed "electric conduction in solids."

"To my amazement," Dr. Bush wrote, "he told how his theory could be applied to make an insulating material of far greater dielectric strength than existing materials. This woke me up in a hurry, for if what he described was correct, it would revolutionize the design of electric machinery and power cables."

Bush told Marshall, whose interest was aroused, and discussions were started with Amtorg, the Russian trading agency in New York City. An option on Joffe's developments was acquired, with time allowed to check out all the details.

Marshall was pleased. He had already suggested several expansions to the board. At one time he thought the refrigeration patents, filed and obtained by C. G. Smith and Dr. Bush—with some improvements of his own—should be exhumed and made the basis of a new effort. Marshall hated to lose those years of intense concentration, and the refrigeration market had grown large in the nation.

Raytheon itself had grown to the point where Marshall was eager for new ventures. In April 1927, the board had enlarged, by the additions of William H. Claflin, Jr., and Edward C. Thayer, to nine members. Business had become so complex that two board members—Jefferson Coolidge and Colonel Dillon—were appointed to meet with Marshall on a regular basis, between full board meetings. Marshall also began to talk about the need to hire a chief engineer to supervise production.

In June the Joffe deal—or more precisely, the Soviet deal—was presented to the board and approved. If the discoveries of the famous scientist could be brought to application, they could lead to far-reaching commercial properties. Unfortunately, Dr. Vannevar Bush was having difficulty in reproducing Dr. Joffe's test results. He thought they should go to Russia and see Dr. Joffe at the Technical Institute in Leningrad. Marshall agreed.

The Marshalls and the Bushes arrived in Leningrad in November 1927, and Bush noted "there was tension in the air." But they were well received in the Institute and he was impressed by the high quality of the young technicians who hovered solicitously about the Director. "One had to remember, many of that group were alive," Bush said, "just because they were a part of Joffe's organization and protected by him . . ." The words, across the gulf of years and space, bring a quiet horror. The grimness of the regime, in which murder was commonplace, had somehow established itself as a weirdly normal state of affairs, even to a man as civilized as Dr. Bush.

But Dr. Bush, a perceptive man, also came to realize that Joffe's theory was fallacious. He pointed out a flaw, on one occasion, expecting to be refuted, and met only silence. On the train to Moscow, accompanied by Joffe, Bush studied another of the professor's physics papers, found it completely erroneous, and said so. Joffe, to his surprise, agreed completely, and seemed grateful for the critique. Bush decided that Joffe was starved for an equal give-and-take. It did not seem to occur to him, then or later, that the older man had more serious concerns.

Later the American party was given rooms in a hotel where the furniture was decayed, cockroaches scurried from the light, and "the window draperies were falling apart." Moscow was crowded; the Communist Party was meeting, they learned later, in a historic session that resulted in the fall of Trotsky and the triumph of Stalin. It was, of course, a coincidence—but Bush, like Raytheon, was forever to be at the scene of great events.

They had the usual experiences. Since one of the members of the Presidium had retained a prerevolutionary taste for the aristocratic ballet, it was the only vestige left of the real grandeur of historic Russia. All visitors went to the ballet; the Bush and Marshall couples were no exception. "The audience was made up of soldiers of the Red Army and peasants in their high woolen boots," Bush says. "Marshall and I may have had on the only white collars in the place." The performance was glorious; the radiance of the stage shone brighter by contrast with the drab audience.

Before they left Dr. Bush had a brief conference with Joffe, who understood that his fraud had been penetrated. Bush, aware that his disclosures might cost the older man his life, assured him he would wait six months, as far as the public was concerned. The professor nodded; that would be time enough to float another promise before the authorities.

Their departure was delayed, but after some mild adventures they arrived in Berlin and in due course back at Cambridge. Bush's later conclusion was that one should not attempt inventions in isolation—which seems to indicate that he could not, like most Americans, grasp the extent to which terror will drive men.

Marshall, Bush, and their wives returned to the United States in early 1928 to discover the country in a curious condition. It was experiencing the final stages of what Frederick Lewis Allen later called "the great Bull market." [22] The late boom was a phenomenon that had little basis in reality. Business had slowed in the nation; unemployment had increased; inflation had become so serious that it eroded the living standard of what was then still called "the working class."

Yet the stocks on the nation's exchanges soared. Eminent economists warned that there was no reason for this; Moody's and other investment services counseled caution; but prices continued to rise as though inflated by C. G. Smith's beloved "celestial gas"—helium.

General Motors, AT&T, Montgomery Ward, and other "household name" stocks soared toward the stratosphere. Dividends in those days were as high as managers chose, and could range from none at all to as much as $7, $8, or $9 a share. But hundreds of thousands of newly converted speculators were not concerned about long-range dividends; the market began to leap upward in jumps of several points a share. So rapid was this progression that stocks began to resemble fish jumping upstream on their way to spawn, driven by some peculiar intuition within themselves.

By midsummer the phenomenon began to falter, but quickly resumed at a quickened pace. Not since the days of the Great Tulip speculation in Holland centuries before, or the heyday of the Great South Seas Bubble, had speculation become so divorced from reality. Fortunes were made in defiance of logic. The nation entered a national election year with fever coursing through its economic system.

The campaign itself took new turns. Al Smith, a respected governor of New York and a man of inherently conservative bent, was an anti-Prohibitionist and a representative of the big-city masses. His campaign, actually based on a shrewd recognition of the new strength of metropolitan voters, of the value of the big-city machines, and of deep changes in the nation, was the first to use radio extensively. Some sectors of opposition, however, stressed Smith's Catholicism. The identification fueled prejudice and helped swing the South into the Republican column.

The Republican campaign managers, on the other hand, chose to ignore flagging business conditions and serious inflationary threats to the economy, and to pretend that all was well. As a consequence Hoover was depicted as a man who would continue a boom already in decline.

Neither Marshall nor Bush, however, was much interested in politics. They had more immediate concerns, for one batch of colloidal rectifiers—the product of Dr. André that C. G. Smith and some others distrusted—had proven disastrous in the marketplace.

"The iron we employed was not pure," Marshall said later, "and when it was attacked by the sulphuric acid, it caused the tubes to collapse." [23] That was putting the matter gently. In reality they exploded with a considerable noise.

Billed by Raytheon as the "A" Eliminator, in honor of the fact that it was designed to eliminate the use of the A radio battery, the new rectifier became known inside the company as the Baby Eliminator, on the basis of a complaint by some unfortunate lady who blamed the explosion inside her radio set for her miscarriage.

"One blew up in the office of the president of the National Carbon Company," said Laurence Marshall. "Acid poured out and flowed across his expensive Oriental rug, causing irreparable damage." [24] This could have had more serious consequences, for Marshall was, at that very moment, deep in highly confidential discussions with National Carbon.

*44*

And because Raytheon had persuaded several small manufacturers to produce and market some subsidiary equipment to be used with the Baby Eliminator, its explosions in various living rooms and establishments throughout the country were having reverberations in other offices than those of National Carbon. Lawsuits popped into the air as quickly as the tubes.

Dave Schultz, the youthful assistant treasurer, who had moved with his family to nearby Brookline, proved invaluable in the crisis. Schultz traveled about with a satchel of cash and authority to make settlements on the spot. That was very helpful, and his transparent honesty made him very successful.

"He went to each plaintiff," wrote C. G. Smith, "and coaxed each of them into an easy settlement. However, the last suer was an Irishman, and he brought his case in Boston. He won a verdict of about $10,000." Then Smith added, with a shudder, "Had he been first on the list, then Raytheon would surely have been completely liquidated." [25]

The faulty tubes were the result of one bad batch—one week's factory production—but the claims took many weeks to settle.

As though this accident was not enough to worry Marshall, RCA brought out its own rectifier tubes. That was a real crisis, which no satchel of cash could settle. All radio sets at the time had to have at least some RCA components, for the firm had a very strong patent position. RCA followed its usual practice: those who bought its parts and tubes would have to include its rectifiers in their orders, or all other supplies would be cut off. This development could slice Raytheon out of the business far more effectively than the bad batch.

At this sinister crossroad, Marshall made some brilliant improvisations. Fortunately a fortuitous circumstance arose to provide him with a life raft. Most men would have seen it as such, and been content to grasp it blindly. Marshall, in contrast, used it as the basis upon which to build an entirely new corporate ship.

The life raft bore the unlikely name of the Q.R.S. Company. Headquartered in Chicago, with offices in New York and San Francisco, it listed itself as a manufacturer of player piano rolls, radio tubes, neon sign tubes, amateur movie cameras and parts. Piano rolls were going out of style, but radio tubes and amateur movie cameras were growing industries.

Unfortunately Q.R.S. had decided to take some shortcuts to fortune, and had created a booming radio tube business for itself by manufacturing and marketing thermionic tubes based on Raytheon's patents without going through the expense of paying royalties. In this effort it met with truly startling success, and sales jumped from a meager $23,000 in 1925 to a startling $550,000 in 1926.[26]

When combined with the emergence of RCA as a rectifier manufacturer, the piracy of Q.R.S. would have given many men the material for dramatic despair, or at least some self-pity. But Marshall was made of better material than to allow himself such indulgences—and he was also too intelligent. Business is a rough and rapid river, with many riptides, crosscurrents, shoals, and perils. Riders on these waters have to maintain strong nerves and a sensible balance. Besides these philosophical realities, there was every reason in 1928 to consider the radio tube business one of the best in the United States in which to be engaged and in which to have an established position. After all, Americans had paid $400 million for radio sets that year. One hundred tube manufacturers had sold fifty million of these essential components, and some of them at prices as high as $5 or $6 each.[27] Even a blind man, it would seem, could see that the enormous potential of radio had not yet reached a foreseeable end. Sales would continue to rise for years, for everyone wanted a set of his own.

Marshall was so sure that Raytheon would expand and prosper that he hired M. Fred Williams to head a sales effort at the then impressive salary of $25,000 a year. Williams, who received a two-year contract, was also offered an added 1 percent commission if net sales fell between $1.5 and $2 million a year, a commission of 1.5 percent if sales went over $2 million—and was warned his contract would be canceled if sales fell below $1.5 million.

Marshall then made some oblique moves. He had the Raytheon lawyers file a suit against Q.R.S. He waited until their lawyers were convinced that the evidence was irrefutable and had time to acquaint the Q.R.S. managers with the fact that they confronted ruin. Then, carrying young Dave Schultz along to pick up any stray details that he himself might overlook, Marshall left for Chicago. Behind him he left Raytheon president Billy Gammell, Vannevar Bush (who had become a director), Colonel Dillon, Jefferson Coolidge, Thayer, and the balance of the board in a state of hope. They were not disappointed.

In Chicago Marshall convinced the Q.R.S. managers not only that he was not narrowly punitive, but that their best course was to share in the enlargement of Raytheon. Only by that step could they both settle a potentially ruinous lawsuit and emerge with a potentially profitable position in the radio tube industry.

As a result an agreement, dated May 5, 1928, was reached fairly quickly. In essence it called for Q.R.S. to pay Raytheon $25,000 in cash and turn over all its machinery for manufacturing, its completed inventory, its engineering know-how, its patents, and its customer lists in the radio tube business. In addition, Q.R.S. agreed to become a part owner in a new, expanded Raytheon to be formed out of the pooling of both its former and its new assets, and to share in the sale of stock in this new enterprise, to be listed on the Chicago exchange, and handled by Harry C. Watts & Co.

In one stroke Marshall had succeeded in converting a lawsuit into an acquisition, a merger, and the basis for a complete corporate reorganization. As an out-of-court settlement, this surely ranks as one of the most unique in the annals of business.

When completed, the details of the changes were dense, and before completion underwent a number of transmutations as the lawyers and financiers huddled. Nevertheless the outlines of the May 5 agreement were met, and on May 22, 1928, in Wilmington, Delaware, a new Raytheon manufacturing corporation was formed. When all the legal details were complete, the new president was, properly, Laurence K. Marshall. Billy Gammell, who had been president through the previous incarnations of the venture, had decided that it was now too large and its operations too complicated for the time he could afford from his own Lonsdale Textile Company. He had shepherded the financial fortunes of the firm very astutely, however, and there is no question that without Mr. Gammell there would have been no Raytheon to reorganize in Wilmington. Mr. Gammell remained on the board, and his contributions were to continue. Vannevar Bush, whose name was becoming well known, also remained as director. Harry C. Watts and Charles D. Dawes represented the Q.R.S. interests in the new company. Colonel Dillon and Havens Grant remained from the older Raytheon. Marshall himself, Schultz, Le Roi Williams, the patent attorney, and Fred D. Williams, the sales manager, constituted the insiders.

The new firm was launched in good auspices. It had $100,000 in cash for operating capital and $300,000 in surplus. It intended to sell 25,000 shares on the Chicago Exchange out of 75,000 shares of no-par common stock capitalization, though it would list 75,000 shares. Marshall thought, a little later in the year, that it would be best to increase the capital shares to one hundred thousand and sell fifteen thousand. He calculated that fifteen thousand shares, sold at $40, would yield $547,000, minus a broker's commission of $52,000.

Big dreams; large sums; big business. The atmosphere had changed in a few short years in a dramatic and unmistakable manner. Raytheon Manufacturing Company, with its expanded assets and its larger plans, was now really in business. Marshall's salary was set at $15,000 a year, Schultz's at $20,000, attorney Le Roi Williams' at $17,500. These were reasonable levels for corporate executives handling large responsibilities. They were not comparable, it was true, to the salaries of men at the top of really large corporations, but they were substantial in 1928, when $10,000 a year was considered success.

But Marshall had only begun. If he was to continue in the radio tube manufacturing business, he could no longer—at least openly—buck the club. He admitted this and came to terms. These constituted a cross-licensing agreement with RCA, General Electric, Westinghouse, and AT&T in which they could employ the Smith patents and others that Raytheon might develop, and Raytheon could manufacture the club products for a 10 percent royalty; the agreement also committed Raytheon to manufacturing $3.5 million worth of these a year. This was the first such agreement reached by any manufacturer with RCA in the United States.

Then, while his men leased the Old Saxony Mills in Newton, Massachusetts, for $22,500 a year—for three acres of land, a building, and an option to buy the property, including remaining buildings, later—Marshall turned toward the National Carbon Company, Inc.

This large, highly respected firm, makers of Eveready batteries and other well-known products, believed it could successfully enter into the marketing of radio tubes through its great national distribution organization.

Ordinarily one would expect that the president of a relatively small, newly reorganized firm of the size of Raytheon would consider himself lucky to make a simple marketing arrangement with such a strong, established group. But Marshall obviously considered himself, his associates, and Raytheon as capable as any other firm in the world.

*48*

He had years before thought of dealing with the great Dutch firm of Philips on an equal level; he approached National Carbon in that same spirit.

Since the world often accepts men at their own evaluation, he succeeded in making another unusual arrangement. Raytheon and National Carbon agreed, in 1929, to form a new corporation known as the Raytheon Production Company. Raytheon's share of this company was paid by its giving National Carbon a license to produce Raytheon products. National Carbon's share was paid by an initial $500,000 in cash.

Together, the two parties agreed the new firm would be capitalized by National Carbon's initial $500,000, plus fifty thousand shares of a Class A common, fifty thousand shares of a Class B common, $1 million in first mortgage bonds secured by indenture; that all the stock was to be held in escrow and National Carbon was to have an option on its purchase, and a further option to buy Raytheon Manufacturing Company itself for an additional $19.5 million.[28] This surprising conclusion was held open, however, until July 1, 1934.

Meanwhile, the net profits of the Raytheon Production Company were to be divided equally between Raytheon and National Carbon, though National Carbon was also to have an option to buy Raytheon Production for $15.5 million at any time up to October, 1938, at which time the price would increase by $2.5 million a year for every year thereafter.

No more amazing document exists in the files of Raytheon than this agreement, drawn up, signed, and approved by the boards of both companies in the heady days of early 1929.

Despite the fact that events were jumbled, 1929 seemed much the same as the year before, and the year before that. The Soviet Union was rationing food, and inhabitants of the larger cities were restricted to one pound of bread a day—but the Presidium took steps to stabilize the situation by exiling Trotsky. Later Stalin would handle his opponents more summarily, but he was still moving with caution.

In Chicago two men wearing false police uniforms and two men in ordinary business suits staged a mock "raid" on an installation maintained by the Bugs Moran gang, lined six men against a garage wall, and shot them all dead. The president of the New York Stock Exchange—E. H. H. Simmons—made a four-hour speech calling stock purchases on margin "the safest form of investment known in this country," and the Hoover Economic Survey reported seventeen million Americans were engaged in "playing" the market.

The mood was equally mixed on intellectual levels. Ernest Hemingway's *A Farewell to Arms* appeared to both critical praise and popular success; its setting was World War I. That conflict, which had ended over a decade before, still obsessed both the literary world and international politics. The Kellogg-Briand Pact, signed the year before, had "outlawed" war as an instrument of national policy; in 1929 the U.S. Senate, with only one dissenting vote, ratified the pact. *All Quiet on the Western Front*, by Erich Maria Remarque, created a literary sensation and started a long run through the various forms of entertainment.

These activities seemed far away, almost unreal, to Dr. C. G. Smith in the Raytheon laboratories, now transferred to the new quarters in Newton. With his developments in the rectifier tube overtaken by other researchers in RCA and the giant firms, he and Percy Spencer, Vannevar Bush, and others concentrated on developing new tubes. One was a tube that was improved by the addition of metallic cesium. But "these tubes," Smith wrote, "were like a doped horse . . . they beat all competitors—for a few hours." [29]

Smith, anxious to obtain new cesium, traveled about New England in vain. Finally, hearing that the waters of the Great Salt Lake in Utah were rumored to contain cesium, he sent for a gallon. When it arrived he bent over the spectroscope while Percy Spencer and Vannevar Bush lounged nearby idly. To C. G.'s excitement, he saw "two telltale lines in the blue were bright—indicating lots of cesium." He looked up jubilantly and Vannevar Bush not only congratulated him, but shook his hand. That was so unusual Smith decided to check his observation.

He looked in the spectroscope again, searching for rubidium, which is always found in conjunction with cesium. Not a trace. Then he became stern and conducted an investigation. He learned that Percy Spencer had, a few days before, been seen with a capsule containing four grams of cesium that were now, unaccountably, missing. Smith was not pleased and would hear no explanations. Instead, he sent for a hogshead of Salt Lake water, which was distilled—the salt removed—and became the object of endless examination; he found no cesium.

Percy Spencer, on the other hand, was having more success. He developed a tube—the BA—based on Smith's short-path principle and using an inert gas, that was extremely valuable for the amateur radio set market. This was profitable, and he began to forge ahead in tube development. His ingenuity was endless. He created photo developer lamps, kino lamps, and then a line of photocells. But the special tube for the amateur set builders was a breakthrough. Marshall, impressed, put Spencer in charge of the engineering and production of new tubes in the expanded Newton plant. Spencer, in other words, was becoming established as a new star; C. G. Smith—modest and retiring—began to move, gradually and without sound, into the background.

With the company in a larger and better financed position than ever before, and with the Eveready Raytheon tubes appearing in the marketplace through the National Carbon organization, Raytheon was well able to move forward. If the economic situation remained healthy, endless radio industry vistas beckoned.

But warning signs appeared. Paul Warburg, the financier credited by some with having been the guiding spirit in the initial creation of the Federal Reserve system, said in March 1929 that the Board had lost control of the money situation. He flailed "incorporated stock pools," and declared that the Federal Reserve—consisting of 120 men on twelve separate boards—was "bewildered" by political influence and could not operate efficiently.

Banker Warburg's complaint seemed too deeply rooted in old ideas about the need for a strong central bank controlled by a few men to be generally heeded. Many more voices were raised denying the truth of old economic theories, and claiming that a new system of expanding production, created new markets, and generous credits had been developed that would lead to eternal prosperity and progress. The land teemed with people—122 million—factories, skills, money, cities, and energy. It seemed inconceivable that this great advance—the most impressive in the history of mankind—could be seriously disturbed by mysterious economic forces . . . especially when so many economists claimed that new instruments had been developed to banish slumps.

The bubble broke in October 1929 from a variety of causes too numerous to trace. The reaction was the same—no better, no worse—as that of the Hollanders when the Tulip speculation came to an end, and of the long-dead speculators in the South Seas promotion of John Law. Older men and previous generations had a grim name for it. *Panic.*

Its span ran three weeks—from October 3 to October 29. When that first, frantic phase came to a close, $30 billion in values had vanished, leaving people exhausted, facing a landscape littered with economic wrecks and personal bankruptcies.

The cataclysm was so huge that it could not be grasped. Years later, when *Time* magazine republished excerpts from its issues of 1929,[30] its later editors were astonished to see that not even the journalists of the day realized the extent of the collapse. After all, the surface of America appeared much the same: trains ran, the highways were crowded with cars, factories were still standing, and 122 million people went about their routines in the same ways as ever.

But in the stock exchanges, brokers stared at mountains of paper representing closed accounts; millions confronted ruin; industrialists were appalled as orders were canceled. The President of the United States, only seven months in office, called a series of conferences. Lights burned late in the offices of financiers around the world.

*Laurence K. Marshall* (LEFT), *one of the company's three founders, with Miles Pennybacker, assistant general manager (Photograph: about 1928)*

*Dr. Vannevar Bush* (RIGHT), *another of the founders, consults with French physicist M. André* (CENTER) *around 1927.*

*From left are C. G. Smith, the third cofounder, Percy L. Spencer, and T. Kenyon in the Raytheon laboratory around 1927.*

*In 1928, this Raytheon factory in Cambridge, Massachusetts, was turning out thousands of rectifiers daily.*

*John A. ("Al") Spencer, head of manufacturing in the late twenties, watches as an employee seals the glass bulbs of Raytheon rectifiers.*

*The Raytheon BH tube of the twenties enabled the radio to operate on household AC current instead of depending on bulky, short-lived batteries.*

*William Gammell, who figured prominently in Raytheon's founding, was a long-time director and once served as president. (Photograph: around 1950)*

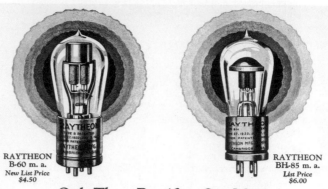

RAYTHEON
B-60 m. a.
*New List Price*
$4.50

RAYTHEON
BH-85 m. a.
*List Price*
$6.00

## Only These Rectifiers Can Meet The Big Replacement Demand

With 590,000 Raytheon-equipped B-power units in use and many of them now ready for new tubes, it is evident that the dealer who exhibits Raytheon will get the cream *and the bulk* of this business. Makeshift tubes will be "out of the picture," for Raytheon—and *only* Raytheon—can be used satisfactorily in these

*The Following Manufacturers Have National Distribution on One or More Complete Units Especially Designed and Approved for Use with Types B or BH Raytheon Rectifying Tubes.*

ACME APPARATUS CO., Cambridge, Mass.
ALL-AMERICAN RADIO CORP., Chicago, Ill.
AMERICAN BOSCH MAGNETO CORP., Springfield, Mass.
AMERICAN ELECTRIC CO., INC., Chicago, Ill.
BREMER-TULLY MFG. CO., Chicago, Ill.
CORNELL ELECTRIC MFG. CO., Long Island City, N. Y.
THE CROSLEY RADIO CORPORATION, Cincinnati, Ohio
ELECTRICAL RESEARCH LABS., INC., Chicago, Ill.
FREED-EISEMANN RADIO CORP., Brooklyn, N. Y.
GENERAL RADIO CO., Cambridge, Mass.
GRIGSBY-GRUNOW-HINDS CO., Chicago, Ill.
KING ELECTRIC MFG. CO., Buffalo, N. Y.
KOKOMO ELECTRIC MFG. CO., Kokomo, Ind.
MAYOLIAN RADIO CORP., Bronx, N. Y.
THE MODERN ELECTRIC MFG. CO., Toledo, Ohio
NATIONAL COMPANY, INC., Cambridge, Mass.
SPARKS-WITHINGTON CO., Jackson, Mich.
THE STERLING MFG. CO., Cleveland, Ohio
TIMMONS RADIO PRODUCTS CORP., Philadelphia, Pa.
VALLEY ELECTRIC CO., St. Louis, Mo.
THE WEBSTER COMPANY, Chicago, Ill.
WISE-McCLUNG CO. LTD., New Philadelphia, Ohio
ZENITH RADIO CORPORATION, Chicago, Ill.

well-known units. Order Raytheon B and BH from your jobber now.

When making replacements remember this —accurate service records show that only about 3% of Raytheon tubes fail within the guaranteed time of one year or 1000 hours of service. If you are convinced that your customer is entitled to a free replacement, give him a new tube and return the defective one to your jobber. If the jobber does not render prompt service on adjustments, send tubes direct to Raytheon Manufacturing Company, Service Bureau, Cambridge, Mass., or to the Raytheon Service Branch, 2007 S. Michigan Ave., Chicago, with the jobber's name.

# Raytheon
## THE HEART OF RELIABLE RADIO POWER

*This Raytheon advertisement appeared in 1927.*

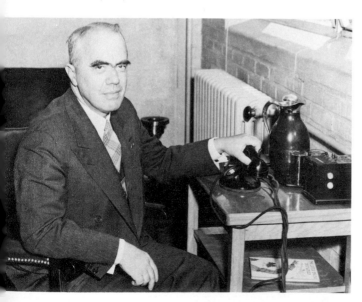

*Mr. Marshall in the thirties*
*Book on telephone table is*
*The Little Engine That Co*

C. G. Smith one of the cofounder's. In the mid-twenties, he developed the rectifier tube that made the radio a plug-in appliance and, at the same time, gave Raytheon its start. (Photograph: 1946)

Acme transformer was among theon's early successful products.

Percy L. Spencer, who joined Raytheon in 1925, developed mass production of magnetrons for use in World War II radars. Before his 1964 retirement, he was a senior vice president and a director of the company. (Photograph: 1946)

*Laurence K. Marshall, was president of Raytheon until 1948, after which he served two years as chairman. (Photograph: 1946)*

*Raytheon Eveready Tubes, first major product widely marketed by National Carbon, Inc. and RCA in the thirties.*

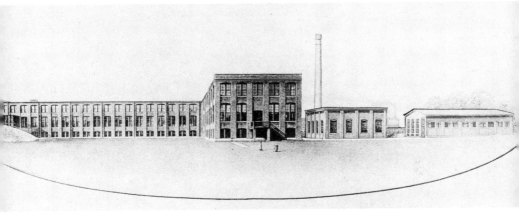

*In 1934, the company occupied this building, a former button factory in Waltham, Massachusetts.*

*Vannevar Bush, one of the three founders, gained fame as a scientist, administrator, educator, and author. Dr. Bush is shown here in 1935 with the differential analyzer he built for solving differential equations.*

Posing in the thirties are (FROM LEFT) *John A. ("Al") Spencer, Mrs. Spencer, Mrs. Laurence K. Marshall, and Mr. Marshall. Mr. Spencer, brother of Percy Spencer and inventor of the snap-acting thermostat, supervised manufacture of Raytheon rectifier tubes.*

*In a company testing laboratory, Fritz A. Gross operates a high-frequency fatigue-testing machine. (Photograph: 1937)*

# *Chapter 4* THE THIRTIES

EARLY in 1930 Ruth Babb's first job, with an engraving firm, collapsed when the company went bankrupt. She left, still owed several weeks' back pay she was never to receive, and joined thousands of others who trudged from one seedy employment agency to another in downtown Boston looking for work.

Dispatched to a temporary clerical post, she wrote in the space headed "Previous Employment" the words: "Eng. Company." Someone later read that and misunderstood. Because it was assumed she was familiar with engineering terms, therefore, Miss Babb was one of the very few lucky enough to land a new job that season. It proved to be permanent indeed: she was to remain the rest of her working life. Her employer was Raytheon.[1]

Raytheon, which had six hundred employees in 1930, was like a man who had built a storm basement, remodeled his home, converted his spare property into cash, and laid in provisions just before a storm struck.

One would have suspected Marshall of second sight, or of a deep, sophisticated knowledge of economic trends. That would have been flattering, but untrue. In large part he placed Raytheon in an excellent position deliberately, through the arrangements he conducted with Chicago financier Harry C. Watts regarding the acquisition of the Q.R.S. assets, with National Carbon regarding the promotion and marketing of the Eveready Raytheon radio tubes, and with RCA.

But in another sense it was an inherent conservatism that saved him. He did not ever think in the Blue-Sky terms so popular around him during the late twenties. If he had, he could have levered the reconstructed Raytheon into another of the endless stock promotions then underway. That course would have led Raytheon down the same drain others had flowed in early 1930.

Since Marshall did not contemplate such an action—though he certainly had as much basis in the reconstructed Raytheon as did many others who took that course—his firm was not caught out on a limb. And by ignoring that pattern, Marshall also showed a strong, conservative streak in the manner in which Raytheon reported its expenses, profits, and reserves in 1929. On sales of $1.3 million, the statement shows, on the bottom line, a loss of $33,000. That sounds dismal, but a closer look shows a better picture. The company paid out $120,000 in dividends to its shareholders during the year and took extremely large amounts from its profits for depreciation and reserve contingencies.[2]

Marshall's approach, in other words, was not designed to make the company look good, but to make sure that the company had as much money in hand as possible and paid no more taxes than were absolutely necessary. The tax aspect is one that promoters often overlook in their eagerness to make earnings appear impressive. Such tactics often, ironically, lead to higher tax payments and less actual net earnings. But Marshall, though many of his associates so regarded him, was not really a promoter. He was an engineer with a flair for business. The difference is considerable.

One result was that Raytheon entered 1930 with money in reserve, a sound product line, and an arrangement with National Carbon that forced the larger firm to spend, in all, $465,000 advertising [3] the Eveready Raytheon radio tubes that year. Meanwhile, Raytheon sales were increased by its arrangement with RCA and the other giants of the industry, while the efforts of Percy Spencer and C. G. Smith and their associates in the laboratory continued to show innovative promise.

Marshall's enthusiasm for these activities was high. He spent much time in the laboratories, and often took part in research efforts personally. He, C. G. Smith, and Vannevar Bush were, after all, products of a generation steeped in the belief that America's progress was due to its technological innovations. Through the latter part of the nineteenth century and the early part of the twentieth, the nation's incredible achievement in receiving millions of immigrants from all over the world, in building great cities, industries, and an educational system to absorb them with unprecedented rapidity, seemed attributable mainly to technology. The political structure that encouraged and maintained the climate for such innovation was, for Marshall's generation, largely taken for granted. They credited Science, for it was a period when both politics and religion seemed to have lost luster.

In 1930, discussing research possibilities with his board, Marshall ticked off a number of fascinating new directions. These included Percy Spencer's photoelectric cells, glow tubes, the potential of electric home phonographs and radios, and new transmission equipment—more advanced than that employed by the telephone industry—that might lead to "exclusivity" in the field of communications.[4] This last prospect was one that entranced Marshall and was to dominate his imagination for many years.

But as the year 1930 proceeded, it was clear that innovations and new pioneering efforts might have to be set aside for better times. Survival became the key to effort. Month by month industrial production fell, unemployment increased, money tightened, and the situation grew more grim. The United States, which had ridden what appeared to be an eternal upward spiral, was now in reverse and riding a cycle downward.

The twenties had started with a scramble in which each man had sought to ensure his own position and had ended in panic. A conference in Geneva on tariffs came to no conclusion; England, Canada, and some other nations lifted their tariff walls higher—and the United States government, ignoring the protests of economists and the clear responsibility it had to international trade, followed suit. No single step could have been internationally more damaging.

A stream of hollow assurances issued from the White House and from leaders of business and industry, but these had lost credibility. A nation that had been too credulous now became too incredulous. The newspapers, featuring the phenomena of distress, grew sarcastic about the drift of events and the abilities of the Administration. A vast national search for scapegoats began. Brokers, bankers, industrial leaders fell into disfavor and, as a series of peculations and shoddy practices were revealed, into odium. Democratic leaders were quick to place the responsibility for the catastrophe upon President Hoover, whose recent campaign promises had concentrated on boasts of prosperity and the promise of "a chicken in every pot."

On Broadway John Wexley launched the first of what would become an endless stream of social protest plays with *The Last Mile,* a passionate argument against capital punishment that contrasted oddly with grim newspaper accounts of gang war in the streets.

The movies, unable to switch their emphasis quite so quickly, played *All Quiet on the Western Front, Journey's End,* and *Hell's Angels*—all antiwar dramas that now seemed, automatically, a part of the sudden anti-industrial atmosphere. Despite the increasing distress of millions, theaters and movie houses played to large crowds, as people simultaneously sought escape and explanations of the strange events underway that had so suddenly changed the pattern and circumstances of their lives.

By mid-1930 Raytheon's report showed a loss of $329,000.[5] This appeared to be a startling sum, but Marshall, in his Message, explained that $300,000 had been set aside for reserves. Nevertheless the firm, like all others in the radio tube and set manufacturing industry, was hard hit. Prices dropped like stones in water; every firm was stuck with inventory losses.

Around the world the situation worsened. England, whose economy had been crippled by the expenses of World War I, had long had a dole and was limping badly; the crash did not make a great qualitative difference. Germany, however—a nation where American investments had been huge—suffered greatly. In September 1930, against a turbulent backdrop of economic distress exacerbated by violent political dissension, the Germans held a significant election. The results showed the Socialists, long the ruling party, with a majority of 143, the Nazis in sudden second place with 107, and the Communists with 77 seats.[6] Such a division did not bode well for any part of the population. France, meanwhile, began the creation of the Maginot Line.

In the United States a phenomenon long associated with mass distress, shortages, and economic misery appeared: the queue. Long lines of people waited patiently for hours in front of emergency food stations, while financial institutions continued to collapse. One person, seeing a line in the street, asked, "Is that a bread line or a bank line?"

By the year's end 1930, unemployment was officially set at 4.5

million,[7] though many persons believed the real figures were much higher. Suicide jokes became, briefly, popular.

Most of the panics of previous periods—at least in the twentieth century—had been brief. By early 1931 it might have been possible for the American economy to begin an upward turn, but it lacked leaders.

Had the nation's bankers rallied to restore confidence and to extend credits to a shaken nation, the situation might have been restored. But the elder J. P. Morgan, who had once led such a recovery during the administration of Theodore Roosevelt, was long dead. His son, though competent, lacked the older man's fire and genius.

The crash had wiped out the speculators who had bought stock on margin; had decimated the ranks of successful exchange merchants and hit the lower levels of the population hard; but it had left the majority of the middle class in a still relatively sound position. But the bankers, looking to the situation of their own firms, decided to hoard money by cutting off the flow of funds to Europe. This set off a new train of powder. The Paris banks, pressed, called on their notes in Austria. In response the Credit-Anstalt, in Vienna, began to quake.

While a new storm was gathered in the stratosphere, Raytheon was having difficulties in the marketplace and—not unnaturally—with National Carbon. The hopes of both firms had been that their mutual efforts would become significant in the radio tube replacement market. "National Carbon never quite understood that the set manufacturers dominated the radio business," Marshall said, years later.[8]

In the wake of the crash and its immediate impact on the working man, pawnshops and secondhand-goods stores were bulging. Virtually everyone cut back on all unnecessary spending; radios were eminently expendable. Set prices fell to incredible lows. Simply stated, there was no market for Raytheon and National Carbon to rely upon.

Nevertheless the company managers argued on side issues, as people tend to do in difficult times. They redrew the agreement on patents and argued about advertising expenditures. National Carbon, to its credit, maintained a budget for these purposes, which soared over $375,000 during the year.[9] But its enthusiasm for the joint venture clearly sagged.

Raytheon reduced its employees from 600 to 450, and cut back on production. Though the Annual Report for 1931 showed a surprising gross profit of $733,000, Marshall pared that figure by withdrawing large sums for contingencies, reserves, depreciation, and "provisions for tube replacements, etc." The grim conclusion was a net loss of $250,000. Though somewhat overstated, there is no reason to dispute the obvious management view that conditions had worsened.

The reasons for pessimism could be, in part, traced to failures of nerve and intelligence on the part of national leadership, though not only the leadership in Washington. The discredit for the debacle that followed seems to lie equally at the doorsteps of Congress, the White House, the bankers, and the nation's press. All these circles followed selfish and shortsighted policies, failed to take a large view of the nation's needs, and led the people over the precipice.

Of them all, the bankers deserve the tallest ass's ears. By withholding funds from Europe at a critical moment, they worsened the crisis. The French were pressed by the Americans and in turn pressed the Austrians. As a result, the Credit-Anstalt of Austria collapsed in May.[10] Few Americans knew its name, but its collapse pulled a linchpin from the economy of Central Europe.

In Washington President Hoover sought to stem the flood by announcing that the American government would suspend European war debt payments for a year and asking all bankers to declare a "moratorium" on their notes. It was too late: a slide had started that could not be stopped.

In July the German Danatbank collapsed, and all the banks of Germany closed.[11] In this crisis the leading industrialists of Germany held meetings with Adolf Hitler. In September England abandoned the gold standard [12] and the international banking system, centuries in the creation, was in virtual ruins.

As the backlash of their actions returned to frighten them, American bankers compounded their error by panic. Seeking to save their own institutions, they called for the first time for more collateral to cover loans secured by stocks, by mortgages, and by inventories. This had the effect of draining the resources of the middle classes and creating another silent crash, larger and covering more people, businesses, and communities than the highly publicized market fall of October 1929. It was as though, on the heels of a disastrous harvest, men had sought to obtain and to hoard all the seeds of a nation's food supply.

By 1932 the situation had grown horrible. Over 1,300 banks [13]

58

and many times that number of businesses had collapsed completely. Unemployment was at astronomical figures; nobody knew exactly how many were out of work. Some said ten million; some said thirteen million. Boxcars studded with the figures of homeless men traveling from no place to nowhere rolled through towns. Knocks on the back door from persons seeking food became commonplace. Communities strained their resources to provide emergency aid; no national system of relief existed. Not the least of the calamities in 1932 was that it was an election year.

"There is no more sordid chapter in recent years than the attacks by Charles Michelson during the 1932 campaign," [14] said Dr. Vannevar Bush. But Dr. Bush gives too much credit to the former publicist of the Democratic National Committee. Articles and speeches, plays and demonstrations, lectures and dissertations were mounted against the Administration, the entire conglomeration of industrial and business leaders, and the Republican past.

One result was the destruction of the personal reputation and effectiveness of an American President while he was in office during a time of great national emergency. Waves of sarcasm swept across the land, with Hoover as the target. The newspapers used by a beggar to wrap himself at night were called Hoover blankets. The wretched collections of shanties and lean-to's that appeared on vacated lands, in which millions huddled and which appeared everywhere, were called Hoovervilles. A pocket turned inside out was called a Hoover flag.

It was a revolution conducted by the pen in a nation where the sword was no longer fashionable.

In 1932 Raytheon reported sales of $1.2 million and a loss of $163,000. [15] The payroll had been pared to 338 persons. "We did not work at all some weeks," Marshall said later. [16]

But, surprisingly, Marshall was still willing to hire bright young men of outstanding merit. He was eager to add new brains to his research efforts, and still more attracted to new development activities than to any other phase of operations. He went about with a cheerful air, though Dave Schultz—burdened as treasurer with the grisly details of declining sales and a vanishing market—showed grim seriousness.

That was, at least, how the leaders appeared to young Henry Argento, who was hired in August 1932.[17] He was, of course, jubilant. He had looked for work everywhere and everywhere been refused despite the fact that he had graduated from Harvard with a major in physics. The sole advantage he brought to Raytheon was a year spent in a radio frequency lab, but it was enough. Marshall was intent upon improving Raytheon's radio tubes.

Once inside the Raytheon lab, where he worked with C. G. Smith —a name he had encountered in his academic studies—Argento became aware that Marshall and Bush were the "guiding angels" of the research effort. They hovered over all the projects and had numerous suggestions and comments about the work.

Sid Standing, another newcomer hired in 1932, was more modestly situated but had similar observations. Standing had graduated from Northeastern University and was hired by Paul Weeks, the chief engineer. "Mr. Weeks was very stern but very fair," said Ruth Babb, who was working for him at the time as a secretary.

"The atmosphere was very informal," Standing recalls. "There didn't seem to be any formal organization whatever." [18] Assignments were made on the basis of whatever seemed most immediately necessary, without regard to status. Being an engineer in those days, at Raytheon or elsewhere, was not considered a mark of special distinction. Standing, who is still with the firm, looks back at that period with retrospective wonder.

"I kept meeting older men who had worked with Thomas Edison," he recalls. "Today, an engineer expects an office, an assistant, and a secretary—and sends his calculations to a computer group. At that time the state of the art was primitive. Trade journals were far behind real developments, and few books were available.

"Everyone worked on a trial-and-error basis," he says, adding, "The range was immense; the subject mysterious."

Like Argento, Standing soon became aware that Marshall was acutely interested in all developmental work. "He would stop and ask questions," Standing recalls. "He would make comments and give suggestions. I don't know how the others felt about this, but it helped me." Like Argento, he was intensely ambitious.

"Everyone watched the other guy and kept an eye on his progress," he says. "Everyone read everyone else's notes." [19]

❉     ❉     ❉

Marshall managed an enterprise that on one level coped with a poor market situation and economic stress in the usual way, by reducing overhead costs, cutting back production, paring inventories, and sparking sales efforts. The joint venture with National Carbon occupied some of his time. He plowed relatively large amounts into developmental and even basic research. To a later generation that does not sound extraordinary, but it should be kept in mind that in 1932 the entire United States War Department listed only thirty-four existing research projects.[20] The age of research had not yet dawned upon national governments, and only the most advanced industrial firms made such efforts. Laurence Marshall was well ahead of the spirit of the age.

An important effect of Marshall's method was that he kept the interest and participation of men in MIT's electrical engineering, physics, and mathematics departments, who sent a stream of graduate students into the Raytheon labs, and who themselves followed to keep track of their activities. Men were also lured to Raytheon from Tufts and Harvard. Later all these contacts, friendships, and connections were to prove crucial.

On a third level—for Marshall had a multilevel mind—the leader struggled with the oppressive market presences of RCA, General Electric, and Westinghouse. He had filed a suit claiming RCA had violated the Sherman and Clayton Anti-Trust Acts, and asking for $15 million in damages for injuries RCA had inflicted upon Raytheon prior to 1928. In response, RCA, aware that Raytheon was not making its royalty payments, filed a suit asking for these sums, plus penalties. While these actions were pending, both firms had no better course than to continue dealing with one another as though these Damoclean swords were not suspended over their relationship.

Complicated lawsuits, a declining market, heavy advertising costs, and disappointing sales were not factors to encourage National Carbon to continue its joint venture with Raytheon. By 1932, according to Henry Argento, Eveready Raytheon radio tubes had only one significantly large customer: the Commercial Credit Corporation. That was not enough. National Carbon began to look toward the exit.

National Carbon's disillusionment with the radio tube manufacturing business was no secret to Marshall. But instead of looking for another large company to pick up National Carbon's option on Raytheon or seeking another well-heeled partner for the marketplace, Marshall began to travel about examining manufacturing sites. These trips took him, on one occasion, as far afield as Kenrod, Kentucky, where he watched girls on an assembly line at a lamp factory with great interest. Lamp manufacturers then were still making tubes. Years later, Marshall recalled the dexterity of those girls, and the recollection was most timely.

Another area of attraction was the tiny Acme Delta Manufacturing Company in Cambridge. "We had some commercial links," [21] said Marshall. This was not unusual, but the links proved, on examination, to be more technological than commercial. Today we would describe them as joint research efforts.

Apparently they grew out of some connections long in existence that were reinforced by efforts made by Percy Spencer when he was in charge of tube operations. His projects, which included the creation of photocells, also extended to the design and engineering of transmitting tubes and tubes created especially for mobile radios. In turn these efforts led to a contract to build radio transmitting equipment for the Newton and Medford police departments.[22] Spencer, discovering the Acme Delta firm was well ahead in the construction of transmitters and magnetic components, farmed some of his effort over to them. This collaboration led to closer contacts, and Marshall was attracted.

Acme Delta had grown out of a previous venture called the Acme Apparatus Company formed shortly after World War I, at about the same time that Marshall and Bush had begun their efforts, but its founders had less success. Although both Ashley Zwicker and Claude Cairns of Submarine Signal made an early success out of building radio transmitters for the embryonic radio industry in the days when sets were put together by amateurs and continued this success later by selling transmitting equipment to set manufacturers, the depression and the death of Cairns effectively ended the effort.

In 1930 Dr. Frederick S. Dellenbaugh, formerly on the faculty of MIT, G. E. M. Bertram, formerly with Submarine Signal, and Charles W. Gaskell combined to buy the remnants of Acme. Together they reestablished a small radio equipment manufacturing business under the brand name of Acme Delta.[23] In 1932, their operations were modest: none of them had the flair, in terms of management, of Marshall, and certainly they lacked his prestigious backers.

Nevertheless Percy Spencer, working with Acme Delta, realized that some of the Raytheon rectifiers had a potential for power applications, and Marshall's imagination was captured. He saw promise in Acme Delta's magnetic components combined with Percy Spencer's potential power tubes. He had, at about the same time, discovered, in Percy Spencer's disgusted words, ". . . a new genius named Jim Le Van, a Harvard graduate," whom he had placed in charge of the Raytheon laboratory at Cambridge. Much to Spencer's dismay, he was ordered back to that laboratory, told to work under Le Van, and also told to concentrate on the power applications of rectifiers. Percy looked about, disheartened, for another job, but managed only to verify what he already knew: that there were very few opportunities in the vacuum tube field. "I went reluctantly to Cambridge," he wrote later—but he went.[24]

The potential of power applications, however, was an interesting area upon which to concentrate. Marshall thought so, and he would not have kept his thoughts a secret from the researchers. He thought that these applications might be used in welding—an industry slow to change. By the time he finished describing what that might mean, the Acme Delta people were excited. And by the time he had them excited, Marshall had already brought them under his spell.

As 1932 neared its close, therefore, Marshall was creating new combinations in anticipation of increased difficulties with National Carbon. As before, they took highly creative, unexpected forms.

In the larger world, other men were moved toward new objectives. It was a time of distress, and times of distress usually evoke both apocalyptic prophecies of the imminent collapse of the world, and clouds of panaceas purporting to guarantee a blissful future. Such an atmosphere is one in which demagogues thrive—and 1932 was a year of loud voices and, in many parts, the demagogue.

The greatest modern demagogic voice arose in Germany that year, and belonged to Adolf Hitler. With almost six million unemployed,[25] violence in the streets, banks in decay, and their nation disordered, the Germans listened to that voice, and many rallied to its banner. A series of elections finally reached a near deadlock, but the Nazis gained in many regions and established local control in Bavaria and Prussia. Toward the end of the year it became clear that Field Marshal Paul von Hindenburg—a relic of the monarchy and the only prewar national leader remaining—would make terms with the Nazis.

France veered in the opposite direction, as did Spain, and listened to the left. States in between were torn between the two extremes. In Finland a Nazi rebellion was mounted but subdued.[26]

Elsewhere there were ominous signs that the peace terms of Versailles were crumbling. Japan, taking advantage of Europe's disorder and the weakness of the United States, moved boldly in China and carved out the colony of Manchukuo.[27] The United States filed a protest. The League of Nations was impotent, most Americans indifferent. The attention of the United States was transfixed by the presidential election, which pitted Herbert Hoover against Franklin D. Roosevelt. Mr. Hoover's reasons for seeking reelection do not bear analysis. His chances were remote.

The nomination of Mr. Roosevelt, who had been a competent governor of New York, an Assistant Secretary of the Navy under unworldly Josephus Daniels in the Wilson administration, and a vice-presidential candidate in the ill-starred Cox effort of 1920, was the result of compromise. The nominating convention of the Democrats, with victory apparently assured the standard-bearer, had in fact split the party. Al Smith, the nominee in 1928, stalked out, followed by a large contingent of conservatives. Those who remained represented many new figures: college professors, literati, old Wilsonians, trade union leaders, and many from what would later be called the New Left.

The results were predictable: Mr. Roosevelt's victory was overwhelming.

But a sign that the nation had abandoned its old tradition of coming together after an election was provided by the President-elect's refusal to see Mr. Hoover or to work with him during the interim. This meant the nation had to wait till at least March 1933 before new steps could be taken. In the meantime, Congress and the White House remained bitterly deadlocked.

While the nation endured the five long months between the election and the actual seating of a new President,[28] Marshall huddled with National Carbon representatives, Raytheon attorneys, and the Raytheon directors. In February 1933,[29] at the offices of the First National Bank of Boston, at 67 Milk Street—a site the company seems to have

preferred whenever it had topics of unusual importance to discuss—
Marshall showed the board the details of his agreement with National
Carbon. Although the minutes do not show it, it seems likely he also
discussed a topic he was apt to raise whenever a sharp turn of the road
was reached: reorganization.

Amazingly enough, Marshall was optimistic. He must have been
one of the very few businessmen in the nation—if not the world—to
have this buoyant attitude. Around him economic earthquakes were
continuing. The bankers were distraught, and their institutions continued to crumble. By March 1, six states had declared a bank holiday [30]—an odd euphemism for a forced closing of all the banks within
their borders. On March 4 President Roosevelt was inaugurated. The
following day, a Sunday, he called a special session of Congress, and a
bank holiday was declared for the entire nation.[31]

During the next ninety days a series of sweeping new regulations
and agencies were formed by the new President and his Brain Trust.
They covered almost every conceivable aspect of national life, but
the average citizen was aware mainly of new relief measures which
were infinitely larger, more extensive and ambitious than anyone had
expected. They included appropriations of $500 million for emergency
relief, a Civilian Conservation Corps for unemployed young men and
the reforestation of the land, and special agricultural measures to assist the farmers.[32]

The nation's banks and stock exchanges were subject to new regu-
latory agencies; sweeping housing measures for the poor were instituted, and the National Industrial Recovery Act regulating wages,
treatment of unions, hours and conditions promulgated.

The atmosphere of the nation changed almost beyond belief. A
surge of confidence coursed through the land, and business took an
upturn, though many neither understood the new rules nor the deep
changes they would make in the pattern of national life.

It could not be said that Laurence Marshall or his associates were
part of this great effort, politically speaking. They were technologists,
not ideologists. But Laurence Marshall's changes in the company did
take place at the same time that these great and far-reaching changes
took place in the nation. In that sense they were well-timed to take
advantage of the sudden lift of the national mood.

There is no doubt that the National Carbon agreement negotiated
by Marshall made the difference in its ability to survive the dark days

of 1930–32. National Carbon had paid Raytheon $500,000 down, and agreed to "advertise and market to the best of its ability" their joint products known as Eveready Raytheon radio tubes. These expenditures amounted to another $500,000. By 1933, however, National Carbon wanted to be free of the obligation to continue. Marshall pointed out it could not simply toss its pledges out the window without abandoning the assets it had helped build in the joint venture called Raytheon Production Company.[33] National Carbon gulped at that: it had hoped to divide and divorce. But in business as in personal life, the partner most anxious to get out of the arrangement usually has to pay the most for the privilege. Marshall, a rocklike negotiator, pressed the point home.

As a result National Carbon withdrew entirely and left all the assets of the Raytheon Production Company in the hands of Marshall, his associates and shareholders.[34] These assets included $150,000 of the original $500,000 National Carbon had paid for an option on Raytheon Manufacturing Company in the days when they lusted after it. That onetime prospect, in which National Carbon would have paid another $19.5 million, of course went by the board. So did National Carbon's prospect of acquiring the entire Raytheon Production Company for another $14.5 million. But these desires had shriveled, long before, in the chills of the depression.

The retreat of National Carbon made it possible for Raytheon Manufacturing to issue an Annual Report, as of May 31, 1933, showing a profit of $267,000 on sales of only $841,000. Such figures, even though they represent a one-time occurrence, nevertheless glowed brightly against the Stygian gloom of the year.

Marshall's next step was to reorganize Raytheon Manufacturing Company so it could absorb and efficiently apply its new assets. That involved a complete restructure and the combined thoughts and talents of many minds. Understandably, the details were complex.

In essence, Raytheon Manufacturing Company, as part of the reorganization in June 1933, revised the capital structure by issuing 140,000 shares of preferred stock at a value of $5 a share and 260,000 shares of common stock at fifty cents a share.[35] All the assets of Raytheon Production and Raytheon Lamp Company, including machinery, inventories, and patents, were included in the new structure.

The patent list is interesting. It reveals that Raytheon had applied for fifty-six patents and owned fifty-three in the United States, as well as a long list of patents held in France, Germany, Italy, Japan, Great Britain, Norway, Sweden, Czechoslovakia, and Switzerland.

Raytheon's position was both improved and weakened. It had over $400,000 in cash in its treasury, was listed on the Chicago exchange, and had no great debts. Financially and organizationally its position was far better than that of most small firms in 1933. The retreat of National Carbon, however, left Raytheon in a weakened condition in the marketplace. Its major assets, after the dust had settled, centered around the unique intellectual position it had achieved in the state of the art in electronic engineering, as applied to radio. Outside special circles it was not well known, though inside such circles it was held in high esteem.

Marshall's immediate task, after the end of the National Carbon agreement, was to strengthen Raytheon's market position. He moved in that direction by hiring Edward Riddell as sales manager and assigning Henry Argento, who had a clear commercial flair, to be his assistant. But Marshall's driving thought, at all times, was not to attain a slow, steady commercial success, but to strike what Argento—who studied him closely—calls the "Big Blow." [36] To Marshall, that meant a creation that would transform the landscape—a technological miracle. The desire to develop a Big Blow impelled him toward Acme Delta.

In 1933, most men thought of personal security. Millions whose lives had been made insecure were willing to pay almost any price to be given the illusion of security again. In Germany, at the exact moment that Franklin Roosevelt was delivering his inaugural address, the voters went to the polls and cast their ballots for the Nazis.[37] By making this choice, they entered a trap in response to the bait of security, in which the price was abject obedience to authority. An indication of the retrograde nature of that authority was provided the world when the new German leadership made persecution of Jews official [38] for the first time in the modern history of Europe.

At the same time the Nazis pulled Germany out of disarmament discussions and joined Italy in vitriolic denunciations of the terms of the Versailles Treaty. The United States and Canada, in part as a result of the collapse of a world monetary conference in Geneva, abandoned the gold standard.[39] Throughout the world nations withdrew into economic and political nationalism.

In the United States Senate Gerald P. Nye of North Dakota—a region noted for the unworldly views of its elected representatives—launched an investigation into the munitions industry. With the able assistance of his staff director, Alger Hiss, Senator Nye sought to prove that wars are created by munitions makers.[40]


By September 1933, Percy Spencer had reason to believe his efforts would, once again, serve as a springboard to catapult Raytheon forward. He had developed a mercury rectifier—a tube that, in practice, served as a power switch and as the basic component in newly designed welding machines.[41] Delta, whose experts had been pulled into this effort, had created special transformers and ten experimental models neared completion.

Marshall described these to the Raytheon board and recommended the purchase of Delta and the acquisition of its people. The purchase price was a modest $16,000.[42] In Marshall's view, this was far less important than the services of G. E. M. Bertram and Dr. Dellenbaugh. Bertram was a superlative production man. Dr. Dellenbaugh towered six feet six inches into the air, weighed 240 pounds, and had a knowledge of magnetic components and filters that was, in the words of Dr. Edward L. Bowles of MIT, "beyond measure." [43]

The entire roster of Delta Manufacturing was small but impressive. It included Robert Quimby, an acquaintance of Vannevar Bush, who had helped J. Jenks develop the world's first cardiograph.[44] During the years, this was not the only significant effort upon which Quimby and the other men at Delta had worked. They had produced tubes that converted light into sound, known as Excito Lamps, for the talking-movie industry. Quimby, then a test engineer, recalls that he himself was so excited when this tube was demonstrated for Warner Brothers that he made an error in the hookup and the apparatus blew up in front of the assembled dignitaries. Nevertheless, it later sold successfully.[45]

Delta had also constructed the new WNAC broadcasting station in Boston, and its activities in general were very advanced. To the engineers of Raytheon the acquisition of this small group of talented men looms as one of the great intellectual landmarks in the history of the company. These men not only opened new avenues, but streets, lanes, and boulevards in the technical sector. The management decision to buy Delta, however, was made mainly because the sum involved was modest, and the Marshall description of the possibilities in the welding industry intrigued the directors.

Indirectly the Delta acquisition brought youthful attorney Carl Gilbert onto the scene. His participation began when he was called into the office of Thomas Nelson Perkins, a senior partner in the prestigious Boston law firm of Ropes, Grey, Boyden & Perkins. Mr. Perkins "kept an eye" on the Boston area interests of J. P. Morgan, who had remained an important shareholder in Raytheon throughout all its divagations since he had sold it the S tube patents a decade earlier.

Gilbert's first task at Raytheon, on behalf of Ropes, Grey, Mr. Morgan et al., was to investigate the validity of the Raytheon efforts in creating a new welding process—in other words, a patent search. It was not an easy task.

"At the time," Gilbert said later, "there were very few persons who knew anything about electronics (the term itself had not yet been coined), and even fewer of those who knew anything were patent lawyers. General Electric, naturally enough, had the outstanding expert in the field in Mr. Teller. Harrison Lyman, a Boston lawyer, was another." Unfortunately Gilbert could not go for help to either of these; he had to learn from scratch.[46]

He learned well, and was able to assure the management that Raytheon's patent position appeared sound. He also learned enough about the personalities and problems of Raytheon to become fascinated and engaged, though neither he nor any other young man could quite appreciate the difficulties that confronted business at the time.

In later years the many achievements, or at least activities, of the New Deal had the effect of obscuring the recollection that it had campaigned and been elected on a program of thrift, governmental restriction, and modest promises. Once in office, President Roosevelt unveiled a vast array of programs that had never, until then, been presented to the people.

Almost all the New Deal programs were presented as reforms, made necessary by practices that had led the nation into a depression. The argument overlooked the fact that a state of political civil war, conducted in Congress against the previous administration, had contributed greatly toward the depression. Descriptions of many of the new measures were also misleading because some of the most significant were not reforms but revolutionary changes.

One such change, although only one, was the new "excess profits tax." This rule made it mandatory for a firm to distribute reserve funds either in the form of dividends or in the form of tax payments. On its face, it seemed well designed to force hoarded money into circulation. Philosophically and politically, however, it amounted to an assumption, new to the United States, that the government had a right to force the legal owners of a property to handle its revenues not as they chose, but along lines considered best by the government.

That new rule affected Marshall's managerial approach very directly. It was only one of many that confronted both Raytheon and every other business enterprise in the land. Furthermore the new rules were not, as in the past, issues in law that had been debated in Congress and approved by the community, but were hurriedly created and enforced by special agencies equipped with sweeping powers. The men in charge of these agencies could both make rules and sit in judgment over those to whom the rules applied. This was a serious break with tradition, which had held that those who make rules should be separate from those who sit in judgment.

In all, these changes were so diverse, so sweeping and numerous, and involved so many people, issues, material matters and concerns, that their totality constituted a most unusual revolution—for those who brought the revolution kept denying that one was underway.

In all, it was a time of confusion and emotion. No man wanted to deny the need for strong action during the depression, but few men could say, in truth, that they knew where the new tide was carrying them, their business, or their nation.


The New Deal did not differ from its predecessors in being antimilitary. Presidents Harding, Coolidge, and Hoover had all disdained the army. The nation had, after World War I, returned to its prewar conviction that the great space of geography constituted its largest protection. In 1923, Franklin Roosevelt, writing as a former Assistant Secretary of the Navy, had declared that any threat from Japan against the United States was "unthinkable," because of the great ocean expanse that separated the two nations.[47]

The only argument against this verity was the growing menace of air power. In Italy, shortly after World War I, a theory had arisen that air power would determine the wars of the future. Newspapers and magazines in the years between had run countless articles on the hysteria and the destruction that would rain upon civilization from the air in a future war. This argument had great effect, and spurred many peace movements. A great number of people accepted it so entirely, in fact, that they considered wars obsolete and the subject closed.

Nevertheless, the United States had, during the Hoover period, allowed funds for the construction of aircraft carriers to strengthen its naval protection. One of these was commissioned in 1934. Beyond that, the military was neglected.

Chief of Staff General Douglas MacArthur complained, in 1934, that the assignment of regular army officers to Civilian Conservation Corps facilities had left the U.S. Army so reduced that ". . . training inside the continental United States has been brought to a virtual standstill." He added, bitterly, "The secrets of our weakness are secrets only to the American people." [48]

MacArthur felt so strongly he carried his case to the President and the order was changed. Reserve officers were called for the purpose, and a few years later that proved a fortuitous strengthening of the army. But some New Dealers were annoyed, and a directive emerged calling for the dismissal from the army of those officers who had not been promoted for a long time. The reasoning, apparently, was that the army "establishment" needed to be changed. Had that order gone through, the United States would have lost the services of Lucius Clay, Leslie Groves, Albert Gruenther, James A. Van Fleet, and Matthew B. Ridgway, all of whom were still then only first lieutenants after fifteen years in the service. Congress intervened and blocked this move.

Militarily, MacArthur had reason to worry, and so had his counterparts in England. A resurgent Germany, a bellicose Italy, and an aggressive Japan made it plain that the world order as established by the Treaty of Versailles could be challenged. These three nations, however, were not the only trouble spots on the horizon. In Spain a left-wing government began to arouse growing resentment; in France strikes, riots, and political violence brought the nation to the brink of civil war; the Balkans were seething.

Ominous events began to occur with increasing tempo. The death of Hindenburg in Germany made Hitler dictator of that nation. The Austrian chancellor, Dollfuss, was murdered by Nazis, and more Nazis and counter-Nazis rioted in London's Hyde Park.[49] The secret association between the Germans and the Soviets collapsed, as a result of Hitler's rise. Inside the USSR, barely over a famine in the years 1931 and 1932, a vast purge of Communist Party members began.

But by far the most significant development, to the U.S. armed forces, was the development, at least in design, of long-range bombers.

No military men believed, no matter who did the persuading, that peace was either eternal or assured. Inside the United States, however, it was long considered that the two oceans comprised an unbreachable moat of protection. Upon learning that aircraft designers and manufacturers could create vehicles to bridge those spaces, the air corps announced a "competition" in such designs and accepted the Boeing B-17 and the B-29 as a result.[50] It was planned to use these vehicles in the defense of Panama, Hawaii, and Alaska. The B-29, however, was not delivered for ten years.

In England Winston Churchill arose in the House of Commons to declare that Germany was capable of threatening the safety of Great Britain. He called for defensive measures and was shouted down by the majority. His influence behind the scenes, however, was so strong that a silent, discreet, and highly important search began to examine and refurbish the state of the island defenses against air attack. Suddenly some British scientists active in the area of radio communication, such as Robert Watson-Watt and Ralph Tizard, found themselves involved in these very sensitive considerations.[51]

A similar process, sparked by the U.S. Signal Corps, was launched in the United States. In its beginnings only a very few men, like Vannevar Bush and Dr. Edward L. Bowles of MIT's electrical engineering department, and their counterparts in the physics and mathematics departments, were involved.

In turn they bent a close eye upon the developments in Raytheon's labs and factory, and it was as a result of this quickened interest and these larger considerations that youthful Henry Bernstein, one of a group of U.S. naval officers taking postgraduate studies at Harvard in the hard sciences, found himself, with some fellow officer–students, being conducted through Raytheon's Waltham installation.

"I was very impressed," Bernstein wrote later, "with Raytheon's research and development of power tubes." His guide, Percy Spencer, "showed us the RK pentode power tube series, which was in production." [52]

A combination of factors had brought Percy back from the Cambridge laboratories and out from under the supervision of the "newer genius, Jim Le Van."

Metal tubes, replacing glass, had emerged in the industry and Marshall determined to go into volume production. Since engineering skills of a high order were needed, he transferred Percy back to Waltham and put him in charge of the change-over.

"We discovered," Percy says, ". . . in metal tube manufacturing, that the electrical resistance welding, as used, required large ignitrons and thyratrons that were unattainable."

"Unattainable" was a provocative word. Percy set about first to discover the details of existing ignitrons and thyratrons and then to improve them, so Raytheon could make the new metal tubes. He succeeded in creating two new power types of ignitrons and three of thyratrons. They worked so well Raytheon decided to market them as new products, and did so successfully. [53]

These advances were paralleled inside Delta. Fritz Gross, a young design engineer hired by Raytheon in May 1934, disclosed a previous knowledge of theater sound amplifiers. [54] When the Delta group hit a snag in these efforts, Gross became involved and found the solution. As a result he remained with the Delta group and found himself working well with another young man, named Dave Coffin, who was designing large transformers, and with Bob Quimby. The trio became the nucleus of what would, in time, become a great seedbed known as the equipment division.

Power tubes had caught Henry Bernstein's eye, but they were only one part of an entire spectrum of developments underway. Such efforts, coupled as they were with production changes and market introductions, are extremely expensive. The 1934 Annual Report disclosed a payroll increase from 554 to almost 900 persons, but the company was again losing money.

Such a situation creates tensions, but Marshall remained buoyant

*73*

and confident. He and the directors debated a possible loan from the First National Bank of Boston; [55] the staff was urged to more innovations. Meanwhile the enterprise, engaged in novel efforts and becoming known for innovations, attracted a steady stream of talented young engineers.

"The larger companies wanted security-oriented men," Marshall recalled later. "We wanted men who wanted to do things." [56]

They toiled in the Old Button Factory at Waltham through the winter and into 1935. The button manufacturers of the past century had long ago left, but they left behind great mounds of shells in the yard, each of which showed a small hole from which a button had been cut. Years later Fritz Gross would recall looking out the window at these mounds, which represented, he says, "the life span of a vanished industry. They seemed to me like a graveyard of the past." The sight spurred him into renewed efforts.

The winter of 1935 faded and spring arrived. The Annual Report showed Raytheon with a healthy sales of $2.28 million, but puny earnings of only $1,359.88. If this seemed ᵣnall comfort, however, it was more than many other firms enjoyed. An economic chill had returned, and the political climate had grown unexpectedly stormy, as a result of several rulings of the U.S. Supreme Court.

One ruled the NIRA, which regulated sweeping sectors of commerce and industry, unconstitutional by restricting the application of the interstate commerce clause of the Constitution. The ruling cast doubt on the legality of the numerous New Deal agencies by questioning the legality of their creation. The justices, taking note that the New Deal was operating largely on the basis of executive authority, reminded the Administration that since the days of John Locke lawyers had agreed that though an office might be invested with special powers, it could not create, by delegation, other offices with the same powers.[57]

In time this reasoning led to congressional action and, ironically, resulted in converting New Deal emergency agencies into a permanent part of the U.S. government—but that conclusion took time to reach.

Meanwhile the nation fell into an angry debate more sweeping and bitter than any since the days of the Dred Scott decision prior to the Civil War. Half the nation raged at the Court for its reasoning; the other half raged that the New Deal attempted to shortcut legal procedures.

The division was reflected in the arts as well. On Broadway Clifford Odets, a left-winger, had three of his plays on the boards at once—and each was a searing indictment of capitalism. A Left Wing Book Club arose. Communism became fashionable in some circles. For the first time influential persons in the literati in the United States began to sound as ideological as their counterparts in Europe.

From the opposite pole came bitter accusations that the New Deal was, at one and the same time, Communistic, Bolshevistic, Socialistic, and anti-American. The D.A.R. and the American Legion demanded the institution of loyalty oaths, and the various associations of manufacturers and businessmen mounted a heavy barrage against the Administration.

Meanwhile the New Deal continued to pour new legislation upon the nation. The Social Security Act, the National Labor Relations Board, the Agricultural Adjustment Act for farmers, and other agencies increased, rather than relaxed, the movement for change. The labor unions, vastly enlarged and strengthened by new political power, joined the fray.

Although business had improved, the situation did not really allow the waste of political strife. Unemployment was still very high; the Federal Emergency Relief Program was spending millions but its effects—although certainly beneficial to the recipients—did not seem to "prime the pump" in the way New Dealers had predicted.

Getting a job was still a difficult achievement in 1935, as young Norman Krim discovered.

Originally from New York, Krim had graduated from Cornell at the age of twenty-one, with a B.S. in electrical engineering, and had then attended MIT and studied under Dr. Bowles. He had met Vannevar Bush at Raytheon's lab, located near the Institute, while working on his graduate studies, and also knew Percy Spencer.

While completing his master's thesis—on the Japanese progress in microwaves—Krim looked for a job. With his connections, which included Bowles's recommendation, he should have had an easy time if anyone did. He did not, even though he was introduced to Marshall by W. B. Overbeck, an MIT professor who had worked, at one period, at Delta.

Marshall looked at the young man grimly and took him through a grueling three-hour interview. "He shot questions at me, such as: 'Why do you think you want to work at Raytheon?' " Krim said, "and would sit there, stern and silent, while I stumbled through my answers."

Eventually he was told to report to work on September 15. During the interval he was employed at a summer camp and toiled over his thesis. When the date drew near, Krim thought he'd like more time and called Marshall long distance to ask for a delay.

"There are lots of young men available," Marshall said into the phone. "We expect you here on the fifteenth." He reported, and went to work in the Old Saxony Mills buildings at Chapel Street, at fifty cents an hour.[58]

Yet though life in the United States during 1935 was harsh in many ways, it was still far easier than in most other countries; Americans spent more time escaping than confronting reality in art, in entertainment, and in their mental lives.

*Mutiny on the Bounty* appeared that year in films; so did *Lives of a Bengal Lancer* and *A Tale of Two Cities*. These costume dramas, far removed from everyday cares, were paralleled by much of the popular literature. Thomas Wolfe's *Of Time and the River* evoked classic American themes. On the stage, *Porgy and Bess* outdrew the proletarian dramas so highly praised in *The Nation* and other small-circulation, politically oriented publications.[59]

Elsewhere life was harsher, in some places, virtually murderous. The Soviet Union mounted a series of spectacles that were to amaze half the world and bewilder the other half. Although called trials, they resembled none the West had seen since the days of the star chamber under the Tudors. In them, the judges questioned and denounced the defendants, and the defendants ranged from Zinoviev,[60] a member of the Presidium, through a number of other Old Bolshevik leaders of the revolution, through thousands upon thousands of lesser party members. Most persons in the West never fathomed, until the information became historic, the reasons for this purge. It was twofold: to consolidate the authority of Stalin, and to eliminate those who knew too much about previous crimes conducted by the authorities against the people. The ostensible charge was treason.

Had it been the practice of the world press to report events in the

Soviet Union in the same caustic and skeptical manner it reported events in the West, there is little doubt that this horrifying charade would have greatly reduced the prestige of the USSR among many of the world's intellectuals. Unfortunately, the practice of glossing over all the weaknesses of the Soviet Union while emphasizing all the defects of the West had already become settled. Only correspondents sympathetic to the regime were allowed to work inside the USSR at any time; by 1935 the newspapers that employed such correspondents had long since lost the habit of calling attention to the censored nature of their dispatches.[61]

Some other decisions were made that did arouse more analytic press attention, though. One was the promulgation of the Nuremberg Laws against the Jews in Germany; another was the creation of a coalition government by Léon Blum which brought Communists into high authority in France; and still another was Italy's invasion of Ethiopia.[62] All these decisions deserved attention, for all were to lead, directly and inevitably, to larger world problems. For calling those to universal attention the press deserved, that year, due credit.

To Sid Standing, Raytheon was a happy place, no matter what troubles it seemed to have. "There were weeks when Earl Wood would come out of the office to announce that everybody's pay would be delayed 'till next Wednesday,' " Standing recalls, "and everyone would go about their work as if nothing had been said. We stayed because this sort of delay was not uncommon during the depression. Besides, there was no place to go." [63]

If there had been, it is doubtful if Standing would have left. Standing worked under Paul Weeks, the chief engineer, and he grew to admire the older man tremendously. "He knew how to draw people's abilities; he never pulled a man down—he pulled him up. He had a way of saying, 'While you were thinking of this, did you happen to think of that?' "

But the man who made Raytheon happy, to Standing, was Marshall himself. "He always gave the impression of being happy. He pulled everyone into his enthusiasms, his involvements."

Dr. C. G. Smith, on the other hand, was a *muted* man, though "immensely learned and highly respected." Jim Le Van, who worked in a cellar laboratory next to Smith, told Standing it was "a little like

*77*

being in the Little Red Schoolhouse." Like working, in other words, with a schoolmaster.

As a rule the average scientist is apt to take a lofty view of engineers, and to regard them as merely so many jumped-up mechanics. Engineers in turn are apt to consider scientists a group of otherworldly dreamers whose calculations, more often than not, end in a quagmire of disproven assumptions. But at Raytheon the scientists of MIT, Harvard, and Tufts moved in and out easily, and an atmosphere of close cooperation developed between the theoreticians and the engineers. This extended the firm's position to a unique scientific and engineering promontory far beyond the usual commercial enterprise.

If technologists in the United States harbored what resembled class antagonisms within their ranks, these were mild compared to the vast gulf that existed between technology generally and such organized groups as the military. In England—where differences of education, accent, and class are deep and, in 1935, were very wide—boffins, as the air force termed them, seemed most unlikely types. But necessity presses men together, and in 1935 the English military, and in particular the air force, was sufficiently alarmed about the possibilities of long-range bombers to put together a group of scientists and to appoint a Director of Scientific Research to develop a defense against air attack.

The boffins learned the British War Office had constructed "two huge concrete mirrors, each two hundred feet long" on the coast. Theoretically these would catch sight of invading aircraft and allow a warning to be raised, upon which fighters would rise in defense. Experiments proved such a warning would give "two or three minutes time." Investigation showed the War Office had also thought of raising balloons as a line of aerial defense. Beyond that, its ideas grew cloudy. Someone asked H. E. Wimperis, of the air ministry, about the possibilities of developing a "death ray"—favorite of science-fiction buffs. The scientists laughed; their name for such ideas was—and is—the Black Box.[64]

Watson-Watt, to whom the death-ray query was addressed—in writing—replied the idea was impossible. But, he explained, it should be possible to measure the position of an aircraft from the ground by sending a pulse of electrical energy, at the speed of light, and by measuring the interval of its rebound from the aircraft. The echo could be measured on a cathode ray oscillograph. Scientists had for some years been experimenting with such beams, to locate electrically charged clouds for other, more esoteric purposes.

A group of British scientists headed by Tizard was able to track a plane for seventeen miles in June 1935. By July the range had been extended to forty miles. In order to do this "a transmitting station illuminated an area with radio waves—pulses of energy." The aircraft within this area reflected some of these waves back to the watcher's station, where they were observed on the cathode ray oscillograph. By mid-September 1935, an airplane flying at an altitude of 7,000 feet was located to a position within 1,000 feet. At that point the British realized that more power was needed, that their transmitting station could easily be jammed by an enemy, and that their work had barely begun. But they had enough upon which to move, and with Winston Churchill, Sir Philip Cunliffe-Lister, and Sir Warren Fisher behind them, they received relatively large funds for their efforts.

This contrasted sharply with the state of air defense in the United States, where in early 1936, the research and development funds of the American military establishment were cut from $9 million to $7 million.[65] Of course, there was an equally considerable difference between the English Channel and the Atlantic Ocean.


The nation moved into another election year—1936—with a demonstration of the power of radio that verified the initial hopes of its importance by its pioneers, but that would have shocked them by its real-life use. As far as many Americans were concerned, the radio had become a dream machine, in which soap opera substituted for reality and a large array of new people whose talents centered on the nuances of speech became important.

On another, higher level, the radio grew into a potent political force. President Roosevelt had launched, within a fortnight after his election in 1932,[66] a series of "Fireside Chats" to the nation. Seldom had such a gifted orator been able to enter into the hearts of his countrymen so swiftly. The radio presence of Mr. Roosevelt, his warm tone and upper-class Hudson River Valley accent, which perfectly matched the expectations of the electorate of being led by an aristocrat of democratic tendencies, was an overwhelming experience. It counterbalanced the fact that the nation's editorial pages thundered against the

New Deal, but paralleled the warm tone in which the President was reported by a sympathetic press corps in the news columns.

In an odd and not entirely rational way, the United States seemed to be living in realms of fantasy that deflected its powers of hard reason regarding the actual state of the nation, the world, and the drift of events.

The drift was dismal. Japan left an international naval conference —a clear indication it no longer felt bound to an inferior status militarily. Britain increased its defense budget and planned to add 250 aircraft.[67] By May 1936, the Italians completed their conquest of Ethiopia, and the League of Nations—revealed as impotent—was shattered as an instrument of world stability. Spain moved toward a civil war as the newly elected Popular Front government, consisting of a combination of all the parties on the left, introduced a series of sweeping changes in the national life. In Belgium, England, and parts of Central Europe, Nazi mini-parties arose. Inside Germany the Nazis tightened their grip; German forces occupied—without challenge—the demilitarized zone of the Rhineland.

But though wars and rumors of wars swept around the globe, the biggest book of the year in the United States was *Gone With the Wind*. With eight million still unemployed, the nation's movie houses played to their largest crowds since early 1929. Over five hundred feature films were produced and over two hundred imported to entertain the people. Athletic events evoked immense throngs; football reigned supreme. Sit-down strikes were introduced and during the spring and summer seven political parties, ranging from the Socialist Labor through the Prohibitionists, the Socialists, the Union Party, the Democrats, Republicans, and Communists held conventions and nominated their candidates.[68]

Meanwhile Raytheon learned a harsh commercial lesson. The welding equipment manufacturing industry, long dominated by a small group of firms, had countered Raytheon's new tube-powered welding machines by simply dropping the prices of their traditional motor-powered units in half.[69] By that swift and certain stroke, they made it impossible for Raytheon to manufacture or sell its hard-won innovation at a profit. The Big Blow could not be delivered.

Directors Billy Gammell, Havens Grant, Richard S. Aldrich,

Harry C. Watts, Vannevar Bush, Miller Brainard, Colonel Dillon all held firm. Marshall and Dave Schultz—his alter ego in those days—were terribly disappointed.

Carl Gilbert, the young attorney from Ropes, Grey, Boyden & Perkins told his employers about this development, but defended Raytheon stoutly. "This small firm," he said, "broke new ground in an old industry and introduced basic modifications. In itself that is a great achievement." [70] He then went on to explain that in the course of these developments, Raytheon had discovered a wide range of improvements that it was applying, with considerable benefit, to its regular production of radio tubes and components.

One such area, interestingly enough, was in the welding of new combinations of metal, in which former "skin welds"—which affected only the surface of the different metals being bonded—were improved to a "deep weld"—or complete fusing. Other developments ranged through an array of special tubes made possible in part by this new approach to welding, and included a miniature tube that proved very valuable in automobile radios.

There was an immediate effect on the welding experiment in other parts of Raytheon's production, therefore, that approached the serendipitous. A few years later, these effects would prove to be crucial in the creation of products upon which not profits but the lives of millions would depend.

But in May 1936, these were considerations that were either unknown or relatively unimportant alongside the more immediate and crushing fact that great developmental expenses and uncounted man-hours had gone into a considerable achievement whose value had been rendered worthless in the marketplace at the stroke of a strange pen.

In the 1936 Annual Report, which showed sales of $3.2 million and a loss of $80,000, Laurence Marshall included a footnote reminding shareholders that Raytheon still had an important antitrust action pending, involving "a substantial sum." [71] The years had not lessened but rather increased his belief that RCA had attempted to stifle competition and he believed his case was strong. The settlement he sought—$15 million—would not only alter the situation of Raytheon, but improve the competitive climate of the entire radio manufacturing industry. Marshall contemplated that prospect and felt his spirits rise again.

Nevertheless the fate of the welding innovations of Raytheon, so

*81*

arduously discovered and so expensively engineered and produced, illustrates the many pitfalls that surround industrial research and development. Such stories are legion: they far outnumber, and greatly exceed in terms of man-hours, money, dreams, and destinies, those that succeed. To the world, Raytheon's change of the welding industry joined the immense legions of nonevents—innovations that never appeared.

Through the balance of 1936, therefore, the firm's radio tube production continued and sales improved, but no great changes took place.

In the larger world, the downward slide continued. A rebellion started in Spain under the leadership of Franco that created a crisis of nerves in Paris and London.[72] Germany and Italy announced they would support and recognize the rebels. In Paris, where a Popular Front government might have been expected to support a Popular Front Spanish government, which had, after all, legal title to its position, cowardice intervened. The French determined to remain aloof and hoped by that tactic to remain safe; by December the British joined in this position. This refusal to accept the gauntlet thrown down by the Fascists and the Nazis was received in Rome and Berlin with jubilation and contempt.

In the United States people remained largely unaware of the implications of these events. Their attention centered mainly on the election triumph of President Roosevelt, who was swept back into office with the majority votes of all but two states. The result was an unmistakable mandate to the New Deal to continue its programs and was so received, at least in the White House.

The year 1936 ended, however, on a note that seemed borrowed from the radio soap operas. In England, Edward VIII announced he would resign the throne [73] rather than part from twice-married Wallis Warfield Simpson.

At Raytheon, production and sales continued to increase, and the number of persons employed rose to over 1,600. It seemed, in early 1937, as though the firm would do well to concentrate on the commercial marketplace. Marshall reported that glass tubes still comprised the largest percentage of those sold and produced, which seemed to indicate, at that moment, that the hard-won advances in metal tubes had still not paid for their expense.

*82*

He told the board that the firm needed additional capital, and discussions—which were to extend for months—began on the form of such an effort. The directors thought a new issue of common stock would be best. Brokers were contacted, the market sounded, and plans drawn up to sell approximately fifty thousand shares at $6, since Marshall believed that about $400,000 would be needed.

Before this plan could be put into operation, an alternate, more complicated plan was drawn. On the second effort, the directors approved a plan to sell 400,000 shares of common stock at fifty cents a share and 140,000 shares of preferred, at $5 a share. Then the experts took another look at the market and decided the time was still not quite right.[74]

They had reason to hesitate. The United States was in a curious condition. Both the Administration and its critics seemed exhausted, unable to create any new ideas, and exacerbated by all the old ideas.

Mr. Roosevelt, in a rare misreading of the climate, offered a plan to alter the judiciary branch of the government which was received as an attempt to "pack" the Supreme Court. A great outcry arose in opposition.[75]

A wave of strikes rippled across the land disrupting industry and crippling the pace of commerce. To compound confusion, the drift of international events led to the Neutrality Act, which set off an avalanche of protest from the intellectuals.

In effect, Washington not only washed its hands of the Spanish imbroglio, but joined with Britain and France to blockade the beleaguered Spanish government. The act was based on the weakness of Britain, the fact that most Americans were unwilling to see the nation entangled in European matters, and the knowledge that the Loyalists had become creatures of the Kremlin. The choice was unpleasant in every direction, for the rebels were supported by the Nazis and the Fascists. The press compounded the confusion by glossing over the Communist orientation of the Loyalists and emphasizing rebel ties between Franco and Hitler. Arguments over the issue became bitter and emotional.

In such a murky climate it was difficult to define either the international or the domestic direction of the nation. The business index dropped, prices began to sag on the stock exchanges. The Raytheon plan to issue more stock to raise needed capital was delayed by these uncertainties.

*83*

By the end of May 1937, the Annual Report showed that sales had risen, but the company as a whole had lost $80,000.

Such results certainly contained little to attract new investors. In his message Marshall somewhat lamely fell back upon the antitrust suit against RCA—an item that had been on the corporate burner since 1931, that was barely mentioned in previous Annual Reports, and that only the year before had been buried in a footnote.[76] The company, like the nation, was drifting.

Yet this surface was deceptive. Inside Raytheon, as well as inside the research facilities of many other firms, entire series of scientific and engineering developments were waiting upon outside conditions to emerge. In Akron, where the rubber industry had its business center, processes for creating synthetic rubber waited for the right moment. In Bell Labs, in RCA, inside Westinghouse, complex series of discoveries similarly waited.

In England, advances by the boffins had resulted in special early warning installations along the Thames Estuary at Dover and near Southend. Much progress had been made and planes could be detected over the North Sea. Unfortunately the intricate tasks of calibrating their precise location and course was replete with error and confusion.[77] Nevertheless the military men were encouraged and the government placed orders with Vickers and Cossor for the manufacture of components, and planned the construction of twenty more such stations.

In the United States the National Research Council created a special Committee on Scientific Aids to Learning,[78] whose members represented a glittering group. They included the president of Bell Labs, Professor Conant of Harvard, and many others, including Dr. Vannevar Bush. On a wide front, the American scientists and military men began, in a muted fashion, to coordinate their efforts in the same direction and for the same reasons as the British.

The men inside Raytheon, aware that matters were not going too well commercially, worked harder. Marshall's mastery of the mysteries of leadership evoked this sort of response without any obvious efforts.

Young Norman Krim, back in the labs, would put in a full day and then retreat, after a hasty bite somewhere enroute, to the stacks at MIT's library.[79] There, being youthful and unencumbered, he often toiled until late in the night taking notes. One of his colleagues, Steve de

Laslo, an MIT graduate, son of a famous English painter, left Raytheon to return to England. Krim, a somewhat lonely figure, found work more interesting than play.

Percy Spencer, whose contributions ranged across an amazing spectrum, from the scientific in the lab to engineering on the production floor, gradually assumed a position of leadership in operations. Dr. C. G. Smith, still gentle and absorbed, faded into the background as a respected, almost revered figure, but one no longer in the forefront, or even the cast, of top management. Smith had, unfortunately, sold most of his stock during the darker moments of the depression and seemed more interested in research than in other areas.

Marshall, on the other hand, recalls himself as being "aglow with electricity." [80] Suggesting, prodding, and seeking new avenues, he ranged restlessly through every aspect of the company. Ruth Babb, working as a secretary for Tom Thompson, the one-man purchasing department, was situated across the hall from Marshall's office, which was next door to Dave Schultz's. Peeking in,[81] she noted that Marshall operated from behind a huge circular desk whose top was kept gleaming and bare. He seemed able to memorize anything he read; he was able to pass it along and retain its contents indefinitely. On a side table stood a book usually seen only in children's rooms: *The Little Engine That Could.* When men said something was impossible, was beyond them, Marshall would point silently at that book. The message was unmistakable.

Traveling about, looking for new ideas, Marshall unearthed a small firm in Peterboro, Vermont, that had developed a process to fuse different woods together electrically. He grew enthusiastic about this, saying it could "revolutionize the furniture industry," [82] and tried to interest Western Union and AT&T into joining with Raytheon in a marketing effort for the process. They were not interested; he was disappointed.

Regarding the telephone company installations he toured, Marshall said, "They reminded me of so many miles of sewing machines, all ticking away." He wondered, aloud, what tubes would do to automate and quicken such fixtures, but turned aside, convinced the telephone people were behind the times.

But the telephone company's decision not to adventure with him was not so much determined by the quality of his project as by the commercial realities of 1937. In autumn a wave of selling overtook the exchanges, and by October a full-scale slide was underway. On the nineteenth, the largest number of shares since 1933 was sold in one great tidal movement—all at lower prices. It was the worst market crack since 1933.[83]

Events in the larger world were equally disquieting. The Japanese, after staging some provocations, launched heavy military efforts in China. Mussolini traveled to Berlin and the merging alliance between Italy and Germany was more firmly welded.[84] In England the Labour Party announced its loyalty to the League of Nations and demonstrations for peace appeared on college campuses throughout England, peated their long-standing argument that wars between capitalistic France, and the United States. In Paris and elsewhere, Marxists renations were based only on the profit motive.

As though responding to invisible cues, the press of the western world began to feature articles on the impregnable nature of the Maginot Line and to emphasize the reputation of the French Army as being the best in Europe.

On high political levels in England, where Neville Chamberlain had become prime minister, a parallel argument, equally reassuring, began to emerge. If Germany's demands for a revision of the provisions of the Treaty of Versailles were met, this argument ran, all difficulties would subside, central Europe would be protected against the Soviets, and the West would be relieved of anxiety. Lord Halifax, visiting Hitler, heard this proposition presented with convincing passion.

In December 1937 the people of the United States were surprised to learn that an American gunboat, the *Panay*, had been bombed and sunk by the Japanese. Many Americans voiced anger that the *Panay* was in Chinese waters in the first place; others shrugged the incident away as an error. In Tokyo, where this action had been ordered as a start in a long-range plan to destroy European dominance in Asia, the American reaction was regarded as significant.

It was not until early 1938 that the genie escaped from the bottle and America belatedly realized the world was closer to war than at any time since World War I. The news seemed almost too large to grasp. Twenty years of steady denunciation, of arguments that war is senseless and never rational; twenty years of soaring pacifism expressed in an endless stream of plays and poems, lectures and books, movies and analyses were too strong for most people to overcome. Millions closed their minds against war and refused to credit their senses; others launched organizations to keep the United States disengaged.

When President Roosevelt called for "collective international sanctions" against aggressor nations, he was, for once, out of tune. His speech startled the nation, and many applauded a response by former President Hoover, who warned against international alliances. A great national debate began.[85]

At the same time the New Deal at last turned its attention toward the nation's military condition. After years of neglect it was in a state of decay. Some idea of the extent of the decline can be gathered from the fact that 1938 was the first year that army expenditures for armored vehicles exceeded sums spent for horses, mules, harnesses, and wagons.[86]

Early in January the President asked Congress for huge appropriations to build up the army and navy.[87] The naval plans were especially sweeping and called for increased forces on both oceans. At the same time, the administrators of the New Deal switched from their search for those who needed help to a search for those who could help the nation. It was as though a great treasure house, previously disregarded, was entered for the first time.

One particularly glittering group of resources—both human and scientific—clustered about MIT, Harvard, and Tufts in New England. Raytheon was a part of this constellation. Many of the areas of research undertaken by this group paralleled those being made by the English scientists. Dr. Vannevar Bush, who had become head of the MIT department of electrical engineering, served as a connecting link between many of these efforts and the Raytheon facilities; Dr. Edward L. Bowles, who had known the Raytheon personnel, facilities, and management since 1922, was another; Dr. William M. Hall, of MIT's electrical engineering department, still another.

Bowles and Hall were part of a scientific group that conducted experiments and theorized on ultra-high frequency radio waves, the radiation of electro-magnetic waves through hollow pipes, circuit theory, and dielectrics, among other esoterica.[88]

Bowles had even persuaded Colonel E. H. R. Green, son of the famous financier Hetty Green, to allow them the use of the vast Green estate at South Dartmouth, Massachusetts, as a research station. From

*87*

that location they worked on the use of radio beams for airplane landings, the dispersal of fog, and other matters of absorbing interest.[89]

Raytheon's facilities and personnel were considered so great a resource by these scientists that early in 1938 Fritz Gross was assigned
to one of their important development projects. Dr. William Hall
himself, deeply involved, became a consultant on the effort and in
time it became of national importance. At the time it linked Raytheon
to the forward wave of the state of the art in microwaves.

Raytheon was not, of course, the only commercial enterprise engaged in advanced work. The Submarine Signal Company of Boston,
where Dr. Fessenden and others had made scientific history by advances in underwater sound equipment, was another. SubSig was unusual in having, as its largest and most important customer, the U.S.
Navy. That situation was, however, a mixed blessing, for many of
SubSig's achievements were classified secret and kept off the commercial market. Nevertheless the firm was important and significant. It had
developed depth-sounding equipment and was far ahead on sonic detection devices.

A series of forward steps took place in early 1938, therefore, that
brought a number of younger men forward. At Raytheon these included Fritz Gross, Dave Coffin, and Robert Quimby, among others.

Raytheon, the scientists at MIT, Tufts, and Harvard, and the New
England sector were stirred into new efforts, but they were not the
only region so affected. The power of the White House in 1938 had
grown far beyond the realization of most Americans. Its decision to
energize the resources of America coursed through the land like an
electrical charge. Business responded, the stock exchanges began to
improve; some war orders began to flow from Britain.

Even young Norman Krim—twenty-four years old—went to Marshall with a new idea. His former coworker, de Laslo, had returned to
the United States for a visit and had dropped in on Krim at Raytheon.
During lunch he described how he had, in England, developed some
new miniature radio tubes that were being produced for new and less
cumbersome hearing aids. Krim came to attention.

Marshall listened to this suggestion with a heavy frown, but Krim
had taken the precaution of first persuading Percy Spencer. Spencer
beamed; he liked the idea. Marshall was dubious.

"If it does not pay for itself within a year, you will be fired," he told Krim. The younger man gulped but nodded his head. It was a deal.[90]


Ordinarily Marshall might have been more receptive but he had received severe disappointments. First, the earlier decline in the stock market—a circumstance beyond his control—had destroyed his hopes of selling a new stock issue and raising more capital. Then, as a result of the decline in the market, the First National Bank of Boston—an institution with which Raytheon had outstanding loans—called for more collateral. That call was a consequence of the decline in the market, but the knowledge did not make the demand any sweeter to swallow.

Finally Marshall was forced to abandon a dream that had sustained him for years: the antitrust suit against RCA. The complaint was complex, as is any dispute that had so many years to fester. In effect, it claimed damages from RCA for injuries to the Raytheon firm, as it existed prior to 1928. In the interim, Raytheon and RCA had become entangled in suits and a countersuit for damages regarding royalties RCA claimed were owed by Raytheon. In that respect, the court ruled that Raytheon was liable to the extent of $425,217, plus interest charges of $45,400.

RCA, on the other hand, was ordered to grant Raytheon—and Raytheon was ordered to grant RCA, Westinghouse, and AT&T—release from all claims except royalties and except for patent infringements outside the radio field. In addition, RCA was ordered to give Raytheon a new licensing agreement to extend from January 1, 1939, to January 1, 1945, to cover radio vacuum tubes, for a royalty of 5 percent. In turn Raytheon was ordered to grant RCA a nonexclusive license for all its patents in all countries. Finally, the court concluded, RCA would have to pay Raytheon $410,000 for the licensing agreement it obtained from Raytheon, and Raytheon would pay RCA $392,000.[91]

All the years of argument, the conferences and promises, discussions and hopes, had ended in a standoff. Marshall reeled and had not yet recovered from this shock when attorney Ned McClellan submitted his bill. It was for $150,000.[92] Marshall promptly went into a towering rage.

❖    ❖    ❖

While deep-rooted changes were taking place inside Raytheon, New England, and the United States, the rest of the world was undergoing more sweeping changes.

In England the prime minister had finally accepted the doctrines of what later became known as the Cliveden Set. Boiled down, they amounted to the argument that the Treaty of Versailles had been poorly drawn. Therefore Italy and Germany had a right to demand changes. Once these were effected, Italy and Germany would no longer threaten the peace and would constitute, in their larger and more powerful forms, a Third Force, capable of being both a barrier and a balance between the West and the Soviet Union.

Beneath this geopolitical argument ran another, even deeper rationalization, based on popular social theories. These theories were predicated on the assumption that nations, like individuals, will cease to disrupt if the causes of their anger are defined and the conditions that maintain resentment are removed. Unfortunately the essence of that assumption rests on the accuracy with which underlying causes are defined. But in 1938, with the formidable forces of the entire intellectual left mobilized for peace, it seemed very persuasive to Neville Chamberlain.

Chamberlain's decision to treat with Hitler and Mussolini created a rupture on the highest political levels of Britain. Anthony Eden resigned as foreign secretary and was replaced by Lord Halifax; Winston Churchill led a rebellion against the policy of appeasement in the House of Commons.[93] Chamberlain, however, had the majority of the press and public on his side, and the rebels were howled down.

Hitler wasted no time in taking his advantage. Nazi troops, displaying terrifying armored forces, crossed the borders of Austria and that nation was declared part of greater Germany within two days.[94] Before the world could absorb the meaning of that swift conquest, Nazi Germans in the Czechoslovakian Sudeten territory began a series of riots, demonstrations, and demands to have their province transferred into the Reich. The sound of drums and marching feet became almost audible throughout the world.

Against the heavy backdrop of great events, the news that Raytheon, despite a formidable reduction in its personnel, had increased its sales during the fiscal year 1937–38 to $3.4 million and could, at last, report a respectable profit of $427,000, aroused little attention outside the company.[95] Too many other changes were taking place.

One change, which would have a profound effect on Laurence Marshall, was the departure of Dr. Vannevar Bush. Dr. Bush had been appointed president of the Carnegie Institution of Washington, D.C.— one of the nation's top scientific organizations. The appointment carried Vannevar Bush away from Raytheon and toward the heights.

In time, Dr. Bush was to become one of the most powerful scientists in the history of the world. His decisions and attitudes would have a profound historical impact. But in 1938, all that was visible was that he had received a plum and was to head an organization that was, though highly respected, still considered outside the mainstream of events.

He wrote a brief note, dated June 3, 1938.[96]

*Dear Laurence:*

This new post, and my location in Washington, will make it advisable for me to drop out directorates. Reluctantly therefore I ask that you present my resignation from the boards of the Raytheon companies. Needless to say I will maintain interest even in the absence of formal connections.

*Very truly yours,*
*V. Bush*

In a personal sense this was a very important change. Dr. Bush had been a partner with Marshall in the Raytheon effort. He had, in reality, been the first to see, and to call Marshall's attention to, the potential of such an effort. In the French term, Dr. Bush was the intellectual author of the venture: in the American, a cofounder. In a more immediate and human sense, in 1938, his departure meant a personal loss to the president of Raytheon. His presence, his stream of suggestions, his analysis, and his shrewd assistance would be sorely missed.

At about the same time Charles Francis Adams, Jr., a partner in Paine, Webber, Jackson & Curtis, received a call in his Boston office from Henry S. Morgan in New York City.[97] Morgan, a younger son of J. P. Morgan, had married Charlie Adams' sister, but the call was on business.

The immediate reason was the illness of Thomas Nelson Perkins, a partner in the law firm of Ropes, Grey, Boyden & Perkins. That illness, Morgan explained, was serious enough to require that the Morgans obtain a new man to keep an eye on their investments in the Boston area. Would Charlie Adams mind watching a small firm in which the Morgans had money? Adams asked about the firm and was told it was Raytheon. He agreed.

In retrospect the timing was amazing. Next to Vannevar Bush, no man would have a greater effect on the career of Laurence Marshall than Charles Francis Adams, Jr., who joined the board of Raytheon in August 1938.

August was the month of Munich and the season of Hitler. He began by mobilizing the armed forces of Germany, while diplomatic arrangements were made for Neville Chamberlain, prime minister of Britain, and Edouard Daladier, premier of France, to make a pilgrimage to Berchtesgaden.

A few days after the dictator alternately raged and promised at this initial meeting, Chamberlain and Daladier met with Hitler and Mussolini at Munich. There they signed an agreement to transfer the Sudetenland and all important Czech military strongholds to Germany. Mussolini received international recognition of his occupation of Libya, which joined Ethiopia as part of a new Fascist empire in the Mediterranean.

Multitudes gathered in London and Paris to greet their national leaders when they returned from this ceremony, and hailed them as victors for peace. A few weeks later a Gallup poll in the United States showed that the majority of the American people agreed.[98]

Though most of the applauding millions did not seem to realize it, the agreement made Germany the strongest power in Europe. The French chain of alliances in the Balkans, designed to prevent this, was shattered. Czechoslovakia, having lost its crucial defenses, was dismembered by its neighbors. Poland, which repeatedly sought world sympathy as a beleaguered smaller power, demanded—and received—Teschen. Hungary annexed southern Slovakia. Ruthenia and Slovakia seceded.[99] All that remained to the Czechs was a shell.

While these grim proceedings were taking place, the British military worked feverishly to improve its strength. The British navy mobilized; an army draft was started. A. P. Rowe, in a book written about the scientific side of these efforts, said, ". . . five stations manned by R.A.F. personnel guarded the Thames Estuary. Then came a winter of mud and wind; mud for the scientists, engineers, and fitters who installed the stations in the more desolate spots of Great Britain; wind for the men who worked hundreds of feet above the ground installing towers and aerial arrays . . ." [100]

The results of Munich were a terrible disappointment to the White House. President Roosevelt had, at the last minute, attempted to avert the outcome by sending a private memorandum to Chamberlain, Daladier, Hitler, and Benes of Czechoslovakia, suggesting international arbitration. Less than a week after this appeal, which he ignored, Hitler was touring his new territories in Sudeten Czechoslovakia.

President Roosevelt, announcing that the king and queen of England would visit the United States for the first time, sought to behave as though all was well. But he recalled the United States Ambassador to Germany,[101] whose reports about German military strength added to his concern.

There were other Americans, however, who believed that matters were improving. A flood of war orders poured from Britain and France to stimulate the economy of the United States; the marketplace reacted by an upswing.

The war orders, though, did not arrive to a completely receptive American market. The previous war had, after all, been almost a generation in the past, and the United States had been through not only the fires of the depression, but also deep, traumatic political changes.

Roger Damon, then a rising young executive at the First National Bank of Boston, who was assigned to the Raytheon account among others in 1939, recalls the atmosphere vividly. "Raytheon was just a tiny little thing," he says. "It had no financial expertise—but it didn't need any; it was too small." [102]

Other firms, better equipped for large-scale industrial production, were in a technical position to profit but lacked funds to fill orders. "Most of the Boston banks did not encourage firms to become involved in United Kingdom war contracts," Damon recalls. "As a result, many opportunities went by default—especially in the New Hampshire, Providence, Rhode Island, and Springfield areas." The First National of

Boston did believe in such orders, however, and took the long chance. As a result, it made an early contribution not only to the economic improvement of the region, but to the war effort.

More conservative bankers were not being indifferent: they were attuned to the national mood; perhaps to a national malaise, developed by years of negative conditioning. In the United States Senate, despite a January recommendation by the President calling for a defense budget of $535 million [103]—a huge escalation—some members of the U.S. Senate still saw no world menace. Senator O'Mahoney of Wyoming was far more interested in concentration of monopoly power, and was conducting a full-scale investigation, as though the early days of the century had not passed and huge trusts were still in existence.

In the same January 1939,[104] Vannevar Bush attended a meeting on theoretical physics sponsored by the Carnegie Institution and George Washington University, where the topics concentrated on the future. Niels Bohr had arrived from Denmark to meet two scientific refugees from Germany: Otto Frisch and Frisch's aunt, Lise Meitner. Both nephew and aunt were leading physicists and had described experiments that, as Bush puts it, "indicated a neutron could knock a uranium atom into relatively large pieces and release great energy in the process." He also learned that two other ranking physicists, who had remained in Germany—Otto Hahn and Friedrich Strassman—had proven one of such pieces "was undoubtedly barium." Listening, Bush thought that Germany "might have been in a decided head start." That conclusion, according to Werner Heisenberg, a German physicist who remained in Germany through the war and afterward, was accurate. Germany was, indeed, ahead in this area in 1939.

Later Bush concluded that the Nazi racial theories, which banished many brilliant Jewish scientists, plus a lack of coordination between the Nazis and the German scientific community, led to failures in the German scientific effort.

At the Washington meeting, however, the Americans were excited when Enrico Fermi arose to speculate that "if a neutron knocked uranium apart, more neutrons might be emitted in the process. If so, there was a possibility of a chain reaction, the release of atomic energy and a bomb." A special advisory committee consisting of eminent physicists, the Director of the National Bureau of Standards, and several military men was established.

❊    ❊    ❊

*94*

Although Raytheon was a commercial enterprise and had, under Marshall's leadership, almost miraculously survived the most severe depression in the economic history of the United States, it had no clearly defined goals. It was almost like an advanced part of academia, in which the major working area of radio tube production and sales was held to be of a lower order of interest than the laboratories and experiments it supported by its operations.

Laurence Marshall's rationalization for this emphasis was, in part, based on the very successful course of the Spencer Thermostat Company. During the years Spencer had been merged into a firm called General Plate, with facilities in Attleboro, Massachusetts. Launched to commercialize a technological discovery, it had prospered—had returned large sums to its founders and shareholders, though during the thirties it had experienced uneasy moments.

Billy Gammell and several other directors and shareholders of Raytheon were also directors and shareholders in General Plate. So was Vannevar Bush. Mr. Marshall, president of Raytheon, was also president of General Plate, though admittedly not very active.[105] His success in one venture had a natural fallout, in terms of influence and persuasiveness, on his activities in the other.

Nevertheless Raytheon in early 1939 was still a strangely mixed bag of interests, projects, products, and potential. Its explorations in the welding area, thanks largely to the brilliant John Dawson—an engineer who could translate the physics into practical engineering—had expanded into large welding machines that could make precision-controlled welds in industrial applications. It had also pioneered other products.

The Raytheon OZ 4 rectifier tube, developed by Percy Spencer, was a distinctive improvement to the automobile radio business, and Henry Argento, who was in Chicago between 1935 and 1939 as a sales engineer, was proud of the sales volume he reached with this product.[106]

Norman Krim, after a hesitation during which he resigned from Raytheon, accepted a job with RCA, and then returned to Raytheon within a month, launched another new product with his miniature tubes. Krim made a fast tour about the United States talking to hearing-aid dealers and discovered that market was very anxious for improvement. It was necessary for special production equipment to be constructed before the tiny tubes could be turned out in volume, but an arrangement was made with Western Electric to have these components placed inside W.E.'s hearing aids. This constituted a new and profitable section.[107]

Yet by the spring of 1939 it could not really be said that Raytheon had grown into a large manufacturing organization whose research and development efforts were geared to a special market position it had attained. After seventeen years of existence it was still an experiment, though one of the most impressive experiments on the horizon. It had a high reputation in certain circles; its laboratory abilities were on a par in some areas with immense establishments of great renown. Yet unlike these enormous competitors, it was not supported by a commercial base of profitable business.

When Henry Argento returned from Chicago to become an assistant chief engineer in production, he observed that Laurence Marshall was still searching for the Big Blow. The only business-oriented man in the establishment was Dave Schultz. Schultz, liked by everyone, handled the bankers, the suppliers, the creditors, the cash flow, and other grim matters. He had an office next to Marshall's, and the two were sometimes called "the twins." [108] They appeared everywhere together, excepting that after the day was done, Marshall could be found in one laboratory or another, toiling with researchers and engrossed in some wonderful new possibility, while Schultz's day had ended.

In 1939 Dave Schultz moved back to New York City with his wife and family. Thereafter he commuted. He would leave Boston on Friday night, on what was then a crack train—the Merchants' Limited— and reach Grand Central Station five hours later. Each Sunday night he boarded the train for the reverse trip. During the week he lived in the University Club in Boston.[109]

Inside Raytheon the Schultz routine was taken for granted. It was, after all, only one of many idiosyncratic patterns at the firm. But it was an excellent reflection of the fact that Raytheon was more like a university in business than anything else.


Inner contradictions on a far greater scale seemed symptomatic of the entire United States that spring. The vast majority of the people were disturbed and unsympathetic to the Fascists and the Nazis, but at the same time wanted to remain neutral. In literature, historical novels—especially those dealing with the American past—became very popular. Yet *The Grapes of Wrath*—a social protest about the plight of mid-1930's Okies—created a sensation, while *DuBarry Was a Lady* packed the house on Broadway, and *Life with Father* delighted millions.[110]

In Europe, Mussolini denounced Italy's pacts with France and made demands for Corsica, Algeria, and Tunisia. Neville Chamberlain, rapidly becoming an anachronistic figure with his wing collar and umbrella, scurried to Rome to placate the dictator. In February Franco completed his successful rebellion in Spain. Both Britain and France promptly recognized the new government; after the briefest of hesitations, the United States followed suit. The Nazis moved into the Czech provinces of Bohemia and Moravia and established a "protectorate." In unison Hungary annexed Ruthenia. Hitler then took Memel from Lithuania, and denounced the peace treaty between Germany and Poland.[111]

These moves awakened Chamberlain from his trance. He conferred with the French, and both nations made a joint announcement that they would guarantee the borders of Poland. The news astonished Hitler; he could not credit a guarantee by nations that had no access to Poland, and that had previously ceded defensible territories much closer to their own.

Mussolini, now caught in the race and moving past recall, invaded Albania. Britain and France then announced they would guarantee the borders of Greece and Rumania. Their meaning was clear. Hitler had reached the limits of their tolerance, and so had Mussolini. Any further power grabs would mean war.

By the end of May 1939—although the figures were not completed and presented until July—Raytheon not only had not improved its position, commercially speaking, but had lost ground. Its sales had dropped slightly, to $3.1 million.[112] Instead of the healthy profit it produced the previous year, it announced a loss of $78,000. A Note D gave some indication of Marshall's humor, as it growled, "This amount includes $50,000 . . . to cover the estimated unpaid balance of counsel fees incurred in the litigation with Radio Corporation of America. . . . Counsel has suggested they should be paid a much higher amount. While the matter is under discussion, the Board of Directors believes now, as

*97*

it believed in 1938, that this amount (with the $25,000 paid in 1934) is adequate." Since it represented exactly half what attorney McClellan had asked, he obviously did not agree; the argument continued.

That was a minor, though vexing problem. By mid-1939, Marshall had far more interesting matters in mind. They revolved, as they had so often before, around the activities of the MIT scientists with whom Raytheon worked so effectively. On a grand, national scale, a gradual confluence of scientists was underway, with the approval—and even the urging—of the government, academe, and private industry.

There was no center to this movement in a scientific sense, but Vannevar Bush played a pivotal organizing role in Washington, D.C., from his position as president of the Carnegie Institution. At MIT, Dr. Edward Bowles took part in efforts in radio transmission as it applied to aircraft detection and landing, explorations in ultra-high frequencies and dielectrics. In these, Raytheon was among the resources that Bowles and his associates counted most heavily. They had a long background of mutual effort and had achieved some outstanding successes together. These had included the design and construction of special shortwave communications equipment used by Admiral Richard E. Byrd in several Antarctic expeditions, beginning in 1929.

Raytheon, however, was a working partner rather than a sponsor. In order to get funds for their experiments, Bowles and other scientists had to appeal to a broad group of private firms, and in some plausible fashion connect their projects with the needs or goals of industry. ITT, for instance, was a sponsor for researches into ultra-high radio frequencies and dielectrics. Sperry, on the other hand, sponsored efforts in aircraft detection.

Robert Watson-Watt, a leading British scientist in this sector, took a long and objective view of the American efforts. They were, he said later, "rather like a string of beads, the beads being separate little groups secretly pursuing a hope of detecting aircraft by the use of microwaves, tantalized by minor successes, frustrated by the major obstacle of lack of power and limited receiver sensitivity." [113]

The English were ahead of everyone, but they were far from having resolved their problems. Their radars used against low-flying aircraft emitted echoes that were confused in the clutter the instruments could pick up from the sea. But they knew, or rather were fairly certain, that they were far ahead of the Germans and the Japanese.

At this point, Watt read an article in an American journal that indicated some significant advances had been made. He led a small contingent of boffins to the United States to pursue this discovery. By the time Watt, who was accompanied by British scientists Cockcroft and Bowen, arrived, Dr. Edward Bowles and his group from MIT had already moved into the new area.

Bowles had learned that Dr. Varian of Stanford had developed a new tube, called a Klystron, that vastly improved radar capability. He called this to the attention of Compton and to the managers of Sperry, and obtained funds to extend experiments accordingly. He and Compton had also, according to Watt, enlisted the influence and support of Alfred E. Loomis, a New York attorney interested in the hard sciences, who had an encyclopedic range of acquaintances and friends, and who was very wealthy.

The scientists collected on Loomis' imposing estate in Tuxedo Park, New York, and Watt learned the Americans had detected a small aircraft at a two-mile range working with principles developed by the British. Loomis, an interested party to the discussion, described a new, special microwave laboratory established at the Radiation Lab of MIT.

While they were at it, the scientists and Loomis also agreed to develop a long-range navigational aid, later called the Loran. It was very similar to Britain's shortwave ASDIC, but the coincidence was merely that. One was not a copy of the other.[114]

A most interesting part of these efforts was that they were conducted on almost an individual, personal level by citizens interested in the subjects and anxious to prepare the forces of freedom against the monstrous tyrannies that were menacing mankind. These efforts were underway at a moment when many Americans obstinately refused to recognize that the realities of the world could not be banished by turning one's head.

Yet the ordinary citizen could hardly be blamed for this attitude. In the White House President Roosevelt, in the summer of 1939, tried to convince Idaho Senator Borah of the danger. The Senator, an awesome figure with his great shock of hair, heavy eyebrows and fiery eyes, snorted at the argument. "All this hysteria is manufactured and artificial," he said.

Anyone who judged the world by the American surface would have to agree. A World's Fair opened in New York, evoking reams of description and pages of pictures, and another opened in San Francisco as a counterattraction. Millions flocked to both and were ecstatic over the exhibits and rides, the restaurants and the cheerful crowds.[115]

In June the king and queen of England arrived in Washington, D.C., and memories of the conflict and divisions that had once parted the two nations faded into antiquity. The Roosevelts delighted the nation by serving hot dogs to royalty on the lawn at Hyde Park, the President's home; the newspapers grew unwontedly sentimental.

Overseas the Soviets, their purge suspended, replaced their longtime foreign minister Litvinov with Molotov, a member of the Presidium.[116] The change was a sign that the highest Soviet level—Stalin—had entered into international negotiations personally. His initial step was extended toward Britain. He suggested a defensive pact against Hitler. In the British House of Commons the longest, most outspoken and famous critic of the Soviets, Winston Churchill, arose to proclaim his opinion that such an alliance would be good.[117] As if by magic, the world press, which had ignored Churchill for twenty years, suddenly rediscovered his virtues and began to proclaim his abilities.

In August a British military mission, pursuing the alliance, arrived in Moscow.[118] Hitler stormed, and for the first time it appeared as though the Nazis might be ringed.

Chamberlain issued another warning that Britain would stand beside Poland, and Hitler took to the radio. Millions of people throughout the globe listened to his voice, which traveled around the world with almost the speed of light on the instruments of science. Despite the interval of space, millions of Americans spent Sunday afternoons huddled in their living rooms listening to an orator whose language they could not understand, and whose arguments, as translated by the announcers, made little sense to them. But the cadence of that voice as it rose toward a shriek—interrupted by the deep, visceral response of German multitudes as they roared *Sieg Heil!*—sent shivers through the land. Suddenly life no longer seemed as simple or as safe as before.

Toward the end of the month the English began to evacuate women and children from London, and on Setptember 1, 1939, Hitler invaded Poland and seized Danzig.[119]

The newspapers in the United States ran headlines inches high; the British appointed Churchill First Lord of the Admiralty; Britain and France declared war on Germany; and within one week the Nazis held all of western Poland. On the seventeenth of the month the

Soviets, by prearrangement, invaded the Poles from the east, and the world learned to its horror that the Nazis and the Communists had joined for a kill.

By the end of the month Poland had ceased to exist as an independent nation and was divided between the Germans and the Soviets. Hitler then asked Britain and France for peace.

President Roosevelt, by now grimly aware that the United States lacked the means to intervene, made a radio address and assured the nation of America's neutrality.

Behind the scenes a frantic effort to catch up began. In Washington, Vannevar Bush found himself deeply engaged in the National Defense Research Committee, composed of civilian scientists and engineers, to develop weapons, systems, and organized avenues to strengthen the nation. War orders began to pour through the land; the wheels of industry began to move. What the New Deal had been unable to accomplish in six years, during which it spent—in seventies' terms—the equivalent of $70 billion dollars, was now accomplished in a matter of months. The nation had entered 1939 with over two million people still receiving federal relief.[120] Their numbers began to diminish rapidly.

Radio tube orders and other special demands began to pour toward Raytheon, but the improvement was not immediate. There are no magic wands in this world. The systems of civilization are circuitous and complex; the translations of change take time to course through its passages.

Outside the United States, however, the movements of war struck upon the consciousness like so many bolts of lightning. A British battleship, the *Royal Oak*, was sent to the bottom by a Nazi submarine in the naval base of Scapa Flow. Magnetic mines, strewn in the waters around Britain by the Germans, sent twenty-six British merchant ships to the bottom in a month.[121]

The rulers of Belgium and Holland, aware their nations were now confronted by the armed might of Germany, asked King George VI of England to suggest peace terms with Hitler.[122]

❖     ❖     ❖

The decade had opened with the collapse of the world economic system and the beginning of a great depression. It closed amid the collapse of international law and the beginning of war on a scale the West had not seen since the days of Genghis Khan and the Mongols.

This time the barbarian, as Ortega y Gasset, the Spanish philosopher, had warned, had risen from within.[123] And it is curious to reflect that the barbarian rose, at least in part, armed with instruments devised and provided by the highly civilized and gentle men of science.

Until World War II, most men had still accepted, with little reflection, the centuries-old assumption that inventions and discoveries would, by their very nature, improve both the conditions and the behavior of men. It was not until World War II that it began to dawn upon many people that this sequence is a non sequitur. An invention is a neutral instrument, which men apply according to their natures and their goals. In Germany, the radio had become an instrument of evil in the hands of Hitler, whose gift was eloquence. He was the first German politician to use radio as a means of reaching the people directly. His arguments, broadcast without interruption or analysis, made a mockery of reason and history but swayed the uneducated masses.

The decade ended, therefore, with a world transformed by the very improvements that Dr. C. G. Smith, Dr. Vannevar Bush, and Laurence Marshall had helped usher into birth, with the assistance of Billy Gammell and his friends. They were, all of them, well aware that this transformation was far different from the one they had hoped would occur. But if the instruments of science can be used for wicked purposes by limited men, then better men can make better instruments for better ends.

Because the world usually moves slowly, it had always before been part of the work of a succeeding generation to devise ways to overcome the unexpected results of its predecessor's efforts. It was the unusual destiny of Marshall, Bush, and their associates to find themselves in the forefront of the effort to launch a second scientific revolution to overcome the effects of one they helped create. That is a very special destiny indeed, and their efforts took novel shape.

# Chapter 5 THE WAR OF THE WIZARDS

T H E British braced against an immediate attack from the air, but Hitler, a master of surprise, talked peace and struck from the sea.

The new German submarines were able to dive deeper and stay down longer, could travel faster and had heavier weapons than ever before. The Nazis also sowed the water around Britain with new and very efficient magnetic mines of a sort never before seen, against which the minesweepers of the Royal Navy were helpless.[1]

Finally some specimens of these horrors were fished, intact, from the chill waters and given to the British scientists to unravel. They toiled to create countermeasures. Meanwhile a heavy loss of ships continued.

Churchill, First Lord of the Admiralty, was told about this situation and his quick imagination was caught by the new reliance of the military upon the abilities of scientists. "A wizard war,"[2] he said, and wondered if victory would eventually go to the side with the greatest, or most efficient, wizards.

The phrase went the rounds, delighted the scientists, and encouraged their efforts. Perhaps it was so intended. Mr. Churchill was aware of the importance of human qualities—and they were at war.

That meant a high pitch of emotion—a time when men are no longer cautious and no longer count the cost. It is also a time when inaction, as well as action, can weight the scale of events.

That is why, in retrospect, the resistance of Finland against the endless armies of the Soviets lit the winter landscape of 1940 like a rocket in the night, and made contemporary newspaper descriptions of a "phony war" seem misleading.

People in Britain, France, and the United States were astonished when the Finns stopped the Communists at the Mannerheim Line and inflicted severe losses on them in several engagements. It was not possible that Finland, with its limited resources and manpower, could hold out against the monolith indefinitely, but its resistance was the first against the dictators.

In preceding months the Soviet Union had swallowed half of Poland and sent its troops into Latvia, Estonia, and Lithuania. All three Baltic nations had once been under the yoke of the tsars. With the new Soviet occupation they again vanished into captivity.[3]

Finnish resistance created admiration among the people of the West, but their leaders had even larger reasons to be impressed. A second front in Scandinavia would provide the British and French navies and air forces with bases from which to strike the Nazis. It was true the Soviets might regard aid to Finland as a warlike act, but that was not a total deterrent. Even national leaders are human, and the duplicity of the USSR—with its incessant propaganda for peace and its cynical alliance with the Nazis—had created a deep anger.

Finland issued an open appeal for help,[4] but the Nazis were too deeply tied to the Communists at that point to answer the appeal. Britain could, and began to organize an expeditionary force. The British asked the Swedes and Norwegians for permission to cross their territories to aid Finland.

Had that permission been granted it might have altered the course of the war, and pitted Britain and France against the Nazis, Fascists, and Communists. With all the free world fighting against all the dictators a clear intellectual line would have been drawn. But that is idle speculation, for both Sweden and Norway announced a position of strict neutrality.

While the British hesitated and argued over whether to respect that neutrality or not, Hitler decided to strengthen his northern flank. These plans, which constituted a diversion for the German military, inadvertently provided Britain, France, and the United States with more time to prepare their home defenses.

Each of the three nations used its time in its special way. France drifted. Soldiers sunned themselves, read newspapers, hung out washing, and went on sit-down strikes inside the massive forts of the

Maginot Line. The newspapers featured these activities, and that is how the term phony war originated.

In the United States the President was aware the nation needed instruction in the nature of the threat posed by the Nazis and Fascists, Communists and—in Asia—the Japanese. But he had himself only recently realized the serious technology gap that existed between America's highly advanced industries and its defenses. The gap seemed to yawn under observation. War orders, flowing from Britain and emerging from Washington itself, disclosed a serious shortage of trained workers. Years of depression and unemployment had left millions of young men without skills.[5]

That was only one phase of the problem. Another was conceptual. The American industrial system was a marvel, but a peacetime marvel, created to serve the needs of a peaceful society. To convert this immense system into a war machine was an engineering challenge of a very high order.

Finally there was an area of science that had to be translated into engineering realities. During the thirties the laboratories of academia and industry had amassed an immense trove of uncoordinated information. New formulas, new systems, new approaches had been devised that had not been applied either for lack of funds or because they were not commercially promising. Dr. Vannevar Bush of the Carnegie Institution; Dr. Frank Jewett, president of the National Academy of Sciences and former head of Bell Labs; Dr. Karl T. Compton, president of MIT; Dr. James B. Conant, president of Harvard; and Dr. Richard Tolman, of the California Institute of Technology, and others met regularly to define, organize, and coordinate these unused scientific resources.[6]

In early 1940 such efforts were still individual, unofficial, and funded from private sources. However, in October 1940 the Radiation Lab at MIT came into existence, and investigations into microwave instruments began moving well. Dr. Edward Bowles believed he had under his supervision the most advanced microwave group in the nation, next to Bell Labs. In this estimate he included, as a prime resource, the Raytheon men and facilities.[7]

The British made the best of their time. When the war had started the preceding autumn, Britain had a string of radar stations in place that stretched along the coast from Aberdeen in the north to Southampton. Each had a steel transmitting tower that stuck 350 feet into the air, and a wooden receiving tower that loomed 240 feet, sturdy enough to withstand wind and snow. The stations operated on long radio waves that sent continuous beams into the sky. If an object struck one of these beams, its echo was reflected and shown on cathode ray screens visible to observers in central coordinating stations. The observers could radiotelephone information to the defending forces that invaders were present at a particular height, traveling in a certain direction at a specified speed. Friend was told from foe by having defending planes emit a regular signal.[8]

The system had defects. It was, as Dr. Edward Bowles said later, "huge and primitive. It could discern activity but could not define its nature." [9]

Another defect was its inability to detect low-flying planes. Repeated confusion regarding friend or foe, lack of complete coverage, and the complexity of the informational sequence impelled the scientists to further effort. They turned from long wave to short, or microwave.

Microwave instruments were easier to handle, operated—as their name implies—on shorter wavelengths, could produce sharper beams and high resolution. The heart of the new microwave system was a special power tube called a magnetron, machined from copper, that contained many intricate cavities of extremely close tolerances. Its development was a major achievement.

The British scientists and engineers designed and installed special microwave equipment in planes. This entailed struggles with aircraft designers and manufacturers and the resolution of a seemingly infinite chain of consequences that stretched to mind-boggling lengths. Nevertheless the boffins succeeded. By the summer of 1940 the R.A.F. had seven hundred planes equipped with radar. As the weeks passed, these were modified and improved to become increasingly efficient.

With the advent of war the need for more radars, for greater volume, for microwave instruments to improve the efficiency of other areas became pressing. The magnetron tube, the heart of radar, was a complex product. An investigation of British industrial resources was launched, to determine how many could be manufactured. The results of this inquiry dismayed the scientists. Britain did not have enough machinists for the job.

In the interim Hitler moved with demonic energy. In early April, beating the British by a matter of hours, aided from within by the treacherous Colonel Quisling, his troops landed by sea and air and conquered most of Norway in a day.[10] Simultaneously Nazi armored forces invaded Denmark and settled for the duration. Scandinavia had its peace, but it was the peace of captivity.

Acrimony developed on high British levels. Neville Chamberlain was accused of a lack of will, of insufficient personal force to lead a nation at war. There was a change, and Winston Churchill became prime minister.[11]

On the tenth of May Hitler turned his forces upon the West, and those who had ridiculed his posturings were stunned into silence. Holland was conquered by a combination of motorized forces, paratroops, and dive bombers in five days. Belgium took eighteen days. France's "first army in Europe" lasted six weeks.[12] The British counted it an accomplishment to get the bulk of their troops away alive at Dunkirk. By the end of June 1940 Hitler bestrode western Europe, and only Britain remained to halt his advance.

Events in Europe had an explosive effect in Washington. Dr. Vannevar Bush, who had courted the mighty in an effort to obtain support for his ideas of coordinating the scientific community to the defense effort, found himself suddenly borne aloft. Harry Hopkins, with whom he had become friendly, hustled him into the White House.

"The whole audience lasted less than ten minutes," Bush said later. When he emerged he had "OK-FDR" scribbled on the side of a one-page memorandum and the National Defense Research Committee was in existence.[13]

It may have been unceremonious, but the event was momentous. In the following weeks Bush realized he had been made, in effect, scientific advisor to the most powerful American President in history. As such, he was endowed with an enormous influence and with authority that was more effective for being undefined.

The NDRC became an arm of the government. Its leaders divided spheres of influence and became barons of the intellectual community. Compton of MIT headed radar and allied matters; Tolman, chemistry and explosives; Jewett, communications and transportation; Coe, patents and inventions. Boards were created; top military men joined; funds appeared. Official channels were outflanked. The scientists were operating from the Executive Office—the presidency.

Shortly afterward, Radiation Lab was empowered to grow to whatever size its leaders desired. Alfred Loomis became a section head. Compton was also a section head—he was in charge of the atomic effort. But it was the microwave committee of the radiation lab that was of special interest to Raytheon. Its composition was interesting, and included Brown of Bell Labs, Willis of Sperry, Beal of RCA, Metcalf of GE, Hutcheson of Westinghouse, and Ernest O. Lawrence (director of nuclear physics). Dr. Edward L. Bowles of MIT was its executive secretary.[14]

Raytheon was not represented in this glittering assembly. "That tiny little thing," in the phrase of young bank executive Roger Damon of the Boston First National, was known, but did not rank with RCA, Bell, Westinghouse, or GE. They were powers.

In fact Raytheon appeared to be a respectable commercial operation, but not much more. It had 1,400 employees and its sales, as of May 31, 1940, were a little over $3 million.[15] It was fighting the tax collectors, but so was every other firm. Under the New Deal, tax collectors had grown noticeably more difficult. Raytheon had lost Richard S. Aldrich, who had been called away on urgent matters elsewhere, and it had also lost Vannevar Bush as a director.[16]

But Raytheon had been steeped in shortwave efforts for years. Marshall himself was very keenly interested in microwaves and had independently decided that microwaves could create a revolution in communications. In his mind's eye, he could see a string of transmitting stations across the land that could have sweeping impact. He and Fritz Gross and Percy Spencer had experimented with simple magnetrons and transmitters, had already worked on television problems.[17] Marshall was serious enough to talk to the telephone people about a cross-licensing agreement so he could advance in the microwave area.[18]

Well aware that great changes were afoot, Marshall also made many trips to Washington in an attempt to have Raytheon included in the new programs being mounted. He received some help from Vannevar Bush, but not for Raytheon. Dr. Bush, after clearing himself of any possible conflict of interest by checking with the attorney general's office, steered some projects to the General Plate Company, the latest incarnation of the Spencer Thermostat effort that he and Marshall had launched years earlier.[19] But there seemed no necessity, or room, for Raytheon in the large programs underway. Marshall, however, refused to accept that situation. He was not going to have Raytheon shiver unnoticed in the cold.

In the fall of 1940 the United States was faced with an election choice between Franklin Roosevelt and Wendell Willkie.[20] The Rooseveltian decision to stand for an unprecedented third term was a break with a tradition that had been honored since the founding of the nation. The open assumption of the White House that no other American was fit to take the helm in the days ahead created bitter reaction in the opposition. It took, in many people, the form of opposing the interventionist policy of the Administration. America First sentiment rose to a peak. Prominent persons rose to preach the doctrine of a fortress America which held strong emotional appeal for many.

In Britain Churchill hoisted an opposite banner. He had encouraged de Gaulle. Now he recognized the French, Polish, and Czechoslovakian governments in exile.[21] Privately the Prime Minister vowed to fight on, if necessary, from Canada.

At this juncture Hitler, informed that an invasion of Britain was not possible without control of the air, instructed the Luftwaffe to "overpower the English Air Force in the earliest possible time."[22]

As the long-awaited onslaught started, the defensive system created by the British scientists and engineers was put to the test.

The Nazis had more than a thousand bombers and over a thousand fighters. They were at first so confident that they sent bombers over without fighter escorts. They bombed a few installations but never realized the importance of the radar early warning, tracking, and intercept system, and left the majority of these stations untouched. But in the beginning, in August, when they centered their efforts against shipping, harbors, rail facilities, and other military targets, they inflicted grave injuries. On one such sortie the Nazi planes mistakenly dropped their bombs on a London suburb. In retaliation the R.A.F.

was sent over Berlin on a brief bombing raid. This action, which amazed the Germans, had an overwhelming effect upon the dictator.[23] A series of unprecedented victories had convinced him his forces were irresistible. In the flood of this hubris, Hitler ordered the destruction of London.

His decision had two major consequences. The first was to allow the British time to repair their military injuries.[24] The second was to harden the resolution of the British and simultaneously to turn world opinion forever against the Nazis. The raids over London created immeasurable misery and distress. Americans, listening to radio descriptions of the holocaust in the eloquent tones of Edward R. Murrow and other American newscasters, were appalled. Some sense of the nightmare quality of dictators began, at last, to seep into many previously closed minds.

Radar made the crucial difference. The R.A.F. planes were slightly faster, but fewer. Their most important advantage was that they could see, while the Nazis were virtually blind at night. The warning system worked superbly; the British pilots were cunningly rotated to spare their strength for the long haul. The struggle was titanic.

As the Battle of Britain began, the boffins were dismayed to learn that if every machinist in Great Britain was taken off his other work and assigned exclusively to making magnetrons, the nation could still produce only ten thousand a year. It was obvious they could not spare every machinist; equally obviously, ten thousand magnetrons were insufficient.[25]

Henry Tizard, Robert Watson-Watt, J. D. Cockcroft, and the other scientific leaders conferred over this impasse. They turned their eyes toward the United States and its immense industrial establishments. But if they brought the magnetron to America it meant the disclosure of Britain's most closely guarded secret, the heart of its defense against the Luftwaffe.

They had, however, no real alternative. That conclusion and recommendation was sent to the highest levels of the government, and approval came back. Watt, Cockcroft, Tizard, and the others prepared for the journey. They would have been less than human if the necessity did not make their hearts heavy.

*       *       *

The British opened their Black Box on the evening of September 19, 1940, at the Wardman Park Hotel in Washington, D.C. The Americans crowded around eagerly. They had assembled in numbers for the occasion; their ranks included Admiral Harold Bowen of the U.S. Naval Research Laboratory and the leadership of the NDRC.[26]

Shortly afterward the British brought their magnetron to Bell Labs. That was their choice: they wanted Bell Labs and Western Electric.

"Bell looked at their 10-centimeter elephant," Dr. Bowles said.[27] In short order the technicians reported that the British magnetron could deliver between 750 and 1,000 times the power of any existing American-designed tube.[28]

The news created a sensation on the top levels of the radio industry. Until then GE, Westinghouse, and Bell had concentrated their efforts on lower-frequency radars. One result was that the newly formed Radiation Lab sent out a call to over six hundred experts and began to conduct interviews. It was obvious that microwave efforts would begin on a huge scale, and in time the Lab became one of the nation's best equipped for the task. Before long it would recruit five hundred specialists.[29]

Nobody needed any instruction on the significance. The need for air-warning, coastal-warning, and harbor-warning systems was common to every nation in the world. All the arms of the services needed improved sensing and fire-control systems. New uses and applications rose in the mind like dragon's teeth.

At this point Laurence Marshall received a call from the telephone company. His cross-licensing agreement was in the mail, but there was one small, last-minute change. Raytheon would have to agree not to make tubes that operated on more than 1,000 megacycles. Marshall was astonished. Such a clause would forbid Raytheon to work in microwaves.[30]

Puzzled, Marshall discussed this with Karl Compton and probably learned then that the British disclosures had completely altered the perspective of the industry. Someone at the phone company with more commercial shrewdness than intelligence had sought to bar Raytheon from the new field altogether.

The effort was foolish and would have horrified the scientists at Bell Labs had they known it was attempted. Raytheon was far too valuable and too close to the Radiation Lab, too advanced in the state of the art to be ignored.

Dr. Edward Bowles, executive secretary of the microwave committee, intervened. There is little doubt that he discussed his ideas with Compton and his associates, and it was he who recommended that the British bring their magnetron to Waltham. They were reluctant, but he put his reasons forward, as usual, entertainingly.

"It is not good to give a large company an exclusive," he said. "It should always be pitted against a smaller one. Small firms are mobile, and can be quick in an emergency." [31]

The British were not so sure. They had many small firms of their own; they had sought the help of the American giants. Their plan had been that Bell Labs would develop radars and Western Electric—which, Bowles says, could "then do no wrong"—would make the magnetrons. They had no objection if the less demanding components were farmed out.

But a suggestion from the Radiation Lab was not one to ignore, and the British acceded gracefully. In due course John D. Cockcroft arrived, bearing the marvel in the proverbial black box. In the Raytheon laboratory Percy Spencer rose to the occasion, was at his beguiling best.

Cockcroft liked Spencer at once. He showed him the magnetron and the American regarded it thoughtfully. He asked questions—very intelligent ones—about how it was produced, and the Britisher answered at length.

Later Spencer wrote, "The technique of making these tubes, as described to us, was awkward and impractical." [32] *Awkward and impractical.* Nobody else dared draw such a judgment about a product of undoubted scientific brilliance, produced and displayed by the leaders of British science.

The conversation took place on a Friday afternoon. As the men talked, shadows began to lengthen, and at some point, Cockcroft later told Carl Gilbert, Spencer looked up.

"I wonder," he asked, "if I could take this home with me over the weekend?"

Later, Cockcroft could never quite explain why he consented. He was, after all, carrying Britain's most valuable secret. It was possible he had been followed by enemy agents. Spencer could have a car accident on the way to or from home, could have a heart attack—anything might arise. In the event of any of these or any other possible problem, Cockcroft would have been hard put to explain why he allowed the magnetron out of his hands. But at the moment assent seemed natural.

The following Monday they again met in the laboratory. Spencer was smiling and optimistic. He thought Raytheon could produce magnetrons; he implied that some improvements might be possible in the manner in which they were turned out. He discussed some of these and Cockcroft, who was himself a notable scientist, grasped their implications immediately. He was surprised but impressed.[33] Raytheon received a contract to make copies of the British magnetron.


Marshall pitted Percy Spencer and two machinists against huge Bell Labs and MIT. On its face, the gamble appeared slightly lunatic, but Marshall believed Spencer was a wild card, able to sweep all others off the board. He had reason for his faith. Over the years Percy had shown remarkable ability. The magnetron project had, in fact, interrupted a project of great importance, whose origin sheds some light on his personality and abilities.

Percy liked people and liked to tinker. He combined these at Raytheon and would fix anything anyone brought to him. Broken clocks, irons, appliances—anything at all.[34] That is not the sort of activity that important eggheads are apt to encourage, but Spencer was an original man; his lifestyle was not an imitation.

One project he undertook was to install radio controls in some toy airplane models for his sons. That called for the use of several types of receiving tubes and a fairly heavy battery. The load was too much for the model; it couldn't get aloft. Percy then created some miniature tubes. One, he said, was "the equivalent of a thyratron." Myers, one of the men in the lab, took a look at it and was impressed.

Later Myers went to work in the department of terrestrial magnetism at the Carnegie Institution in Washington, under Dr. Vannevar Bush, and was placed on developmental efforts centered around the creation of a proximity fuse for artillery shells. Someone mentioned that a similar fuse would be useful against aircraft, if the components could be miniaturized. Myers recalled Spencer and the toy planes, and told Dr. Bush. In turn Bush sent a physicist to talk to Percy.

One result was that Percy became one of the developers of the proximity fuse.[35] Norman Krim, whose miniature tubes were going into hearing aids, worked on aspects of the problem with him.[36] The project was fascinating. The tiny mechanism and tubes had to withstand great centrifugal forces until the projectile in which it was contained neared its target and the charge detonated.

By the time Spencer turned from his proximity fuse work to concentrate on the magnetron, he had already made enough contributions to the state of the art to have achieved a formidable reputation in any university, but he was not a man with a university background. At an earlier period that would not have made a difference, but by 1940 the scientific community had moved to very high academic levels, heights which few nonuniversity men could attain.

In the autumn of 1940, therefore, Spencer was regarded as a superb technician, but by no means a scientific personage.[37] It is possible that his standing might have been improved if Dr. Vannevar Bush had still been present, or in the region, of the Raytheon laboratories. But Dr. Bush had moved to the heights: the most enjoyable of all locations. There one meets so many interesting, articulate, and intelligent people that one is apt, in time, to receive an elevated view of the human species, and to forget the smaller, hindering jealousies below.

But Percy Spencer had a strong and remarkable supporter in Laurence Marshall. Marshall, whom some men regarded as a mere promoter, was in reality more like the director of some huge, sprawling research institute. He could step into any laboratory and grasp the sense of its activities. He could share an insight and a vision, and understand the scientific principles of a project.

There is no doubt he helped Spencer. He went to the U.S. Patent Office and looked up American magnetron efforts. On his return he said, "The configurations are obvious." [38]

That was entirely possible. The sands of science are dotted with the remains of discoveries that were ignored until a need for them arose. But there were few corporation presidents who could make such a search, come to such a conclusion, and return to a Percy Spencer with observations and suggestions.

Their first task, which was to produce copies of the British magnetron, was simple for this pair. Their goal was to improve and eventually to mass produce the tubes.

Western Electric, which had opened a special facility in Chicago to manufacture magnetrons, allowed Marshall to come out and tour the works. "They even let me see that they were having trouble drilling into copper," Marshall said. "That was to prove how difficult it was, to convince me the task was beyond Raytheon." [39]

The demonstration had the reverse effect. Marshall returned convinced that there were better ways to solve the problem.

The task of manufacturing the magnetron in larger volumes impelled Spencer, assisted by Palmer Derby and others, to an examination of every detail and to a series of improvements. One was the development of a better way to seal copper to glass. Another was the elimination of gold solder on the covers to the body of the tube.[40] As each modification was devised, men from the Radiation Lab entered the situation to make their evaluations and add their suggestions; the results were sent to Britain, in the form of samples, for approval.

The British had strapped their magnetrons with wires, in an effort to reduce the tendency of the tube to generate "spurious" frequencies (frequencies other than the desired frequencies) and to improve its general performance. Percy Spencer set rings, called straps, into the tips of the tube, and achieved better performance and higher efficiency. Palmer Derby then doubled the rings and achieved even greater efficiency.[41] Later, describing these developments, Spencer said the result was a forty percent improvement.

These were very significant improvements, and it is noteworthy that they emerged from a relatively small corporate laboratory. Some of the scientists at MIT and Bell Labs were surprised, but there is no doubt everyone was pleased. Word was received that the British shared this reaction, and both Raytheon and Percy Spencer began to achieve recognition.

While scientists toiled on both sides of the Atlantic, the Luftwaffe continued its savage strikes against British cities. The list lengthened daily: Coventry, Birmingham, Bristol, Southampton, Manchester, Glasgow.[42] The news of these flaming cities and the fierce air combat over them contrasted oddly in the American newspapers with sports, entertainment, and political argument.

Nevertheless America grew increasingly aware that Hitler was not simply a menace to his immediate neighbors. The continent of Europe was occupied; Nazi U-boats were using French Atlantic ports; Hitler threatened to become a world conqueror.

Against this backdrop the President won election to a third term with surprising ease. Although the isolationist movement remained highly vocal and influential, it was obvious the people did not want any drastic change and considered Franklin Roosevelt the best available man for the future.[43]

This news gave Hitler reason to pause. The possibility of American intervention was now evident. Peace feelers to the British had been rejected. His first move was to make an alliance with Japan. His purpose was clear. Japan provided a back-door menace to the USSR, and confronted the leaders of the United States with the ominous possibility of a two-ocean war if they moved against the Nazis.[44]

Hitler's next move was to ask the Soviet Union its price to join with Germany, Italy, and Japan against the West. Its price was high. Had Hitler met it, the combination would have been difficult, perhaps impossible for Britain—even joined with the United States—to overcome. But it would have left the USSR in a far more dominant world position than the Nazis could accept.

The Soviets wanted guarantees in the Balkans that Hitler would come no closer. They wanted all of Finland. And they wanted the Persian Gulf.[45]

The last demand was impossible for Hitler to meet. The Fascists, who had sought to create a new empire in North Africa, were contending with British troops in that arena. To cede the area to the Soviets would demolish Hitler's agreements with Mussolini and truncate the Nazi's own plans for world domination. The Soviets had overstepped. In December Hitler ordered his military men to prepare plans to invade the USSR by May 1941. He estimated the conquest would take five weeks.


In early 1941 the United States was in a position similar to Britain's two years earlier. The threat of war was coming close and its services were feverish in the effort to prepare.

The U.S. Navy was particularly hard pressed. General Electric, a major supplier, was overloaded and falling behind in its deliveries.[46] A switch from high-frequency radar to microwave radars, as well as fire control and other electronic systems, was underway. A scramble took place. The navy had to have new equipment right away.

Bell Labs—everybody's favorite—was given the responsibility for creating new microwave fire-control radar systems. The next need was search radar.[47] Laurence Marshall, haunting the corridors of Washington, came forward.

He could see the war was close, but he was not alone in that. It was his vision regarding Raytheon's choice that was, in retrospect, interesting because it was so uncommonly clear. ". . . the demand for [radio] tubes would be very great," he said. "A conventional expansion of this business would be easy, safe and profitable." [48] What more could a businessman want?

"An alternative was presented," he said. "It involved the development of electronic devices employing microwave tubes and components for radar—then in the laboratory stage—for military purposes. Although not possessing the certainty of profitable operation, Raytheon elected to accept the challenge." [49] Of course, Marshall would always accept a challenge rather than turn to something "easy, safe and profitable."

He could not reach admirals, but Marshall could reach captains. He found some receptive ears in the U.S. Navy's Bureau of Ships, among them a pair that belonged to Captain Sam Tucker. Tucker, at Marshall's suggestion, went to the Radiation Lab and asked Dr. Bowles whether Raytheon was capable of building some surface-search radars—ship radars. Dr. Bowles talked to Karl Compton and they agreed the firm had the technical ability.[50]

Marshall meanwhile had to obtain and equip a building. That was easier said than done. Banks do not lend money when no business is in hand; the government could hardly give Raytheon a contract when the firm lacked facilities to fill it. In this extremity Marshall recalled the days of his youth when he worked for contractor Pat McDonough. Wistfully he recalled the days when arrangements were made to construct buildings almost on the backs of envelopes.

That was an inspiration. He put on his hat, climbed into his modest car, and drove to the offices of the largest contractor in New England. He explained his problem and persuaded the contractor to go to Washington and say that he had an available building, waiting to be inspected and approved, for the use of Raytheon to meet navy orders.[51]

All these efforts, all this anxiety, resulted in an agreement for Raytheon to produce one hundred SG radars. "All he had," said Argento, who watched sympathetically, "was an agreement—a slip of paper saying the money would be furnished later—but Marshall had tears of joy in his eyes." [52]

Other men might have been in business, but Marshall was, really, in the war. Nobody seemed to realize that.


During the first six months of 1941 the Administration signed the Lend Lease Bill providing for assistance to Britain and its allies in return for "services," and created a great number of instant agencies to put the nation on a war footing.

New systems, new men, new approaches appeared as though evoked from the air. The Office of Production Management was given charge of the nation's material resources, the Office of Price Controls given authority over wages as well. The Office of Scientific Research and Development,[53] headed by Vannevar Bush, was established to coordinate scientific efforts.

During the Wilson administration in World War I, the United States had, briefly, experienced this sort of control from the top. President Roosevelt had served under Wilson and been a part of that earlier effort. But his own steps exceeded Wilson's, were more detailed, and penetrated even more deeply into the life of the nation.

At first, however, the new systems held large elements of informality. Vannevar Bush recalls that General George C. Marshall, chief of staff, gave instructions for, in the interests of speed, "direct informal contacts between interested individuals." [54] But week by week the government moved to create and strengthen its formal machinery with truly remarkable speed and efficiency, though the nation was not officially at war.

The air was suffused with a sense of change and motion. Colonel Theodore H. Dillon, a longtime director and strong Marshall supporter, was recalled to active duty with the Quartermaster Corps and submitted his resignation to Raytheon's board.[55]

Fiscal year results, as of May 31, 1941, showed sales of $4.4 million and profits of $151,000.[56] In June the contract for shipboard SG radars finally arrived, although work on this project had been underway for months. It called for the delivery of "certain radio devices" by April 1942, at an overall price of $1.2 million.[57] It was not a large order in a dollar sense, and the intellectual demand it constituted was not visible in its outline. Years later investigators would not realize that these radars had to be *created;* microwave shipboard radars were not in existence when the order was originally contracted.

The Axis had also been busy during these six months. Mussolini, eager to extend his "empire," had invaded Greece—and was shamed when his forces were driven all the way back to Albania. Simultaneously, his huge armies in Libya, which had been gathering, in a leisurely and somewhat elegant way, to invade Egypt, were interrupted in their efforts by a small British force. In Churchill's words, this resulted in the capture of "five acres of officers and two hundred acres of other ranks."

Shortly after the British entered Libya, Hitler sent Rommel and the Afrika Korps to that area, invaded Greece, fell upon Yugoslavia.[58]

At the same time he resumed the bombing of British cities and intensified the U-boat campaign against Britain. That effort, he declared, would accomplish the final destruction of that stubborn island power. The U.S. Navy, equipped with new bases in Iceland, found itself engaged as an ally with Britain, in a secret anti-U-boat war. Commander I. L. McNally, then a junior officer, was one of six to receive orders signed by Admiral C. W. Nimitz to "receive instructions in Radar by attending sessions at Westinghouse, RCA, Western Electric, BTL, MIT and GE." [59] Following this assignment they were sent to sea on the U.S.S. *Roe* to test radar equipment.

It is significant that Raytheon was not on this list. Yet Raytheon's high-frequency tube production was rising rapidly. Raytheon tubes appeared in such volume, with so many modifications, that rumors started. One, quite persistent, was that Raytheon tubes *would leak.*

Henry Argento recalls that Raytheon's executive offices received a call from an admiral in Washington who had heard these rumors and was greatly distressed. "If they're right, I'll be cashiered," he said agitatedly. He was assured there was no truth to the gossip.[60]

On June 22, 1941, the Nazis, joined in war by Finland and Hungary, invaded the Soviet.[61] The news astonished everyone but Winston Churchill, who had scented such a possibility.

The event sent the world Communist movement into reverse. Peace demonstrations, until then noisy and numerous, abruptly halted.

Agitation for a second front to relieve the strain on the worker's paradise began.

In Asia the Japanese, coordinating their moves with the Nazis, first threatened and then, in July, invaded French Indo-China. President Roosevelt froze Japanese assets inside the United States, incorporated the Philippine Army into the U.S. military establishment, and called MacArthur back to service as a lieutenant general.[62]

The White House then made arrangements to meet British Prime Minister Churchill.

Their rendezvous took place off Newfoundland in August 1941. President Roosevelt traveled aboard the heavy cruiser *Augusta*, Churchill aboard the *Prince of Wales*. Both vessels were accompanied by numerous escorts—"enough," said *Time* magazine later in the week, ". . . to fight a major sea battle if an enemy appeared."

The major result of the meeting, as far as the world was later told, was the Atlantic Charter, a document worthy of Woodrow Wilson at his peak. It called for abandonment of the international use of force, disarmament, a system of general security, the right of all people to choose the form of government under which they would live, and other soaring goals.

In terms of press and propaganda the Charter was well received. The meeting itself made it clear the United States would stand beside Britain, but that was hardly news. The Charter did not describe the actual proceedings, which had undoubtedly centered on whether or not Britain should become an official ally of the Soviet Union and whether the U.S. should extend lend-lease to the commissars.[63] This tremendous topic, of immense significance from every angle, was lost from view in paradisaical rhetoric.


On November 1, 1941, Commander McNally writes, "I was ordered to Pearl Harbor to establish a Fleet Radar School by Admiral Nimitz. I departed San Francisco on 21 Nov 1941 and arrived at Pearl Harbor on 28 Nov 1941 via the USS *Republic*. I was assigned to the USS *Pennsylvania* to assist in the installation and checkout of several radars being installed in the fleet. At this time the shipyard was drawing up plans for the radar school, and I must say, in a very routine fashion . . ." [64]

Japan's plan was not to destroy the United States, but to reduce the effectiveness of its Pacific fleet by a hit and run, and then to obtain control of Malaysia, the Dutch East Indies, and Thailand. Around these central areas it planned a strategic ring of lesser conquests, a string of islands that could serve as a defensive bastion and as bargaining counters in later negotiations.[65]

The reasoning was careful and astute. Malaysia, the Dutch East Indies, and Thailand, when combined with French Indo-China, which the Japanese already occupied, produced 90 percent of all the rubber in the world. Without this vital commodity neither ships, nor planes, nor tanks, nor cars, neither armies nor navies could move. Japanese observers in World War I had listed lack of replacement rubber as one of the factors that immobilized the Kaiser's army and made it necessary for Germany to sue for peace. Based on the Japanese evaluation of this commodity, the United States, without rubber, would never be able to mount the machinery necessary to win in Asia.[66]

In Washington political leaders discounted such mundane considerations. The military men had their eyes fixed mainly on tactical possibilities. The assumption was so strong that Japan would move only in Asia that when Secretary of the Navy Knox was told Japanese planes were striking Pearl Harbor he cried, "My God! That can't be true. They must mean the Philippines." [67]


There were five mobile radar stations on the northern perimeter of Oahu, and each was linked to an information center at Fort Shafter. The warning system was capable of detecting oncoming aircraft 150 miles away.

The system was in good order when shortly after seven o'clock on the morning of December 7, 1941, Privates Lockard and Elliott, stationed at Opana, saw so many blips on their screen that they thought the set was broken and deranged. They watched uncertainly for a time. By the time the blips had moved from 133 miles away to 113, they decided to brave censure and call the information center.

Their call was answered by Private Joseph McDonald, who relayed the message to Lieutenant Kermit Tyler. Tyler, aware a number of B-17's were due from the States, told him not to worry about it. In turn McDonald called Opana and told them to forget it.

Worry removed, Lockard and Elliott decided to track the planes just for practice. At 7:25 A.M. they were 62 miles away. At 7:30 A.M., they were 47 miles. At 7:39, 22 miles.

A "dead zone" created by nearby hills hid the rest. At 7:45 their breakfast arrived and Lockard and Elliott left the screen. At 8 A.M. they learned, in common with the rest of America, that the world contains enemies.

The Japanese attack on Pearl Harbor lasted two hours. U.S. battleships, lined in a neat row, were the central targets. The *Arizona* was blown up, *West Virginia* and *California* sunk, *Tennessee, Nevada,* and *Maryland* damaged. One hundred eighteen U.S. military planes were destroyed on their fields. All told, the United States lost 2,375 military dead and 1,143 wounded; 68 civilians killed and 35 wounded. The city of Honolulu suffered forty explosions, and damage was estimated at $50 million.

The Japanese lost twenty-nine planes, one large and five midget submarines, and approximately one hundred men.

As the Japanese flew away, the Opana radar station tracked their direction and phoned this information in to the information center, where it was ignored. Otherwise the high command would have discovered that the Japanese carriers were only 190 miles away.[68]

Pearl Harbor was a strategic error for the Japanese, a blunder that its transient success would never repay. It galvanized the United States, fused the nation more firmly than any other possible action. Had it not sent its planes against Hawaii, Japan might have proceeded to conquer the Dutch East Indies, Burma, and Malaysia—even Singapore and Hong Kong—without deeply stirring the American people.

In early 1942, however, the Americans plunged into the war effort with a seriousness that could hardly be equated with the land that had rated Fibber McGee and Molly, baseball standings and the movies as more interesting subjects than foreign affairs only a few days earlier.

The change was abrupt but deep. Mrs. Laurence K. Marshall, dropping by to see her husband at his office, was stopped, allowed only to make a phone call from the guard's booth, and then sent on her way.[69] Other wives had similar experiences. Raytheon was suddenly among the war firms; its government activities were henceforth to be shrouded from view.

The change was like a dash of cold water to the people of Raytheon. Through the years the firm had been a compact, close-knit, almost familial organization.

"We had wonderful Christmas parties," said Mrs. Robert Quimby, wife of one of the firm's most talented engineers.[70] Under the new exigencies of war, the enterprise suddenly seemed cold and impersonal. The old camaraderie remained inside the buildings, but the men were miserably aware their secrecy oath forbade even their wives from learning about their efforts. For a time this created a chill inside some homes, but the men were engrossed and absorbed, and were keeping incredibly long hours. Their partners, seeing them so driven and withdrawn, forgot their curiosity and settled into the new regime. Still, it was a sign that the atmosphere of America—so long a fresh contrast with other parts of the world—had irrevocably changed.

Percy Spencer had been an active radio shortwave ham for many years and kept in touch with others throughout the world. One was a Catholic priest who was also an Arctic explorer; another was Herbert Hoover, Jr., head of communications for TWA. Percy, together with some other Raytheon men, was a member of the American Relay Radio League, and of its inner circle club, the IGBA (I Want to Get Better Acquainted). Shortly after the war started, Percy appeared at the league headquarters and sat down to chat with Clark Rodiman, editor of the league's publication, the *QST*.

He talked about a great opportunity in somewhat mysterious terms and tones. "I can't tell you what it is, but I can tell you that it's important," he said. Rodiman listened eagerly. By the time Spencer left, Rodiman was hooked.[71] He applied for a leave of absence from the league to join Raytheon.

Once on the scene, Rodiman learned from Marshall that Raytheon "engineered" radars. His task would be to organize a field engineers group to install, maintain, and instruct the services in their use wherever they were placed—on ships, shore stations, or anywhere else. Marshall's heavy eyebrows emphasized the need for secrecy and the reality of danger. The field men would have to go to sea in destroyers and other ships, travel to combat areas, be articulate enough to instruct and agile enough to bear these burdens. It was, he stressed, a heavy responsibility. Rodiman nodded, thrilled to be in the heart of the war effort.

Rodiman's selection was a stroke of genius. He had been with the league almost his entire working life and, as editor of *QST*, was one of its best-known names. He was personally acquainted with hundreds of its members. Most of them were, in 1942, young men, for their hobby had not been possible before the mid-twenties. They built their own sets from diagrams and could both understand and diagnose equipment troubles.

He recruited expertly. Some of the men came from NBC and other communication firms, but many from other sectors as well. He even raided the league's own technical staff, and that cost him his leave of absence. He received word he was fired. But Rodiman didn't care. Radar fascinated him, as it was to fascinate the men he collected.

He joined Raytheon at a time when it was small, but it rose like a rocket around him. His day started, he recalls, at eight in the morning and stretched until midnight. His first efforts, however, were to learn about radar himself. He was told to report to Fritz Gross and became involved in the creation of the SG-1.

Like his associates' work, his new efforts were shrouded in secrecy; a security program far more sweeping than any ever before seen in America had been drawn across its war effort.

With over five million aliens in the country and a divided political climate until the very moment of Japanese attack, the American government could not afford to take unnecessary chances. Its intelligence system was obsolete and its people naïve. The State Department was reduced to requesting civilians to mail in whatever snapshots and information they had from their individual travels regarding North Africa, China, the Pacific, and other areas of new importance to the nation.[72]

The American military establishment, only recently scorned as an enclave of loafers and civilian rejects, was confronted with awesome responsibilities. The country faced a two-ocean war with fronts scattered around the globe. Both Washington and London were aware the demands of the situation would strain the resources of their nations to the breaking point. They took the most immediate and sensible step possible, and made a formal alliance with the Soviets.

On an ideological level this had the effect of blurring distinctions. One dictatorship, older, as malignant and far more influential than the others, was joined to the forces of freedom, and a veil was drawn over the atrocities of the commissars. In time this would lead to serious political, cultural, and intellectual problems, but in early 1942 it was clear that only the endless steppes of the USSR kept Hitler's full power deflected from the West.

In the Atlantic, Nazi U-boats ranged practically at will. Some American merchant vessels were shelled and sent to the bottom within sight of their native shores; every U.S. Naval vessel was needed in a dozen places at the same time. Unless the Nazi submarines were subdued, Britain would be isolated and the United States would be unable to maintain a flow of matériel and men to its allies in Europe.

The situation in the Pacific was equally stark. The Japanese had sent carrier-based planes against the Philippines the day after Pearl Harbor, surprised and destroyed American B-17's on the ground. In the opening months of 1942 Japan invaded the Philippines, forced the flight of General MacArthur, and besieged U.S. troops at Bataan and Corregidor.

In March 1942 Japan had taken Singapore and Burma from the British, Malaysia from the Dutch, and Indo-China from the French. In the process they had eliminated the Royal Navy as a fighting force in the Pacific. Their occupation of the Dutch East Indies gave them possession of the world's rubber-producing area as well as immense resources in tin and petroleum.[73]

In other words, the United States was in peril of defeat by sea: a defeat that would cut the nation from both its European allies and its Pacific allies and possessions. Where Britain's crucial battle had been at home, and where its defense had relied on a land-based radar network and the creation of aircraft radars for land-based planes, the Americans had to mount new radar defenses for use at sea. That meant that the creation of radar for ships was as crucial for the United States as the creation of a radar warning system had been for Britain on land.

It is in the light of that far-flung need that the efforts of Laurence Marshall, Percy Spencer, Fritz Gross, and others must be evaluated. They not only took the products of the laboratory and were able to suggest and prove innovations, they were able to translate the most advanced products of the state of the art into engineered devices that could be mass manufactured. In the beginning, their efforts were launched at a time when the needs of Britain were paramount. Before they had proceeded far, they were working toward the survival of their own country as well.

Wartime secrecy, the pooling of patents, the absence of individualized records, the complexity of the group tasks shrouded the individual contributions of the men at Raytheon who put together the SG radar, as well as their later improvements and modifications. Certainly the Japanese later learned the importance of their efforts. But in March 1942, when G. E. M. Bertram, the chief, Fritz Gross, the designer, and Clark Rodiman, head of the installation group, gathered on the deck of the heavy cruiser U.S.S. *Augusta*, they attracted no attention whatever. In their severe business suits they were as inconspicuous and seemingly as far removed from the arena of war as all the rest of the great industrial system they epitomized.

The three men watched as a sling hoisted Raytheon's first seagoing radar—the SG-1—from the dock to the deck of the cruiser. All were aware the moment was somewhat historic: the *Augusta* was already familiar to them as the ship that carried President Roosevelt to the Atlantic Charter meeting. But as they watched, the sling broke.[74]

The first part of the delicate mechanism fell with a heavy thud to the steel deck of the *Augusta*, and the men rushed forward. Bertram felt for injuries with all the concern of a physician searching for broken bones. To their relief, he straightened and reported that only a few easily replaceable tubes had broken. The loading proceeded, the radar was installed, and a short time later the *Augusta* left for the African coast.

Back at Raytheon Marshall's attention centered on the production of magnetrons—tubes that were integral to all radar assemblies. The government, acting on the consensus of expert opinion at Western Electric, MIT, Bell Labs, and other informed quarters, had set magnetron production at a maximum one hundred a day. Spencer was told to find a way to achieve higher volume.

Spencer turned toward one of his favorite techniques: lamination. Using the General Plate facilities in Attleboro (Marshall was also president of General Plate), Spencer began with sheets of copper instead of the solid blocks previously used. And instead of having machinists carefully hollow cavities, he stamped cavities from each sheet with machines. Then he stacked the sheets in sequence, separated them with silver solder, and ran them through a continuous hydrogen oven. The result, after many experiments with stamping, stacking, and fusing, was an indissoluble unit completely formed by machine methods, capable of being infinitely and perfectly reproduced.[75]

Estimates were made of the types and cost of rolling equipment, punch presses, and other machines necessary to automate production. The largest single item was the continuous hydrogen oven. That single piece of equipment alone would cost $750,000.[76]

Finally samples and production plans were submitted to the government. To Marshall's chagrin he met with skepticism. The government, following its usual pattern, polled experts in the industry, and these experts declared the Raytheon production plan was impractical. Typically Marshall then decided that Raytheon would buy and install the equipment at its own expense to prove its point.

By ordinary standards, Marshall's was an amazing decision. Without Washington approval Raytheon had no priority and had to scrounge to collect the necessary equipment and material. It was not possible to borrow money against orders when no orders existed—and when the possibility of such orders seemed remote. Certainly it was not the business of an ordinary business firm to undertake a governmental program the government itself did not consider practical. But Marshall was not ordinary and had not gathered ordinary men around him. Schultz was told to forget the rules, to raise money from every possible and even impossible source, to stall creditors and suppliers, to cut corners—but not to sacrifice quality. Schultz protested and Marshall's heavy eyebrows came together: he pointed at *The Little Engine That Could.*

The Japanese had managed to injure the mystique of the Europeans in Asia and take possession of a vast empire. The last step in consolidating these victories was to create an immense line of defense that would stretch from the Aleutians in the north to Midway—an island northwest of Hawaii—in the center of the Pacific, down to include New Guinea, the world's second largest island, northeast of Australia. Such a line would sever Australia and the United States and disrupt cooperation between those two nations.[77] Only one obstacle remained to be destroyed before this plan could be complete: the U.S. Navy.

In the first week of May 1942, the Japanese were in the act of invading Port Moresby in New Guinea when they were surprised by the U.S. Navy. The surprise was not an accident: the Americans had cracked the Japanese secret navy code. This achievement, which the Japanese forever considered impossible, was accomplished by the use of computers developed at MIT by Vannevar Bush and two assistants just before the war.[78]

The Battle of the Coral Sea, as it was later called, was remarkable among other reasons for the fact that none of the naval vessels involved ever came within sight or firing range of one another. The issue was decided entirely by planes operating from carriers. The aircraft of both fleets inflicted heavy damages: the United States lost the *Lexington*, and the *Yorktown* was seriously hurt. The Japanese lost a light carrier and a large number of planes. Later both sides claimed victory, with some reason. The Japanese could truthfully say they had inflicted grave injuries. But the fact remained that for the first time they failed in an invasion attempt.[79]

The significance of this strategic victory was overshadowed, unfortunately, by news of the fall of Bataan and Corregidor, and the surrender of the American forces. In the following two months the world gradually learned of the Death March at Bataan, in which hundreds of Americans were slain or died enroute, and 22,000 later died in the first two months of captivity.[80]

In June 1942, only a month after their first engagement, the Japanese and American navies met again at Midway. Again, the United States had the advantage of knowing the major outlines of the Japanese plan and was therefore not fooled by a feint made at the Aleutians. The Japanese, on the other hand, were again surprised in the midst of a major invasion.

As on the first occasion, planes operating from carriers proved to be the major instruments of battle. The first strikes of U.S. torpedo planes proved ineffective: the heavily armed Japanese were able to cut down twenty-five planes out of the first forty-one launched against them. Nevertheless U.S. commanders ordered more such strikes, and American pilots proved, to the amazement of the Japanese, capable of using their aircraft as projectiles. Their suicidal assaults diverted the attention of Japanese gunners to the point that American dive bombers were able to swoop down and sink three Japanese carriers. A little later the tactic was repeated and a fourth Japanese carrier sunk. The Japanese admirals ordered a retreat. They had lost four carriers, over two thousand men, and 250 planes—and again been halted in a major invasion effort.[81]

The American high command, examining these results, was both pleased and disturbed. The outcome had been far from certain: timeless factors of human courage had turned the scales. Far more certain means were needed.

A call went out from the navy for more and better radars for both ships and planes. Dr. Edward Bowles, summoned from MIT's Radiation Lab to become scientific advisor to new Secretary of War Henry L. Stimson, was told his first task was to "do something about the German submarines that are roaming the East Coast almost at will." [82]

Bowles got in touch with the U.S. Army Air Force and established a Sea-Search-Attack Development Unit. Land-based bombers were to be equipped with radars developed at the Radiation Lab, radar altimeters, magnetic detectors, odographs, radio sonobuoys among other devices. All were needed in quantity—right away.[83]

It is in this climate and context that the true value of Marshall's volunteer efforts, in which the fortunes of Raytheon were put to the hazard, must be judged.

Captain Henry Bernstein, who had last visited Raytheon in the thirties as a junior officer taking advanced training at college, returned from the Pacific in June 1942 as the officer in charge of radar design at the navy's Bureau of Ships. He was touring all the firms that made shipboard radar and was in the forefront of the naval effort to increase, improve, and quicken production to meet urgent needs.

Bernstein was given a tour of Raytheon's facilities at Waltham by Marshall, Fritz Gross, G. E. M. Bertram, and Percy Spencer. He found a series of astonishing sights, learned of surprising developments. He was thunderstruck to see that "magnetron lathes had been built by Raytheon out of parts, including bicycle chains, purchased at Sears when they could not get them elsewhere." [84]

Marshall was, of course, in the process of proving that mass production of magnetrons was possible, and was operating an assembly made up of whatever elements he and his men had been able to scrounge outside priority channels.

Bernstein learned of this and was horrified when Percy Spencer told him "production of Maggies was about to stop." Bernstein wanted to know why, and "Spencer said the Chase Copper and Brass Company would not ship the last order for oxygen-free copper."

Back in Washington this information was so distressing to Bernstein that he picked up the phone and called the president of Chase Copper and Brass himself. In answer to Bernstein's inquiry, the head of Copper and Brass replied that "Raytheon was a poor risk; it had taken a long time to pay for the previous shipment." "I told him," Bernstein wrote later, "I could not speak for the Bureau but the material was vital to the war effort. I would personally guarantee payment to the maximum extent of my resources—about $12,000. He replied that if I felt that strongly about its need he would ship it at once—and did."

In other words, Raytheon had broken through to the Bureau of Ships. Captain Bernstein, in a position to gauge both the needs of the navy and the grim nature of the situation, lost no time in acquainting such associates as Captain Hull, also in BuShips, of the potential and importance of the Raytheon effort.

Bernstein scouted the state of the art and learned that other firms did not believe Spencer's magnetrons could be produced by lamination in volume. Nevertheless Bernstein studied Spencer's magnetrons and was convinced. He argued the case at the Bureau of Ships, and won.

Meanwhile Spencer showed Bernstein other developments. Bernstein was so impressed he was able, years later, to describe them in detail. "Raytheon designed and built the first megawatt magnetron that would put power into a waveguide without arcing. Percy tried at first to follow the Radiation Lab's design, and output from the Maggie arced to the waveguide. Other suggestions were tried, but it still arced." Then Spencer asked Bernstein if he could design the Maggie himself. "When I approved, he put the necessary length of feed inside the Maggie in the vacuum and it worked without arcing."

In other words, the great hazard Marshall had undertaken at the expense of the firm, to prove his point, succeeded in convincing Captains Bernstein and Hull at the Bureau of Ships. These men then urged the navy, over the negative opinions of larger and more prestigious firms in the electronics industry at the time, to fund a $2-million, three-story facility for Raytheon's volume effort.

Months later the Raytheon men proudly escorted Bernstein

through the results. He stared and wondered why the ceilings were twice as high as necessary.[85]

Raytheon was not the only company to perform miracles. On the West Coast Henry Kaiser produced a Liberty ship in less than five days; vehicles poured out of Detroit in phenomenal quantities and variety; aircraft manufacturers, steel producers, textile manufacturers, chemical firms all produced in prodigious volume at unprecedented tempos. Even agriculture—a sector that some mistakenly associate with a lack of progressive techniques—forged beyond previous records, thanks in large measure to the self-propelled combine that had replaced the tractor-driven model.[86]

The situation was replete with ironies. New Deal theorists had long argued that the American economy had reached its limits and had devoted far more attention to the regulation of industry than to encouraging its growth. Social programming had occupied the Administration far more than discovering the mainsprings of industry.

This approach spread across a span of eight years had not succeeded in restoring full employment, business confidence, or the industrial momentum of the nation. Had President Roosevelt not chosen to run for a third term, his administration might well have gone down in history as an experiment that failed, a misreading of the American temperament and system. Instead the war transformed the New Deal into an administration that headed the greatest concentration of industrial power in the nation's history, the crucial difference being that the concentration was placed in the hands of Washington rather than the private sector. In the heat of the moment few could afford to philosophize, however—the need was too great and the peril too near.

In the summer of 1942, Hitler, who had spent the lives of one million men in his initial drive against the Soviets, remanned his armies with divisions culled from the Italians, Hungarians, Rumanians, and other satellite peoples, and renewed his offensive. The front extended almost two thousand miles inside the USSR, whose forces steadily retreated.[87]

The war with the Soviets, however, did not reduce or diminish the fierce war in the Atlantic, where the Nazi U-boats were deadly and effective. Convoys then took seventy days to make a round trip from the United States to Britain; all were constantly menaced. The

Nazi submarines were so well armored that depth charges could not affect them short of a direct hit. U-boat defenses included the ability to eject a chemical that would create bubbles that reflected sonar echoes behind which the submarine could submerge and escape.[88]

The Nazis had a fleet of 360 U-boats in 1942 and kept an average of eighty operating at sea at all times. They were equipped with torpedoes that could track a ship by its propellor sounds; with others that detonated only upon impact, still others that could travel in loops through a convoy until they found a target. They sank U.S. and U.K. ships at a ratio of 20 to 1. Allied ship losses in 1942 averaged 130 a month.[89]

Raytheon's leap into the production of essential radar and sonar components on a mass volume basis arrived at a fortuitous moment for the nation. The sea war alone could have brought Britain down, had the instruments to overcome the U-boats not become available.

As the summer drew toward its close, the White House was concerned enough about Japan's conquest of the world's rubber-producing land to assign Dr. Karl Compton of MIT, Dr. James Conant of Harvard, and elder statesman Bernard Baruch the task of inventorying U.S. supplies.

Their report, delivered in September 1942, was a shocker. "The situation is so dangerous," they said, ". . . that unless corrective measures are taken . . . the nation will face both civilian and military collapse." [90] Years of insouciant disregard of industrial realities were coming grimly home to roost.

To a large extent the situation was saved by the farsighted actions of an industrialist whose repeated warnings had been previously ignored: John Collier, of B. F. Goodrich.[91]

Collier, a man as stubborn and patriotic as Laurence Marshall, had similarly spent his company's funds to prepare for what he considered a national need. Working against the clock before the war, he had sponsored large-scale researches into methods of creating synthetic rubber and constructed a large synthetic rubber plant that served the nation as a prototype when the crisis arrived.

Alarmed by the September report of "the three wise men," Washington ordered funds for a crash synthetic rubber program. Men were called in from the rubber manufacturing, petroleum, and chemical businesses to create an entirely new industry.

The New Deal, however, revealed that it had not changed its ideas or lost its zest for a controlled economy. The new synthetic rubber industry, for example, was deliberately structured to avoid integration, was divided between the petroleum, chemical, and rubber companies— and Washington announced it would retain ownership of the new facilities.[92]

In similar fashion the Administration moved to establish new controls over large areas of industry, impossible in peacetime but essential to the war effort. Yet these controls were so extensive and burrowed so completely through the economic and organizational life of the nation that it was not till later that it became clear they could not be extracted without creating havoc.

Thousands of business and industrial leaders who eagerly answered the emergency call of the government; hundreds of thousands of firms that surged into extra hours and efforts; millions of men who dedicated virtually their entire waking hours to the emergency could be proud of the fact their aggregate skills helped turn the tide during those dark days. Ironically, they were less aware that the industrial renaissance they mounted also helped enshrine the New Deal in both history and control.

Inside the new Raytheon plant at Waltham the production of magnetrons and other high-frequency tubes soared from one hundred to well over a thousand a day. The tables at which girls sat in assembly and the rows of equipment lengthened. Orders poured in to the firm; no competitor could match its output.

In naval yards and bases throughout the nation Raytheon field engineers toiled to install SG radars. One was Milton Mix, an old friend of Clark Rodiman's, enlisted by Raytheon in September 1942. Mix, formerly an engineer with radio station WTIC in Hartford, Connecticut, received two weeks' training and was in charge of installing SG radars in the busy Brooklyn Navy Yard.

At the Bureau of Ships, Henry Bernstein learned that radars were needed for PT boats in the Pacific. He canvassed the larger firms and was told that radars could not be created to function inside these small vessels because of the way they bounced in heavy seas. He immediately decided to visit Raytheon, accompanied by John Smith, a senior designer from BuShips.

Once on the scene Bernstein and Smith huddled with Gross and discussed design, sizes, and production systems. Gross seemed quietly confident that radars could be designed for PT boats as well as larger ships: why not? This calm acceptance of what other designers had rejected took even Bernstein aback; he suggested that Gross ride a PT boat out of Newport harbor first, in order to get a realistic idea of the problems involved. Gross took the suggestion seriously—as he took most suggestions—and rode out, clutching his fedora. He then went to work and in a few weeks called Bernstein to report that he and his team had made preliminary sketches of a design they thought would do the job. Bernstein promptly ordered fifty over the phone, sight unseen.

Six months later the first Raytheon PT boat radars had been designed, tested, produced, and were being delivered. Bernstein was astonished. "That was the quickest radars had ever been delivered—even on repeat orders," he said.[93]

That was only one of the special efforts. Other firms were still making an essential component—oscillator klystrons—by hand. "That was a bottleneck," Spencer said. "We devised a method of making envelopes with the grid discs sealed in a single machine operation, and were able to manufacture . . . in a volume equal to the magnetron."

In the Brooklyn Navy Yard the meaning of these efforts and the impact they were having on the battle of the Atlantic was relayed to Milton Mix by the crews of destroyers and destroyer escorts returning from sea. The SG radar was regarded by these men as superior to the radars carried in planes because the German submarines could tune in on the frequencies used by the planes, but not those used by the ships. One destroyer escort crew told Mix the SG enabled them to track down and actually ram a submarine that had surfaced to recharge its batteries.

At Raytheon's headquarters the navy forwarded more official reports and comments on the value of the SG radars. Unlike the results of the British scientific radar efforts, Raytheon's took effect far out of public view and were screened from general knowledge by wartime secrecy regulations. Yet the men were aware their efforts could play a key role in the war. That lifted their spirits.

*     *     *

Nevertheless the situation in the autumn of 1942 was grim for the Allies, and the outlook was uncertain. The Nazis drove into Russia destroying a number of armies, took huge crowds of prisoners, occupied immense territories, and encircled the city of Stalingrad.[94]

The attention of the western world—including Washington—seemed transfixed, even hypnotized, by the events in Russia. But the situation in the Pacific was equally grim and equally important. The Japanese moved to strengthen their island bastions in the Solomons and to attain control of New Guinea. The United States learned Nippon was building an air field on Guadalcanal and simultaneously mounting an overland assault on Port Moresby in New Guinea.[95] It moved to counteract both efforts, and the ensuing campaigns—Guadalcanal and Papua—were the most ferocious, protracted, complex, and bitter possible to imagine. In overall importance the struggle ranks with Stalingrad, though it did not receive equal attention, either at the time or in later histories.

The Guadalcanal sequence, though tangled, is fairly clear. On August 7, 1942, the navy, employing a task force collected around three carriers, landed a marine division on the island in the first amphibious assault by the United States since 1898. The landing was marked by air attacks from the Japanese that were defeated, but that nevertheless sent the carriers away from the immediate vicinity, leaving the marines on half-rations and a thirty-day supply.

On August 10, 1942, the Japanese sent a naval force of five heavy and two light cruisers into The Slot—a body of water separating Guadalcanal from neighboring islands. This flotilla surprised a U.S. naval force of four cruisers and three other warships at night and succeeded in sending all the American vessels to the bottom without suffering any noticeable damage of its own in the process. The Battle of Savo Island, as it was called, was the worst defeat suffered by the U.S. Navy since Pearl Harbor—and one of the worst in a surface engagement in its history.

While this disaster was still trembling in the air, Japanese army forces in Papua marched up the Owen Stanley mountains toward Port Moresby. This effort seemed incredible: even more incredible was the fact that eleven thousand Japanese forced their way through dense rain forests over narrow foot trails up towering, saw-toothed peaks thirteen thousand feet high after proceeding through matted jungle and stinking swamps heavy with malarial mosquitoes, snakes, and other

*135*

horrors. On August 12, 1942—two days after the U.S. Navy was humiliated in The Slot—the Japanese took Kokoda and its airstrip from the Australians.

On August 18, 1942, the Japanese landed reinforcements on Guadalcanal, attacked the marines and were annihilated. A week later, on August 24, the Japanese sent a major task force of sixty-four vessels, including three carriers and three battleships, down The Slot; it was driven away with the loss of a carrier by U.S. planes, in the Battle of the Eastern Solomons.[96]

On October 9, 1942, a cruiser force under Admiral Norman Scott sailed up The Slot to ward off attack from a transport group carrying U.S. reinforcements to Guadalcanal. The engagement is noteworthy for several reasons, not the least being the fact that Admiral Scott, in common with many other high commanders of the U.S. Navy, had not yet grasped the full utility of the new SG radar. "He made the mistake," said Admiral Nimitz later, "of choosing as his flagship the *San Francisco*, which was not equipped with the new SG surface radar." [97]

Admiral Scott was, in fact, proceeding without much thought of radar at all. The older SC radars, with which his flagship and many of his other vessels were still equipped, could be picked up by Japanese receivers. Scott had, therefore, ordered them not to be turned on. Instead he relied on searchlights to sight an enemy.

Yet one of the light cruisers in the U.S. force—the *Helena*—did have an SG radar, whose frequency could not be detected by the enemy. The *Helena*'s SG radar located the enemy, which proved to be a formidable force far outnumbering the Americans. The *Helena* relayed a warning but unfortunately its message and Scott's subsequent order to fire became garbled in a communications misunderstanding.

Nevertheless the outcome was a defeat for the Japanese, who lost three cruisers and a destroyer. The Americans lost one cruiser and one destroyer. The Japanese were forced to retreat; their attempt to attack the U.S. forces on Guadalcanal was aborted.

Scott's victory at Cape Esperance cheered the navy and the United States. He might, it was true, have achieved greater success, but he cannot be criticized for what was then a general informational lag. After all, as Admiral Morison wrote later, "His ignorance of the varying capabilities of the different types of radar was almost universal in the U.S. Navy in 1942. Later commanders learned that the proper use of radar could eliminate the searchlights and recognition lights which attracted enemy fire as a candle attracts moths." [98] But that was later. At Guadalcanal, where this and other lessons were learned, the cost of learning had first to be paid.

During October the Tokyo Express began record runs down The Slot, landing new troops. The United States, aware of the buildup, created a cruiser-destroyer task force around the battleships *Washington* and *South Dakota* and the still-damaged carrier *Enterprise* in response.

On November 12, 1942, Admiral Callaghan took a U.S. naval group consisting of five cruisers and eight destroyers up The Slot. He did not know it, but he was headed straight toward a Japanese force consisting of a cruiser and fourteen destroyers, trailed by the Japanese battleships *Hiei* and *Kirishima*.

As in the Battle of Cape Esperance, Admiral Callaghan had chosen the *San Francisco*, with its inferior radar, as his flagship. Admiral Scott, who on this occasion was second in command, led the cruiser force in the *Atlanta*. As on the previous occasion the light cruiser *Helena*, equipped with the SG radar, sighted the enemy first. Its warning was relayed but before a proper response was completed, formation was broken and battle joined. It consisted, said Admiral Nimitz later, of "a half-hour melee which for confusion and fury is scarcely paralleled in naval history." [99]

The United States lost all but five of its thirteen warships; both Admiral Callaghan and Admiral Scott and most of their staffs were killed. The Japanese lost two destroyers immediately, but Admiral Abe's flagship—the new battleship *Hiei*—was damaged.

That battle, known somewhat misleadingly as the Battle of Guadalcanal—a term that could better describe the whole protracted, complex, and almost continuous series of engagements around the island—created dismay in Nippon. The warlords ordered a withdrawal not only from Guadalcanal but also from Buna, in Papua. The Tokyo Express remained in operation, however, for the Japanese held other positions and possibilities in the Central Solomons. Their strategy remained essentially unchanged; they paused mainly to review the lessons learned and to plot new efforts.

The lessons, however, were not all on one side. Milton Mix, Raytheon's field engineer at Pearl Harbor, heard about some others when he clambered aboard the war-damaged U.S. battleship *South Dakota* on its return from Guadalcanal.

"A five-hundred-pound bomb had landed on the Number Two gun turret," Mix recalls, "and splinters had reached and killed several officers on the bridge. But the SG antenna, made of cast aluminum, had lost only a wingbolt. That was easy to repair."

Mix then examined the radar itself, inside its steel case, and found it undamaged. Crew members of the *South Dakota* told him that the radar cable had been severed, but that they had been able to splice it together. The radar had then resumed functioning and worked so well it enabled the vessel, at the last moment, to avoid going aground on a reef. "They were really superstitious about the SG," Mix remembers, "and didn't want me to touch it." Mix told them it might be off alignment; and of course it was.[100] But the attitude of the men on the *South Dakota* reflected a respect regarding the SG radar that had spread through the entire U.S. Navy.

On the highest levels, where the lessons of Guadalcanal were being evaluated and new plans drawn, the command had grown similarly aware that the new instrument allowed new tactics. The review of the early engagements in the Pacific was summarized by Admiral Nimitz, who wrote, "The new SG radars then being installed in American vessels could have offset enemy binoculars and night training had more American commanders understood its capabilities." [101] That misunderstanding was ended by late 1942.

The struggle in the Pacific made it clear that the era of easy European dominance in the Pacific was over. But the world did not pay too much attention to that change—momentous though its implications—because its attention was attracted to the situation in the West.

Britain, former mistress of the seas, fought for survival in the Atlantic aided by the United States. In the Soviet Union the Russians struggled to hold the Germans back along a two-thousand-mile-long front in which Stalingrad was pivotally located.

During the first half of 1942 the U-boat came as close to becoming an ultimate weapon as was then possible. During the year before, Nazi possession of French ports on the Atlantic and Italian ports in the Mediterranean enhanced their power. During the first six months

*138*

of 1942 U-boats sank 360 merchant vessels from American ports alone.[102] That did not include those destroyed around Britain or in other locations. Only a miracle, or a chain of miracles, could save the Allies in the Atlantic.

The wizards, as Churchill called them, could conceive of weapons. But, as in the instance of the magnetron and radar assemblies, it was necessary to transform these concepts into engineered, mass-produced realities. Britain was limited in its ability to do this; the United States appeared to have no limits.

Firms like Kaiser, Todd, and others dusted off old dreams, unused ideas and concepts to produce not only more ships, but ships in more variety and design than the enemy could sink. A similar phenomenon emerged in the aircraft industry, which made Flying Fortresses, Liberators, and other long-range planes in huge volumes.

But it was radar and radio and their ramifications that were most useful to the navy in the battle of the Atlantic. It was essential to protect convoys, but equally essential to be able to search out and destroy the U-boats.

By the last half of 1942 all these efforts converged to equip the sea and air forces of the nation with better instrumentation. Gyro controls were developed that enabled sonars—search and detection underwater—better to find and remain fixed on target submarines; airplanes equipped with improved radars could scour the skies and simultaneously detect submarines below; shipboard radar made surface searches easier, quicker, and infinitely more certain.

These methods and instruments meant that convoy escorts were better armed to protect their flocks. Planes, ships, and even Allied submarines began to range the seas and skies in search of U-boats. Once pure predators, the Nazis began to experience the sensation of being hunted in their turn.

Toward the end of the year the change in circumstances became so marked that Berlin was unable to stop, or even delay, the huge American armada that converged, from various U.S. and U.K. ports, upon French North Africa.[103]

Hitler was astonished and infuriated that the Allies could move 400,000 men on fifty transports, with hundreds of supporting vessels, through the narrow channel off Gibraltar. Admiral Doenitz, who created the greatest U-boat fleet in history, promised to improve his methods.

The U-boats began to organize into groups. If the defenders had discovered new ways of meeting single onslaughts, perhaps they would be less able to protect themselves against a pack. Because they so resembled animals in their sleek gray, their cunning, their ferocity, and their approach, these new and deadly combinations were soon called wolf packs.

Nevertheless, the scales of battle in the Atlantic were nearing a balance. The curve of Nazi sub killings, which had been going straight up, faltered and plateaued.

In the Soviet Union the Nazis had poured men and munitions without stint at Stalingrad, a linchpin in their two-thousand-mile-long line of attack. By late 1942 the Nazis succeeded, at terrible cost, in entering the city, but defenders continued to fight at every street corner, building, and intersection.

As the struggle continued, the Soviets brought forward new armies under the curtain of winter snows and dark nights. These silently surrounded the Nazi army that was intent, like a beast of prey, on its effort. Nazi reinforcements could not reach the besiegers; the Soviets closed the ring. In January the Nazi Sixth Army before Stalingrad found itself pocketed and subject to destruction. It surrendered.[104] Though the shaken Nazi high command strengthened the balance of the two-thousand-mile-long line, the German thrust into the USSR had been halted.

That achievement, combined with the new balance in the North Atlantic, victories in North Africa, and the halting of the Japanese in the Pacific by the United States meant that the Axis powers had, at last, reached their peak of expansion. Now the bitter effort to push them back could begin.

By spring 1943 most of the combat ships of the navy had been supplied with Raytheon SG radars, and these instruments were proliferating into new and improved models. Captain Henry Bernstein, of the navy's Bureau of Ships, delighted with the first deliveries of PT boat radars, ordered many more. In addition BuShips ordered other versions of these SO radars.[105]

With this increased volume, one would have expected a great expansion on the managerial level inside the company, but all that happened was that the small inner corps added huge sections of operations to its work. Marshall, tireless and omnipresent, remained on top of everything.

His financial efforts were highly mixed. With huge war orders arriving from every direction the banks of Boston were available for short-term financing, especially the First National. Navy contracts assisted greatly; the navy created pool accounts, which relieved the strain of swelling payrolls.[106]

The directors' meetings, attended now by the remaining hard core, which included, as always, Billy Gammell, as well as Havens Grant, Marshall himself, Schultz, and Harry C. Watts, took up the question of dividends. The firm had been in existence for many years with the distinction of not having paid any dividends since the halcyon days of the late twenties, when it briefly held an edge with C. G. Smith's rectifier tube. In early 1943 Marshall told the directors, for the umpteenth time, that it had been necessary to create and install new and more expensive and complicated test equipment, special tools, and other additions to such an extent that no dividend was possible.[107]

The directors sighed. It seemed extraordinary, but that was the way it was.

It *was* extraordinary. Marshall had extended and expanded every aspect of Raytheon to huge proportions, as though the firm were a balloon. His payroll had blown from one thousand to well over four thousand people and more were being hired by the hour. His managers were no more numerous than before, but each seemed able—like Napoleon's soldiers—to pull a field marshal's baton from his knapsack for the emergency.

G. E. M. Bertram, for instance, had always been considered a top engineer and production man, capable of turning out in quantity whatever was needed. But under the pressure of the war and the unprecedented orders that poured down upon him, he proved to have superlative qualities. Captain Henry Bernstein, who at this period was intimately acquainted with the insides and the abilities of all the competitive firms, including giant RCA, Western Electric, Westinghouse, and General Electric, said Bertram had "the most efficient production lines I saw during the war. It could make changes quickly without a lot of new drawings and red tape. Their testing and repair, when required, was also most efficient. I will always remember the two lighthouses in Bertram's office—one green and the other red. The green was usually lit, but whenever any production line was stopped, the green was turned off and the red was lit." [108] Its glare, the men found, was a reminder that was hard to ignore. If they slackened, they soon found the production manager, John Beedle, a tireless driver and stickler for detail, at their side.

Raytheon had somehow obtained the use of Charles Eliot's old home situated atop a bluff overlooking the restless Atlantic from the point of Nahant. There it operated its radar school, whose graduates, all members of its field engineers, were sent around the world to instruct servicemen who themselves became instructors.

Rodiman recalls evenings when he would be in his office at six or seven o'clock and Laurence Marshall would come to him and say, "Let's go to Nahant."

"We would stop on the way to get lobsters and wine," Rodiman recalls, and then proceed to Nahant. They would stay "two or three hours, during which Marshall would get acquainted and talk to the new men. He was interested in people," Rodiman said, "and in turn he interested them. People loved him; he was stimulating company."

A question arose about insuring the field engineers. They were civilians but were being sent to combat areas; ordinary insurance firms wouldn't cover that. Lloyds of London would accept any risk, but its rates were high—so high Rodiman went to Marshall for permission. The company head listened and looked up, eyes blazing, to say, "Nothing is too good for these men. Nothing." [109]

Meanwhile the war was changing attitudes and shifting the grounds of old assumptions. The second year of American involvement opened to a flood of war books: *Guadalcanal Diary, God Is My Copilot, Thirty Seconds over Tokyo*. After twenty years of unremitting muckracking about the American past, patriotism had, once again, become popular. *Oklahoma!*—a musical whose lilting songs lifted the hearts of the audience—swept across Broadway like a fresh breeze.[110]

These themes were joined by another. Wendell Willkie, defeated Republican candidate for President, wrote a book in six weeks called *One World* that sold two million copies in two months. It was a raft in a vast, almost euphoric tide of propaganda about a different, better postwar world.

The shift was remarkably similar to the change that had taken place in World War I, which had also started as a resistance to German military expansion and been transformed rhetorically into a movement for world reform. In World War I, however, democracy as a concept had described only those nations whose people had a limited government, a free press, open and free elections, and parliamentary rights.

In World War II the clarity of that concept of democracy dissolved in the wartime alliance with the USSR. At a time when the Soviets were holding huge Nazi armies locked in combat, that seemed a matter of only minor intellectual importance.

A curtain fell over the nature of the Soviet regime and the realities of life under the commissars. A rash of articles appeared in the western press stressing the patriotism and homely virtues of the Russian people, their basic similarity to the people of the West.

The world Communist movement, long covert in the arts and in academia,[111] emerged into respectability. By its association with the West against Nazis and Fascists, communism succeeded in separating itself from the general denunciation of totalitarianism.

Many persons, therefore, came to accept the idea that a better postwar world would be one without Nazis or Fascists, but one that would include Communists in the new, expanded definition of those who believe in democracy.

By May 1943 the Nazis had committed a string of atrocities that horrified the world. In April they leveled the Warsaw ghetto and murdered all its inhabitants.[112] They brutally mistreated prisoners of war, people in conquered territories, and even their own citizens. Their concentration camps grew notorious, and their anti-Semitic activities represented a barbarous step toward an unspeakable goal.

Partly in retaliation, partly to draw Nazi power away from the Soviet, partly to sap Nazi ability to fight, the British and Americans launched a heavy bombing of Germany.[113] The step was highly popular—too popular.

The expansion of Allied bombing from factories, harbors, transportation, and other legitimate war targets to the saturation bombing of German cities constituted a breakdown in western ethics and the

*143*

traditional western attitude toward civilians in time of war. But definitions were crumbling, fine distinctions being lost.

These undercurrents and their significance were, however, remote from the daily life of the average American. The "arsenal of democracy" was moving into high gear. On Friday, May 14, 1943, in response to an official notice sent by Under Secretary of the Navy James V. Forrestal, Raytheon received the official army-navy "E" Award. The E was for excellence.[114]

The pennants were handed over at appropriate ceremonies by Commander Lewis L. Strauss of the navy, and Colonel James H. Van Horn of the army. They were accepted on behalf of the company by Lillian Driscoll, Frank Vonel, and Margaret Lavery.

It was a proud moment. The ceremony was broadcast, and all involved were immensely pleased. Afterward everyone went back to work.

Some idea of the intensity of that work and its meaning can be gained from the statistics of the Annual Report, as of May 31, 1943. Gross sales were $37 million. Profits were $719,000.[115] In a single year Raytheon had expanded over six times. It was moving up and outward, like a rocket.


In the first half of 1943 the Nazi wolf packs made some heavy strikes against Allied shipping. On one occasion forty U-boats attacked a huge double convoy and sank twenty ships in one fell blow. On another occasion a wolf pack attacked a convoy of thirty-three ships and sank twelve—more than a third.[116]

This aroused the attention not only of the naval forces, but of the wizards. One of the British savants, Dr. P. M. S. Blackett, developed a "probability theory"—a sort of special application of theoretical mathematics.[117] In a sequence that was to become almost repetitive, British scientists discussed the mechanization of this theory with their American counterparts. And a new combination of academe, the services, industry and technology came together in an anti-submarine approach.

This called for the coordination of a play-by-play description of all the activities conducted each day, including sub sightings and attacks, defenses, areas, locations et al, of the submarine situation. The information was fed into computers and statistical probabilities, as well as defensive tactics and choice of weapons, began to emerge as a result.

Admiral Doenitz, head of the world's largest underwater fleet till that time, unwittingly opened the door to other effective counter-measures when he ordered U-boat commanders to radio a shortwave report to Berlin once every twenty-four hours while they were at sea. Allied radio monitors happened upon the shortwave band the Nazis used. With this lead they exhumed the principles of a high-frequency radio direction finder created years before by the remarkable Robert Watson-Watt. Building from these early patents and adding improvements, ITT created instruments known first as HF/DF's and, soon, more euphonically, as Huff Duffs. These were mass manufactured, placed in ships and planes, shore stations and carriers. In short order they targeted Nazi submarines.[118]

Had Huff Duff been developed and placed first, the probability theory might not have emerged. But in the long run the probability theory proved more important. Before Huff Duffs were operational, statistics were used to direct antisubmarine searches. In May, June, and July 1943, 108 U-boats were located and destroyed by this system. That contrasted dramatically with the fact the British had been able to sink only 192 in forty-four previous months, even though they had had U.S. aid in the previous eighteen months.[119]

The probability results made Washington sit up. A new factor had emerged in the ancient game of war: one that was to lead to the famed Game Theory and all its ramifications.[120] This was, eventually, to affect other sectors of human behavior as well as military considerations, but in 1943 that was still in the future. That season held more immediate problems—such as the quality of U.S. naval torpedoes.

These had fallen far behind the advances of the Japanese and Italian navies, and those employed by the Germans. Word was sent through the ranks of science and the military to change this imbalance. Many groups were ordered to create solutions.

Other sectors of the U.S. government were active on the torpedo problem. The Office of Strategic Services, later described as "half cops and robbers and half faculty meeting," learned that the top echelon of Italian leadership was wavering in its loyalty to Mussolini. That was vital news, and it was partly in response that the Allies invaded Sicily in July 1943. The command of naval and land forces was divided among the British and Americans; Eisenhower was top commander and the plans were drawn by Montgomery. Results in a military sense were mixed, for the Nazi forces escaped intact in the resulting confusion.

In a political sense, however, the invasion of Sicily had shattering results. It led, immediately, to the downfall of Mussolini. Since his rule was really based on rhetoric more than a structured political system, his fall marked the end of fascism, Italian style.

The downfall of Mussolini dealt a deadly blow to the system Hitler headed in Europe, and broke the myth of the "iron ring." Instead of an ally, the Nazis now had a nation to their south secretly dickering to surrender and change sides. Scenting this,[121] Berlin planned to occupy all Italy and defend this territory at all costs. That made a massive transfer of military force necessary for the Nazis.

Meanwhile the OSS, in probably its best stroke of the war, spirited Vice Admiral Eugenio Minisini, head of the Italian Torpedo Works and the man directly in charge of that highly skilled and advanced sector of the Italian naval technical effort, out of Italy and to Washington.[122] There he was interrogated by youthful John M. Shaheen, a U.S. Navy lieutenant, to whom the unpredictable OSS had given responsibility for executing the project. Shaheen, a notable bargainer, persuaded Admiral Minisini to hand over the technical details of the advanced Italian torpedoes being used by the Nazis, as well as a list of the best Italian technicians. The OSS then put Minisini, who was actually signed up by Shaheen, at the disposal of research groups and their industrial contacts in the United States. These included Raytheon among others.

The coup aroused intense satisfaction. The OSS, with Lieutenant Shaheen still in charge of what was, for unknown reasons, termed Project McGregor, began to lay plans to spirit the technical experts —and, if possible, the whole Italian Navy—out of Italy.


These and other developments had echoes inside Raytheon. The army wanted a radar and its need centered, at first, on a radar designed for amphibious forces. Raytheon went to work and created the SG-2. The army was pleased with the design but wondered if Raytheon had sufficient facilities to manufacture the new device. It was then that Bernstein learned why the original three-story building had such high ceilings. Marshall simply slid new floors halfway in each story and, with one stroke, doubled his manufacturing space—and got the army SG-2 radar order for Raytheon.[123] It was obvious the Raytheon president had not wasted his youth in the construction industry.

Marshall also found ways to absorb a continuing stream of new employees made necessary to fill the larger orders. Raytheon's roster soared close to ten thousand and the dollar volume of the firm's war effort neared that of Western Electric, until then the unchallenged leader. That was astounding.

One newcomer, barely noticed, was floor tester T. C. Wisenbaker. He had been chief engineer of radio station WQAM in Miami, and was eager to join the war effort more directly. Once inside the Raytheon plant at Waltham, he looked about with satisfaction. "A real war plant," he concluded.[124]

Mrs. Laurence Marshall became involved in the Cambridge Community Center, a neighborhood house located in a black district. The CCC operated a salvage shop, but its activities were somewhat limited until Laurence Marshall sent down some damaged magnetrons to see if they could be disassembled and their tungsten—an expensive and rare material—could be extracted for further use. The women were deft and the task was simple; he was delighted with the results. He sent more and set a price upon the effort.

In a matter of a few weeks Mrs. Marshall was highly pleased to discover that the salvage shop had been converted into a virtual Raytheon annex and was performing useful and remunerative work.[125]

In March 1943, the Japanese under Admiral Yamamoto put the Tokyo Express into high gear down The Slot to pour troops into the central Solomons. It met disaster from the air in the Battle of the Bismarck Sea when American planes using slow fuse bombs sank eight fully loaded troop transports and four destroyers, and downed twenty-five Japanese planes.[126]

Alarmed, Yamamoto went to Rebaul, gathered three hundred planes, and sent them against shipping in The Slot. This air fleet struck hard and sank a U.S. destroyer and a corvette, a tanker and two transports, but lost forty planes in the effort. One American response was outstanding, however: having broken the Japanese code, it was able to trace and shoot Yamamoto himself out of the sky when he made a trip to Bougainville.[127]

By June 1943, when the Japanese struck in The Slot again, they lost twenty-four bombers and seventy Zekes, at a cost of six American planes. Yet the Americans had reason to wonder about their opponents. In May Admiral Kinkaid, a most efficient commander, had been sent to root out some 2,600 Japanese isolated on Attu, in the Aleutians. Kinkaid arrived at Attu with three battleships, six cruisers, nineteen destroyers, five transports, an escort carrier, and eleven thousand troops. They landed without opposition on the north, and then placed two thousand more ashore on the south. The idea was to drive the Japanese defenders into the eastern tip of the island, where the naval forces could pound them into surrender. Instead the Japanese holed up in the mountains and fought till they were out of ammunition.

On the night of the twenty-ninth of May, one thousand of the remaining Japanese came silently out of the mountains armed mostly with knives and bayonets, came through the American lines, overran some outposts, killed all the sick and wounded, and then—when finally surrounded—killed themselves. When completed, the conquest of 2,600 Japanese on Attu cost the United States 600 killed and 1,500 wounded, as well as immense expenditures of matériel. Another 1,500 American troops were hospitalized because of the cold, wet climate of the area. In all, a nightmare.[128]

The Japanese proved as difficult in the tropics as they had been on Attu. The first Allied landing in New Georgia was virtually uncontested on sea and in the air, but once the troops entered the jungle they found an entrenched, slippery, and deadly resistance that tied up over 33,000 troops in weeks of exhausting efforts to subdue 4,500 enemies. That was in June 1943.

On July 6 and again on July 13 Ainsworth, heading a cruiser destroyer force in The Slot, located the enemy twice. On each occasion he sank only one destroyer and one cruiser, and in each battle lost a cruiser himself. One was the *Helena*. In reviewing his performance, Nimitz decided the use of SG radars was still not fully mastered: the commanders paid most attention to the largest targets on the radar screen, and ventured too close to the enemy before opening fire. Part of this could be traced to the often defective U.S. torpedo, whose longest range was only three miles at 45 knots, as against the Japanese Long Lance that could travel nearly eleven miles at 49.

Nevertheless, when another Japanese cruiser-destroyer came down The Slot a few nights after the second engagement expecting easy pickings, it received a surprise. A PBY "Black Cat" equipped with radar sighted the force and flashed the alarm, and bombers appeared at once. They sank two destroyers, damaged a cruiser, and sent the Japanese into retreat. For the first time it was clear that radar had changed the rules of night naval engagement, rules the Japanese thought they had invented.

Admiral Nimitz later compared the effort with the "usually ill-prepared, often hastily assembled scratch teams that had fought in Ironbottom Sound during the Guadalcanal campaign. . . . Dependable radar," he said, "had now become generally available on Allied vessels, and fleet personnel had learned how to use it effectively. The scopes were housed in a special compartment known as Radar Plot, where contacts were plotted and analyzed. Gradually other information, from radio and lookouts, began to be correlated here, and Radar Plot became the Combat Information Center. Possession of the CIC gave the Allies a tremendous advantage over the Japanese, whose radar, still primitive by American and British standards, had by this time been installed only in their largest vessels." [129]

The array of electronic devices that emerged from Allied laboratories and the industrial establishment of the United States made almost as much qualitative difference in the Atlantic as in the Pacific.

Yet the Nazis still held command over the highly advanced scientific establishment of Germany. It had been weakened by Hitler's racial theories and totalitarian controls, but still functioned on a very high level. German scientists managed to unscramble the radiotelephone code used between Churchill and President Roosevelt in their transatlantic conversations and taped them for analysis and information. They also mounted an effort toward creating an atomic bomb, and Allied intelligence directed a number of daring strikes against their Norwegian sources of heavy water, a vital component in such experiments.[130]

In the Pacific, on the other hand, the Americans and Australians confronted an enemy whose huge advances since 1895 "had been fired by a technology imported wholesale from the West." [131] The Japanese did not seem able to improve this markedly during the war. They had prepared their plans carefully and well, but they kept them relatively unchanged.[132] The United States, in contrast, proved able to improvise, to shift, and to learn lessons quickly.

Among the lessons learned by the military tacticians was that the Japanese military had a tendency toward suicidal attacks when their positions became untenable. This was a decidedly nonwestern reaction and one that was to influence American policy regarding Japan.

In September 1943, the Italians surrendered. In October—a month later—they declared war against the Nazis and became allies of the Allies.[133] Combined British and American forces landed on the ankle of the boot and began a slow crawl up the leg of Italy. The Nazis savagely contested every inch.

In Rome the situation was tangled, uncomfortable, and dangerous. The Nazis treated the Italians as not merely another conquest, but as betrayers. The Gestapo watched all Italy, and the air was heavy with mistrust, suspicion, and mutual hatred.

Meanwhile the American OSS and various branches of British intelligence scrambled for Italian scientists and experts. The OSS had the edge. Its coup in reaching the Italian admiralty under Project McGregor was energetically pursued by Lieutenant Shaheen and his associates. These included James Rand, Serge Obolenski, Henry Ringling North, and a number of other names since famous.

One target was Captain Carlo Calosi, a scientist who had developed the trigger mechanism on the deadly Italian magnetic torpedoes. Calosi was contacted by the OSS the day before Christmas in Rome, in his hideout—a convent. Following a complicated route prepared by the Italian Secret Information Service and the OSS, he proceeded, dressed as a priest, down the Tyrrhenian coast to join a group that included two U.S. Army Intelligence officers and two other Italian naval officers.

Beginning the night after Christmas, the small party went to the beach nightly for a week to signal toward the sea. On January 3, the eighth night, a PT boat arrived and carried them away to Corsica. From there they were airlifted to Algiers and interviewed by OSS Colonel Obolenski. Calosi was not sure how much he could reveal, so he was taken into the presence of Admiral DeCourten, secretary of the Italian Navy. DeCourten gave him permission to cooperate and even to go to the United States.

Calosi also met the legendary U.S. Colonel Pash, who was in Italy as head of the American Scientific Mission, following the faint but very real spoor of the Nazi atomic bomb project.

Finally Calosi was flown to Washington, where his arrival was a matter of satisfaction to young Shaheen. The McGregor Project had succeeded marvelously well. Though certainly the OSS had not negotiated the surrender of the entire Italian Navy, it had succeeded in removing a large part of its nervous system and whole segments of its brain, excisions that led to its surrender.[134]

In time Calosi was established inside the Submarine Signal Company, where he was put to work to develop defenses against his own naval devices.[135] His arrival was, understandably, slightly mysterious. Later he was to enter the Raytheon circle—but that was later.

Production at Raytheon continued to soar, and employment went over twelve thousand. There was a problem, Laurence Marshall told Mrs. Marshall, in obtaining all the help that was needed. She was interested; her salvage shop operation had grown prosperous. Marshall, having discovered that tungsten could be recovered, decided the entire operation—including Mrs. Marshall's workers—should be transferred into the Raytheon factory.

To their pleasure the experiment worked better than they had planned. The black women came in and were, at first, placed at their own tables to salvage tungsten. But Marshall assigned instructors to them to teach them the other areas of assembly that were underway. At those tables other women worked on piece rates. On occasion a worker would not appear, and the entire table's quota would suffer. The white women, on such occasions, began to invite their new co-workers to join them; soon the entire department was integrated as a natural matter of course, without any management directives.[136]

Other changes were underway. T. C. Wisenbaker, the new test man on the factory floor, aroused attention by redesigning the test equipment. The engineers gathered around interestedly and Wisenbaker was moved to the laboratories and was put to work on radar assemblies.

Wisenbaker was, in fact, a lucky find. His background was very southern. He had graduated from a Bible school and attended college for two years in southern Georgia. Later he took some special courses in mathematics and electrical engineering at the University of Miami and had become chief engineer of a radio station. "There weren't many available jobs in the thirties," he says softly, and that was certainly true. Wisenbaker was one of the many hundreds of thousands, perhaps millions, of young men of talent whose time was wasted during the depression by circumstances beyond their control.

At Raytheon he found his abilities recognized, but Raytheon's ardor was not returned in equal quantity. Wisenbaker found New England, with its cold climate and tart people, not entirely to his liking. Mrs. Wisenbaker was even less enthralled; she did not have the fascination of new professional vistas. As a result, Wisenbaker, always called "T. C. Wisenbaker" in recognition of some indefinable quality of innate dignity, asked to be made a field engineer. That, he reasoned, would carry him back to his beloved South. He even selected his areas: Montgomery, Alabama, and Miami. His timing was good and his superiors agreed willingly enough. Raytheon had recently developed a new precision indicator for its radars; Wisenbaker—who was familiar with its principles—could easily supervise its installation and instruct the military in its use.[137] Off he went, and other new faces arrived.

Three belonged to a trio who would become famous in Raytheon. Their leader was Royden C. Sanders, a young man with longish hair and restless eyes who fidgeted and rambled about conversationally and physically. He was, in the almost universal opinion of everyone who saw him, a typical "mad scientist." He was trailed by two more orthodox but equally dedicated types: James Ludwig and William Mercer. All three had left RCA because they had ideas of their own they wanted to pursue. RCA, a structured organization, could not find room for them, was not interested in their thoughts.

Marshall, however, was willing to listen. Sanders talked; the others nodded solemnly. Later, after Marshall had ordered they be given laboratory space and "all the tubes they wanted," someone asked him if he really understood their ideas. He said he wasn't sure he did. His questioner expressed surprise and wanted to know, in that event, why he had hired Sanders in the first place.

"His burning eyes," Marshall said briefly.[138]


Pressures were beginning to show. Fritz Gross, who had been working around the clock for years, developed a constant low-grade fever that left him dragged and thin. It is doubtful if Gross had ever taken an extra day off in his life. Clark Rodiman says he only recalls, during this war period, two official holidays a year: Thanksgiving and Christmas. It was no wonder Gross sagged.

To his surprise Marshall appeared before him and said, "You need a vacation." The Grosses were even more surprised to learn the president had not only discovered an undeveloped island off the coast of Florida he considered suitable, but joined them with Mrs. Marshall for two weeks of swimming, fishing, and just plain loafing. They had not dreamed the chief executive would accompany them: Gross did not, ever, seem to realize the extent and great importance of his contribution to the firm. The cure, however, worked like magic. Fritz's fever vanished, never to return.[139]

The timing of the vacation was significant. The war was still in progress, but the tide had turned. In the east the Soviets recaptured half their lands from the Nazis and were marshaling huge forces. In the Pacific, American submarines were taking a fearful toll of Japanese shipping, and U.S. amphibious forces were moving from island to island in a deadly progression.

American industrial production was so effective the Administration relaxed some of its rigid controls over material priorities.[140] But though speculations about the postwar economy were beginning to arise in top management circles, forecasts were not easy to formulate. The wartime cost of living had risen almost a third.[141] Arguments about the nature of the postwar economy were beginning to emerge. If the past was any measure of the future, victory would be accompanied by massive dislocation and a slump.

With wartime business still rising and creating heavy internal pressures, the Raytheon situation reflected, in microcosm, the perplexing problems confronted by leaders on the world stage.

The war was rising to a crescendo. Hitler still held the Balkans and all western Europe in a mailed fist. Roosevelt and Churchill had made it clear they would never negotiate a peace with the Nazis. Japan had been publicly warned it would be stripped of all its advances in Asia, going back to before 1914.[142]

It was clear, therefore, that industry and the military would find themselves entering the final stages of a vast conflict that would be savage beyond all modern parallel. It was equally plain that nobody, on either high, low or middle levels, had any clear idea on what would happen after that.

The war was changing all mankind. Penicillin had not only been discovered, but a method found to manufacture it in quantity; DDT was removing that ancient curse of all armed forces, typhus.[143] The American air force, which barely deserved the name before the war, had expanded into a great, almost global instrument. One arm was in Italy; one in England. A strategic command was created, and American planes, in the spring of 1944, began to range from the Balkans through southern Germany, over Italy.[144]

Berlin was bombed nightly for months; by spring it was bombed during the day as well. Questions about saturation bombing began to arise in the British House of Lords; despite the denials of the government, it seemed to some that civilized barriers were crumbling, that war was becoming total. In the month of April the Allies dropped almost 85,000 tons of bombs on Germany and Occupied Europe.[145]

The Nazis, however, were still dangerous. The dictator, who was never really informed in depth on the possibilities of an atomic bomb, had ordered the creation of flying bombs; self-directing missiles. Peenemunde, launching site for German missiles, was spotted and the Allied Air Force ordered to demolish it. The Nazis, however, had other missile sites along the French coast. The bombers managed to injure but not to kill the program.[146]

In the Pacific, American forces planned an assault on New Guinea strongholds of the Japanese and to take the Japanese mandated Mariana islands in midsummer.[147]

In Britain the high command clustered around weather and tide charts. Huge forces had been collected, and the long-awaited leap to the Nazi-held continent of Europe drew near.

At Raytheon production rose to a tremendous peak. By the end of May 1944, sales had risen by a factor of three to go over the $100 million a year mark. Profits were $2.6 million.[148] Raytheon was even with Western Electric in war orders, and still hiring, training, and expanding.

Early in the year Marshall had conferred with directors Billy Gammell, Havens Grant, Harry C. Watts, and Dave Schultz to discuss the possibility of a new stock issue. Paine, Webber, Jackson & Curtis, as well as White, Weld & Co., thought the time propitious. Raytheon's stock, which had sold for only 13 on the Chicago Exchange in 1942, had risen to over three times that price and was still heading straight up.[149]

But the directors, who could have estimated the firm's capital needs on the back of an envelope only a few years before, demurred. Raytheon had grown huge, but it had only one huge customer. They wondered how long that customer's needs would be so gargantuan; they were anxious about the shape of the future. Marshall, of course, never lacked for plans at any time. He had ideas, and as usual they were sweeping. The meeting left matters at that point for the nonce, but the record leaves a curious taste. It was a sign—faint and so far subtle—that the board might have begun to believe that improvisations were no longer sufficient, and that longer-range plans would be preferable.

Such plans were still difficult to conceive. The highest circles of science in the United States were as absorbed in weaponry as the workers at Raytheon. Dr. Vannevar Bush, for example, sent another emissary—a physicist—to talk to Percy Spencer. Spencer was ordered to work on a project so secret he was not permitted to engage in it at the Raytheon Labs.[150] Since every man in those labs had been rigorously screened, that alone was surprising.

Nevertheless Spencer was willing, and he enlisted Robert Quimby. They worked in Quimby's home with lab equipment especially obtained for the two of them. Their task was to create a gas-ignition firing mechanism; they were not told its final purpose. Theirs was one section of a vast jigsaw puzzle whose parts were being made in several installations, fabricated by men blindfolded against the overall pattern.[151]

On June 4 the Allies entered Rome.[152] On June 6, they landed at the beaches of Normandy in the largest amphibious assault in the history of the world. Though planned by the British, it was commanded by General Eisenhower.[153] Unlike huge invasions of the past, it involved not only sea and land but the air as well.

On June 15, less than a fortnight later, the Americans assaulted Saipan, a Japanese stronghold in the Mariana Islands in the Pacific.[154] It had been planned to assault Guam three days later, but stiff resistance on Saipan and news that the Japanese fleet was headed toward the engagement caused a change in plan.

The Battle of the Philippine Sea was won by the American Navy—but more by the use of planes and submarines than by surface warships. U.S. pilots were highly trained, had the better equipment, and downed more than three hundred enemy aircraft the first day, losing only thirty from their own number. Two Japanese carriers were sunk by American submarines. On the second day the U.S. planes made more heavy strikes and sank a third Japanese carrier, forcing an enemy withdrawal.[155]

Despite this naval victory, the land battle on Saipan was ferocious. Every inch was disputed; the struggle went on for weeks. The strain was deadly on the Japanese, but the U.S. forces suffered command disputes that revealed serious flaws. In the end the island was taken; it could hardly have been lost since the U.S. had sea and air command around it. But the Americans had almost 3,500 dead and 13,000 wounded. The Japanese lost 24,000 dead.[156]

The news led to the resignation of General Tojo in Japan, and for the first time a presentiment of possible defeat permeated the Japanese high command. Peace groups began to form, but the war group managed to retain control.

The world press, however, continued to devote more attention to the war in Europe. On June 12, 1944, the Nazis sent a self-propelled jet missile twenty-five feet long, with sixteen-foot wings carrying a two thousand-pound explosive warhead through the air over the English channel to London: the V-1.[157] The Buzz Bombs, as they were called, created great alarm. Aircraft found they could be shot from the skies but were able to down only about 10 percent. General Marshall asked Dr. Edward Bowles, in Washington, D.C., if he had an immediate answer to this new menace. Dr. Bowles, acting on his own initiative—since Air Force General Arnold was away—ordered 165 of the newly developed 584 antiaircraft, gun-laying radars, developed by a team under Dr. Ivan Getting of Radiation Lab, sent to England immediately.[158] These radars were able to locate and lay a barrage that destroyed 90 percent of the buzz bombs before they could land and do any damage. Men at Raytheon, who had worked with Dr. Getting on the devices, were highly pleased; the British were relieved. Allied wizards, as Churchill had hoped, were outdoing their Nazi counterparts.

In June 1944—a busy month—the Allies discussed the future course of the campaign in Italy. Their forces had passed Cassino and Rome;

the path through northern Italy loomed ahead. The question was whether they should hold, thereby pinning down Nazi defensive forces, or move on. Churchill wanted to penetrate northern Italy, enter Hungary, and combine forces with prowestern Hungarian partisans.[159]

His purpose was clear: Britain did not want the Soviets to occupy all the Balkans. American military men, who avoided political issues like the plague, bucked their response to Washington. Word came back from President Roosevelt that Project Anvil, as it was called, should remain where it was; he forbade U.S. forces to fight in the Balkans.

Churchill, bitter, renamed the project Dragoon, to indicate he felt dragooned into it.[160]

The Soviet Union moved on June 23, 1944. It used one hundred divisions, but no other specific statistic has ever been revealed. Thousands of tanks, tens of thousands of cannon, numberless planes are described. Stalin permitted no statistics of Soviet war industries or production, resources, reserves, or facilities. "A riddle," said Churchill, "wrapped in a mystery, inside an enigma."

In a month the Soviets broke through the Nazi lines, surrounded and destroyed a Nazi army of 350,000 men. That was a larger figure than Stalingrad.

In late July, an attempt—masterminded by the German generals—was made to assassinate Hitler.[161] It failed. Had it succeeded, the Germans planned to surrender to the Allies in advance of the Soviet arrival. Though the news swept the world, the Allies ignored the cue.

A fortnight later the Soviet armies were outside Warsaw. Their radio urged the Poles to rise against their Nazi occupiers. On August 1, the Polish underground army, acting on suggestions from London, rose and mastered the city. A few days later Nazi SS troops arrived and for almost a month the Poles fought against the Nazis while the Soviet army camped across the Vistula and refused to intervene. The entire city of Warsaw was razed. Appeals to the Soviets from Churchill and Roosevelt were ignored.[162]

The event alerted the British. Afterward, no British leader trusted the Soviet intentions. Washington was more hopeful. President Roosevelt remained convinced the United Nations would resolve all difficulties, bind all wounds.

Unfortunately the world was not falling into easy categories. In

September the Nazis sent V-2's into London. They were rockets 46 feet long, carrying 1,650 pounds of explosives that moved faster than the speed of sound.[163] They made, therefore, no noise and could not be seen. Dr. Getting's gun-laying radar defenses were of no avail against these; no defense existed. The phenomenon was shuddery and deathly, like arrows that fall after the archer himself has been mortally wounded.

While these events were underway, the production of radars and tubes at Raytheon continued to soar. Wars consume weapons, men, and matériel. Firms devoted to the supply of the military are almost as dependent on the course of engagements as are the troops themselves.

In the autumn of 1944 Raytheon's production of magnetrons rose to over two thousand a day in a plant originally designed to produce one hundred. Over $3 million in special testing equipment had been designed and installed by the company for its operations.[164] Its field engineers, stationed in combat areas and on naval bases, served as a communications belt by which reports of performance, suggestions for improvements, and needs for new features poured back to the company to guide the efforts of the engineers.[165] This sequence was then well ahead of its time.

Sales had risen to over the $150-million-a-year level and were still rising.[166] Laurence Marshall, looking about, had good reason to believe that he had in hand an organization capable of competing with the giants that had always overshadowed the fortunes of Raytheon: General Electric, RCA, Westinghouse, Western Electric.

In October, at a board meeting held in the offices of Jackson & Moreland in Boston, Marshall talked to the directors about the future. First they took care of routine business, setting aside $50,000 from profits for charitable purposes. That was not new; the firm had always contributed to charity whenever it made any money. Neither Marshall, Gammell, nor their associates would have been good New Englanders otherwise.

Then Marshall suggested the board create an executive committee. That was good politics. Further, he thought it time to set a director's fee. There were no objections to that.

Then he suggested, and the directors approved, a change in the corporate charter to enable Raytheon to "conduct and maintain high-frequency broadcasting stations," and to file an application with the FCC to construct a high-frequency station in the very near future.[167]

Microwave communications, in Marshall's opinion, could lead toward the creation of relays for television, facsimile reproduction, FM broadcasting, and nationwide police and weather networks as well. There is no question that he was right in all these assumptions. The tools were at hand and needed only to be assembled. Raytheon, with its new, expanded professional groups, its expertise, its scientific connections and knowledge of the state of the art, could establish the first beachheads in this area and compete—at last—with the giants on an equal basis.

The directors were impressed. It was the season of the wizards, and Marshall's visions were worthy of the time.

At about the same time that Marshall discussed his ideas for launching a revolution in communications, the U.S. and Japan joined in battle over the Philippines. Certainly no two events could have seemed farther apart, either geographically or intellectually. Yet, in the new world dominated by wizards, they were actually to become interconnected. And in the long run, by ironic twists of unpredictable fate, it would be the events at Leyte that would have more ultimate impact on Raytheon's postwar future than the dreams of Laurence Marshall.

All that was visible in October 1944 was the immense armada assembled by the United States for the effort. Since the loss of the Philippines would have severed their lines of supply and endangered their control of all lands inside their inner defense circle, the Japanese brought up their main fleet for the defense.[168] The ensuing sea and air battles were marked by confusion and accident on both sides. The Japanese, however, lost heavily and withdrew.

The Americans landed in force on Leyte. The Japanese rushed troop reinforcements. Their need was crucial and they revealed the mainsprings of their culture in the nature of their response. The Nazis, confronted with a long-dreaded invasion, had turned toward highly advanced mechanical horrors—the V-2's. The Japanese turned toward suicidal heroes: the Kamikaze.

Kamikaze means "divine wind"; the term was taken from an event in Japanese history, which records that the island was once saved from invasion by a providential typhoon. There was something very near the Grecian idea in the way the Japanese went about creating their new weapon. Their pilots competed for the honor of selection. Ceremonies that stressed the glory of sacrifice were held, and the chosen ones flew off to immolate themselves in their aircraft against the Americans.

The Americans had no real defense against these human rockets. Two U.S. aircraft carriers were sunk, and a great many of Halsey's ships severely damaged. The U.S. radars had difficulty in picking up low-flying craft in the first place, and the Japanese devised a number of maneuvers that created even more confusion in the second. They flew low over the ground before appearing at a harbor; they intermingled with American planes in the air; they could maneuver faster than a ship.

Three out of every four Kamikazes were shot down, but the fourth landed. One out of every thirty-three sank a ship.[169] Word raced through the American navy and a call went out that some better, surer means of protection against this new menace had to be discovered. The call soon reached Raytheon, among others.


Hitler's attitude toward the German people reveals a change dating from the abortive assassination attempt. His decisions seemed no longer based upon the long-range future of Germany.

The greatest peril confronting the dictator was the Soviet juggernaut. It had recaptured its own territory and ground over Estonia, Latvia, and Lithuania again. It had pushed back the borders of Finland and signed an armistice with the truncated remainder. It entered Rumania against only token resistance, and the Rumanians switched sides. Bulgaria, also compliant, switched too. By October the Soviets were in Yugoslavia and joined forces with partisans led by Tito. Belgrade was encircled by the end of the month, and the Soviets turned toward Hungary. During December they encircled Budapest. Churchill, alarmed, flew to Moscow.[170]

Hitler, instead of withdrawing and regrouping his troops, ordered all eastern armies to fight to the death at their stations. Then he ordered a last convulsive draft and distilled his remaining resources to create one last army.

As though determined to punish the United States for thwarting his plan to reach a negotiated settlement with Britain, and to punish his own people for their evident attempts to surrender to the West, Hitler chose to use this last army not against the Soviets but against the Allies.

Washington, still jubilant over the election of President Roosevelt to a fourth term in office, was astonished. The Nazi offensive, mounted by twenty divisions, struck along seventy miles of the Allied lines, centering on U.S. forces. The line held in the north and the south, but the middle was thinly defended because the Ardennes Forest was considered nearly impassable. The Nazis used that route and the Battle of the Bulge was joined.

Heavy weather aided the attackers and impeded the ability of U.S. planes to play an effective part. The attack was in full fury when British troops in Greece met resistance from Communist-led partisans. Churchill flew there.[171]

By the end of the year 1944, the Battle of the Bulge was being won by the Americans, at heavy cost. Before it finally ended in January 1945, the United States had suffered 77,000 and the Nazis over 100,000 casualties.[172]

Larger results were less easily calculated. By stripping Germany's last internal resources, Hitler had delayed the advance of the Allies and, perhaps as a punishment to a people he believed had failed him, had opened the gates to an unimpeded Soviet drive to Berlin.

Early in 1945 Laurence Marshall leaned forward and looked at some Raytheon executives who had gathered in his Cambridge home. "Time," he said, "is of the essence. I estimate the war will end this year—probably between July and September—and we must be prepared."

Norman Krim scribbled this prophecy down; it was one that struck him deeply. Later he looked back at it with restrospective awe. "Hit it right on the button," he said. "I don't know how." [173]

Marshall, however, was not in a contemplative mood. He had large plans, and he spurred them into suggesting other, subsidiary, lesser activities. Krim recalls discussions of cooling systems—air conditioning, in other words—mobile radios, portable recorders, and "at least a half dozen other products."

By early 1945 Raytheon had increased its production forty times

over 1940 and was producing 80 percent of all magnetrons—now pro-
liferated in great variety—as well as huge amounts of other high-frequency tubes. Its mass production systems were advanced; its engineers
had proven capable of extraordinary achievements. Its stock had risen
180 times in value on the New York Curb, going from a low of 50
cents in 1940 to $90 a share in January 1945, though it had not paid a
cash dividend since 1929.[174] Many careful market-watchers had made
fortunes following the rise of Raytheon—whose products during the
war were neither described nor known to the general public.

Marshall, with sixteen thousand employees,[175] examined the future
with all the intensity of a commander whose army had grown sixteen
times and whose future seemed immeasurably brighter than before.
The board approved, in February 1945, a split of the common stock
three for one. The price per share diminished proportionately but the
overall price did not waver.

Examining commercial needs, Marshall's eye fell upon Belmont
Radio Company of Chicago, one of the last two independent receiving-
set manufacturers left in the industry. Belmont, established since 1930,
had an excellent earnings record and had handily survived the depression by building sets that were marketed under their own brand
names by Montgomery Ward, Western Electric, and Gamble-Skogmo.
During the war it had received contracts from the government. Its
latest annual report, as of November 1944, showed sales of $38 million
and a gross profit of $3.4 million.[176]

Marshall swept Belmont off its feet by offering 270,000 shares of
Raytheon common—issued for the purpose—in exchange for Belmont
stock. The Belmont principals—P. S. Billings, H. C. Mattes, Charles M.
Hofman, Sigmund Freshman, and John Robertson—were agreeable.
Later Marshall rated the purchase at a modest $2 million; Raytheon
historians have since put it at $4 million; stock prices at the time would
give the purchase a going rate of $5.4 million. In actuality, discounting
the relatively minor dilution of the Raytheon stock structure, the acquisition cost Raytheon practically nothing in terms of initial purchase. It was announced April 1, 1945.

In commercial terms, it seemed at the time a flawless move. Belmont was an established radio receiving-set manufacturer with a strong
independent position. By its acquisition, Raytheon had extended from
regional toward the national market. It hoped, in the future, to supply

Belmont with the results of advanced research and volume manufacturing support to enable it to grow.

The acquisition of Belmont was, however, only one part of a vast program to carry Raytheon forward in the sort of future that Marshall foresaw. He explained this future to the directors, placing it against the context of wartime developments.

First he reminded them of how swiftly research advances in radio had been translated into commercial realities. This phenomenon, which they had all witnessed in their lifetimes, had resulted in sprouting broadcasting stations and millions of home receiving sets.

During the war the government had funded research into radio for the first time, at least on a national and serious level, to the extent of $75 million.[177] (That was a sum equal to several hundred millions in the seventies.) These funds and efforts had led, in turn, to "deep studies and the use of new frequencies." One result was that television was now commercially practical.

Marshall also planned a network of microwave and shortwave relay and television broadcasting stations across the nation. The East would be blanketed with stations atop tall buildings in major metropolitan centers: New York, Boston, Washington, Miami; the Midwest by similar stations in Cleveland, Detroit, and Chicago; the Far West in Los Angeles, San Francisco, and Seattle. Microwave relay stations thirty-five to forty miles apart would serve as connecting links.

The area between the Mississippi and the Pacific would be served by stations on top of mountain peaks ranging from three to five thousand feet in height. He ticked them off: Adams in Washington; Shasta, Tamalpais, and Whitney in California; Wheeler in Nevada; King in Utah; Gray in Colorado—among others.[178]

Possible uses multiplied as he talked. They could be air traffic control relays, transmitters of newspaper facsimiles; they could broadcast on UHF private bands for police and government; for television entertainment, news programs, special messages; they could be relays for areas too remote for telephones. The name of the network would be, appropriately, Sky Top.

This program, combined with Belmont, envisioned a net so wide it was almost unworldly. Broadcasting on one end, marketing receiving instruments on the other—and manufacturing all the components in between—would leave no communications sector uncovered.

It was a vaunting ambition, sovereign in its sweep and unlimited in scope. Years later Henry Argento looked backward and said, "He seemed to believe he could do anything; anything at all. Once he had listened to Dave Schultz, but toward the end of the war not even Dave could slow him down." [179]

There seemed some surface merit to Argento's observation, but there was more to Marshall than success alone could affect: he had been successful for years. It was simply that he could see the whole great panorama of change opening in the world of communications as clearly as daylight. It was coming; the parts were at hand to put it together. Who could tell a man who had already accomplished the seemingly impossible that what he clearly knew to be possible was beyond his reach?

From the East the Soviets, with 180 divisions, swept through Poland and into Germany. From the West the Allies broke through the Ruhr and captured almost 320,000 Nazi troops. [180]

A few months before, in February, Roosevelt, Churchill, and Stalin had met at Yalta and come to agreements; the Soviets were already breaking them. A deep discussion arose between the British and U.S. military men. Montgomery, with Churchill's backing, wanted to take Berlin. Eisenhower, supreme commander, decided instead to have Bradley and U.S. forces drive through central Germany. He feared last minute pockets of resistance. [181]

The decision could have been determined by President Roosevelt, but "some weeks before he died," Vannevar Bush noted later, he received a letter from the President. "From its nature, and from the shakiness of the signature, I knew he had not dictated it, and I doubted if he had read it before signing." Bush realized, apparently from the contents, that Secretary of War Stimson had received a similar letter. He went to see the Secretary and they compared the letters. Finally, after a long pause, Stimson said, "Van, I hope we are not in for another Wilson episode." [182]

They parted on that note; it was clear the President was not himself.

At that juncture the decision of General Eisenhower to allow the Soviets to enter Berlin remained standing. On April 12, 1945, the President died of a sudden brain hemorrhage in Warm Springs, Georgia.

The following day the Soviets entered Vienna and, a week later,

Berlin. Nine days after that, on the twenty-eighth of April, Communist partisans captured Mussolini and his mistress in northern Italy, shot them dead, and hung their bodies upside down in a meat market. On the thirtieth of April Hitler committed suicide in his underground headquarters in Berlin,[183] and the war in Europe ended.

The situation vis-à-vis Japan was far different. In early 1945 the Japanese spent 21,000 men defending Iwo Jima and the United States lost almost 7,000 dead and over 19,000 wounded. On April 1 the invasion of Okinawa, largest amphibious effort in the Pacific, was started.[184] The initial landings were lightly contested because the Japanese military had decided to send Kamikaze planes from Japan to drive away the U.S. Navy and isolate its troops.

On April 6, seven hundred of these suicidal vehicles descended from the air against the Americans. It was the first of ten such attack waves. According to historians, these succeeded in damaging nearly four hundred ships, sinking thirty-six, wounding almost five thousand sailors and killing another five thousand. The U.S. Navy lost seven hundred planes fighting against the Japanese at Okinawa.

Yet the United States accounted well for itself. On April 8 its pilots sank the Japanese battleship *Yamato*—the largest and most deadly ship afloat at that time.[185]

The battle for Okinawa was still being fought when President Truman met with Churchill and Stalin at Potsdam, on July 16. That same day the atomic bomb was successfully ignited near Alamorgordo, New Mexico.[186]

The top-level conference between the three major survivors of the war was laced with strain and tension. The Soviets held all Eastern Europe in its grip; its forces were menacing Turkey and Iran in the south; pro-Communist partisans were creating disorder in Italy, France, Greece, Austria, Czechoslovakia. Stalin held an agreement, concluded earlier with President Roosevelt, guaranteeing the USSR concessions in Asia if it entered the war against Japan after the defeat of Germany.

The British, whose resistance to the Nazis had bled their empire, were undermined when Prime Minister Churchill learned, during the conference, that his party had been defeated in elections at home. He departed and his place at the table was taken by Clement Attlee.

Publicly the major accomplishment of Potsdam was a joint announcement to Japan calling for surrender and acquiescence in an occupation, and the end to its militaristic regime. The alternative was stated to be "prompt and utter destruction."

The Japanese response to the ultimatum was evasive, and on August 3 the first atomic bomb was dropped on Hiroshima. Even then the Japanese sought to avoid surrender. A diplomatic mission was in Moscow, seeking Soviet support in negotiating better peace terms. The Japanese government awaited the results hopefully.

On August 8 Molotov met with the Japanese and told them the USSR would declare war against Japan the following day. He was accurate: Soviet troops did invade Manchuria the following day. That same day the United States dropped a second atomic bomb, this time on Nagasaki. The day after that the Japanese sued for peace, but laid down one firm condition: Emperor Hirohito must retain his throne.[187]

Meanwhile the people of the world—told about the atomic bomb on August 6—staggered under the implications of the development. The wizards, as Churchill had predicted, had won the war. But they had destroyed the sense of peace historically associated with civilization.

# *Chapter 6* THE FORTIES

RAYTHEON engineer Robert Quimby, who had worked with Percy Spencer on a supersecret ignition design, was sitting in his living room at home when President Truman's voice came over the radio announcing the atomic bomb. Mrs. Quimby saw her husband turn white. For a fleeting moment she thought he was having a heart attack, then guessed his reaction had something to do with the radio broadcast.

"Bob, did you help make that?" she asked. He nodded, unable to speak.

In due course he received a framed certificate headed:

ARMY SERVICE CORPS—CORPS OF ENGINEERS

MANHATTAN DISTRICT

ROBERT S. QUIMBY

*has participated in work essential to the production of the Atomic Bomb, thereby contributing to the successful conclusion of World War II. This certificate is awarded in appreciation of effective service.*

STIMSON

SEC OF WAR

Greatly distressed, Quimby hid the certificate.[1]

Actually neither Bob Quimby nor Raytheon had been told the specific purpose of his effort. During the war, three different departments of the company had been contacted and asked to design what

*167*

Percy Spencer later called a "gas discharge device" and others a "firing tube." Each time the department contacted had rejected the order. Finally a call came from a highly placed official on the Manhattan Project, who ordered the work done under circumstances of secrecy so extreme it was necessary to outfit a special home laboratory for Quimby.

Working there, Quimby had designed and built a firing mechanism that enabled the fuse of the world's first atomic bomb to operate in 1/1,000 part of a second.[2] He guessed, of course, the nature of his assignment, but he was an engineer, not a physicist. The reality had been so awesome, so swift, and so deadly, that he was conscience-stricken. A great sense of guilt suffused him.

Many persons shared that sense of guilt, including some of the men who had been most eager to press the atomic project when the goal was to use it against Hitler. Yet few paused to realize that the Manhattan Project would never have been mounted had it not been for experiments conducted by German physicists working under the Nazis. Information about those experiments was brought to Britain, to the United States, and probably also to the USSR at about the same time, by scientists who were forced to flee from Germany and Nazi-dominated nations by Hitler's racial policies.[3]

The Manhattan Project, therefore, was only one of four such national efforts in competition, in as many countries. Because the American effort was hugely funded and could draw upon the world's most advanced industrial complex, it forged ahead of the others. By 1943 it was so far ahead the British wanted to merge their efforts into the Manhattan Project and to share its results. Vannevar Bush had a difficult argument with Winston Churchill on the subject, and in the end the prime minister had to settle for an exchange, on an equal basis only.[4]

Inside Germany the physicists continued their nuclear effort on a far more modest level. Their failure to continue their initial head start was due to administrative decisions inside the Nazi national administration, which tended to concentrate on weapons efforts. This led to the development of the V-2 rocket, which, ironically, was based on the initial discoveries by the American scientist Goddard. They also produced the jet aircraft, but that came too late in the war to help Hitler.[5]

The German nuclear physicists were afraid to promise too much

to the Nazi leadership because they feared being placed under un-
bearable pressures. Another underlying but nevertheless real factor
was the considerable disaffection that coursed through the underside
of German life during the war. Nevertheless they were too intrigued,
as physicists and as Germans, to abandon their promising beginning.[6]

Nobody outside the Kremlin knows how the Soviet project fared
during this period, because no information about it has ever leaked
from that airtight, sealed establishment. But when the Nazis collapsed
in April and May 1945, there was a race between the United States,
British, and Soviet scientific teams to arrest as many of the German
physicists involved in the nuclear effort as possible. The U.S. team,
headed by Dutch-American scientist Goudsmit and the redoubtable
Colonel Pash, managed very well—but so did the Soviets. They carried away a number of Germans who had worked on the uranium
project.[7] Certainly they did not do that by accident.

Much of the surprise felt throughout the world regarding the
atomic bomb, therefore, was in nonscientific sectors. The world's
physicists were not as surprised as all that. German physicists in-
terned in Britain when Truman's announcement was made realized
they had been headed in the right direction as soon as they heard
the word uranium. Their conversation, which was recorded, reveals
that they were bitter at losing a game in which they thought they
had held the trumps.[8]

For the ordinary citizen, however, the news was mind-boggling.
It verified long-standing myths that scientists are some sort of modern
magicians, working with powers and elements beyond the ken of ordinary men. That in itself was sinister enough, but the timing of the
event was even worse.

Had the atomic bomb been developed and dropped on Japan
when the European war was at its crest, it might well have been
differently received. It would have removed Japan as an opponent at
a time when Hitler still held Europe and threatened the life of both
Britain and the USSR. But that was a time when passions were running high. They ran high as late as February 1945, when the British
Air Command deliberately chose to make an example of Dresden,
teeming with miserable refugees, and bombed more people to death
than in Hiroshima and Nagasaki combined.[9]

Instead the bomb was dropped when rhetoric about the United
Nations had soared into the stratosphere, and was shimmering before

*169*

the eyes of the world. Peace had been brought to Europe; Hitler was dead. The contrast was simply too much; many minds reeled in shock.

The shock was so great that for many it seemed to dwarf the war itself. The greatest war in history, which had cost forty million lives and $4 trillion,[10] suddenly seemed antique. That had the effect of casting all sorts of developments and persons into the shadows.

In England, for instance, British scientist Dr. A. P. Rowe, a leader in the radar effort, was very proud of his Hall of Magic, where films and models had been created to display the development and the effectiveness of wartime radar. After the hostilities he invited the press.

"We showed them to all the Cabinet ministers and other distinguished visitors," he said later, "and they were enthralled. But when we showed them to the journalists we failed to impress more than a few of them. While demonstrations were being given, some stayed in the background exchanging stories that were apparently funny. Others were interested in what radar might do in the future but not at all in what it had done in the past."[11]

Much the same sort of situation existed on this side of the Atlantic. People were suddenly made aware that their own futures were imperiled by the A-bomb; the past was no longer of interest. The newspapers carried long columns of material explaining various developments and stages of the war. Page after page appeared listing the merchant vessels that had been sunk by the Nazis, with columns carrying the names of their crews. This information, formerly suppressed by wartime censorship, surfaced briefly and then sank out of sight again, carrying with it the public realization of the meaning of the SG radars that Raytheon had, with so much effort, helped to create and produce.

There were other ripple effects of more immediate concern to Laurence Marshall and his associates. The bomb had been held secret from the lower ranks of the armed services until the moment it was dropped. And until that moment, plans for the invasion of Japan, with all the immense forces it required, proceeded. Once the bomb was dropped, the navy canceled pages of radar and component orders. These cancellations poured in over the Raytheon transom.

One sequence flowed into another, with no time for the management to readjust, at a dizzying rate of speed. The May 31, 1945, figures were put together and issued on a mimeographed sheet first, and then printed and included in a glossy Annual Report later, so that the great wartime growth of the firm, which had reached its peak at the end of May, could be described, and also new problems of converting to peace could be discussed. Sales by the end of May had risen to $173 million—over twenty-five times that of 1941. Profits were $3.4 million.[12]

The bulk of this business had been wartime contracts. In the report, Marshall said "both Raytheon and Belmont have received notices of termination of the major portion of their Government contracts." His great achievement was beginning to melt like a snowball in spring.

To balance this shrinkage, Marshall moved swiftly toward building his microwave communications network. Headquarters were established in the Lincoln Building in New York; Joseph Pierson—former president of Press Wireless, Inc.—hired to head the effort, was made a vice president and director. In turn Pierson hired Cap Smith, formerly with RCA, to head the engineering end. Application to construct a pilot system between New York and Boston was filed and others submitted to operate FM stations in Boston, Washington, New York, Chicago, and Los Angeles. Agents were sent out to lease mountaintops and strips; Pierson bought donkeys to carry equipment up the slopes.

Marshall's plans were not only large but diverse. It was obvious lots of money would be needed, and the board approved a new issue of 100,000 shares of Raytheon preferred at a $50 par. The sale went briskly: Raytheon's standing in the market was high.

As soon as this sum appeared, however, a good part of it was spent in the purchase, on September 30, 1945, for $1.1 million, of the Russell Electric Company, a phonograph parts manufacturer. The purchase was made at the recommendation of Belmont's managers,[13] who argued it would cost $400,000 in the next year to purchase equivalent production equipment and take at least a year to get into operation, while Russell could be made an immediate, functional, and helpful subsidiary. The argument prevailed, and the purchase was in cash.

Other changes were on a personal, human level. New faces began to appear on every level from the board of directors downward. That was a real change. Marshall had managed Raytheon since its inception as a virtual one-man show, as ringmaster to a small group of highly talented technicians. And from the beginning he had benefited from the support of a prestigious board, whose members were highly placed, substantial, and knowledgeable. Of this group, by late 1945, only Billy Gammell and Harry C. Watts remained. Havens Grant had resigned for reasons of health; the others had departed during the war.

As replacements Marshall invited two investment counselors—George L. Langreth and Emmons Bryant—to join the Raytheon board. That was reasonable; they were New York men and the market had become important to the firm. They could contribute a financial expertise comparable to the technological abilities of director Ralph D. Booth, an engineer and partner in the Boston firm of Jackson & Moreland.

Marshall also invited Parnell S. Billings, Harold Mattes, and Charles Hofman—all of Belmont—to join the board, and included vice presidents Ray Ellis and Joseph Pierson, two new men whom he had hired. In all, the new roster was less impressive than Raytheon's old board, less able to resist Marshall's plans, and less equipped to contribute its own. Emmons Bryant decided a conflict of interest existed when his firm (Reynolds & Co.) decided to underwrite Raytheon's new preferred stock issue, and resigned.

Other changes involving people occurred behind the scenes. One was quite important and painful. During the war Raytheon had added more than two hundred improvements to the SG radar alone. Percy Spencer had improved the design and altered production of the magnetron and created more than fifty variations of this essential component. Other advances made by the firm were of inestimable value.

Marshall took it for granted that these discoveries would be Raytheon's property after the war and would strengthen its patents. He underestimated the extent of the changes the war had brought to the nation, to its government, and to the attitudes of officials toward traditional property rights.

During the war the Office of Scientific Research & Development, headed by Dr. Vannevar Bush, had set new rules regarding this sector. The reasons, as explained by Dr. Bush later, seemed sensible. The OSRD had funded immense efforts at MIT and elsewhere, which called upon the inventive energies of thousands of scientists. "It would have been absurd for MIT to own patents on the inventions which emerged," says Dr. Bush. But it was also absurd, he believed, to have individuals obtain patents on such group efforts. His solution was to have patents filed by the OSRD that were then "by me dedicated to the public." [14]

Dr. Bush was not completely at ease about this, although he was very clear about its wartime necessity. He was undoubtedly correct in assuming that the regular rules would have allowed individuals to file for inventions they might not have themselves conceived and that horrendous postwar patent fights could have resulted.

In his autobiography he remarked on the inconsistency into which he, as a believer in patents, was impelled by the war. "I suppose," he said ruefully, ". . . I personally destroyed more property in the form of patents than any man living."

His reasoning is now generally accepted. "The purpose of a patent," he concluded, "is not to reward an inventor, but to enable the investment of capital." Since "the inventions on which I destroyed patents had no need for venture capital in their development," he concluded that no inherent inequity took place.

Marshall did not agree. Raytheon had signed over, for the duration of the war only, "a royalty-free license to the Government for all its patents, even though at the time it was negotiating with all the big companies for license arrangements which would have resulted in benefits . . ." [15] That was done out of a sense of patriotism, and Marshall did not begrudge it, but it constituted a considerable offering from a small firm in considerable need of "venture capital." During the war Raytheon men had made many more inventions. Marshall sat down and compared these developments with the contracts Raytheon had signed with the government, and saw no reason why the firm should reassign these rights to the government. He saw, in fact, a legal right to file a whole sheaf of patents, a step that would enhance and improve Raytheon's postwar position. He informed Dr. Bush of his intention, and the two old school chums, partners in business and close personal friends, came to a turn in the road.

Dr. Bush had been careful during the war to keep his official duties and his private interests far apart. "Raytheon was a *contractor*," he said. "I had no contact with the firm. I dealt only with the Radiation Lab." [16] For Raytheon to file for patents when others had lost the right would constitute a serious embarrassment, in view of Dr. Bush's well-known past association with the firm.

Marshall triumphantly produced copies of the Raytheon contracts and pointed out the absence of any restrictive clauses. Dr. Bush had the matter explored, and learned that Raytheon's first governmental contract had been a subcontract, where the matter of patents did not arise. All the further contracts the firm received had fallen within the realm of the first. "An accident," Bush growled. "A slipup on the part of some junior government attorney." [17] He grew angry.

A determined Vannevar Bush was formidable. He had risen very high, had become the most important scientist in political history. At one point, he had faced down Winston Churchill.[18] On many other occasions he dealt with five-star generals and full admirals on a basis of equality. As a consultant to the most powerful President in all American experience, Dr. Bush had grown used to the ways and the use of pressure; he was not the sort to allow an embarrassing situation that might cast a shadow on his career to develop.

"I told Marshall I would take the matter to court and fight him all the way," he said later, and there was no doubt that he meant every word. Marshall did not back down; that was not in his character. But he could see that his path was blocked and that the struggle might cost more than he could afford to pay. The men decided, therefore, to select an impartial committee of men to go over all the patents involved and to make a selection of those to which Raytheon would have a clear and unimpeded right. Both Marshall and Bush agreed to abide by the selections.

The committee made its choices and that ended the matter so far as the corporation was concerned. But sad to say, it also ended the long, close friendship of Laurence Marshall and Van Bush.[19]

Change coursed through the organization. T. C. Wisenbaker, still a member of Clark Rodiman's network of field engineers, watched these activities dwindle and came to his own conclusions. "It looked as though Raytheon's days of glory were over," he said. Later he recalls he was planning to return to Miami when he received a call from Fritz Gross. Gross, by then acting chief engineer of the equipment division, wanted T. C. to come to headquarters to talk to him and to Roy Sanders.[20]

T. C. knew Sanders had developed an admirable altimeter for RCA and considered him a genius. Talks with a genius always hold a special allure, so Wisenbaker made the trip.

The men sat down in Sanders' domain: Lab 16. It held little beyond Sanders, Bill Mercer and Jim Ludwig, a secretary and some scattered equipment; but the mental climate was impressive, the subject absorbing.

Leaning forward intently, Sanders discussed how the echoes from sea waves and ground contours created clutter on pulse radar screens. Low-flying Kamikaze planes, merging into this clutter, could not be detected by pulse radar.

It was his opinion, Sanders continued, that continuous-wave radars should be developed, capable of tracking moving objects through this clutter. Scientifically, he was talking about the Doppler Effect.

Named after its Austrian discoverer, the Doppler Effect is used as a basis to measure the speed and direction of a star moving toward or away from earth. Analogies are slippery, but if a man is compared to a continuous radar, such a man would notice the Doppler Effect if he were standing on a station platform, heard the rising sound of an approaching train, its crescendo as it reached him and its shift into a lower register and diminuendo as it proceeded past him. He would make that observation, incidentally, despite the fact that the train made a steady sound as it traveled and despite background noises.

Working on the basis of Doppler's principle, Sanders and his team had received a small developmental contract from the navy. They created what Wisenbaker calls "an excellent basic design for a seeker that could separate a fast-moving object from surrounding clutter by its speed—and that could then lock on that object."

The navy was sufficiently impressed to award Lab 16 another contract to proceed further. At the same time it gave airframe manufacturers Convair and Fairchild contracts to design a missile the seeker would direct, and called that missile-in-the-making the Lark.

Sanders was convinced they were a long leap ahead of all competitors in creating the seeker, or guidance system of that missile-to-be. His eyes glowed as he described his progress to Wisenbaker and urged him to join them. At that point Wisenbaker asked Sanders how he knew he was ahead. Sanders said the navy had said so. Wisenbaker shook his head pityingly, and pointed to not only the number of competitive efforts underway, but the formidable nature of the competition.

"There is MIT and its advanced group," he said. "The Applied Physics Lab of Johns Hopkins is working on a beam rider system; Sperry Rand is developing an air-to-air beam rider; Martin Aircraft is working on a seeker system. Someone," he concluded, "will win. And that someone will be the best technical group." [21]

The others fell silent. He was, of course, right. Other firms were spending huge sums in the most advanced laboratories on the same quest. Lab 16 was a pygmy entering the arena against giants. Wisenbaker made the point sternly and then announced he would help. If the effort was that difficult, wild horses could not have kept him away.


Charles Francis Adams, Jr., returned from the navy in 1946. In four years of war he had risen from a lowly lieutenant jg to a full commander. He had spent his time in service aboard destroyer escorts and destroyers, had ended on the staff of Admiral Ingram, CIC of the Atlantic Fleet. In these posts he had learned, at first hand and under unforgettable circumstances, the significance of radars, sonars, and the other electronic mechanisms produced by Raytheon and Submarine Signal. Both had achieved a reputation in the navy for superb equipment: advanced, efficient, and essential. Adams would never so put it, but he was proud of them.

Both firms had been intertwined in Charlie Adams' background. His sister had married into the Morgan family, and Morgan money—despite the talk about its being a purely Boston venture—had helped create Submarine Signal as well as Raytheon.

Of the two, SubSig had the longer and more glorious history prior to World War II. Its activities, replete with bell buoys, depth sounders, iceberg warners, and underwater submarine detection, were of a sort to fascinate all sea buffs—and Charlie Adams might well have been dipped in salt water at birth.

His father was a famous yachtsman who had sailed the *Resolute* to victory against Sir Thomas Lipton's *Shamrock IV* in the America's Cup race of 1920 and later served in President Hoover's cabinet as Secretary of the Navy. His father's mother had been a Crowninshield of the famous shipbuilding family. Charlie Adams himself was an expert and enthusiastic sailor.

In 1946 Submarine Signal had become not only important—it had been important for years—but a substantial commercial New England enterprise.

Its wartime sales had grown to over $50 million a year; its profits hit a peak $1.7 million. SubSig and Raytheon had long enjoyed a close relationship; SubSig bought many millions of dollars' worth of Raytheon tubes and components; they shared some very advanced research projects.

Once settled again as a partner in Paine, Webber, Jackson & Curtis, it was only natural for Charlie Adams to pay a call on Harold John Warren Fay, the seventy-year-old president of SubSig. He found the older man pleased to see him; as intelligent as ever, but "confused about the turbulent postwar world—and with no successor in sight. His board was worried about that."

Laurence Marshall, on the other hand, was bubbling with plans and greatly interested in the commercial prospects of marine radars. Adams brought the two men smoothly together and got them launched on a merger discussion.[22] Both boards of directors hailed the prospect; all sides sat down for some protracted New England haggling.

Adams, pleased at having started this highly constructive development on its way, then decided to take, at last, a much-needed vacation.

By 1946 storm signals flew over the world again. The press in the United States had reflected a vociferous clamor for the immediate dissolution of the armed forces and the return of all U.S. troops to the country. The campaign fit precisely inside the desires of the USSR, which settled over eastern Europe like a vast locust, intent upon repairing its enormous wartime losses by the acquisition of a new empire.

The new theory that communism was simply a variant of democracy propelled Communist sympathizers into positions of influence in the West; subverted de Gaulle in France and the new government of Italy; created an impossible coalition in Czechoslovakia; placed puppet rulers in East Germany, Poland, Yugoslavia, Hungary, Rumania, Albania, and the Baltic.

In the United States, where the Administration had retained the wartime Office of Price Controls, inflation had, nonetheless, held wages below the cost of living. Many shortages existed and people demanded goods to purchase with their backed-up wartime savings. But the nation's industrial machine, confronted with the need to convert into new products, was stalled by nationwide strikes.

It seemed very likely, for a time, that the Communist movement would engulf Western Europe as thoroughly as had the Nazis—but with a qualitative difference. The Nazis had earned the condemnation of the entire world; the Communists had achieved widespread support. In part this was a natural result of the wartime alliance in which the Soviets suffered huge losses. That alliance, which eventually pitted the Communists against the Nazis, was adroitly used by party propagandists to level the charge that anticommunism was, in effect, profascism.

The leaders of the United States, whose people were not ideologically sophisticated, had only two special advantages in the new contest. The first was the atomic bomb, in which it held a temporary monopoly. In the hands of the USSR, the world was well but subconsciously aware, such a weapon would have settled all issues. As it was, the commissars had been exposed to President Truman's caliber at Potsdam, and could not be sure he would not resort to its use if pressed too hard.

The other advantage was America's great wealth, and its use better fitted the American temperament. There was a widespread myth in the United States that communism grew largely from economic need, despite the clear evidence that its practitioners seldom operated from economic principles. The myth was a projection, for Americans are respectful of economic realities.

It was natural for President Truman to use the nation's economic resources first. He canceled $30 billion in British war debts and extended another $3.7 billion in immediate credits, contributed over $2 billion to war-ravaged Europe through UNRRA (United Nations Relief and Rehabiliation Administration).[23] He conferred with the nation's most experienced and probably best top-level military establishment in its history regarding other moves, but turned toward Winston Churchill for help in explaining the new state of world affairs to the people. Mr. Churchill did this, in masterly fashion, at Fulton, Missouri, in his famous Iron Curtain speech.[24]

In time the American approach would work, but at the moment confusion reigned, with strikes and shortages choking the system with bottlenecks. Lower governmental echelons added to the confusion by undertaking to rewrite many wartime contracts retroactively.

Raytheon was particularly hard hit. Washington canceled $150 million worth of orders out of $200 million.[25] That was bad enough; it forced layoffs of thousands of people and sent ripples of economic distress through the community. But what was even worse was the new government renegotiation policy, in which all the money earned during the war was reexamined to see if it fit within yardsticks created, with chilling efficiency, after the heat of the emergency had passed.

Nevertheless, Marshall had plans and needed new men to help carry them forward. Though his army was melting, his men were busily staffing the ranks of the company's intellectual cadre.

One man contacted in this effort was Paul Hannah. Hannah, a lawyer in civilian life, had risen to colonel in the U.S. Signal Corps. At one time he had been in the Chief Signal Officer's office in Washington, but when he received a cable offering him a job with Raytheon he was on General MacArthur's staff and was living in Frank Lloyd Wright's masterpiece, the Imperial Hotel, in Tokyo. He was very fond of the hotel because the doors, rooms, stairways, and other features had all been scaled to the Japanese height. As a short American, Hannah found this feature marvelous.[26]

He was pleased at the cable, which was signed by Ray Ellis, whom he had met in Washington. Part of Hannah's duties during that tour had been radar evaluations. He also recalled Harold Mattes, onetime head of Belmont Radio. When Raytheon was on the verge of buying Belmont, Hannah recalled, Mattes had brought Laurence Marshall in to be introduced. The introduction was one of the strangest of Hannah's career, for Marshall shook hands, smiled, sat down—and remained mute throughout the entire ensuing conversation. When the pair departed Hannah stared after them in surprise, for Marshall had never once spoken.

He recalled all this while sending back his acceptance of the offer to become Raytheon's treasurer. By the time he arrived in Boston a few weeks later, however, he learned that that post was no longer his to have. Marshall—who proved quite able to talk—was engrossed in his effort to create a microwave relay system. Hannah found himself immediately immersed in lease details and other legalities, and—just as well satisfied to be a lawyer instead of a financial man—settled in with great pleasure.

*     *     *

That was only one aspect of Marshall's activities, however. In late 1945 he and Fritz Gross had come together on the basis of a brilliant observation by Percy Spencer. A great many men knew that a magnetron radiated energy which could generate heat in various substances when it was in use, but remained incurious. Only Percy Spencer, intrigued, sent out for a bag of popcorn and placed it in front of the wave guide—a horn that was about the size of a sandwich. He watched in fascination as the kernels popped as though before a fire.[27]

The next day he brought a raw egg and placed that before the wave guide. One of the engineers became so engrossed he leaned too close and was splattered when the egg suddenly exploded. The men were caught by the fact that the *inside* of the egg had cooked first, causing the shell to explode. But all were more impressed by the larger fact that Spencer had discovered one could cook by *radio*—by microwaves.

The discovery filled Marshall with enthusiasm. He knew a great deal about the problems attendant on serving food to large numbers of people—cooking it, transporting it, and keeping it properly warm. Early in the war he had realized that the great numbers of persons employed in the expanded Raytheon factories needed warm lunches and were located too far from restaurants. He had persuaded Herbert Marshall (no relation, but a Boston restaurateur whom he had known, it seemed, forever) to enter the catering business to handle that part of Raytheon's needs.

After examining Spencer's discovery, Laurence Marshall's boundless imagination foresaw a complete revolution in furnishing cooked food, piping hot, to large volumes of people. He could visualize central kitchens where food could be cooked to the edge of completion in minutes, transported to satellite locations, heated to completion in seconds, and served to a rushed and busy world in a tempo that fit its needs.[28]

He ordered the engineers to design a cabinet for the magnetron with inside trays in which cold sandwiches could be heated and served almost without interruption. A contest was held to name the new device. Knowing it had emerged from the components of radar, the winner suggested Radar range. The words were merged so the origin was slightly blurred: Radarange.®

At the same time someone suggested other uses for radio heat, and

*180*

designs were made to create diathermy machines, a genuine contribution to the medical industry. This was to prove useful and profitable—but Marshall's attention was most caught by the potential of the Radarange in the food business.

With renegotiation sessions underway with the government, a microwave relay system in the process of construction between Boston and New York, applications for radio and television stations pending, the Radarange, new diathermy machines, new machines for electric welding, sweeping plans to produce broadcasting and phonograph equipment, receiving-tube manufacture, pioneering plans to introduce television sets to the nation—one would have thought that Marshall was busy enough.

That would have been an underestimation. Marshall pushed talks with Submarine Signal with all the vigor of a man who needed even more products to make and market, more people to supervise, more executives to merge into his own senior group—and more projects to worry about. By May 31, 1946, Marshall was able to announce a new agreement. Each Submarine Signal share was worth 5½ shares of Raytheon common in the surviving corporation. Overall, the deal represented about $8.5 million of Raytheon's market value. The result was a full merger, with Raytheon left with outstanding stock composed of 99,930 shares of $2.40 cumulative preferred at a par value of $50, 1,053,158 shares of common in the hands of premerger Raytheon stockholders, and 394,295 capital shares in the hands of Submarine Signal's former stockholders. It had become the owner of all of SubSig's properties, products, and patents, and the employer of its people.

More important even than the figures of the merger, however, was the fact that a new board of directors was created. It had eleven members. Both Laurence Marshall and H. J. W. Fay, the former president of Submarine Signal, were flanked by four men who had formerly sat on their previous boards of directors. On Marshall's team, if the term can be used in this context, were Billy Gammell, Harold Mattes of Belmont, George Langreth (a relatively new director), and Ralph D. Booth, who was also relatively new. Mr. Fay, an elegant figure, brought in Ralph Hornblower of Hornblower & Weeks, James V. Toner, the president of Boston Edison, Amory Coolidge, a senior executive with the Pepperell Manufacturing Company, and William H. Raye, a SubSig executive.[29]

Both men agreed on inviting the eleventh director, who had brought them together: Charles Francis Adams, Jr.

The announcement of the merger was made on May 31, 1946. That was the date of Raytheon's fiscal year end. Fortunately its figures did not emerge for a time, or they might have affected the terms of the agreement. From a wartime high of $173 million in sales the year before, Raytheon had plunged to sales of $105 million. And where it had shown a profit the year before of $3.4 million, it showed a loss in 1946 of $333,000.[30]

The figures did not reflect the acquisition of SubSig and the expanded products and markets, sales and contacts that it represented. But they showed such clear indications of Raytheon's terribly swift problems that many of the men in SubSig, who found themselves, like Russian peasants of a bygone day, sold by their corporate owners to new masters, thought they had grounds for bitterness. They muttered that Raytheon had made the purchase out of desperation.[31]

Such comments would have outraged Marshall had he heard them. In his view SubSig was a firm that not only had worked on underwater problems, but had itself operated underwater for years. It had developed, it was true, remarkable advances. Created in 1901, it had enlisted the energies of Dr. Elisha Gray, of telephone fame, and first installed a network of underwater bells whose signals could be picked up by submerged microphones and heard through telephones on shore stations or in wheelhouses. In 1912 the firm had had the acumen to hire Professor Reginald A. Fessenden, a huge, leonine, red-haired scientist addicted to long black cigars, capes, boundless enthusiasms, and a flair for invention.

Fessenden, who never received the scientific recognition to which he was entitled, created an oscillator-transmitter. His original version, about the size of a bushel basket, had a range of fifty miles and was a basic breakthrough. By 1922 SubSig and Fessenden had proceeded to the use of a cathode ray tube and developed submarine detection devices based on pulsed acoustic waves [32]—in other words, sonar.

Then SubSig was enveloped in comfortable captivity. The U.S. Navy declared its developments military secrets and sequestered all information about them.[33] The firm received large contracts to equip the navy, worked closely with the naval research laboratories, the Carnegie Institution, and other carefully selected, screened, and discrete groups in a variety of developmental projects.[34] But in effect it virtually vanished from the commercial marketplace and became an unofficial arm of the state.

Later—such are the fortunes of science and industry—SubSig exchanged information on sonar and underwater instrumentation with many firms. During the war Raytheon and SubSig had many contracts and mutual efforts; both firms were counted among the nation's assets. But by the time SubSig merged with Raytheon, it was the informed consensus that it had passed its peak. The Cocoanut Grove fire in Boston in late 1942, in which 492 people died, had also wiped out several of SubSig's most promising younger executives. Fritz Gross, who evaluated its engineering groups, discovered they contained a number of very talented men. Harold Hart, Ed Turner, Laurence Batchellor, and Paul Skitzki were especially outstanding. However, SubSig as an entire organization had not developed clear alternatives to wartime projects and was entering the postwar period with no clear goals.[35] It is true the firm had money in the bank, but it is not certain that it would have prospered had it remained independent.

In the evening, after almost everybody else had gone home, Laurence Marshall would leave his president's office, with its great oval conference table that served him as a desk, and appear in the equipment division laboratories. There he was transformed into an engineer once again. Fritz Gross, the chief engineer of the division, acted as his partner.

A cabinet for the Radarange oven had been created, but Marshall, it seemed, was dissatisfied. It leaked; it was too large. It worked, in his view, too slowly. He and Gross would create a new, better model.

They began with the idea that the energy should be radiated into a closed cavity containing the food. Casting about for such a container they left the building, and the nature of their search is difficult to imagine, because they brought back a large galvanized garbage can. They began by coupling a magnetron to the inside of this unappetizing object and began to heat water. They would pour a cupful into their improvised pot, then turn on the current.

"Not good enough," Marshall said after a while. "We'll have to use real food." He rushed away and returned with an armload of gingerbread mix, a product then just beginning to appear in grocery stores. They cooked this in batches, varying the magnetron coupling

*183*

and the amounts of mix. First they would cook, then munch the results—and then cook some more. Gradually the scent of gingerbread permeated the premises, seeped into their clothing, and surrounded them. "A sweet, sickly smell," says Gross, shuddering. It was a smell he grew to hate as they worked, night after night, until eleven or twelve o'clock.[36]

Although this was a private, intense, after-hours effort conducted at the end of busy and complex days, they succeeded in establishing the principles of a functioning Radarange oven in the speeds that Marshall considered the best attainable. Sam Hathaway helped refine the design. Then they decided to turn the project over to a regular group effort. John Dawson was chosen to supervise the next stage.

Dawson created large ovens and control circuits. G. E. M. Bertram headed the engineering and production system; the power tube division created a special magnetron.

This approach to the microwave cooking was a Marshall classic. He had realized the potential of the discovery immediately, had rushed upon it to improve it, had pulled together the elements of manufacturing it in volume with miraculous speed. The swiftness with which he moved and his uncanny ability to evoke special efforts from his engineers was as impressive as ever. The pace at which he worked was that of a young and tireless man. It was that sort of perception and drive that had pushed Raytheon into a huge national resource during the war—but during the war a huge and anxious customer had been waiting impatiently, order forms at the ready.

In microwave cooking developments no such customer was either at hand or visible on the horizon. And in the crush of his effort, Marshall had overlooked some key commercial elements inherent in peacetime markets. Who would sell the Radarange oven? How would salesmen be selected and organized? How would the Radarange oven be distributed? Finally, to whom would it be sold?

The equipment division was, meanwhile, engrossed in an effort to develop, sell, and install commercial radars for ocean liners, tankers, and freighters, commercial fishermen—the entire marine industry. The effort was difficult because Westinghouse, GE, RCA—the giants—could produce these devices as well as Raytheon, had established sales presences, and lower prices. One reason for their lower prices was that at

Raytheon, price was considered secondary. During the war, Raytheon's exacting and expensive standards, and the rigor with which the firm maintained them, had shocked even government inspectors.

That approach was understandable when quality was paramount and costs of no consequence—but the consumer marketplace does not really need to be served with indestructible objects. Newspapers are not carved on stone; a modest commercial fisherman did not need a radar that would outlast his vessel. There must be a certain obsolescence if new products can find a market: objects too permanent can prevent improvements from finding entry room. Generally speaking, businessmen like to produce sound products that will last a reasonable period; at Raytheon the emphasis was on reaching, if not perfection, at least as close to it as possible.

The multiplicity of projects, the flow of new men into the company, the inevitable arguments about priorities, direction, selection, and approach, created intense internal pressures. Henry Argento was stricken when Marshall said casually, "I just hired Bill Gray to handle your job. Why not find yourself some other work to do?" He meant inside the firm, but Argento was deeply hurt.

He went to Percy Spencer, of whom he was very fond, and said he was leaving the company. Spencer trotted him back to Marshall and said, "If Henry leaves, I'll leave too." Marshall calmed them down. Soon afterward he sent Argento to Chicago, to establish sales for broadcast transmitting equipment.[37] The incident was a sign of dishevelment, though to all outward appearances Raytheon was making impressive moves.

*Fortune* magazine drew attention to the dominance of engineers at Raytheon in an article that season, which appeared in its issue of October 1946. It was a good article, very flattering to Marshall, who was portrayed grinning widely in his office. He was described as "short, compact and heavy-browed," and looking "like a friendly and uncommonly intelligent wrestler."

After giving Raytheon due credit for its immense wartime contribution by quoting Commodore Jennings Dow, electronics head at the U.S. Navy Bureau of Ships, who said, "Raytheon radar had a marked effect on every major sea engagement of the war," an only slightly hyperbolic statement, the article concluded that the firm's "most formidable competition comes from companies that can, in a sense, take their electronics or leave it alone. GE, Westinghouse, and

Western Electric all do a huge business in 'conventional' electrical equipment." If, *Fortune* said gently, "the electronic age proves to be somewhat slow in arriving . . . these companies can wait it out." That was the rub.

The Raytheon directors were well aware of these realities. Billy Gammell, in addition to his other interests, was at the time first vice president of the Providence Institution for Savings and had been watching Marshall's pattern of management for many years. Ralph Hornblower, legendary partner in Hornblower & Weeks, was especially astute regarding financial matters and tended to be somewhat acerbic in his opinions. He termed Marshall "a genius—but not a businessman." [38]

In addition there were some other problems a *Fortune* writer could not, in the course of a half-dozen or so interviews, hope to uncover. Foremost among these was the formidable question of renegotiating the wartime contracts and their profits with the government. Washington's experts had laid down some guidelines based on the amount of a firm's prewar investment. In line with this thought, contracts were examined and profit margins pared back. Perhaps the scarifying hearings in the Senate during the thirties—that famous era of pacifism in the face of tyranny—had permanently seared more minds than was realized. At any rate, large numbers of bright young men in gleaming glasses appeared to ask sharp questions.

Captain Henry Bernstein, called in to testify regarding Raytheon's wartime business, praised its performance highly and stressed the value of the more than two hundred improvements it made, voluntarily, on the SG radar alone during the course of the conflict. "I'm afraid," he said ruefully, "my statements didn't help much. The [Renegotiation] Board gave much consideration to the amount of capital a company had invested in their sales and Raytheon did not have much of its own capital to work with at the start of the war." [39]

That being so, the renegotiation committees and experts were determined that wartime profits would be pared to the bone. Argento, who attended one of these chilling sessions with Marshall, recalls that the older man, grilled regarding some high development costs, had answered huskily, "I only wanted to improve the state of the art."

Later, when they left, Argento saw Marshall's eyes were filled with tears, realized that the real answer had been that Marshall had wanted to help the country. Such an answer could hardly have been

*186*

made to efficiency experts after the event: they would have considered it irrelevant, frivolous.[40]

As always, internal difficulties impelled the board not only toward sharp questions, but to intervention in management decisions. One result was that the board, shortly after the SubSig merger, said that Raytheon should "separate itself from the direct operation of microwave communications systems, as contrasted with the manufacture of microwave communications equipment." Charlie Adams was asked by the board to "explore the possibility of finding persons interested in supplying capital and management for such operations."[41] That was a loud alarm bell.

A Raytheon microwave station had been erected in New York, another in Boston, and plans were well along to broadcast educational programs. Marshall, operating on his usual assumption that intelligent men could do anything and everything, had tapped various men to appear on the network with their own programs. Since it was educational, he thought in terms of teaching and lessons. Fritz Gross was told to prepare to give a course in mathematics; Cap Smith would teach physics. Cold sweat broke out on Gross at the thought of appearing before the camera. He also had no idea of the level on which he should teach and had to consult with his wife regarding that rather crucial point.

Obviously the board did not agree that television programming should be approached in quite such a cavalier manner.

Western Union was willing to buy the system, but Marshall thought their price was not worth considering. "I will not," he is quoted as saying, "give up my heritage for a mess of pottage."[42]

Meanwhile the Raytheon board, concerned at the downward trend, created both an executive and a finance committee, whose members worked long extra hours delving into the situation. For the first time in several years Dave Schultz's influence rose, largely due to his detailed knowledge of the firm's financial situation, its internal costs, and other specifics of the sort that a director is apt to probe.

That does not imply Marshall could not answer the same sort of questions, but Marshall was not a man to suffer exasperating cross-examinations—nor was he of the opinion they served a useful purpose. Marshall thought in terms of goals and achievements: he soared beyond money. In the first part of the year, when Raytheon profits began to sag, Marshall cut his own salary. Money was not his pole star.

But money was a subject that began to dominate the board meetings. Every project cost money and would cost more money to get the first money back. Belmont and Russell, purchased to have a built-in use for tubes and a base from which to launch home radio and television sets, had production problems attendant on the disorderly labor situation, were short of essential plastic—and now needed to buy a building in which to manufacture. For the first time in a number of years the firm turned to short-range financing and borrowed $500,000 from the First National of Boston.

Through the beginning months of 1947 the Raytheon corporate condition continued to worsen. The finance committee reported that money had drained out in huge sums during the previous eight months of the fiscal year. Almost $8 million had vanished in "non-naval" operations. Out of this vast sum, almost half—$3.7 million—had been spent on developing products, projects, and groups for commercial business; almost $2 million to increase inventories; Belmont had cost over $2 million. Added together, these sums had drained the firm's cash to such an extent that Raytheon would not be able to operate in April without another transfusion or some drastic changes in its approach. Storm clouds no longer threatened; the storm itself had arrived.[43]

Joseph Pierson, the vice president chosen to head the microwave relay system, resigned, and so did Controller Trouant. Mr. Toner, of the Boston Edison Co., resigned as a director; Paul Hannah was made corporate secretary.

By reducing sail—suspending supply shipments, replacing a $500,-000 demand note, securing some advance payments—the board began to steady the ship. Funds were obtained from the pool account maintained with the navy against production contracts; Submarine Signal persuaded the navy brass to make a "progress payment."

Belmont finances were improved by a loan; the RFC agreed to finance Raytheon's purchase of the navy-built factories upon which it relied and some semblance of order began to appear. These were, however, merely shafts of light; the firm was still in trouble.

The revenue agent—a term for a team of tax men—had recommended that almost $6 million in additional taxes be levied against Raytheon for the years 1942 to 1944. The directors, alarmed, turned toward Dave Schultz, who calmed their fears. Most of that would, he said, "wash out" in the discussions of the high tax years to come. "But the interest, plus the addition, would probably cost the firm at least $700,000." The directors stared at one another; the agent had not yet looked at '45 and '46.[44]

At the beginning of May 1947 all these problems, considerations, bills, and vexations began to boil over. Langreth, as chairman of the finance committee, announced that Raytheon's problems extended into the management, suggested a new committee to study that. The board elected Adams, Booth, Gammell, Hornblower, Langreth, and Raye, called them a special committee, and made Billy Gammell chairman.

On the eighth of the month Marshall said that he needed "one or more assistants." Then the Minutes record that Charlie Adams and Laurence Marshall reported they had held several conversations, and that young Adams—he was thirty-seven in 1947—would join Raytheon as executive vice president and chairman of the executive committee, at a salary of $32,000 a year.[45]

Inside Lab 16 such top level activities were too remote to attract attention. Sanders and his team, now augmented by the presence of T C. Wisenbaker, were immersed in developmental work. Their efforts were at variance with the approaches recommended by their larger, more prestigious competitors.

"Simplicity is the key," said Wisenbaker. To him this was not simply an aphorism, but a scientific truth. He considers complex approaches to be unscientific. He regarded the decisions of the Naval Research Lab, for example, as being basically unsound. Yet the Naval Research Lab had used the newly developed computers to check out a whole series of probabilities, and developed some persuasive theories. Since a plane reflected multiple echoes, the navy establishment had decided that no radio-controlled missile could home in on such a diffused target, would in fact not be able to come closer than fifty to one hundred feet.

"Martin Aircraft took these computer runs as revealed truths," Wisenbaker recalls, "and dropped the effort to design an accurate missile guidance system. Instead they concentrated on developing a warhead powerful enough to injure a plane fifty to one hundred feet away." Later it proved too heavy to carry.

"Another rathole," Wisenbaker says, "was estimates about the 'roll' system of a missile. Some research groups tried to write computer programs to correct such a roll." Others became engrossed in computer studies of simulated flights using theoretical models. "In time," says the skeptical Wisenbaker, "these studies grew so complex even their designers couldn't understand them." [46]

In contrast the men of Raytheon called in Dr. Charles Stark Draper of MIT. That eminence, termed the "father of inertial guidance" by his admirers and other names by his detractors, proved able to do what no computer could match: find original answers to gyro problems.

By coincidence Hamilton Hauck, a young naval officer who had earned a master's degree at MIT only the year before, was sent at this point to attend a symposium at MIT on guided missiles. Hauck had studied under Dr. Draper and was abreast of the state of the art. He recalls that "speakers from all the larger companies talked until the program was almost over. On the last day Roy Sanders gave a paper on continuous-wave radar. Most of those present were skeptical; their questions indicated disagreement." Hauck, however, was impressed.[47]

He returned to Point Mugu, California, a missile testing center that was then still largely a compound of Quonset huts, dirt paths, and runways. Shortly after he returned, Dr. Vannevar Bush appeared to look over the site. Hauck took him on a tour and later sat with him in a Quonset hut that served as a visitors' lounge. Bush looked about and said, "Reminds me of the old days. I give it ten years. Then *rigor mortis* will set in."

Dr. Bush was, for once, mistaken, and one reason was that Hamilton Hauck had sent a special report to his navy superiors, recommending that close attention be paid to Raytheon's Lab 16. Hauck had reason to remember that recommendation later: its prescience helped his career in the navy.

Many persons, then and later, were puzzled that Charlie Adams chose to leave his comfortable nest at Paine, Webber, Jackson & Curtis to join Raytheon. In the years since, the decision has seemed increasingly reasonable, but at the time it looked more like a man entering a burning building that contained nothing of personal value to him.

His father advised against it, and he was not the only one. But Adams was intrigued.

"Why?" someone asked.

"Electronics was new," Adams replied. "It was a chance to build a new industry at a time when all the traditional industries of New England—textiles, shoes and the like—were in decline. It was a chance," he repeated slowly, "to build a new industry on the ashes of the old, for New England." [48]

The answer is interesting. The heritage of the Adams family—the most consistently eminent in New England—was, when the chips finally fell, inseparable from Charlie Adams' choice.

He had, of course, seen it coming. As a member of the board's financial committee he had done much to help on various problems. He had even conducted a quiet search for someone to assist Marshall, with the knowledge and approval of the board. But nobody he approached wanted the Number Two job at Raytheon. It was not that Marshall was not admired; it was simply that he had not established a line of succession. Dave Schultz, an able man, had not been given responsibilities equal to his talent, and the point was not lost on observers.

That was when the board turned to Charlie Adams, and suggested he think about the post himself. He took his time, gave it real thought. Among others, he talked to Professor Philip Cabot at the Harvard School of Business, where Adams had himself studied.

He explained Raytheon's condition and the description, despite his familiarity with it, sounded both dismal and confusing even to him. "The first step in a mess like this is to reduce chaos to disorder," Cabot told him, and something about the phrase kept it ringing in Adams' ears.

Certainly he knew the task ahead would not be easy, and very probably not pleasant. "The firm had forty-eight projects going," he said, "and each one was undermanned. The latest was introduced yesterday."

Then Adams, with grim practicality, tied a lifeline around himself before plunging into Raytheon's troubled waters. He obtained an agreement—in writing—that he could carry any deadlock between himself and Marshall directly to a board vote. That was shrewd. He also obtained an agreement that he would serve as executive vice president only long enough to learn the inner runways and patterns of the establishment—details not visible to a director—and would then become far more than the "assistant" that Marshall, when painfully pressed, had conceded he might need.

Raytheon's period of crisis, in which the pattern of both its prewar and wartime activities changed almost beyond recognition, was a microcosm of greater changes taking place in the larger surrounding world.

In a series of wartime conferences, President Roosevelt had accommodated the Soviets and was, by virtue of background, inclined to be chilly toward British colonialism. By the end of the war there is evidence he began to distrust the intentions of the Soviets, but there is no evidence that the United States, under either Roosevelt or any succeeding President, ever favored colonial rule.

The major Rooseveltian legacy to the postwar world was the creation of a larger League of Nations under the name United Nations. Eventually headquartered in New York on land purchased for $8.5 million donated by the Rockefellers,[49] the founding membership of the UN favored the West. Subsidiary organizations were formed under the UN banner to assist economic and medical standards of colonial and primitive areas. The organization was launched on a wave of idealistic hope. Some persons were dismayed, however, to discover the Soviet Union more intent upon using the UN as a podium from which to attack the West, stressing anticolonialism while tightening its own grip over Eastern Europe. The propaganda outlets of the international Communist movement provided an unremitting chorus to these expressions, in which the British were replaced by Americans as the symbol of international capitalism.

Some persons assumed this turn of events, described as the Cold War and the Iron Curtain, was a new state of affairs. It was not. The USSR had conducted a cold war against the non-Communist world since 1917, and had persistently curtained its own activities from outside view. It simply restored these practices to their customary priority after the Nazi menace vanished.[50]

What was new was the entrance of the United States on the world ideological stage as leader of the opposition. In May 1947 President Truman announced a $400 million program of economic assistance to Greece and Turkey as part of a new policy of "assisting free nations threatened by subjugation by armed minorities or by outside pressure." [51]

Further evidence of the new American decision to bear the burdens of world leadership was provided a few weeks later in 1947 when General George C. Marshall, in a speech at Harvard, urged a study of European needs and the intention of the United States to provide the West with sufficient economic and military help to enable it to rebuild and remain free. A month after that new legislation was passed unifying the armed services, and James V. Forrestal was made the first Secretary of the Department of Defense.

Many wartime agencies, such as the OSRD headed by Dr. Bush, were simply blended into the new arrangements. Funds circulated from Washington through various university and industrial research groups, the Department of Defense and industry, to create an ongoing system to strengthen the nation's military position. Much of this, unfortunately, was conducted behind a mini-version of the Iron Curtain in the form of new and unprecedented security regulations.

A Presidential Order was signed that banned all Communists from holding office in the executive branch; [52] plants working on government contracts had to meet similar guidelines, and a national movement against Communists was encouraged on all levels. In a move to reduce politically motivated strikes Congress passed the Taft-Hartley Act.

At the same time the House of Representatives created what was called the Un-American Activities Committee, which undertook to investigate Communist machinations and centers of influence.

Unfortunately the investigators, like most Americans, had difficulty in defining communism. Very few could define anticommunism in positive terms. At one time the deadly animosity of communism to religious thought had provided a very clear distinction, but during the thirties the influence of religious spokesmen and groups had almost entirely vanished from the literature, lecture halls, and academies of America, especially in high culture. That left a vacuum whose dimensions were not, at first, generally realized.

At the moment anticommunism seemed sufficient in itself. The new attitude was adopted by many of the thirty-eight magazines whose circulations had soared, for the first time, to over one million; and by a beginning spate of anti-Communist films of indifferent quality. Meanwhile the resurgence of consumer products—including new automobiles, appliances of every sort, the newly popular "ranch home" and split levels and the like—seemed to improve the national mood.

Many people assumed these new goods and products had simply appeared in response to widespread demand, but demand for the better articles of the world always exists; it is purchasing power that makes markets. There seems little doubt that the classical postwar depression would have hit the United States hard after World War II had it not been for the immense lend-lease, UNRRA, and Marshall plans devised by Washington. It was true the Administration did not create these plans in order to employ people, or—for that matter—to enlarge its own ranks and place Uncle Sam in the position of being the nation's largest employer, purchaser, and economic hub. But that is, in effect, what happened. The nation was placed on a new sort of war economy in which its wheels turned out consumer goods as well as new military weapons; taxes soared but employment increased.

Few would call Adams an organization man, for he never had been a part of a corporate management before entering Raytheon as executive vice president. But he had studied at the Harvard School of Business and his knowledge of business was organized, coherent, and systematic.

His background included a naval career that had been compressed into a brief span. In only five years he had served on the lower officer levels and risen to stand near men with overall command responsibility. His war had not been spent ashore. That was important: real war experience should never be discounted. Men familiar with actual dangers are, afterward, hard to scare.

Once established as Raytheon's executive vice president, therefore, Adams moved incisively. With Dave Schultz at his elbow explaining the background and location of every crevice of the firm's financial lockers, he ordered massive inventory write-offs. Belmont, living on advances, wrote off $400,000. Raytheon wrote off $600,000. With this load jettisoned, Adams reported to the board that SubSig had lost $200,000 and Russell $30,000. That would leave the firm able to publish an Annual Report, as of May 31, 1947, showing profits of almost $980,000 on sales of a little over $66 million. That was close, far better than it might have been.[53]

For the immediate future he thought that a draw of $1 million

*194*

from the government pool account, plus a number of new products, the Radarange and diathermy machines, as well as the long-anticipated Belmont television sets, would carry the firm through to the end of the year.[54] Between then and the autumnal season in which he submitted this report, it seemed likely other developments would arise.

One such development was the death, in August 1947, of H. J. W. Fay, the president of Submarine Signal. The event was not unexpected: Mr. Fay's health had been precarious for some time. But it brought the subject of SubSig to the fore, and carried Charlie Adams into a head-on collision with Laurence Marshall.

Adams had chafed under an arrangement that kept SubSig as an independent operation even after its merger into Raytheon. In Boston, discussing the situation with Wallace A. Gifford, a surviving long-time executive of SubSig, he pushed the point. "Why have two machine shops, two controllers, and two everything else?" he asked. "The firms must be combined. Does that make sense?"

The older man nodded. "I hate to see this happen," he said. "I'm very fond of Submarine Signal, and proud of its background. But logically I cannot disagree with you. In fact," he added, "I'll do all I can to help."[55]

Adams was pleased. He knew that SubSig contained some talented men who resented the merger and would even more fiercely resent being integrated into the Raytheon organization. But if he placed Gifford in charge of the effort, they would have him as a court of final appeal, a reassuring presence. Mr. Gifford's cooperation was crucial.

Having once obtained that important support, Adams talked to Percy Spencer and G. E. M. Bertram about the need to integrate the SubSig organization without losing the great talent pool it represented. "Integration," he stressed, "is the way to economy." It was also, clearly, the way toward future profits.

Marshall disagreed. Submarine Signal had developed a close-knit, solid group that had navy financing and approval behind it. Marshall did not believe in "tampering with a going concern." Unfortunately for that argument, the balance sheet showed SubSig was sinking.

The difference between the two ranged beyond the specific, however, into the philosophic. Adams did not think in terms of projects

*195*

but of organizations. Marshall, on the other hand, thought more like an artist than an organizer. In business terms he preferred the revolutionary, and his managerial style was intensely personal.

While the managers were locked in this muted struggle, the corporate vessel continued to plow the business sea. New faces continued to enter the firm. Dr. Edward Bowles, whose presence was familiar and manners congenial, had returned to MIT as a professor. He remained a special scientific advisor to the air force. Marshall, who knew him well, enlisted Dr. Bowles as a part-time consultant at Raytheon. Bowles moved into a small office and was soon involved with Marshall on matters relating to the microwave relay system.

Ernest Leathem, a former naval officer and a lawyer in civilian life, entered as an assistant vice president. Justin Margolskee, an army veteran and a graduate of MIT, a mechanical engineer and expert in hydraulics, was hired and joined Lab 16.

That effort had made great strides. Its new seeker system would work; they were sure of that. Wisenbaker was so sure he announced he was leaving; he had no more work to do. The others were astounded and wanted to know where he was going. "Miami," he answered. "New England is just too cold." [56]

That created great consternation; nobody believed they could afford to lose Wisenbaker. They persuaded him to stay by sending him to the West Coast—to Point Mugu, just outside Oxnard, California, where the missiles were being tested. There he could work under Jake Leiper, recently hired to head the actual testing of the Lark.

Leiper was a man after Wisenbaker's heart: practical, a hard taskmaster, and a man whose information was always reliable, clear, and briskly forwarded. Leiper, like Percy Spencer and to some extent T. C. Wisenbaker himself, was a largely self-taught engineer. He had joined the navy as an electrician, risen to become a chief petty officer, then made the difficult jump into officer ranks and retired as a commander. He had served as a contract officer for the navy and knew the missile situation very well. After he retired, he sought employment with Raytheon because he believed that Lab 16 was on the right track; he was interested in the effort and wanted to join it. He proved very valuable.

Lab 16 detoured Wisenbaker from Florida just in time. Ed Dashefsky, an aeronautical engineer who had been lent to Raytheon to work on Lark developments, recalls some of the difficulties. "Everyone said the safest place to be when a missile was tested was in the drone," he recalls. Missiles were apt to go anywhere except toward the target: had been known to swoop toward cities, turn back toward the test range itself, go flying in circles. Some had had to be shot down as a menace to the landscape.

Hamilton Hauck, who was then a commander at Point Mugu, agrees, but his description is more succinct. "It was terrible," he says. The fact was that neither Fairchild nor Convair had produced an airframe that would fly. The men at Lab 16 were deeply dismayed. What good was their missile guidance system without an airframe?

By early 1948, with many sections of the firm still disheveled, an increasing number of issues arose between Adams and Marshall. Both men were careful to confine their disagreements inside the executive suite, but such collisions have a way of traveling through walls. Rumors of troubles at the top seeped through the organization.

Clark Rodiman, whose field engineers had been transferred into SubSig, believed Raytheon Fathometer® depth sounders were too expensive to be competitive, wanted to make some design changes and lower their prices. He had, in his years with the firm, been accustomed to taking his troubles to Marshall. On this occasion he explained the situation but Marshall did not seem deeply interested. He looked at Rodiman quietly and then said, "I will not swing that ax. You'll have to take care of that yourself." Rodiman realized then that Marshall had either lost or was relinquishing authority and was so disturbed at this change on the quarterdeck that he resigned and left the company.[57]

Other men also found themselves removed from Marshall's guiding hand. Norman Krim, for instance, was told to report to Dave Schultz. He was anxious about that at first but soon grew pleased with the new arrangement: Schultz proved an understanding, intelligent supervisor.[58] The same proved true for Henry Argento, whose admiration for Marshall was profound, but who fretted because he thought he was not being used to his full potential in Chicago.[59]

Nevertheless the firm was busy and many men had high hopes. Dave Schultz, usually cautious, was sure television would introduce a sweeping series of changes into the world. Raytheon, with its expertise, with its facilities to produce tubes in a variety and volume equal to those of any competitor, had entered that industry early and had glowing prospects. He was sure that Raytheon would not only turn the corner, but go on to greater successes than ever.

Unfortunately matters were not so optimistically regarded higher up. On February 8, 1948, a very terse letter appeared before the board of directors. It said:

> I hereby tender my resignation as President of Raytheon Manufacturing Company, effective immediately.
>
> LAURENCE K. MARSHALL [60]

Marshall's eruption was predictable, but untimely. The company condition was still precarious; and Adams and Schultz—now an open team—had just submitted a six months' report. Sales had been a little over $25 million and the firm had a loss of $67,000.[61] Assets had diminished, but government contracts had increased and debts had been reduced. All divisions showed some losses, but the largest had been reported from Belmont in Chicago. Belmont's, however, was being reduced in terms of overhead.

Nevertheless Adams had not yet found all the trouble spots, was far from solving the problems that remained. If Laurence Marshall chose to leave at this critical juncture, when the firm's condition was still uncertain, it could create havoc. He was a great force in terms of both personality and talent—an inspiration to many and the symbol of Raytheon to the public. Yet, as Billy Gammell said, "Genius is hard to live with." [62]

Charlie Adams recalls the situation as "uncomfortable all around." He had learned to know Marshall as a working partner and his comments were dry.

"An orderly setting was unimportant to him," Adams said. "Systems were monotonous; so were schedules. Overruns were uninteresting." Adams came to realize that Marshall "didn't give a damn about money." Then he paused and added, "But he was very creative."

The two had clashed repeatedly. "Time and again the board was dragged into three- and four-hour-long sessions," Adams recalls, "and I always won." [63]

Obviously that state of affairs could not continue indefinitely and it is a credit to Adams' foresight that when Marshall finally blew up, a plan appeared as if by magic to resolve the impasse. It was such a neat, orderly, and reasonable plan—managed so well to retain Marshall's talents where they had always glittered and at the same to move Adams' organization plans forward—that there was no need to name the author. The directors presented the plan to Marshall while Adams, slender, elegant, balding, and taciturn, waited on the sidelines. It called for Marshall to become chairman of the board. That would not only entitle him to head all directors' meetings, but, he was assured, meant he would have to be consulted on all matters of importance regarding the corporation. It empowered him to make top-level deals for the company. Adams would become president, but the powers of the president would be modified.[64] In effect, Adams would be the operating officer, would run the shop, while Marshall pointed new directions from the mountaintop.

It was a plan that fit the situation so precisely that Marshall accepted. He had, in fact, large plans for a Big Blow that would make his value clear to all the world, which seemed to fit well into the new arrangement. Adams was also pleased, which was natural.

Around Raytheon, the nation and even the world showed signs of strain and dispute. Old patterns were breaking; new structures being created. Political differences erupted between President Truman and the Eightieth Congress, which he termed the "worst in history." [65] The air filled with recriminations. Led by Senator Joseph McCarthy of Wisconsin, a modern white-collar witch hunt began, designed to uncover Communists in the government and elsewhere. Over two million federal employees were investigated; 526 resigned and 98 were dismissed as a result.[66]

Newspapers made much of the accusations of Whittaker Chambers, a former editor at *Time* magazine, against Alger Hiss, a onetime State Department official. Many private anti-Communist groups were formed. Since the Administration was actually the first to lead the nation into an international foreign policy based on anticommunism, it was mischievous for the Republican Party to claim priority in this sector, and to adopt the official stance that the Democrats were "soft on Communism."

The fact was that a split level had developed not only in residential architecture but in the nation's political thought. Both Congress and the President had cooperated to appropriate $5.3 billion for the Marshall Plan. There was no great argument over the need to send military aid to Greece, Turkey, China, and other nations threatened by subversion or invasion.

In the spring of 1948 the Soviets staged a coup d'etat in Czechoslovakia. A similar activity on the part of Hitler had led to World War II, but this time the West was too diminished. Britain, France, and the Benelux countries huddled together, signed a mutual agreement to pool their military resources to repel possible "armed attack." [67]

At home Washington, which had sponsored only a handful of such projects ten years earlier, authorized $625 million for research and development.[68] Raytheon was among the firms tapped for such efforts; Lab 16 was a prime example. The new security regulations kept these efforts shrouded from the public. At Raytheon, for instance, only those directly involved knew about such activities.

On a national scale this had the effect of placing many important and far-reaching activities of the nation outside the discussion and beyond the knowledge of its citizens. By a natural progression what could not be described was not explained. What was not explained led in turn to silence regarding the background and overarching reasons for such efforts. It was as though Washington expected the people to follow its reactions to foreign developments on faith alone, as though explanations were no longer to be expected by the people from their government as a matter of right.

This lack of intellectual rationale was behind much domestic confusion. The Democrats had ruled in the White House without interruption since 1933 and in Congress since 1930. In that long period many Americans, especially younger citizens, had grown accustomed to what amounted to one-party rule, but that party grew too large to be contained. In 1948 it split into three parts. The once solid South formed the States Rights party and nominated Strom Thurmond; the big city groups formed the Progressive Party and chose, curiously, midwesterner Henry Wallace. The centrist Democrats unhappily accepted President Truman. Republicans, confident at last, renominated Thomas E. Dewey, Roosevelt's last opponent. The newspapers predicted a Republican landslide.[69]

Unfortunately none of the groups represented a majority of the electorate; all were factions. Few chose to discuss communism rationally or foreign affairs in a manner to clarify international events. The overall impression was of a nation and a world in a state of flux. On

200

the world stage, a blanket anticolonialism irrespective of distinctions seemed sufficient in itself. The Labour Party of Britain and the world socialist movement, the commissars and Washington could all, at least, agree on that. But some Americans believed the UN a better vehicle to assist this development than Washington, and began to transfer the sort of hopes they once held for their own government toward the amorphous world organization.

Washington was convinced the anticolonial movement was a positive force; a Third World view began to arise. News that Burma had declared its independence was greeted with pleasure, the newly gained self-rule of Ceylon with hope. An enthusiastic U.S. response greeted the new state of Israel.[70]

The Soviet Union was also prominent in the anticolonial movement, but its participation had its own flavor. Special schools inside the USSR trained leaders for nationalistic movements, steeped them in the Communist ideology, taught guerrilla warfare and political tactics. Soviet funds poured into underground insurrectionary movements. At the same time the commissars began to pressure the Allies to get out of Berlin.

Outside the electronic and telephone industries and some sectors of government, few Americans were aware of ITT in 1948. It was, however, an interesting and even romantic firm, whose operations resembled a British or European firm more than the typical American corporation.

Its founder, Colonel Sosthenes Behn, had served in the U.S. Signal Corps during World War I and later created an international telephone business. His first large contract was in Spain during the monarchy of Alfonso XIII. In 1925, backed by Morgan, he purchased International Western Electric. Behn, an international type who spoke several languages, was a good judge of wine and the better pleasures of life and fit the world scene during the twenties very well. It was a period when many small monarchies remained, when pre-World War I manners were still recalled and even practiced in some parts, and international business remained relatively unfettered.

In the thirties the ITT situation was complex. Behn had to use all his acumen to keep pieces of his enterprise from being expropriated by the Falange in Spain and the Nazis in Germany, and by the various dictators who appeared and disappeared in the several South American countries where ITT holdings were scattered.

With so many foreign employees in different parts of the world, ITT came under close State Department observation. Nevertheless, the firm was headquartered in the United States, Behn was an American with an excellent record, and in World War II ITT's contribution was helpful to the Allied effort. It was ITT engineers, including many refugees, who created the Huff Duff system by which Nazi U-boats were tracked down during the war. For this and other accomplishments the firm received several E awards. The Colonel himself was awarded the Medal of Merit by the government.

Laurence Marshall, however, kept ITT at arm's length during World War II. "It had too many foreign entanglements," he said. "My feeling was that no secret could be kept secure. The navy knew my sentiments—and appreciated them." [71]

After the war Marshall knew that ITT had healthy reserves. "They had $50 million," he says. That was enough to solve all Raytheon's problems. "My idea was to merge Raytheon with ITT on a share-for-share basis. Together we could build microwave systems— broad bands that could pipe television and completely change the communications system in the nation." [72]

He called on the Colonel, and the two were highly pleased with one another. They were, after all, men from the same time, products of a period when the world belonged to individuals and no enterprise was considered beyond the grasp of a single man. Only a slight shift in the scales of fortune in the past kept Marshall himself from occupying Behn's sort of position. After all, he had made a special trip to Europe during the twenties in the hope of making a cross-marketing deal with the Dutch electrical giant, Philips, when Raytheon was barely a regional company.

The two men sat down together in Behn's ornate New York office, furnished and decorated in the French style with genuine antiques from the old monarchy, and began to talk. Great misty visions of a new empire rose around them.

At Raytheon Charlie Adams proceeded to establish a line-and-staff organizational structure. Before he undertook this task, Raytheon had operated as an extension of Marshall's ideas. During the war the firm had grown large and diverse but its lines were very loose. Marshall himself crossed everybody's line and plunged into whatever intrigued him most. Adams determined that definitions were needed, that goals should be set, that divisions and a management staff should be created that could operate, in one of his favorite words, in an "orderly" manner.

He began, appropriately enough, by issuing an executive memorandum outlining, in eight and one-half pages, *Objectives, Policies and Administration.*[73] It was, and read, something like a working constitution. His forebears could almost be seen nodding their heads in approval. No progress can be made without form. Adams was as sure of that as the Founding Fathers had been.


Hamilton Hauck, the naval commander at Point Mugu, was, inevitably, known as Ham Hock. That lifelong problem did not concern him; he was more worried that the missiles being tested at the base were all failures. He had his own ideas about the reasons, but to have them either proved or disproved assigned an in-depth study of the situation to Dr. Herbert Wagner.[74] Dr. Wagner, who pioneered the ribbed-wing concept and had produced Germany's first air-to-ground guided missile, was one of the German scientists scooped up by the U.S. military after the war. "He worked well on what he didn't know," said Wisenbaker drily. "He was a good sounding board." [75]

As far as Wisenbaker and Leiper were concerned, Dr. Wagner was a consultant the navy had produced to help them. They didn't mind: they needed all the help they could get. But behind the scene Hauck wrote Washington that both he and Dr. Wagner had discovered that the tiny Raytheon subcontracting group, charged only with producing the guidance system for a missile, had ideas superior to those held by prime contractors Convair and Fairchild regarding complete missile systems. He suggested that Raytheon be given ten Convair missile airframes to try out. That meant, of course, that Raytheon would make whatever modifications it chose, a reversal of the previous role. While Washington pondered this suggestion, Hauck encouraged Wagner to encourage Raytheon.

Leiper, Wisenbaker, Sanders, et al. did not need much encouragement: they were already toiling with possible airframes and the idea of making their own missile. Conversations flowed interchangeably and in the end Hauck's suggestion and their own efforts combined in what

*203*

appeared to be natural evolution. Funds appeared, and arrangements and understandings were reached. Raytheon would be able to order prototypes in at least ten varieties for testing. Design was up to them. Jubilantly Lab 16 plunged ahead, heartened enough to hire some new bright young men.

One was only twenty-four years old but had already earned his B.S and M.S. from Virginia Polytechnic Institute, had taught electrical engineering there and at New York University. Originally from the Boston area, he came home to visit his mother before proceeding to a teaching post at the University of Wisconsin. He entered the Raytheon orbit by pausing to visit a friend in the Lab.[76] Their talk turned, as it does so often with engineers, to the state of the art. The visitor was fascinated at his friend's description of the blend of theory and experiment underway. He was trotted past several senior men, who agreed he appeared intelligent, and was immediately hired. Later at least three men were to insist they were responsible, but in the final analysis Tom Phillips seems to have chosen Raytheon himself.

He entered Lab 16 at a most propitious moment. In Berlin the Soviets had abruptly closed to the Allies the highways and railways leading to Berlin.[77] President Truman conferred with the military and ordered that the city be provided with supplies and people conveyed in and out by air. The Berlin airlift, as it was called, made the awesome meaning of U.S. air power clear to the most myopic—and the Kremlin hesitated.

This dramatic display of U.S. power did more, however, than only make Stalin hold his hand. It spurred intense behind-the-scenes efforts by all the military powers of the world to find counterweapons against air power. Missiles fell within that area. Lab 16, therefore, was competing against the world's best.

At the same time Cap Smith and Fritz Gross became engaged in an effort with the navy to design and improve digital computers and test instrumentation for a missile test range. At Raytheon this facility was called Lab 30. Smith's nickname—Cap—had no military significance, but he himself was both significant and prominent in Raytheon. Originally from Bismarck, North Dakota, Smith had started as a telegraph operator, worked his way through college, was a recognized communications expert when he was lured from RCA into Raytheon to head the engineering end of Laurence Marshall's Great Microwave Project. Most of the men hired for that effort departed as it collapsed under various strains and pressures, but Smith had remained to become one of the leaders of the equipment division.

Adams placed Dave Schultz at his right hand as financial advisor, Dr. Edward Bowles at his left as technical advisor, Ernest Leathem as administrative assistant, Paul Hannah as general counsel and Laurence Apsey as patent counsel, Dr. Carlo Calosi as research advisor, and W. Hamilton Walters as sales advisor. In time some names would change, but the staff concept was clear.

His line consisted of seven divisions formed from the mixed groups of the past. Equipment, the largest, was broken into engineering and production under assistant vice presidents Cap Smith and G. E. M. Bertram. Ray Ellis headed an international sales division; Percy Spencer —elevated to assistant vice president—would preside over power tubes; Dr. Carlo Calosi over research; and Norman Krim, also promoted to assistant vice president, would head receiving tubes. Fritz Gross headed government engineering.

Adams' memorandum explained that committees and study groups would be formed to establish the integration of SubSig, Russell Electric, and Belmont, to set up lines of authority and appeal, and to codify, as much as possible, administrative policies. But the memorandum itself did much to meet that need.[78]

It is doubtful if many of the free-wheeling creative engineers of Raytheon, who closely resemble other artists in both their lack of worldliness and their individual eccentricities, ever fully appreciated the Adams accomplishment. New managements are seldom clear or open about their goals and the means they will use to reach them. Later in 1948, when the Annual Report figures were finally put together and published, they gave unmistakable evidence of how close Raytheon was to the precipice at the time of Adams' effort.

Sales of $53 million had resulted in profits of only $380,000 as of May 31.[79] Had the men known that when Adams' reorganization was announced, they might have been more appreciative. But a summer event of far-reaching import, similar in a scientific way to the political significance of the Berlin airlift which had its effect on Lab 16, attracted far more of their attention. In a way, this was to be often repeated in Adams' career: other events would overshadow his efforts in the eyes of observers, though without such efforts the firm would have tumbled over the cliff.

The overshadowing event in the summer of 1948 was the discovery by Shockley, Bardeen, and Brattain of how to use semiconductors to amplify electric signals.[80] Semiconductors was a subject that had intrigued researchers for generations. Marshall had flirted with the subject years before; it had been the basis of his interest in Dr. André.

Krim had heard, through personal contacts, of Shockley's breakthrough; Marshall led a Raytheon delegation down to Murray Hill, New Jersey, and reviewed the event at Bell Labs. On their return, Krim prepared a report predicting that tubes would become obsolete in the electronic industry. That was somewhat sweeping, but it was a moment of high excitement. He suggested a crash program to produce germanium semiconductors for use in the hearing-aid business. That sounded practical; Raytheon had an established and profitable position in that market.[81] Adams gave the go-ahead and Marshall nodded his agreement. More might have been done, but many other pressing problems diverted the attention of the management.

The federal tax agent, a figure that looms as almost sinister, had filed a final bill for $4.2 million against Raytheon for its wartime effort.[82] Some insight is provided into tax policies when it is learned that the agent had described this as a "compromise figure." If it was not accepted without argument, the agent threatened, according to Schultz, to file legal proceedings for a larger amount.[83] Fortunately the firm could pay.

Belmont, which had been hoping to reap a profitable harvest from the introduction of its television sets at year end, was strikebound. Radarange ovens, now introduced in restaurants, were losing money.

Nevertheless Adams pushed through an improved pension plan, and Schultz was able to report that the Boston bankers had restored Raytheon to their good graces. Both Adams and Schultz could take a bow for that. The entente with Marshall was working well enough for Marshall and Adams to agree on extending an invitation to Carl Gilbert to join the Raytheon board of directors.[84]

Gilbert, who had known Raytheon since the thirties when, as a young attorney with Ropes, Grey, et al., he had assisted with its patent problems, was pleased to accept. He had left the private law firm in 1948 and joined Gillette as a vice president and treasurer.

In October Raytheon appeared on the market with its new germanium semiconductors. That was really impressive. The company was the first of those who received Bell Labs' generous information to reach the marketplace with a product. In order to do it Krim had purchased diodes from Sylvania for their germanium content, but that didn't matter.[85] At a time when the new development had depressed the stock price of virtually every firm in electronics, Raytheon had scored a coup. That gave everyone a psychological boost and helped the reputation of the firm.

In other, more personal terms, there were other improvements. Dr. Carlo Calosi, who had been plucked from the shores of war-torn Italy by the OSS, spirited to Washington and from there to SubSig, was a personage in the new Adams regime. A scholar who had earned degrees at the University of Genoa and the University of Pisa, he had been a full professor in Genoa at the age of twenty-seven. His English, though accented, was fluent; his wife was charming; they were both social stars in Cambridge.

Charlie Adams, always keen for the international scene, liked Calosi. Dr. Bowles counted him an esteemed colleague. Calosi had developed effective countermeasures against his own magnetic torpedoes while at SubSig.

Hannah, himself a valued member of the new team, looked about him with pleasure. "It was," he said later, "a high level, candid and intelligent group. They had differences, but these were always openly thrashed out." Hannah was fascinated by the personalities as well as their interplay. He traveled to New York with Marshall on a number of occasions, sat in during the discussions with Colonel Behn. "Ex cathedra," Hannah said. Watching them, he thought Marshall could outwit the Colonel.[86]

Carl Gilbert was not so sure of that. He had studied Marshall for years. "He would have a conversation with a vice president at Westinghouse or some other company, arouse attention regarding some project he had in mind. They'd say, 'Well, that's very interesting. If you go any farther with that, we'd like to hear about it.' That would so enthuse Marshall he'd return and say, '*I have a deal.*'"

Nevertheless, Gilbert found himself included in the visits to ITT. They were interesting, but his opinion was caustic. "The Colonel ran a very fancy establishment," Gilbert recalls. "The dining room was elaborate, and he had a butler; would serve five or six courses at lunch—with wine, of course, in the European style.

"It was a style that made a great impression during the twenties," Gilbert said, "when empires existed. It faded during the thirties, was forgotten during the war, and by 1948 seemed strange."

Gilbert knew that ITT had troubles of its own, both internal and external. It was common knowledge that ITT wanted to expand its U.S. business. Listening to the Colonel spinning great dreams about the merger with Raytheon, Gilbert wondered, as did everyone else, who would come out on top. On one such occasion Gilbert leaned over and whispered to General Harrison, who was then president of ITT, "Who will run it all?" Harrison, looking sideways at him, whispered back, "Damned if I know. I'm almost nuts trying to run things as they are now." [87]

Other large Marshall projects, originally highly promising, were running into similar problems. An exhaustive series of discussions had been underway with different groups regarding the financing and operation of a Boston television station: Channel Two. These were not proceeding well, and the FCC was showing signs of impatience; the franchise would not wait forever.[88]

The fact was that Marshall's programs for the firm had been in trouble when Adams came aboard, and were not particularly forwarded when their author lost control of operations. That was predictable, but not—as in so many other circumstances of the sort—predicted.

With an active, youthful president in charge, a new group of men heading the firm's operations, there had been a quite natural swing toward the new and away from the old. Bowles put it quite succinctly. "I chose," he said, "the future." [89]

Toward the close of 1948, therefore, Marshall took another step, this time a long one, toward the exit. The board received another letter; this time—unlike the year before—Marshall suggested a new plan for himself.

Boiled down, it amounted to a proposal that he cease being an employee of the firm and that his duties be reduced to chairing the board meetings. In every other respect he would prefer, he said, to act as a consultant.[90]

This time the directors did not mount as many demurrals as before. A number of meetings were held whose proceedings were not recorded. As usual, the crisis arrived in December.

Some day someone will undertake an analysis of why so many managements undergo personality crises in December, the Christmas month. It seems inappropriate, in the midst of preparations for feasts and holidays, gifts and sentiment, but it is more common in U.S. business than is generally realized. In any event Marshall threw his second bomb during December 1948 and it was after January 1949 when the directors finally placed into the minutes their reaction and the results.

They had not wasted their time. The powers of the president had been increased to make Charlie Adams the chief executive of Raytheon. It was agreed to retain Marshall as chairman of the board, and to sever his connection with Raytheon as an employee. It established the long-time leader as a consultant at a reduced salary on the basis that half his time would be available to the firm, and that he would be suitably compensated for more of his time if it was needed. This arrangement was to last until 1954—five years. Then he would receive three-quarters pay for the balance of his life. Demands on his time from 1954 would be reduced to one-quarter, and after 1959, not set at all.[91]

It was, clearly, an arrangement in which Marshall's role with the firm was, for the first time, formally programmed to disappear. But it was not ungenerous. Marshall's response was that he would think about it while he was on a trip abroad; he would let them know what he thought when he returned. The directors, clearly annoyed, then formally rescinded his power to make any deal for the company while he was out of the country.[92] They wanted no further surprises.

There are fashions among historians as well as dressmakers, and as a result certain years become better known than others. In these rankings, which seldom seem to change, 1949 is not placed high. It is treated as a transitional year, a year in which the world did not make many deep changes. This is an underestimation. It was a very significant year; many far-reaching moves were made.

In a personal sense it was an important year for Harry S Truman, whose lack of pretensions for high office had caused many more conceited people to doubt his qualifications. He launched his term as President, after his surprising defeat of Mr. Dewey, by announcing on Inaugural Day, January 20, 1949, that the United States would spend $5.4 billion in a Point Four program of assistance to the "underdeveloped" and friendly nations of the world.[93]

Though the Point Four program appeared to some as simply an extension of the traditional liberal conviction that virtually all the ills of mankind could be traced to poverty, it was more complex than that. It was a bid for the support of the Third World against communism, and opened an avenue of improvement as well to the nations of the West who were being pressed to free their former colonies.

Ending the colonial system was not easy. It had been a part of civilization since the dawn of history, and in many instances had lasted for centuries. The United States, however, could point to its own progress as proof that colonialism was not essential to prosperity or power. In 1949 it offered the secrets of both to the nations that would follow its lead.

By virtue of its victory over the Soviet in the Berlin airlift, its atomic superiority, its great wealth and undoubted technological lead, the United States had a persuasive argument. In addition several steps were taken. The first consisted of an economic union among France, Italy, and the Benelux countries. The second—a triumph for Truman— consisted of the creation of NATO, the North Atlantic Treaty Organization. Its members were the United States, Britain, France, Italy, Portugal, Denmark, Norway, Iceland, and Canada.[94]

The United States pledged an initial $1.2 billion in funds for this effort, another $5.4 billion for the Point Four program.[95] Washington would be the financial supporter as well as the leader against the Communist world.

That mysterious world, however, was not still. Moscow announced the creation of a mutual assistance program between itself and the nations of Eastern Europe; Communist insurrectionaries fought in Burma against the new government; a Communist-backed "People's Republic" appeared in North Korea; and in China the Communist forces of Mao Tse-tung gained the ascendancy over Chiang Kai-shek.[96] Some State Department officials saw no danger in that development, but they were in the minority.

It was a time, in other words, when new combinations were forming and the outlines of the new postwar world were at last growing clear.


Inside Raytheon the future was also growing clearer. Laurence Marshall's departure for a trip abroad gave no public hint of the new arrangement he had reached with the directors, but his absence was eloquent. Charlie Adams was in the saddle and was the boss.

One of his moves was to give Percy Spencer a contract that increased his salary and outlined further payments through the age of sixty and past sixty-five.[97] Percy had been with the firm twenty-five years in 1949, had contributed immensely toward its much-heralded wartime success, and still headed the heart of its operations: microwave tubes. Yet he had never achieved the general recognition to which he was entitled and had never before had real security. Adams' move was more than shrewd: it was wise. Spencer's reaction was all one could expect; he plunged into new efforts with enthusiasm. Meanwhile Adams went on to create a salary review board to repair other omissions and establish objective yardsticks.

In a corporate sense, the seas had grown calmer. Raytheon's government business still accounted for most of the firm's sales, but instead of dropping they had begun to increase. The Annual Report prepared later in the year showed that by the end of May 1949 sales had increased slightly, from $53 to $56 million; profits had risen from $380,000 the year before to almost $1 million.[98]

In other words, the turn had been negotiated; the company was not yet headed up, but it was stabilizing. Its reputation for high-quality engineering remained very high in Washington. Its radar and sonar knowledge was still needed. Early in 1949 the firm was visited by General Omar Bradley, who would soon become chairman of the joint chiefs of staff. The Annual Report shows an interesting picture of Percy Spencer standing alone talking on one side of a table piled with intricate Raytheon products, while on the other side the General, Laurence Marshall, Dr. Edward Bowles, and a Colonel Mathews are listening intently. Most intent of all, in their center, is Charlie Adams, his head lowered. He is so serious among the older men he appears their contemporary.[99]

Raytheon had, therefore, established a sort of floor under its efforts consisting of government work. Such contracts, however, were held to low profits. It was in the potentially high-profit area of commercial business that Raytheon was having its greater problems.

Belmont, Raytheon's television entry, had only one real customer: Montgomery Ward. The balance of the television marketplace was dominated by giant firms with household names. In order to compete with these giants Raytheon would have to create a sales organization of its own: a huge and complex undertaking at best, but awesome against entrenched, market-wise firms.

Yet inside Raytheon far more attention was being paid to the technical matters of television. Larger sets were being marketed by the big firms; Raytheon's engineers had to abandon their own special approach and adopt methods the firm had rejected to continue in the race. This was a far less difficult, far less important matter than the need to organize a television sales force, but received far more attention. As a result Belmont was draining profits in an industry where the competition was well financed and tough.

Meanwhile Lab 16 pursued tests and experiments with its ten prototype missiles. At Point Mugu, Wisenbaker and Leiper worked on the pressing problem of incorporating the Raytheon active seeker in the missile airframe. Their efforts were not conducted in any serenity; Wisenbaker recalls monumental arguments with the aeronautical engineers of Convair, who resisted following the designs of outsiders—but nevertheless the program moved forward.

By autumn 1949, the nation began to flock after television sets and the greatly troubled sales of Belmont began to improve. A communications revolution, a new and powerful force, began. But unlike radio, which had entered into the consciousness of mankind to lift and extend its imagination, television in the United States brought the street into the homes of America. It was marked by feverish huckstering.

In such a climate Arthur Miller's play *Death of a Salesman*, which questioned the values of such activities, hit a responsive chord. The nation was also disgusted by the turbulence that accompanied the trial of the leaders of the U.S. Communist Party, and disturbed by the proof that Alger Hiss, a former high State Department official, had committed perjury. In September, to add to the uncertainty of the time, scientists of the U.S. Air Force detected and analyzed a radioactive cloud and the Administration announced the USSR had secretly detonated its own atomic bomb.[100]

In China the forces of Chiang Kai-shek, defeated, began a withdrawal from the mainland to the island of Taiwan. President Truman signed the NATO pact and in West Germany Konrad Adenauer emerged as a prowestern leader.

In 1943,
President Laurence
Marshall (LEFT)
and four other
Raytheon
employees accept the
army-navy "E."

Antennas for SG
radars. In 1946,
Fortune magazine
described them as
"antennas of three
of the 20 radar
models that made
Raytheon."

BELOW: *Gen. Omar N. Bradley visited Raytheon in 1949 as chairman of the Joint Chiefs of Staff, and was briefed on magnetrons. Here (FROM LEFT) are Chairman Laurence K. Marshall; General Bradley; President Charles F. Adams; Dr. Edward L. Bowles, Raytheon's chief consultant; Col. Willis Matthews; and Percy L. Spencer, manager of the Power Tube Division.*

*Operator checks scopes of the Navy SG-1 radar. (Photograph: 1947)*

*The 1949 line of Raytheon Belmont television receivers included this table model.*

*Vice President Henry F. Argento, manag of Television & Radio Division. (Photograph: 1954)*

*Lark* missile, with *Raytheon guidance system*, is shown ready *for launch and in flight. In 1950, the Lark scored history's first interception and destruction of aircraft.*

H. J. W. Fay headed the Submarine
Signal Company, which merged
with Raytheon in 1946, the year
of this photograph.

At the television-tube plant in Quincy, Massachusetts, machine in foreground sealed b
of picture tubes to the electronic gun. (Photograph: 1953)

Assembled prior to shipment are these magnetron tubes for radar and other application
During World War II, magnetron production by Raytheon rose from 17 per week to 2
daily. (Photograph: 1951)

...otographed at the Waltham, Massachusetts, headquarters in the early fifties are
...OM LEFT) Ernest F. Leathem, assistant to the president; Vice President David R.
...ll; John L. Sullivan, former secretary of the navy; Dan A. Kimball, then secretary
...he navy; and President Adams.

...he RAYDAC digital automatic computer was developed by Raytheon in the early
...fties for the U.S. Navy's Bureau of Aeronautics.

*David T. Schultz, Raytheon vice president and treasurer. (Photograph: about 1951)*

*In 1952 Raytheon's early Radarange® microwave ovens were installed in buffet cars of the Pennsylvania Railroad.*

*Presenting the one-millionth transistor made by Raytheon to Massachusetts Governor Christian A. Herter (RIGHT) in July 1954 are (FROM LEFT) Vice President (for research and engineering) Ivan A. Getting; Vice President Norman B. Krim, manager of Receiving Tube Division; and President Adams.*

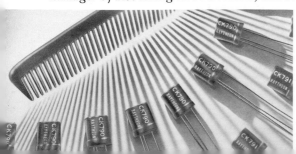

*Silicon transistors introduced by Raytheon in 1955 were designed for high-temperature operation in jet aircraft and missile equipment.*

*Visiting Raytheon with his staff in 1951 is K. T. Keller* (LEFT FRONT), *Director of the U.S. Guided Missile Program for the secretary of defense in the Truman Administration. Beside him is President Adams. Behind Mr. Adams is Vice President David D. Coffin. At far right is T. C. Wisenbaker.*

*A 1955 open house at the newly constructed Wayland, Massachusetts, laboratory occasioned the baking of a giant cake in the form of the building. Pointing is Fritz A. Gross, the laboratory manager. With him are three members of his staff* (FROM LEFT): *Dr. Ronald L. McFarlan, Leonard Bradford, and Dr. William Hall.*

*This launch of the Sparrow III air-to-air missile was photographed during 1958 tests*

*In this photo are (FROM LEFT) T.C. Wisenbaker, J. H. Leiper, Mr. Adams, and Comdr. J. Sliney of the U.S. Naval Air Missile Test Center at Point Mugu, California. Picture was taken prior to a flight to witness Sparrow missile tests.*

*Raytheon's management team in 1957 included (FROM LEFT) Senior Vice President Percy L. Spencer, President Adams, Executive Vice President Harold S. Geneen, Treasurer Allen E. Reed, and Vice President E. Douglas Graham.*

*Posing for this 1958 picture are (FROM LEFT) President Adams, Secretary of the Army Wilber Brucker, Gen. Alden Sibley, T. C. Wisenbaker, Thomas L. Phillips, and Vice President David D. Coffin. Mr. Phillips was then manager of Missile Systems Division's Bedford (Massachusetts) Laboratories.*

*The Hawk missile, shown here immediately after launch, became operative in the fifties.*

*Senior Vice President Percy L. Spencer (LEFT) and Carlo L. Calosi in 1958. Dr. Calosi served Raytheon in several capacities, including vice president for Eur*

Group attending 1958 Hawk missile tests in White Sands, New Mexico, included (FROM LEFT) President Adams; Vice President David D. Coffin, manager of Missile Systems Division; T. C. Wisenbaker, assistant manager of the division; a newsman; Thomas L. Phillips, manager of the division's Bedford Laboratory; and Edward L. Bowles, general consultant.

Vice President W. E. Stevenson headed Machlett Laboratories after its acquisition by Raytheon in 1959. Here, he holds a Machlett X-ray tube.

*Built by Raytheon in 1958, this radar antenna had a forty-foot span.*

The year and the decade moved toward its close in a climate of deepening seriousness. UN deliberations centered around troubles in Korea; the USSR delegates were absent.

The last year of the forties was not one over which historians like to dwell. Yet it was not an insignificant year; it was the year the United States lost its atomic monopoly and communism triumphed in China.

For Raytheon it had been a hard year but a significant one, because Lab 16—that tiny handful—produced, on December 1, 1949, a missile guided by a continuous-wave active seeker that, for the first time, intercepted a target drone.[101]

# Chapter 7  THE FIFTIES

WHEN *Fortune* decided to take a quick look at New England in early 1950, it seemed, at first, surprised to find the region alive and well. By the time writer Hedley Donovan reached the end of an article entitled "Watch the Yankees," however, he was warning that a new technological revolution had been conceived in the old seedbed.

He cited a dozen or more firms created on the basis of advanced research during and after the war. Then he added, "For these and larger companies like Raytheon, a Massachusetts location means direct access to the raw material of the business—technical brains." These were to be found on the north bank of the Charles: at MIT, Harvard, and a long string of industrial research laboratories.

As usual, the article carried copious quotes from a representative sprinkling of leaders and notables. All brimmed with optimism except Charlie Adams, whose picture led all the rest. In a lengthy caption he was credited with saying he never read books about his family because "there has been too much of that sort of thing in New England"; that he believed the company is "making progress in its cost cutting," but that "earnings have been too erratic to create much confidence at the banks." Why had he gone into Raytheon? "I have seen so many New England industries go down or go South with so little being done about it. There are six thousand people working for us in Waltham and Newton. That means a good deal in New England." The magazine concluded he was "painfully honest."

Painful honesty was a quality appreciated by the Raytheon directors and demanded by the moment. A technological hurricane was swirling, and Raytheon was near its center. The firm still possessed an

*214*

immense establishment that was, in large part, an inheritance from its wartime eminence. At Waltham alone this consisted of five large and twenty smaller buildings, many of which had been purchased from the navy on terms that preserved the government's priority for future national need. The power tube and equipment divisions and Lab 16 were located at Waltham. Receiving tubes were produced at Newton, in congeries of ancient buildings, some of which had been leased to other firms as business had contracted. In Chicago the company owned more property, where Belmont produced phonograph, radio, and television sets; these were also produced in a small but modern plant at Oelwein, Iowa.

In opening 1950 it was clear many of Marshall's predictions and expectations regarding electronics were being realized. Microwave relay systems, capable of jumping television programs, telephone messages, and radio services, had been created across the country—but not by Raytheon. AT&T flung the largest into existence, spending an estimated $37.5 million to create a national network. GE had built a smaller, special, 1,800-mile system for Transcontinental Gas; Westinghouse had done still another for the Pennsylvania Electric Co.

The uses of microwave had barely been scratched, but other electronic developments were expanding the industry in multiple directions. Tube production had reached four hundred million in almost a thousand varieties, and forty manufacturers crowded the scene. GE, RCA, Westinghouse, Sylvania, Philco, Zenith, and Raytheon led all the rest—the telephone companies manufactured mainly for their own systems.

The situation was both promising and frustrating. A traditional time lag between advanced research and its translation into engineering and manufacturing had contracted remarkably. Raytheon had been unusual in its relationship with MIT, Harvard, Tufts, and other advanced laboratories in the twenties and thirties. This sort of relationship had been expanded in the wartime forties. By 1950 it had become an established pattern throughout the electronic industry.

As a result inventions, improvements, new products and applications poured out in an apparently endless stream. The firms from which they emerged became entangled in large-scale, bruising collisions in the marketplace.

Raytheon purchased Russell Electric, for instance, in order to be able to manufacture its own phonograph motors, to enable Belmont to reach the marketplace more expeditiously with phonograph, radio, and television sets. But the phonograph business was upset by the invention of the long-playing record at Columbia and the RCA introduction of a different-speed long-playing record. One result was massive confusion in the record pressing, manufacturing, and marketing aspects of the phonograph industry, which pushed some small firms and distributors into bankruptcy.

The television situation was similarly tangled. The government had restricted TV licenses to 105 in sixty-three metropolitan areas; applications had backed up and great arguments raged over the system of allocation and its rationale. Columbia had, in addition, emerged with a color system [1] that RCA disputed, and the marketing arms of these giants were locked in combat. Sets had first appeared with small screens, and a race was underway to enlarge and improve these; new sets with larger, wider screens appeared before the old were sold.

Belmont, dependent on Montgomery Ward and a few other special customers as major outlets for its radio and TV sets, scrambled to create distributors but was forced to accept outlets rejected by the majors; it was therefore handicapped in the marketplace. In addition its juke boxes—a popular prewar item—were rapidly fading from the market. On every hand the Chicago-based operation confronted enormous competitors competing fiercely in a burgeoning, expanding, and tangled new industry.

Dwarfed by the mastodons, Raytheon's microwave relay system, although first to appear, dwindled to pilot proportions. The Raytheon Channel Two television license in Boston had been a coup when first obtained, but was now on the verge of being rescinded for lack of follow-through.[2] Lack of funds had kept the firm from realizing its initial advantages. Raytheon's eyes had been larger than its stomach; it had seen opportunities beyond its reach.

Laurence Marshall's answer to these and other, similar problems had been clear: merge with ITT. In January 1950 he reported his discussions with Colonel Behn to the Raytheon directors and strongly urged this course. To his immense disappointment the board was not swayed; instead it turned toward Charlie Adams and asked him to explore the matter.

This went into the minutes as "No Action," but in truth it was a very significant action. It meant that if the firm were to enter a merger with ITT, it would be Charlie Adams, and not Laurence Marshall, who would lead the way.

Adams did not dally. In two weeks he was back to the directors with the information that he and Dave Schultz had met with Colonel Behn and "exploratory talks had been held." Again, No Action.

Then in early February ITT sent word that it wanted to drop discussions for the time being.[3] The Raytheon directors received that news with notable calm and turned toward other matters.

Ruth Babb had joined the firm in 1930, had been Marshall's secretary since 1942, and had risen to become an assistant secretary of the corporation. She received a shock in February 1950 when Marshall, soon after ITT had suspended discussions, looked at her and asked, "What will you do when I leave?"

"Why, Mr. Marshall," she replied, astonished, "I didn't know you were leaving." To her, he was the firm; it seemed inconceivable without him. He told her to make an appointment for him with Mr. Adams. As she picked up the phone she realized she was the first in the company to know, but Ruth Babb knew how to keep a secret.[4]

Soon afterward Marshall told Charlie Adams, "Well, you've won. I'm leaving."

Adams tried to dissuade him, but Marshall was not to be moved. "I'll find something to do," he said, but his tone was pleasant.

"Damn it," Adams said later, "I hadn't wanted to win in that sense. I had great respect for Marshall. But I knew it had been difficult, and that our relationship had only lasted as long as it did because I wanted it to last. In the end, I could not persuade him any longer; he insisted on leaving." [5]

It was a winter of discontent in many more places than Raytheon, and some of the problems entailed were far more difficult. Communism was on the march, it seemed, everywhere, and great confusion existed regarding its meaning, purpose, and the nature of its internal dynamics. Some observers took comfort from a break that had developed between the Kremlin and Tito, believed it presaged a breakup of the Communist empire. That was an optimistic view, for the argument was based not on foreign policy, but on the internal control of Yugoslavia.

Tito wanted to be master in his own house; in every other respect he and his minions remained commissars—that is to say, men who placed the state above every individual right.

The split had one positive effect for the West, however: it closed Yugoslavian sanctuaries to Greek Communist guerrillas fighting the Greek monarchy. They retreated, but took with them a final 28,000 Greek children whom they kidnapped from their parents in various villages; the intention was to train a future force.[6]

Meanwhile France, attempting to create a union of its former colonies along the British Commonwealth pattern, ran into difficulties from similar forces. An insurrection headed by a Moscow-trained leader who called himself One Who Shines (Ho Chi Minh) started in Vietnam. It appeared likely to succeed soon; the puppet Vietnam emperor Bao Dai had organized only four battalions, four thousand men.

Elsewhere in Asia the Chinese Communists confounded their apologists by invading the peaceful and unworldly land of Tibet. That placed their forces in position to threaten India.

With NATO still a paper plan, attention turned toward the condition of the U.S. military. It was appalling. Secretary of Defense Louis Johnson, announcing he would "cut the fat," seemed bent instead on decapitation. Only one combat division was battle-ready; no defensive radar existed; eleven out of twenty-three marine fighter squadrons were cut, naval carriers had been reduced. The United States had a bomber force and was expanding nuclear weapons.

In answer to questions regarding the U.S. posture in the Pacific, Secretary of State Dean Acheson announced the U.S. defense line would run from Japan south through Okinawa to the Philippines. The Kremlin noted with interest the implication that the balance of Asia would not be defended by the United States.

At home the global situation did not attract as much attention as it deserved, for the press was feeding the public a new diet. It featured the dismal, and centered on prophets of doom and destruction. One series followed the career of Senator Joseph McCarthy of Wisconsin, leader of charges that great numbers of subversives had permeated the government. Another group was alarmed over the perils of atomic energy. Two University of Chicago scientists gained headlines when one charged radioactive dust from Pacific tests "would sterilize New York in five days," and another—Dr. Leo Szilard—predicted hydrogen bombs, recently authorized by the President, could, if tested in sufficient quantity, "ring the earth with a radioactive dust layer capable of killing the . . . entire population." [7]

A third group, whose spokesman was Dr. Norbert Weiner of MIT,[8] prophesied sweeping societal disruption, massive unemployment, and untold miseries from newly developed analogue and digital computers. Nearly all the large universities and many firms, including Raytheon, were experimenting in the design and construction of the new "thinking machines," whose intricacies alarmed the unlearned. Their usefulness in the possible control of pipelines, factories, warehouses, payrolls, and a host of other arduous mechanical tasks, was obvious. Their need for solving problems in engineering, aeronautics, and allied areas was incontrovertible, but scare articles pictured computers as creations of demonic scientists, bent upon the enslavement rather than the liberation of mankind.

This was a strange new tone in a nation once famed for its optimism, that had emerged from World War II physically undamaged, its influence extended, its living standards improved, its population increased. In 1950 the United States had 150 million people whose wages were higher, goods more plentiful, entertainments more varied than at any time in history.[9] Yet the press mounted a litany of complaints and poured scorn upon a President whose simplicity disappointed its hunger for drama. To a visitor the nation appeared much the same; its regions remained strong and distinct, its activities impressive. Most of the people went their accustomed ways. The bountiful countryside looked much as before, but a faint malaise—not yet strong enough to define—began to trickle through the land.

Laurence Marshall's departure took place, officially, in May 1950. By that time his office was empty and he was gone, but his new activity had been announced and was featured in the newspapers. He would lead an expedition, on behalf of the Peabody Museum of Harvard, to study the life of the Bushmen in the Kalahari Desert of South Africa.[10]

That was an astonishing turn, completely different from any of his previous adventures. But Marshall was well off; the commercial race held no new lures for him, and Mrs. Marshall had majored in anthropology.

It would not be accurate to say that he was not missed at Raytheon; he was. There were many men and projects in the firm he had hired and inspired. He was missed at Lab 16, and elsewhere; Charlie Adams missed him.

Adams said, "It's hard for a nontechnical man to track the scene in a technical company." He did not, being Charlie Adams, point out that very few firms were actually headed, then or now, by technical men. Most firms are headed by men with a proven ability for business whose training is in finance or law. He himself had studied business and been in investment banking for a number of years, and this particular skill was sorely needed by Raytheon in 1950, needed far more than any other.

The new Adams organization had been shaped: he was flanked by Dave Schultz as treasurer and Allen Reed—formerly of SubSig—as controller. Paul Hannah headed a refurbished legal department, Dr. Calosi headed research. Adams had Dr. Bowles and others for technical advice—and he also had Percy Spencer.

Spencer had accumulated 138 patents, and some of his discoveries were not only crucial, but made at crucial times. The magnetron and improvements in the klystron were, in 1950, integral to the power tube business. His applications of these tubes, in the Radarange oven, diathermy, radar systems, and other places kept Raytheon abreast of an immense and highly competitive market. He was not alone in these efforts by any means, but he was a key figure.

Nevertheless Spencer was not regarded with the awe, the immense respect accorded university scientists, whose activities were considered untainted by the stains of private enterprise. Universities have an interest in their budgets and the standards of living these afford their staffs, but that is a reality overlooked by common consent. Spencer had been one of the significant contributors to modern radar; of that there can be little doubt. Yet few anthologies bother to include the essential facts of mass manufacture in their histories of this great chain of circumstance.

It was a great moment for him, therefore, when the University of Massachusetts at Amherst offered him an honorary doctorate. The scroll the school prepared is worth repeating, if for no other reason than the high element of truth it contained, in contrast to so many windy effusions bestowed upon men whose main distinction is their ability to pay for flattery.

Percy LeBaron Spencer [it read], inventor and public servant, although from the age of twelve, without benefit of schooling, you raised yourself from a spool mill bench into the highest circle of scientific research and trust, you nevertheless sent a son to this campus and thus entitled us to an interest and pride in your characteristically Yankee success.

Among your scores of patents in the field of electronics, your development of the vacuum tube for use in the proximity fuse and your making "the very heart of radar," the magnetron, manufacturable in quantity at the strategic and critical moments in World War II were notably instrumental in our victory and have been recognized in various national citations, culminating in the Navy's highest civilian award.

The Commonwealth of Massachusetts is proud that such a career is still possible within its borders and the University, graduating its first substantial group of engineers, is happy to welcome you into our society of alumni.

I, therefore, by authority of the Board of Trustees of the University of Massachusetts, confer upon you the degree of Doctor of Science, *honoris causa*, together with all of the rights, honors, and privileges which appertain to that degree here or elsewhere. In token of this, I present you with this diploma and invest you with the appropriate hood.

It was no wonder that Spencer, aware of the whispers, used the title proudly from that day forward. The world being what it is, the whispers, however, did not stop: they switched, to ensure that strangers would soon learn the degree was honorary. Dr. Vannevar Bush, reminded of this, growled, "He has earned it far more than most of the Ph.D.'s I know." [11]

What was not honorary was Spencer's new eminence in the firm as part of top management. Charlie Adams made Percy a vice president; in this, as in other instances, he showed he had an eye for the realities of organization.

Meanwhile Adams was aware that Lab 16 had emerged with a coup and that new, younger, equally brilliant men were beginning to make their marks. He was not inclined to delve into this effort per-

*221*

sonally, however, and looked about for someone to supervise Lab 16, Lab 30, and other special projects. He chose Captain David Hull, who had been an exacting customer of Raytheon during the war from the Bureau of Ships, and whose career included stints as vice president at Capehart and Federal Telecommunications. Between Hull, Bowles, Calosi, and Spencer, the president had reason to believe the technical sector was well covered.[12]

He then turned toward the all-important question of finances. Raytheon needed money. Adams and the directors pondered their course. Should they float a loan or a new stock issue? The need was so urgent they started both efforts, and in the meantime the figures for the end of the firm's fiscal year, May 31, 1950, were put together. They proved neither exciting nor deplorable. Sales had risen slightly to $59 million; profits still hovered a little below $1 million.[13]

Then on June 25, 1950,[14] with no warning and claiming self-defense, the Soviet puppet government of North Korea abruptly invaded the South. The UN Security Council met, but the Soviet delegate was absent, for the USSR was protesting the inclusion of Nationalist China and the exclusion of Red China from the world body.

The Security Council passed a resolution calling for the UN to resist the North Korean invaders. President Truman, leader of the world anti-Communist forces, ordered U.S. air and sea forces to carry out that mandate.[15]

The event, and Washington's response, took place on a weekend. It caught the American public off guard.

Washington made emergency plans while the North Koreans, armed with thousands of Soviet tanks and mortars, assisted by MIG's, made amazingly rapid advances. From Tokyo General MacArthur cabled Washington that neither U.S. bombers nor battleships could stop such an advance. Ground troops, said the General, would be needed, and needed soon.


War is a great pressure cooker in which the pace of all developments is put under strains and raced to capacity. Some idea of what it meant to electronics companies like Raytheon in 1950 is provided by a hasty glance at Percy Spencer's beloved tube industry. In 1950, everything that operated on a vacuum tube was called electronics; transistors were still being developed in the labs, except for a few products like Raytheon's germanium transistors for hearing aids which, as Norman Krim ruefully learned, were too noisy to be immediately practical.

Twenty-five percent of the air force budget for military planes went into electronic devices such as radar, pilot controls, and similar instrumentation. At least thirty separate functions in a combat airplane were electronic in nature. An armored army division, on the other hand, had to carry 120,000 tubes in its operating equipment, with four spares for every one working.[16] From there the imagination can extrapolate other needs for communication, detection, and fire control systems; for equally heavy uses in the navy, marine corps, headquarters, and the establishments maintained both in the field and at home.

The Korean emergency arrived just as Adams had successfully steered Raytheon through an issue of 289,459 shares of common stock—a one-to-five ratio of shares.[17]

The underwriters had included Hornblower & Weeks and Adams' old firm, Paine, Webber, Jackson & Curtis. Raytheon's location may have helped its research, but its background helped equally well in the financial community.

Meanwhile the nation slowly reacted to the reality that it was fighting again, and to the fact that this time the conflict was under new rules. "We are not at war," said the President, "this is a police action." [18]

That meant that the effort was restrained, was not all-out. The Soviets had calculated shrewdly, had hedged their bet. Their probe was extended through a puppet; world opinion—which the United States, unlike the Kremlin, respected—would not be in favor of the use of the atomic bomb. The American effort was, like a policeman's, restrained. No such restriction hindered the aggressor.

As autumn wound toward its close, quarrels arose between the White House and field commander General MacArthur. The President had never met General MacArthur, and the General had not been in the States for many years. In the interim, the U.S. press had described his many exploits in slightly acid tones. Nevertheless the UN troops and the forces of South Korea, known as ROKs, outflanked the enemy at Inchon, regained Seoul, and drove the invaders back toward the 38th Parallel. It began to look as though the issue would soon end when a new element appeared. Chinese Communist troops, massed in large numbers, suddenly poured into the fray.[19] Their combined weight drove the ROK's and their UN allies into pell-mell retreat.

At home these events took on a dreamlike quality. The majority of the nation went about its usual activities; television was the most popular and fascinating novelty in the average home. Belmont's television set sales soared, together with those of the rest of the industry; the Chicago firm cheered Dave Schultz and Charlie Adams by racking up its best months yet.[20]

The power and receiving tube divisions boomed, wartime taxes had been paid and forgotten, and Raytheon moved forward. Robert Hennemuth, who had majored in journalism at the University of Syracuse, spent three years in the U.S. Navy during World War II, then returned to act as public relations director for the chancellor of Syracuse before entering Harvard Law, joined Paul Hannah's legal department in December 1950 and provided a newcomer's appraisal.

"The firm was dominated by two personalities," he recalls: "Charlie Adams and Percy Spencer. Neither of them seemed rank conscious, but Adams was—or seemed to be—aloof. Spencer, whose wife was ill, did not socialize much. Everyone knew his habit of going straight home from work, but everyone knew him at work. He was easy to talk with; was very popular."

Adams was a different sort. He was quiet. Hennemuth, whose time in academia had not been wasted, knew that organizations take their tone, whether they admit it or not, directly from their chief executive. He found Raytheon remarkable in the clear distinction made between work and private life. "Mr. Adams did not intrude into private lives," he said, "he was concerned only with performance on the job." [21] Such coolness can be comforting. Hennemuth had arrived after the Marshall regime, with its enthusiasms, its hot and cold policies, had vanished; he was to benefit from the contrast.

Mike Fossier, on the other hand, soon discovered that not everyone liked the situation; everyone never does. Fossier, who had received his bachelor's degree in science when he was seventeen, was hired to work on the Lab 16 missile program. That program had received an enormous impetus from its intercept almost a year earlier, and had expanded to about six hundred men headed by Sanders. The effort was closely coordinated intellectually but divided geographically between headquarters at Waltham and the missile testing grounds at Point Mugu, where T. C. Wisenbaker and Jake Leiper were in command.

Fossier, a mathematical wizard, was sent to Mugu to work in tandem with Harold Rosen, another youthful prodigy, whom Fossier later termed "the smartest man I ever met." Both were in their early twenties and considered T. C. Wisenbaker and Jake Leiper, who were in their early forties, "real old men." [22]

Despite that generation gap, Fossier grew to respect and admire T. C. Wisenbaker. "He had a strange background," Fossier says, "but great creative talent. He had a feel for the practical and could tell when a paper theory was just—not right." That ability, which approaches divination, was particularly helpful because missiles were designed to self-destruct if they deviated in flight from performance parameters. That left little physical evidence for analysis.

Each test was watched closely in Point Mugu. The resulting information, eagerly awaited in Waltham, became the starting point for new design efforts. Since the overall problem was to create an operational airframe, i.e., a missile that would fly properly, test results led, by a natural sequence, not only to changes in design of the airframe but also changes in the components to fit inside the new configuration. Various disciplines were involved—aeronautical, mechanical, hydraulic—that combined many talents and led down interesting bypaths.

One such path was blazed by Lab 30 and the eventual award of a navy contract to create a large computer to control the missile firing range for Point Mugu. By 1950 Lab 30 was in full swing, was moving well ahead, and clearly headed toward a completion of that contract.[23]

Another involved new Lab 16 missile efforts. The Lark was initially equipped with an active seeker. This meant that radar energy was transmitted and echoes received through a single antenna in the nose of the missile. That clearly limited its homing range. Efforts were underway, sponsored by the navy, to develop a missile with a semiactive seeker. Such a missile would be carried by an airplane that could transmit from its nose; the missile would receive target echoes. The homing range of the missile could be significantly longer. The military advantage was obvious. Following its usual practice, the navy had given developmental contracts to both Sperry and Douglas. Sperry's effort was known as Sparrow I; Douglas had Sparrow II.

Lab 16's semiactive seeker program group used the same general principles it pioneered on the Lark. A handful did theoretical and design work at Waltham, and tested from a hangar Lab 16 had obtained at Bedford, using a B-26 with an antenna in the nose. Their progress was amazingly swift, in part because of their Lark experience.[24]

The navy followed these developments closely and with interest. But it should be remembered that the navy had been the only branch of the service to experience Kamikazes in combat. It was the service branch, therefore, that remained most keenly aware of the dangers inherent in the low-altitude gap in prevailing radar defenses at the time. The military establishment as a whole associated the Kamikazes with Japan—a vanquished and vanished enemy. The Pentagon, like the Capitol, was far more concerned about the emerging military threat posed by the Soviet Union, the dangers of nuclear war, and the potential threat of intercontinental bombers. Far more top-level attention, therefore, was directed toward the high altitude surface-to-air missile being developed at Bell Labs, the Nike, than to the relatively modest efforts underway in Raytheon's Lab 16.

A somewhat parallel situation existed between Lab 16 and Lab 30 and Raytheon as a corporation. Neither the number of persons involved nor the size of their contractual activities was, as yet, significant to the corporation. Far larger sums and greater numbers were engaged in the huge equipment and tube divisions, as well as other sectors of the company. Sanders, who had once reported directly to the chief executive, now reported to Captain Hull. Dave Coffin was brought in to provide administrative strength.

That situation did not please Sanders. He had been hired by the previous chief executive, whom he had interested and impressed. He had been in the habit not simply of reporting to Marshall, but also of enjoying long and enthusiastic talks. Paul Hannah, the firm's legal chief, had listened to them both in the past and was struck by their affinities. "They spoke *mathematics*," he says. "I couldn't follow them." [25]

Nevertheless Lab 16 and its efforts to make a workable subsonic missile based on continuous-wave radar principles moved forward at an impressive rate and reached a crescendo in December 1950. On

226

the eighteenth, a week before Christmas, the Lab 16 team scored a remarkable victory when the Lark made a direct hit on a plane in flight.[26]

That was the first time in the new missile era that a guided missile hit a moving target in the air. Wires burned between Point Mugu in California and Waltham—and Washington, D.C. The event was momentous, outstanding—equal to any triumph made by the firm.

Yet the executive office remained silent, though news was relayed that the management was pleased. Sanders seethed.

While both triumph and strain mounted inside Raytheon's Lab 16, other pressures strained the relationship between the White House and the high command in Korea, between President Truman and General MacArthur.[27]

The appearance of Red China in Korea had turned the tide of battle against the UN and the ROK's. MacArthur, deeply disappointed, aware his own predictions that China would not interfere had been proven wrong, wanted to pursue the enemy across the Yalu River in North Korea. Pressed, he was even willing to use the atomic bomb, if necessary, against that nation—and against the USSR as well, if it honored its agreement to come to China's military assistance.

The General's full position was not made public, but enough was leaked to test public reaction. It was, if such reaction could be accurately gauged by the press, intensely negative. Questions had begun to arise regarding the U.S. presence in Korea; some did not believe South Korea worth the effort, nor communism *per se* a sufficient menace to resist in such a faraway area.

A peace movement had begun to appear, though it was not far advanced. Its initial argument stressed the need to contain the Korean conflict, to emphasize the dire consequences of a full-scale war, stressing the dangers of radiation attendant on the atomic bomb. President Truman was also confronted by the grim fact that the U.S. military establishment, though double in troop size from the year before, was still short of the strength necessary to tackle the USSR. His decision was not made easier by political trial balloons floated by elements in the Republican Party who sought to enter General MacArthur, despite his age, in the presidential sweepstakes.

While the President reviewed overall strategy, however, he took some immediate steps that pushed the nation farther toward a new kind of limbo—neither war nor peace. Acting under authority of a state of emergency, he froze the prices of 200,000 items and pushed through an excess profits tax increase that lifted Raytheon's bill 470 percent.[28]

The step came at a time when Charlie Adams was beating the bushes for money to expand in order to fill government orders. He borrowed $1 million from Morgan & Co., arranged a $10-million V-loan credit,[29] started expansions in receiving tube and power tube facilities, and watched the payroll increase by thousands.

It was by no means the best of times for Colonel Behn to reappear on the horizon; the ITT merger had never gained much favor in Adams' eyes. Nevertheless the Colonel did reappear, and in a typically oblique way.

The Colonel's emissary was John Cutler, an old Boston friend of Adams' who was a partner in Smith, Barney & Co., and an ITT director. Cutler, famous for his charm, pulled Adams to one side at a football game and said, in a confidential aside, "The Colonel wants you to know that if a deal goes through, you'll be the man who will inherit ITT."

Adams' response to the older man was skeptical. "Mr. Cutler," he said, "with all due respect, I'm a simple country boy but I can't buy that one. It won't work."

Cutler smiled at him and said, "Think it over." [30]

Although he had been abrupt with Cutler, Charlie Adams was made uneasy by this new evidence that Colonel Behn was serious about acquiring Raytheon. After worrying about it briefly, he made a trip to New York and looked up George Whitney, head of the Morgan interests.

Once alone with Whitney, Adams described the background of Raytheon—ITT negotiations to date, and explained that the Colonel was now proposing to buy Raytheon with ITT stock. He was candid about his qualms, but added, "There are other interests involved who must be considered. If the deal is a good one for the shareholders and employees of Raytheon, I would feel duty-bound to recommend it." Then he said, "It would help me if I could get an open appraisal of Colonel Behn's character—and competence."

Whitney nodded his head, but said it would take him time to

answer that line of questioning. He assured Adams he would take the time, however, and let him know.

Meanwhile the firm expanded in all directions. Stanley Lovell, head of Lovell Chemical and wartime chief of research at the OSS, had become a director; Norman Krim, now a vice president, exulted over the construction of a new subminiature tube plant under his supervision.

The equipment division was especially busy in a welter of developments, a great swing from wartime radar to peacetime devices. This effort included men from the SubSig organization under Harold Hart, a highly valued engineer who had worked with Fritz Gross on radar problems during the war and who became a leader in the swing. Together Gross, Hart, and others developed a Pathfinder® marine radar system and by May 1951 had designed, engineered, and sold more commercial marine radar systems than all competitors combined. They climaxed this achievement by placing the one-thousandth on the giant liner *United States*, and installed a harbor entrance surveillance radar system in Le Havre, France.[31] From these efforts Gross and Hart, now partners on top of the division, were to proceed to many more achievements.

During this rush of heightened activity Charlie Adams received a call from George Whitney in New York. Whitney had finished assessing the legendary Colonel Behn of ITT. Adams listened to the evaluation with rapt attention.

"It must be admitted," Whitney said in part, "that the Colonel has repeatedly gotten his company into great troubles. But then," Whitney added, "the Colonel has also, repeatedly, shown extraordinary skill and resourcefulness in getting ITT out of these troubles. In terms of stability and leadership, therefore, the Colonel is a most curious man.

"But on the whole," Whitney concluded, "on the basis of the overall record, it must be admitted that ITT's history contains some of the most remarkable moments in business history."[32]

Adams put the phone down little better off than he had been before. He knew the Colonel's record was remarkable and that the Colonel was a fascinating study. "He had sold Marshall," he said later. "But his lures appeared illusory to me."

The longer he thought, the more that particular aspect struck him as critical. "Could ITT endure an audit?" He turned that one

*229*

around and it became increasingly curious upon reflection. According to SEC rules a merger between two firms called for an open disclosure of their holdings and financial condition. That was the only basis on which the U.S. government believed shareholders could make an informed choice. But how could ITT, with part of its properties behind the Iron Curtain, provide proofs for such a disclosure? The fact was that only Colonel Behn himself knew his firm's actual condition.

"The Colonel could entertain one with fascinating dissertations," Adams said later, "but how could these be translated into precise facts upon which one could base a recommendation?" The more he thought about it, the less attractive it appeared. With all due respect to the Colonel, a large matter of business could hardly be based upon undocumented information. Finally he decided he would not be able to "recommend a merger of Raytheon with an ill-defined, or *undefinable* enterprise."

He explained all this to the Raytheon directors very thoroughly in April 1951 and the directors agreed. The ITT merger was, at last, rejected.[33]


Ed Dashefsky, an aeronautical engineer, had been assigned to work with Lab 16 on the development of the Lark. He was aware of the dominance that Sanders and Mercer exercised, but as a specialist did not consider them universally gifted. "They were up on electronics, gyros, and valves," he recalls, "but not on airframes." On the other hand, he himself was not up on everything either. In 1951 he decided his own knowledge of servomechanisms needed improvement, and he took some night courses at Northeastern University. Somewhat to his surprise he found that one of his teachers worked beside him at a desk "on the floor" at Waltham—Tom Phillips.[34]

Dashefsky was one of a number of new men appearing inside the missile group. Not only was the Lark, by its spectacular strike against a target drone, a proven success, but the progress of the semiactive seeker group at Bedford had convinced the navy Raytheon should receive an air-to-air Sparrow missile contract as well. That contract had not yet been awarded, but all the signs indicated it was on its way. Lab 16, therefore, had a double triumph to celebrate. This twin achievement, based on continuous wave radar, should have dispelled Sanders' unhappiness, but it did not.

Sanders talked to his senior men—Mercer, Richmond, and others—and found them sympathetic. In time the discussions grew into plans to leave the company and launch a new business, should Sanders decide to leave Raytheon as he had earlier left RCA.

Sanders then talked to T. C. Wisenbaker and Jake Leiper, who were in charge of the missile effort in California. Leiper, who had transferred a fierce loyalty from the navy to Raytheon, would have no part of it. Wisenbaker was taken aback.[35]

"But you've *won*," he said.

"*Raytheon's* won," Sanders replied bitterly.

"Why not try to work out a new deal?" Wisenbaker asked. "Maybe Raytheon will agree to Lab 16's becoming an independent venture."

Sanders shook his head negatively. He was sure the management would never agree to such a step.

"Well, what about the navy?" Wisenbaker persisted. His implication was clear: the dissolution of a superb team at the peak of its effort could jeopardize a program essential to the nation that supported and needed it.

It was no use. Sanders had made up his mind. He left and took twelve men—the top of the team—with him. T. C. Wisenbaker and Jake Leiper remained, together with a covey of youthful, unknown, and relatively untried engineers. There was no question Sanders' departure created a crisis for Raytheon and the U.S. Navy—to say nothing of the men left behind.


In April 1951 a similar split developed on the highest level in the land when President Truman abruptly dismissed General MacArthur from all posts, in effect retired him from the army. The news was sent to Asia through channels but simultaneously released to the U.S. press. General MacArthur, therefore, heard the news on the radio before the dispatch itself reached him. It was a sad close to an illustrious military career, but the White House had decided its authority over the military had been disputed.

The fact was that the Administration and the nation were embroiled in arguments on many levels, and these arguments were not unique to the United States. In Britain leading members of the Labour cabinet resigned. Harold Wilson and Aneurin Bevan believed free health care should be maintained even if defense spending had to be reduced.³⁶ The British Empire, beset by riots in India and persistent depression at home, was clearly crumbling, and the British no longer seemed to care.

In the United States the Kefauver hearings on organized crime seemed of far more interest than the war in Korea; a paperback phenomenon arose in which more than 231 million reprints were sold; AT&T reported it had more than one million shareholders; *The King and I* played on Broadway.³⁷ Scientifically the nation—and the world— were making great strides. The British, Dutch, and Norwegians were exploring nuclear energy; David Riesman wrote a book titled *The Lonely Crowd* which claimed that new, mass-directed individuals were arising, created a term that would, in time, become a new pejorative for the old American majority: WASP.³⁸

Added together the mixture was unprecedented for the United States in wartime. The action in Korea had cost 100,000 U.S. casualties and was continuing, but had been accepted as less than war—as a police action. Communist propagandists termed the U.S. intervention "imperialistic," but if the United States had become imperial, it was along new, unprecedented lines. By 1951 the direct cost to Americans of lend-lease, Point Four, and military assistance to the free world rose to $35 billion; the indirect costs were incalculable. This seemed imperialism in reverse.

One result was that the American national budget began to reflect strains and deficits. Both Germany and Japan, nations that received industrial and technological and economic aid, began to produce goods with U.S.-designed machinery for sale in America. The first Volkswagens appeared in the United States. Another result was that some firms engaged in direct governmental contracts found their volumes rising. Raytheon was one of these: sales increased by $30 million to reach nearly $90 million by May 31, 1951, the close of the firm's fiscal year. Profits, as a result of the excess profits tax, were less proportionately impressive—below 3 percent on the dollar—and reached $2.1 million. The number of employees rose to over twelve thousand.³⁹

Beyond these specifics, new psychological divides began to open in the nation. The Korean war was remarkable in being the first U.S.

232

action in which neither the White House nor Congress attempted to rally popular support, marked the first time Americans died in combat in answer to their nation's call without the backing of their fellow citizens. No bands played; no streamers or posters appeared; no supportive rallies were held; few admiring speeches made, for these would have been inappropriate in a police action, which by definition is the use of impersonal force. The Korean conflict became an issue of domestic politics. Even the UN, in whose name the action was conducted, turned against the conflict, questioned its purpose and value.

A new federal excise tax sent prices up; the selective price freeze exacerbated inflationary pressures by creating shortages of critical materials. Regulation W hurt the ability of people to buy homes, television sets, automobiles, and other items by making a 25 percent down payment mandatory. Belmont television set sales tumbled. Charlie Adams' countenance, often glum, became gloomy at this. He brightened, though, when his assistant, Ernest Leathem, found the Charles Frost Company of New York willing to pay $700,000 for Russell Electric.[40] That was almost what the subsidiary had cost originally and, more important, ended a steady drain.

"Wisenbaker and Jake Leiper flipped a coin, and Wisenbaker lost," said Mike Fossier, an interested observer. That meant that Wisenbaker, who hated a cold climate more than anything, had to return to Massachusetts to head the Lab 16 missile effort.

T. C. had to return because, as Tom Phillips said later, "The actual working structure of Lab 16 was not visible from the outside." Dave Coffin, placed in charge of the effort, was invaluable in dealing with a management that had known him for years, and was equally able and impressive in dealing with outsiders. But as far as the actual development of a missile was concerned, T. C. Wisenbaker and Jake Leiper were the two men who knew the program best, could grasp its overall pattern in better detail and guide it most expertly, and were considered the technical leaders by the gifted cadre of young engineers who did the creative work.

Once back in Massachusetts, Wisenbaker evaluated the engineers Sanders had left behind, and began a strenuous effort to recoordinate and continue the program. Meanwhile Hamilton Hauck, who had been transferred from Point Mugu to the navy's Bureau of Aeronautics in the Pentagon, received a visit from Roy Sanders. He was most sorry that Sanders had left Raytheon, for it could jeopardize a crucial program at a critical time. When Sanders indicated he might be able to continue the missile effort as head of Sanders Associates, Hauck shook his head adamantly. "You lack the essential supportive resources," he said, "That program will remain, so far as the U.S. Navy is concerned, with Raytheon." [41]

Shortly afterward he called upon Raytheon to estimate the amount of damage Sanders' departure had done, "and to assess whatever vigor remained."

Wisenbaker soon discovered that when he asked questions Tom Phillips could answer them. That marked him in Wisenbaker's quick mind, and he took a closer look. Phillips, twenty-six years old, towered an inch over six feet, dressed with the usual indifference of a young engineer, had a shock of tousled black hair. He was teaching a course in servomechanisms at Northeastern University, was married and had children. He was a bear for work and, to test him, Wisenbaker began to load work on him, to push him hard. The results were gratifying. Wisenbaker decided he had found his man.[42]

By the time Hamilton Hauck arrived for his evaluation visit, he found Lab 16 running hard. Hauck, escorted about by Dave Coffin, was impressed; he liked Coffin immensely. "He was composed and quietly effective," Hauck recalls. T. C. Wisenbaker was, of course, a known and respected quality; Hauck says that Phillips and other younger engineers made similar impressions. He left convinced the navy should continue its contract with Lab 16.[43]

In actuality he did not have great alternatives at hand. Korea was proving anew that low-flying combat planes could not be countered effectively. The Kamikaze problem, therefore, was as bad as the day it appeared. The Nike high-flying missile program notwithstanding, the Raytheon effort was necessary and important. To have arbitrarily canceled a program that had made a promising start might have converted Ham Hock into Ham Burger.


Although only salesmen seem aware of it, secretaries inside corporations not only handle clerical duties and staff the telephone barricades that insulate executives from an importunate world, but watch and assess the men—and often influence their decisions. They comprise a sort of Greek chorus to happenings inside a firm, operate a pipeline that seldom carries financial information but is heavy with warnings of impending personnel changes and the movements of men up and down the corporate escalators.

Their own passages in and out are seldom recorded, but secretaries are, nevertheless, both important and interesting personalities in every firm. When Ruth Babb was no longer secretary to the chairman, it made a difference in the executive suite. Charlie Adams had suggested—and the board had approved—the abolition of the office of chairman of the board as "redundant." Miss Babb wondered what would become of her, and thought it wonderful that the general counsel, Paul Hannah, appeared to lead her toward the legal department.[44]

She found it housed in what had been a private residence in quarters known simply as The Shack; desks were so crowded that whenever anyone tried to ford an aisle coat racks toppled. But in short order the work, already partly familiar from her duties as an assistant secretary of the company, became familiar and she settled in for what would become the duration.

Miss Babb's departure was marked by another arrival on the executive floor: Lillian Ottenheimer. Miss Ottenheimer—or Lillian, as she soon became known—had been, for a number of years, secretary to journalist H. V. Kaltenborn in New York City.

Kaltenborn, who achieved fame, among more substantial accomplishments, for being unforgettably mimicked by President Truman for his persistent radio refusal to believe in Truman's triumph on election night 1948, had grown elderly and was cutting back on his work. Being a conscientious man, he shopped around for a new job for Miss Ottenheimer and was put in touch with Charlie Adams through a mutual friend. He told her to send in her résumé, and she did.

In due course Miss Ottenheimer received a call from a gentleman who said, "This is C. F. Adams of the Raytheon Company." She asked what the company made, and Adams told her electronics. "I don't know anything about the field," she responded, and Adams assured her she would be taught.[45]

It meant moving out of New York, but that was beginning to seem attractive in itself, even in 1951. Miss Ottenheimer arrived, was shown her desk, and soon met Ernest Leathem, Adams' assistant, and Dr. Edward Bowles, among others. She heard about Percy Spencer, the

*235*

firm's resident genius, and was warned he hated that particular word. She was to be Adams' secretary, and she evaluated her new boss. A few weeks were enough to convince her she had gone from one extreme to the other. Kaltenborn had been a journalist—i.e., a man who wore his opinions on his sleeves and changed them often. He had been mercurial, flamboyant, filled with anecdotes and observations, a notable talker subject to many moods. Mr. Adams, in contrast, was grave, quiet and, to her astonishment, "seemed to have no moods at all." But she took sharp notice that he ran the Raytheon ship; there was no doubt whatever about that.

Earlier in 1951 Bell Labs had revealed that Dr. William Shockley, leader of its transistor efforts, had made another breakthrough and produced the junction transistor.[46] The advance was part of a long chain that could be traced back to the quantum theory again, to the speculations of Heisenberg, Sommerfield, Fermi, and others—and was monumentally important. As Norman Krim had predicted originally, the transistor could replace tubes in multiple applications; outlast them; was smaller, more versatile, easier to build into new and more complex assemblies.

Raytheon was onto the junction transistor early, because Krim—in the course of evaluating the practicality of stockpiling proximity fuses for the army—had roomed with Shockley, who told him his breakthrough.[47] That led to conferences in Raytheon and the hiring of Dr. Ivan Getting, at the suggestion of Dr. Bowles, to head research. Getting, formerly of the Radiation Lab at MIT had meanwhile moved to Harvard.

Then Raytheon obtained a Bell license and concluded an agreement with GE to develop its own junction transistors. Two million dollars was set aside for the effort. That was a large sum for Raytheon at the time, and a clear indication of the importance attached to the project. Later in 1951 young George Freedman was put in charge of a special team and work began in a subbasement at the Chapel Street building.

This location was as modest as the aims of the team were lofty. One young man had to carry buckets of water in and out, or rather up and down steep stairs. Freedman took special interest in the fact

*236*

that Dr. C. G. Smith joined his team. He was impressed; Dr. Smith was a hallowed name—one of the company founders.⁴⁸

Dr. Smith wanted to keep busy. He made no special demands beyond requesting a special chinning bar, on which he chinned himself ten times every morning to keep in shape. Soft-spoken, retiring, he astonished Freedman by making his own tools rather than requesting special instruments. Freedman's recollections are also interesting because of the light they unexpectedly shed on the vast cultural distance traversed by the United States since the early 1920's.

When Smith casually mentioned that one of his uncles had fought Indians in the West and that he himself had played in watermelon patches as a boy, Freedman was astonished. He regarded the older man almost as a time traveler, a personage from another age. Yet Smith was only in his sixties. In time Freedman was also impressed with Smith as a scientist; the older man proved an amazingly valuable member of the transistor research-development effort.

The management was also pleased when the group announced its own junction transistor in June 1951. Norman Krim took a swing through the hearing-aid industry and returned with between $2 million and $3 million worth of orders; the production experts swung into high gear.⁴⁹

Around them other electronic firms were engrossed in similar efforts, developing transistors—semiconductors—for other applications. Bell Labs had persuaded the government to remove this subject from the secret category and was running special courses in the subject. The reasoning behind this move was the hope that by spreading knowledge of the state of the art, the entire resources of a burgeoning industry would be attracted to further effort.⁵⁰

This was an astonishing exception in a period when the nation was still embroiled in the McCarthy campaign to uproot subversion; when high-ranking physicists Fuchs, May, and Pontecorvo had been revealed as defectors,⁵¹ and when reasons of national security held much scientific information apart from the community.

Apparently the immense potential of transistors, which could upgrade all electronic instrumentation, was considered too promising to be held back for any reason. Giant RCA was deep in efforts to create transistors for use in telecommunications; others were engrossed in efforts to improve lights, computers—an infinite array. Twenty-five firms took Bell licenses for programs too numerous to list. As usual,

Raytheon was in a crowded field, but the company was also very crowded with ongoing work. Later, some of the men would look back at this particular corner in the road somewhat wistfully, and wonder if Krim's hearing-aid industry, tiny in the total picture, should have overshadowed other possibilities—but that is hindsight.

By the end of 1951 Charlie Adams had arranged for a credit of $20 million from a group of five New England banks and had borrowed more money from the insurance companies.

In World War II Raytheon had taken a giant leap forward, but it had been a leap directed by force of personality. In the Korean war, the firm was once again propelled into expansion and heavy volumes. This time its activities were channeled, its accounts kept clear, its lines of responsibilities clear and structured. There was less drama, but also less waste motion. One of the defects of efficiency is that it does not dazzle; does not attract the imagination; is not spectacular. Adams had achieved, nevertheless, an organization that smoothed the path of many who remained unaware that it was not by chance.

Otherwise, however, matters could quite easily have grown tangled, for the pace was heady. Charlie Resnick, a youthful attorney who joined the firm late in 1951, afterward remarked on the tempo. "It seemed to me that the legal department at the time existed mainly to find and handle the real estate paper attendant on the firm's expansions," he says. "There was a huge lab being constructed at Wayland; buildings were going up in several locations; others being planned." [53]

In addition, Resnick took note of the personalities. Some were of a sort to astound a younger man. "I recall," he says, "listening to Percy Spencer explain his Desk Theory. 'I believe,' Spencer said, 'in having only three desks for every four executives. That way I know someone is on his feet and working.' "

The Spencer theory would have been redundant inside Lab 16, where everyone seemed to be on his feet. Tom Phillips, sharing an office with Wisenbaker, learned invaluable lessons. Wisenbaker, Phillips discovered, had some approaches that cut through fog and confusion.

Their days were long and hours a matter of complete indifference. As before, the missile effort was conducted across the width of the continent and kept together by telephone. Tests at Point Mugu, where seventy men were busy under Leiper, were constant and sometimes extended for hours. Fossier and Rosen, the theoreticians, were generally ahead on the mathematics and analysis; a constant interchange

*238*

was maintained with computer groups. Wisenbaker and Phillips, who had to translate theories into hardware answers, had the task of central coordination and overall direction. Phillips, watching Wisenbaker, learned "to simplify. Wisenbaker would take pencil and paper and get at the essence of a problem." [54] He found the older man stimulating and learned to have great respect for him.

Meanwhile the conversion of an old powder plant at Lowell into a missile manufacturing site was undertaken under the supervision of Rogers Hamel, a navy veteran of World War II and an expert in plant production and management. The task was far from simple, involving not only the job of planning aisle layouts, partitions, and production flow, but the acquisition of new and special equipment to meet the advanced requirements of Lab 16 prototypes, which pressed against the technological state of the art in many areas. Toward the end of 1951 Hamel, having looked about, requested the assistance of Ed Dashefsky as a staff engineer. Dashefsky, recognized, proved able at unsnarling problems and began his rise in the firm.

Like Dashefsky, a number of young men in the missile group were rising; the group as a whole was rising. Lab 16 changed from a peripheral developmental effort based on some interesting but unfashionable theories into a new and important manufacturing part of Raytheon's government business. Wisenbaker had led his cadre of young, unknown engineers into avenues of effort and accomplishment far beyond the stage at which Sanders had left them.

Sanders was, however, charting new pathways of his own. News trickled back that Sanders Associates, established as a going concern in the electronics industry, had obtained a number of important contracts, including some from the navy. Among his backers Sanders could count on Laurence K. Marshall, who had liquidated his Raytheon holdings when he left the firm, and—understandably—backed his former protégé. It took T. C. Wisenbaker, however, to point out the larger irony of the outcome.

"Sanders left Raytheon because he wanted to be free to engage in creative engineering along his own lines," said Wisenbaker. "Now look at what's happened. He's turned into a businessman." [55]

Greater ironies arose on larger fronts. Britain's voters restored the Conservative Party and hailed the return of Winston Churchill as prime minister; in West Germany Konrad Adenauer reigned supreme as chancellor. Both men were representatives of pre-World War I times; in the United States, President Truman himself reflected their indomitable spirit.

Yet the President's position was odd. His foreign policy seemed popular, but the Korean war was most unpopular. He had easily gained approval for a military budget of over $56 billion; NATO agreed to create an international force of fifty divisions.[56] Most people agreed communism was a menace and approved vast expenditures to meet that menace—but were against any physical action. Truce talks, being held in Korea, were stalled and little discussion arose regarding their content. Instead, the U.S. press headlined charges of "cronyism" in appointments and highlighted a series of small-bore instances of influence peddling in Washington.

Inflation created many problems. Employment was at an all-time high of over sixty million, but prices rose fast and labor troubles followed.

Raytheon discovered with shock that some government contracts were converted into losses by the unadmitted devaluation of the currency; the U.S. Treasury announced a national deficit of $4 billion. Yet Raytheon's government contracts and orders kept increasing; by February 1952 they had reached a backlog of over $117 million.

One effect of inflation for companies, as for individuals, is that it forces the need for more capital. In early 1952 Adams, working again through Hornblower & Weeks and Paine, Webber, offered another 434,189 shares of Raytheon common—a ratio of one to every four shares outstanding.[57]

But, as in every war, government demands extended into increasingly broad sectors as time passed. Belmont, whose television sales had been hard hit by new credit rules, turned toward war work, and this volume soon outgrew its previous sales mark. Meanwhile it marked down sets for liquidation.

Adams, scrambling, obtained Certificates of Necessity—a necessity —to create the new Lab 16, now simply known as "missiles," buildings at Bedford, Massachusetts; discussed the impact of transistors with the directors and told them that plans were afoot to build a computer with Minneapolis-Honeywell.

By May 1952, the firm was surprised, but pleased, to discover that it had passed through its best year since 1944, during the heady time of World War II. Sales had jumped from $90 to $111 million (they had been $112 million in 1944), though profits were less than the year before, at $2 million. "Increases in taxes," Adams said in the Annual Report, "amounted to 44 percent." [58]

Corporate psychoanalysts, who seldom call themselves that but should, would be interested in Raytheon's Annual Report for 1952. It was not Adams' first, nor would it by any means be his last. But it provides an almost pure example of what he considered appropriate and necessary to describe. At a time when Annual Reports were still somewhat stark and heavily statistical, his was addressed to the average stockholder.

One page was devoted to Where the Money Went. This feature was a staple in the Adams report. One year the budget breakdown was illustrated by pie cuts, in other years other images were called upon. In 1952 a whole page was used with bars and drawings. There was something basic about this perennial, which fit Adams as the man who husbanded the firm's revenues. In 1952 it showed 48.5 percent of all moneys received going to employees; 40.9 percent for materials. Out of the 10.6 percent remaining, 4.3 percent was paid in taxes, 4.4 percent for maintenance, 1.7 percent for reinvestment, and .2 percent for preferred shareholders. There was no dividend for the common shareholders; the firm could not afford it. Raytheon's management was, obviously, conservative about offering lures toward the stock market.

The text carried many references to the firm's executives and was replete with illustrations of its products. In 1952 the directors were pictured; in other years officers would usually appear. Adams' sense of organization permeated the Annual Report; it gave the impression of a group enterprise. By 1952 it could almost be called a mass enterprise, for the number of employees had increased to over fifteen thousand.

Out of the welter of activity represented by this immense force, retrospect can catch only the peaks of effort. One strenuous arena was the new missile plant at Lowell. It cost $6.5 million, but that does not bring its memory to life. That glimpse is better provided by the recollections of Joe Alibrandi, then a twenty-four-year-old production engineer fresh from MIT and a brief stint at Fairchild, who joined Raytheon expecting to be swallowed in a giant maze and instead found himself in the front lines of a pioneering effort.

Alibrandi, for whom Lowell was his first big project, can still remember the steps that Hamel and Dashefsky took, from original paperboards through to the final production layout; recalls with pleasure swinging around the countryside to obtain machinery, and the time that he escorted Ed Gleason, of the industrial planning division of the navy, through the plant on a rainy day.

To his horror they came upon a lathe operator working under an umbrella; the roof leaked.

"The space is great," Gleason said tersely, "but you'd better do something about the environment." [59]

In the missile tower, meanwhile, Wisenbaker decided he had found the right man at Waltham in the form of Tom Phillips; he could leave New England and return to the sunny skies of California and Point Mugu. No decision could more clearly prove Wisenbaker's indifference to being center stage himself, as far as the world was concerned. He left the younger man with heavy responsibilities, and Phillips was immersed. He later recalled some occasions when he worked from 8 A.M. until 6 P.M.—the following night. One such occasion was in preparation for a visit by Hamilton Hauck.[60] That was extraordinary, of course—but even the ordinary day was long.

Why did he and the others work so hard? Later Phillips said, "It represented challenge." That seems factual enough: opportunity, to men so young they have not yet tasted the fruits of success, is just a word. They worked because they were young and vigorous, because they were in competition against other men elsewhere—but mostly because the nature and the pleasure of the work itself consumed them. In that, they were no different than other young men in art, or science, or medicine. Industry, after all, is an element in which young men work as creatively and selflessly as in any other—and the competitive edge of business gives it a snap of its own.

Meanwhile, despite his physical removal, Wisenbaker remained almost as close to Phillips as if they still shared the same office. They were on the telephone every day; "sometimes we talked for two hours," Phillips remembers. That was a defeat of space and of time, an intellectual partnership of rare quality.

It was not, elsewhere, a period noted for cooperation. It was, of course, an election year, but party lines were blurred and personalities prevailed. General Eisenhower, nominated by the Republicans, spoke in generalities, but his reputation and character made him tremendously appealing to the voters; Democratic candidate Adlai Stevenson seemed unable to shake off the accumulated resentments amassed by the long tenure of his party.

The world situation was scrambled. The decline of colonialism continued, Libya being the most recent in a long string of former subject areas to gain its freedom. Liberations did not diminish international tensions. Riots erupted in India over conditions, in Egypt over Britain's influence, in Paris over communism.[61] The situation between Israel and its Arab neighbors in the Middle East was tense and difficult; truce talks remained stalled in Korea; sporadic fighting continued. The West was moving along its plan to arm against the Soviets, but no clear divide was drawn. The press, literature, and intelligentsia appeared still of the opinion that communism was a variant of democracy. This did much to muddy the waters. In the election, General Eisenhower presented himself as a peace candidate in Korea.

Changes in the world scene mirrored changes at home. Prior to World War I, the United States had functioned with a weak and modest government. During World War I, the Wilson Administration assumed emergency powers that were relinquished, for the most part, after the conflict. The New Deal, however, established sweeping governmental power during the thirties and extended these during World War II. The transition into the Cold War made these powers a permanent part of the nation. By the closing months of the Truman administration, the nation's economy had become inextricably intertwined with its government. During the political campaign, rhetoric about "free enterprise" soared to new heights, but in reality business had been so severely circumscribed that only elderly men, active before 1929, could recall the thrills and the frights of a free market.

When Dave Schultz attended renegotiation conferences between Raytheon and the government in 1952, he did so as a veteran of many previous sessions. He had none of the surprise and shock of Laurence Marshall years before; the routine had become familiar; he knew all its twists and turns.

Much the same could be said about the government itself. Men in Washington, its bureaus, agencies, and subdivisions, had grown used

*243*

to their role vis-à-vis private industry. A symbiotic relationship had developed with no special author, no traceable source. Governmental power had simply grown, like Topsy. The interrelationship of business and government in the United States, down to the smallest subcontractor, had become a way of life and work.

Martin Schilling, "schooled in the early to mid-thirties in the engineering sciences" in Germany,[62] was a fascinated and interested observer of this phenomenon from 1945 onward. His career has been typical of this century, which has hurled many men into unexpected situations.

Schilling started out to become a physicist, then turned toward engineering. When the Nazi leaders plunged Germany into war in late 1939, he was among those who learned the government had already marked his role: he was instructed to report to the Guided Missile Group and there placed on optical measurements. He worked at Pennemunde under von Braun and others, and helped develop the buzz bombs and the other weapons upon which Hitler placed so much reliance until May 1945.

When these and similar bases were overrun by the Allies, Schilling fled to Bavaria. To his astonishment, he was unearthed, arrested, and carried to Paris by the U.S. Army. There he learned that Colonel Toftoy, of U.S. Military Intelligence, attached to Patton's army, had cast a net and pulled in not only Schilling, but von Braun and others of the German missile group. By Thanksgiving 1945—an occasion he might well have joined—Schilling was one of 110 to 120 German scientists treated to turkey and its fixings in a ship anchored in Boston harbor. He had, in his suitcase, a one-year contract with the U.S. Army to help develop a missile.

Schilling and his associates landed at Fort Bliss, to work on the first U.S. V-2 for the Army Ordnance Department. He learned the Americans had "an embryonic" missile program underway at the Jet Propulsion Laboratory in Pasadena, and that work had started on the Corporal. Schilling helped on these projects and also helped create the Redstone Project.

In the same course of time, Schilling became an American citizen and an admirer of Colonel Toftoy. The U.S. style, he recalls, "seemed so simple; so clear." Schilling watched, listened, and marveled. The pace of development was rapid and effective. Von Braun rose; Colonel Toftoy became a general; Schilling himself became an important official in the program management section of army ordnance. He was, in fact, chief of that section when General Toftoy, alerted by the navy approval of Sparrow III, gave a briefing on the low-altitude missile situation.

"He took only one day," Schilling says, "to explain Bell Labs and its manufacturing arm, Western Electric, the work on Nike, and the other factors involved." When he was through, Schilling thought the situation was simple. Air defense needed electronics, processing, and fire-control systems; Raytheon—whom he learned General Toftoy respected—had an organization of "deep competence." Schilling would advise on guidance and control systems and on airframes so the army could have a defense against low-altitude bombers. Other factors were the need to improve radar screens, which had "chicken wire defense" (Schilling has a gift for phrases), and the creation of new and different sensors. All of this was, of course, right down Lab 16's alley.

Schilling visited Bell Labs and "found them interesting. The men were very bright—but they were not interested in the new small missile program." They preferred the large Nike-Hercules—a successor to Nike-Ajax.

Informed about Royden Sanders and his contributions, Schilling visited Sanders Associates at Nashua, New Hampshire, but decided "they did not have the facilities." Nevertheless he recommended a small contract. He visited Raytheon and discovered it was already working in these sectors. So was Republic, but its establishment struck Schilling as more complex, glitteringly new. "Toftoy always said *take the simple way; be direct,*" Schilling recalls, "and here was Raytheon. The men sounded like Toftoy: very clear."

Schilling surveyed their facilities, noted they had "only one building at Bedford with two floors and an unfinished basement; a test group at California that included Fossier, Harold Rosen, and T. C. Wisenbaker."

He recommended Raytheon begin, as far as the army was concerned, with developing a continuous-wave radar illuminator to track low-altitude targets. Then he would see what happened.

The year 1952 ended with an Eisenhower landslide. A feeling of great relief swept over the nation as the press ended its long, almost morbid criticism of the Truman Administration and all its personalities. The business community was jubilant; some persons even dreamed of a restoration of former patterns. Such hopes were unrealistic. The new President had inherited an immense governmental structure that had penetrated virtually every area of national life and that could not be excised without irreparable damage to the body politic.

Though the 1952 dollar was worth only fifty-two cents compared to the thirties,[63] a U.S. population of almost 161 million enjoyed record employment and unprecedented abundance. Despite the grim Cold War, the arts, theater, and literature turned toward entertainment. Broadway showed *The Seven Year Itch;* the movies unfurled *From Here to Eternity* and the new eminence of Frank Sinatra; Hemingway's *The Old Man and the Sea* collected prizes.

Such escapes into fantasy or the past evaded recognition of the actual state of the nation and the world. The Cold War had hardened; the West, losing colonies, struggled to retain influence and put together a defensive alliance. In Egypt revolution swept away both King Farouk and his British advisors; the Mau Mau mounted a bloody Kenya rebellion; Asia was in flux.

The U.S. ship rocked in response to very real tides. The Rosenbergs were convicted of espionage and sentenced to death; the U.S. Communist Party was found to be a creature of the Kremlin [64] and ordered to register as a foreign agency; arguments regarding subversion raged, but most people remained confused regarding the specifics of Communist doctrine and where it differed from the democratic.

Raytheon found itself drawn inexorably deeper into the needs of the government and the nation. Adams told the board the backlog of government contracts had risen to $200 million and that word had been received from the authorities that all the directors of the company would have to obtain security clearances.[65]

Raytheon's president also had some interesting international developments to report. He had been making many trips to Washington and to Europe, and had worked out an arrangement to supply radar technology and parts to Microlambda, an Italian firm located in the suburbs of Naples. Dr. Carlo Calosi, former Italian professor and now one of Raytheon's stars, was instrumental in these new arrangements. Dr. Calosi had suggested that Raytheon accept a minority interest in one Italian venture that had fallen behind in its royalty payments; the

246

suggestion pointed the way toward a relatively painless way into deeper participation in Europe. The directors—and President Adams—were intrigued. This was the beginning of Raytheon's involvement in Elsi.

Traditional areas of Raytheon were booming. Percy Spencer, head of power tubes, proved he was still master of the magnetron and other microwave generators by creating several important new variations of value to military and commercial groups; Krim's receiving tubes forged ahead in germanium transistors and diodes.

The only soft spot was Belmont, whose debts to Raytheon had reached $11.5 million. "Such losses have turned debt into investment," said Adams and presented a plan to make that a reality. One move was to transfer Henry Argento, who had been working under Percy Spencer, over to Belmont as general manager and a Raytheon vice president. Another was to fund special efforts to produce a Raytheon color television tube. The combination would, he hoped, reorganize Belmont efficiently and enable it to pioneer the introduction of color television to the nation. The plan was bold, had the endorsement of Dave Schultz and the assurances of the engineers, and was approved by the directors. Henry Argento was very pleased; it was his big chance.

Argento arrived in Chicago to discover more problems than he had anticipated. "A real mess," he summarized later. "It was running a faulty assembly line, billing single orders at a time with conflicting orders being issued; the employees were engaging in wholesale thefts and there were leakages in the inventory. Great losses were piling up." [66]

Aware the eyes of management were fixed upon him, he "fired droves of men." As he delved into the books he found horrifying facts. "The books," he said, "were in a state. One senior executive was intent on building a private business of his own; the sales groups were indifferent."

Like all new managers, though, Argento was sure these problems could be solved and that he was the man who could solve them. He searched for bright spots and discovered that Belmont's Bill Dunn, the chief engineer, was "highly creative," and came to the conclusion that Harold Mattes, long-time Belmont chief, had "an excellent commercial mind." One result was that Argento's reports to Raytheon's management radiated optimism though their details were grim.

*247*

Belmont was, or seemed to be, the only major problem area in early 1953, however. Equipment, the remaining large division, whose activities extended from engineering and producing radar for marine, commercial, air and land uses in both commercial and military markets, to special microwave systems, Radarange ovens, and a vast array of other special products, was busy. Headed by Captain Hull and staffed by veteran Raytheon engineers, this division was running at top speed. But one corner of the equipment division, now named the missile group, was outpacing the rest in a manner that made its title seem especially apt.

The nation itself was competing on a larger, infinitely more complex level, and the results were mixed. The Soviets proved most effective in propaganda, alarmingly adroit at keeping the West off balance and more capable at keeping its own secrets than any previous great power. Stalin's postwar moves had been masterly: he had succeeded in simultaneously repairing war damages inside the USSR, extending Soviet power in Eastern Europe and Asia, and harassing the West on a global scale. The Kremlin had two weapons denied the West. The first was the existence of pro-Soviet sympathizers throughout the world who glossed over minatory Soviet moves while promulgating its arguments. The other was the ability to make all prowestern comments and arguments inside its own domain not only illegal, but suicidal. The net effect on the world press coverage was to emphasize the weaknesses and discord of the West and to gloss the difficulties of the Soviet Union. The size and extent of Soviet military and technological strength were rarely revealed and seldom discussed, while the military and technological establishments of the West were targets of critical examination.

Early in March 1953, the world was finally granted relief from the presence of Stalin,[67] the last of the top leaders who had pushed mankind into World War II. He had lasted beyond his seventy-third birthday and had been responsible for the murders of millions. His death might well have been celebrated in the streets but instead was reported by the world press with a respect that was later revealed to be misplaced by officials of his own government.

Stalin's death compares with the passing of Genghis Khan, which, when it took place, halted the invasion of Europe by the Mongols,

*248*

and sent all the lesser khans back to Asia to confer. In similar fashion the Soviet leaders gathered at the Kremlin and laid plans to divide the dictator's mantle. Unlike the Mongols, they did not decide to rest upon their victories, but their drive was delayed. The new U.S. President was able to reach a peace in Korea. U.S. Secretary of State Dulles announced the outlook for world peace had been improved.[68]

The end of the Korean action, the knowledge that a top military man was in the White House and able to guard the nation's defenses, the pleasant personality of the President, and the unwonted civility of the press combined to bring a great sense of relief to the people of the United States.

Raytheon, a microcosm of the nation, mirrored this reaction. Its activities by the end of May 1953 were at a record high. Sales had soared to an unprecedented $179 million, profits were $3.8 million.[69] The bulk of its activities represented government contracts; overall sales had increased 66 percent. Its commercial business had also improved; new buildings were being erected at South Lowell and Bedford for the missile group, a new tube plant being built at Waltham, and still another new plant at Quincy. Like the nation, it faced both expanded government and consumer business. The 1953 Annual Report, in addition to the standard Adams page on Where the Money Went, featured the operating managers: Percy Spencer, Krim, Hull, Argento, Nichols (manager of research replacing Calosi, who was busy internationally), Ray Ellis, Dave Schultz, and Allen Reed.

A Twenty-five Year Club had been formed with sixty-one founding members. The organization had a little difficulty in agreeing on the actual date of its birth, since it had begun as the American Appliance Company; settled—for the moment—on 1928, the year it had launched the Raytheon Manufacturing Company.

An impression arises that the firm had, finally, passed its period of reckless youth and entered maturity. It had over twenty thousand employees and sales offices in Europe, Central and South America; it was working closely with advanced university, industrial, and governmental research groups, and had extended deep into the community.

In these respects it greatly resembled the nation overall, whose government and citizens alike had become involved in far-flung international enterprises while improving comforts and standards at home. A season of sunlight appeared, though dangers remained beneath the surface of events. For the time being the country had a comfortable sense of being sensibly governed and having a clear purpose. Raytheon was similarly calm. On both the national and company level, this was a long-sought, hard-won moment.

The end of the Korean war did not end the huge defense effort of the United States, though it did remove this effort from the headlines. President Eisenhower, able to function as his own Secretary of Defense to an extent beyond his immediate predecessors, continued their policy of retaining U.S. atomic secrets but determined to arm NATO with tactical weapons. That decision alone was to spur the exchange of technology and ensure a stream of contracts, as well as to spur a series of efforts to improve, modify, and modernize the U.S. defense arsenal.

In late 1953 the impact of this push was felt inside the U.S. Army, which had grown concerned over its lack of an effective low-altitude missile. The army chief of ordnance, placing Colonel Eiffler in direct charge, ordered development work on such a missile started at once. Eiffler turned toward Bell Labs and Westinghouse almost automatically, which is not surprising. More surprising was the fact that he was also willing to listen to presentations from lesser establishments—among them Raytheon.

Tom Phillips, on his first real sales trip, made the Raytheon presentation to Eiffler and left with a sense that he had hit it off.[70] He was right: Raytheon received a $2.4 million contract—a sum that seems puny today but was considered substantial then—to design a guidance system for an army missile. Interestingly enough, Sanders Associates also received a developmental contract on this program at about the same time.

Before the effort was far along, Eiffler defined the problems that confronted the low-altitude missile design groups into thirteen tasks, or problems. Technically searching and highly demanding, they involved the creation of a search radar to discern an airplane in the midst of clutter and a tracker to illuminate the plane in the midst of that clutter, a seeker for the missile, a working fuse to set off its charge, a radome assembly that would withstand rain erosion, and other equally difficult, abstruse, and arduous problems.

With his other hand, Colonel Eiffler appointed a small group of experts—including Dr. Martin Schilling of Redstone Arsenal—to monitor the progress of the four competing development groups, to grade their efforts, and—if possible—to keep them from falling into bushes and beartraps.

Tom Phillips, as the presentation leader for the new developmental army missile program, was spun off to head the project at Raytheon. Because it arrived on the heels of the initiation of the Sparrow production facilities, and because that program was now large, Wisenbaker again had to abandon California and return to New England.

Phillips, confronted with an impressive challenge in a new and significant area, began to organize his project team. In the earlier instance of the Sparrow, the Raytheon missile group had been like a stable boy that had ridden a two-year-old to victory at Arlington. Now, in the list against Bell Labs in a race to develop a low-altitude missile for the army, it was to ride, with more experience, in the Derby.

Much the same could be said of the firm overall. Its radar systems had extended into the nation's Weather Bureau, into special assemblies such as the navy's Tartar shipboard missile, into supporting equipment for the high-altitude army Nike, into harbor and merchant ship controls and other applications. Radars were essential to both commercial and military aircraft; they were part of strategic weapons planning. With the firm's personnel steadying at around eighteen thousand, both Adams and his top managers were kept busy balancing the Raytheon technical ability against the shifting tides of the marketplace.

One difficult though promising area was color television. Sid Standing, a valuable man at Raytheon in the thirties, had left to work for the Dutch Philips organization during the war. In 1953 he received a call from Norman Krim asking him to return and to help the cathode ray tube group solve the television problem. He returned and was impressed by the changes in the firm. His opinion of the trends in television was interesting.

"As an engineer," Standing said, "I deplored the switch of emphasis dictated by the merchandisers that changed television from a great technological search into a piece of furniture. It slowed the rate of progress and switched the emphasis of the state of the art." [71]

Standing's comments underscored the gulf between technology and entertainment. It had long existed, but for a time the introduction of mechanical marvels such as movies, radio, and then television itself had seemed to close the gap. Hollywood, in early 1954, sought to combat television by introducing wider screens, stereophonic sound, and clearer images—but it did not change its traditional westerns, its final weapon to attract audiences.[72] The television industry, whose programs were rooted in vaudeville, sports, and soap opera, hoped to spur new purchases by color sets rather than by discovering a fresh way to use a new and exciting medium.

Literature, traditionally belated in its response to events, similarly sought to succeed by repeating old themes in greater volume. A rash of atomic bomb novels, war recollections, and journalistic accounts of the past appeared. The public, in response, continued to turn away from books. A survey that spring of 1954 showed Americans reading fewer books per individual than their counterparts in Western Europe, though more books appeared in the United States than ever before.

President Eisenhower's programs, introduced in early 1954, proved intelligent and constructive. He proposed large sums to create the St. Lawrence Seaway, which would open the inland Lake ports to the ocean; to unlock the peaceful uses of atomic energy; and to spur the construction of highways. These were all intelligent, farsighted, and beneficial proposals, for they would strengthen the nation's ability to move forward.[73]

The newspapers, however, fretted for more dramatic material. They turned toward Senator McCarthy of Wisconsin and his investigation into internal subversion, and in short order blew the Senator, his subject, and his targets beyond reasonable proportions. In similar fashion television flowed into new channels to join the theater and art world; provided entertainment in the guise of news that used living subjects for its material.

To Raytheon's missile group these were events in another world; their own was exciting enough to engage their attention.

Many changes had taken place since Sanders' departure. In the wake of that event, T. C. Wisenbaker had held a talk with Charlie Adams, explained the situation and the goals of Lab 16, and concluded by bluntly asking the president if he was behind the effort. Adams, leaning forward, had said he was.

From there until the Sparrow triumph, both Lab 16 and a number of younger men had emerged. Phillips, working with Wisenbaker, proved able "to run without creating resentments. He had," Wisenbaker mused later, "a great facility for putting people at ease." [74]

He had also, working under Wisenbaker, learned some basic and important lessons. Wisenbaker did not believe in relinquishing "sound principles under pressure." The missile group had progressed, in his opinion, "along straight ways, and by being flexible enough to ride with all ensuing problems." That meant, to Wisenbaker, "that men must be strong enough to say No to their managers when they do not agree—and that includes the government."

That was a wonderful lesson for a younger man to absorb, and Phillips had some innate abilities to complement that sort of independence. One was an aptitude for making clear and concise explanations, a reflection of Wisenbaker's insistence on getting to the essence of a matter quickly. Phillips himself credits his experience in this area to his background as a teacher, but that could hardly be true, in view of the large numbers of confusing professors on the landscape.

Added together, however, it meant that Lab 16 appeared before its new judges in the army with a refreshing air of intellectual independence. Dr. Schilling, who had extensive experience with the guiles of contractors, noticed "the Raytheon men had a little light plane. If we called they would appear on a day's notice with their papers under their arms. As soon as the questions and answers were over they left; that little plane flew right back to Massachusetts. No parties; no dinners." Schilling liked that. [75]

From the first, Lab 16 did not regard the army's thirteen tasks as the end of their efforts. They would not only work on a guidance seeker and answer the thirteen tasks, but they would try to create the sort of missile system the army needed. The thirteen tasks, as leading toward such an effort, were foothills: their eyes lifted to the mountains.

They did not regard the basic problems of the army Hawk as different from the navy's Sparrow; the change would be in dimension. The Sparrow was only eight inches in diameter; the Hawk would be fourteen to sixteen inches. The components of the Sparrow were tight; the range of the Hawk would be greater.

Phillips began to repeat the Sparrow experience. That meant the creation of a complete system, including airframes. The team chose a cruciform design—four wings instead of two—with maneuvers to be managed by ailerons. The Hawk would operate on a solid fuel with its seeker in the front and a motor in the tail, the warhead near the motor. Dave Coffin, head of Lab 16, was highly enthusiastic and helpful. "That was one of Coffin's strengths," said Hamilton Hauck, "he let men run."

The effort was more of a gamble than it appeared, for Phillips had gone beyond the limits of the developmental contract Raytheon had received. From the viewpoint of the army that was a bargain. Designs, studies, tests, and experiments were conducted toward a complete systems proposal for a new army tactical weapon.

In February 1954 Phillips and Fossier explained their results and approaches to Colonel Eiffler and the army. They retired after that effort to await the results with considerable anxiety. After all, they did not know what Bell Labs had accomplished, though they had no doubt that great establishment would prove competent.

One midnight Phillips received a telephone call from Colonel Eiffler. Bell Labs, said the Colonel, had been given new responsibilities and would start work on the Nike-Hercules high-altitude missile, to be designed to carry nuclear warheads. An immense project.

Then, continued the Colonel, he had shown the Bell Lab experts the Raytheon low-altitude missile study for the Hawk. Listening intently, Phillips held his breath.

"Bell Labs," said the Colonel, "declared your proposal was better and more efficient than its own." [76] Phillips felt elation coursing through him.

As soon as the Colonel finished, Phillips called the members of his team in Massachusetts and at Point Mugu. "They—Bell Labs—put the national interest first," said Phillips later. "They were completely objective."

Fossier, when he heard the news, responded coolly, "They were right. We're ahead on low-altitude missiles."

It was great news, and Eric Levi, Don Banks, and others on the team rejoiced. It meant that Lab 16 could begin a full-fledged development effort to create an entire new system for the U.S. Army. Ahead stretched weeks, months, perhaps years of work. But for the moment they rejoiced in the fact that Raytheon had broken into the clear, had won the first of a new series of qualifying races—and Tom Phillips was to become Mr. Hawk.

\* \* \*

The achievement of Sparrow and the opportunity to build toward Hawk compared in magnitude and importance to Dr. C. G. Smith's rectifier tube and to Percy Spencer's contribution to the wartime magnetron and Fritz Gross's radar effort.

Missiles are not simply projectiles. They are vehicles that soar into the air in response to airborne intruders detected by their own instruments, that can intercept and strike such intruders without outside guidance. The Sparrow was, in early 1954, ready for production. The quantities would increase, though problems attendant upon producing such complex, compact vehicles would continue. The Hawk was not yet developed, though breadboard designs had been submitted, but Raytheon had received word to begin engineering development: make prototypes.

Both missiles were essentially defensive weapons against invasion or attack from the air. That possibility was regarded in Washington with extreme seriousness. Military analyst Hanson W. Baldwin, writing in the *Harvard Business Review* a year earlier, in 1953, had stressed the situation. "The map," said Baldwin, "has been foreshortened by space-devouring, ocean-spanning aircraft and missiles, by submarines that can . . . launch atomic-headed missiles against our coastal cities. In a strategic sense the United States occupies an insular, not a continental position today; for the first time since the Indian wars we have 'live' frontiers—frontiers of the sea and sky subject to sudden and devastating attack."

One response to that situation was an order from Washington to construct a giant early warning system stretching three thousand miles across the Canadian north: a cooperative defense network undertaken with a friendly neighbor.

But until the Sparrow was proven in the air, no low-altitude missile existed to protect the nation against low-flying planes that might penetrate existing radar defenses. The breakthrough of Sparrow was part of an extension from pulse to continuous-wave radar, and therefore one of the milestones in improving not only defense weapons, but defense itself.

In a commercial sense, the development was immense. Small missiles could be stockpiled and used in greater quantity than larger ones, were more versatile and provided Raytheon with at least the head start in a new manufacturing area of incalculable potential.

This potential appeared at a crucial time for Raytheon. On the first of May the firm appeared with the Challenger line of television sets; in June 1954 it introduced its Aristocrat. The 1954 Annual Report described, with pride, how these new models were using a twin triode miniature tube developed by the company; how a new special cathode ray color tube and new germanium diodes were being produced in pilot quantities.

The firm had also leaped ahead of the industry in volume production of junction transistors and was, therefore, well placed in the van of the transistor revolution.

Annual sales by the end of May 1954 were $177 million; profits had dropped to $2.5 million.[77] The number of employees had also dropped a bit, to seventeen thousand, but operations remained large. Yet no dividends were being paid; competition in radars and their infinite variations, tubes and their design, transistors and the applications, television, radio, marine and military instrumentation was very heavy, well financed, and demanding.

Charlie Adams had entered a tangled situation, had introduced order and built an organization. Its operations were, in most areas, well managed and efficient; stability had been achieved. The firm was beyond its wartime peak, had greatly increased its executive ranks and its abilities overall. Its financial connections were solid, its reputation sound. Adams had backed most of the projects initiated by Laurence Marshall very heavily, but he was too practical to back a losing horse forever; 1954 would prove whether Belmont was worth the time, trouble, and money it had cost.

Beyond that, the firm was working behind the scenes in computer technology that held considerable promise. Lab 30 had advanced beyond missile test-range computers to create larger and more complex computers for a wide variety of uses. That was a promising area, but it held problems as well. After all, the computer industry, though fascinating, was one in which the stakes were huge, the capital requirements heavy, and the competition fierce.

In contrast the Lab 16 effort was not only breaking new technological ground, but achieving a good profit with only a modest capital requirement. No management, asked its secret dreams, could have ordered anything better. Meanwhile, the missile men were engulfed by fascinating though tiring problems.

Fossier recalls that gyros were needed on six-inch antennas to sense and feed stabilization signals to hydraulic actuators, and that Justin

Margolskee designed these so well the firm later listed and sold them as special products. Hydraulic valves had to be built to control the actuators; none were available; the Lab built its own. Both were mechanical breakthroughs.[78]

In early summer 1954 the Sparrow III developed a tendency to veer away from instead of toward its target at altitudes of 30,000 feet. That sent waves of alarm through the military and, "for the ninth time," says Fossier, "the program seemed vitally jeopardized."

T. C. Wisenbaker called Fossier at four in the morning—an hour Wisenbaker obviously considered unimportant. What is more surprising is that Fossier didn't seem to mind either. Wisenbaker wanted recent telemetering data recorded on the Sparrow at 30,000 feet.

Fossier, who knew the circuits, the hydraulics, their susceptibility to the temperatures involved, sent the data. He also took the parts into a cold chamber and watched them, to make some observations of his own. In the course of this he spotted the defect and called Wisenbaker and was hugely pleased to have found the answer before the crew at headquarters had completed their computer run.[79] It was, in other words, a game of three-dimensional chess fascinating in its own right.

Around them the world continued to seethe. In Egypt Nasser abruptly appeared beside General Naguib and the revolution in Egypt took a more nationalistic tone; in Indo-China the French suffered a humiliating defeat at Dien Bien Phu.[80] The latter event created a crisis in France; the government fell and Mendès-France assumed power. Among his first acts was a treaty with Ho Chi Minh ceding North Vietnam to the Communists and withdrawing French forces from South Vietnam, Cambodia, and Laos.

Washington's response to rising revolutionary tides was to push the tactical arming and organization of NATO, and to create a string of defensive alliances around the world, pledging U.S. support to external aggression and internal subversion. It was, in reality, a continuation of a policy established by President Truman, but it proceeded on high levels with less attention paid to the propaganda war than in preceding U.S. international efforts.

The U.S. military program was neither small nor unimpressive. It included the construction of the U.S.S. *Nautilus*, the world's first atomic-powered submarine, which slid down the ways at Groton,

Connecticut, in September 1954; production of hydrogen bombs; and a closely coordinated drive to improve NATO by including West Germany.[81]

By virtue of Lab 16's successes, Raytheon had moved upward in this military program and became the prime contractor for the army Hawk as well as the navy Sparrow. The army missile program, though a later entry, was eventually to outdistance the Sparrow, because it involved not only the missile but its complete supportive system. That meant the firm would make radars, launchers, and loaders as well. In every sense this enlarged responsibility would carry the firm forward and make a quantum leap in terms of dollar business, once production was achieved.

In other words the two missiles and their attendant equipment would carry Raytheon as a corporation beyond the firm's publicized and more visible commercial efforts. They would prove the fulcrums upon which the firm's fortunes would turn.

It would take some time for the company to tool into these programs. The quantity of low-altitude missiles required for the far-flung defenses of the United States by its navy and army were immense; behind these giant domestic requirements loomed others overseas. National security created a curtain over this huge and important effort, however, and only the insiders in the management of Raytheon knew the extent and significance of the role the once tiny Lab 16 had assumed.

On a national effort the military modernization programs were accompanied by a series of alliances around the world. These included a mutual defense pact with Japan, and the Southeast Asia Treaty Organization that gathered together France, Australia, New Zealand, Pakistan, Thailand, and the United States against the threat of Red China in the Orient. At home President Eisenhower finally quieted the noisy, disruptive, and untidy brouhaha that had grown around Senator McCarthy of Wisconsin.

McCarthy's challenge, in the end, centered around the constitutional question of whether a Senate committee could force the executive branch to hand over documents regarding individuals, their backgrounds, and activities. The press of the nation was bitterly against the Senator and personalized the argument to such an extent its intellectual essence was never clear to most Americans. In the end the Senate avoided the issue by censuring the Senator.

With domestic arguments reduced and the strength of the nation being improved, its international position clarified, the year 1954 ended on a note of optimism on all sides.

The firm, now listed on the Big Board, created a new facility at Wayland for its engineering groups and formed a Raytheon Charitable Foundation. Percy Spencer was nearly sixty, his contract was extended. That brought up the question of retirements, and a mandatory age of sixty-five was set. That left a lot of time for Adams; he was only forty-four, but he was aware that the percentage of older employees had increased. Raytheon had to improve its pensions. Adams believed a corporation should operate on a large scale as an enlightened citizen on a small. That meant not only being of New England, but of national value; not only national but international.

Early in 1955 Adams discussed a Raytheon participation with Firar, a small Italian firm, manufacturer of electronic components, and also told the directors that the Missile & Radar Division—a new title for Lab 16—would open a test site at White Sands, New Mexico. That was, of course, the army location where the Hawk would undergo its trials.

In addition discussions were underway with Minneapolis-Honeywell to enter the computer field. In April 1955, Raytheon and Honeywell concluded an agreement to create the Datamatic Corporation. Essentially Raytheon would provide technology, valued at $1 million, for which it would receive 47,650 shares of Datamatic stock. Honeywell would hold 52,500 shares of Datamatic common and 18,975 shares of Datamatic preferred, and put up $1.4 million in cash.[82]

Thereafter each partner would put in capital proportionately, as needed. The first party refusing to put up capital (up to $6 million) would thereby give the other party the right to buy it out. On the other hand, if one party wanted to sell, it had to inform the other and give it the right to meet any offer minus 10 percent on a thirty-day notice. These clauses were later to prove crucial, but at the time all that was clear was that computers had tremendous commercial potential. Raytheon entered that promising market with its technology as a 40 percent partner with a well-established and successful firm. Cap Smith, who had played a significant role in both developing the computers and working out the new arrangement, joined Honeywell as a vice president.

It was in this atmosphere of quickened business that Adams also received a proposition from Lockheed. Lockheed chairman Robert E. Gross and the firm's president, Courtland Gross, wanted to diversify into electronics. They told Adams they thought Raytheon—shorn of its missile and military equipment groups—would be an ideal vehicle.

"In other words," Adams said after several discussions, "you only want the apples and the pears. But Raytheon is a whole basket of fruit." The talks continued and he studied the proposal, but was close to a refusal when he had lunch with Al Gibbons, a senior partner of Hornblower & Weeks, Raytheon's financial advisors.

Adams was surprised when Gibbons began to argue that the Lockheed proposal should be snapped up. He mentioned his growing reluctance, and was both shocked and angered when Gibbons said bluntly, "You'd better make the deal. Raytheon can't survive on its own."

The more he thought about that, the more Adams' anger grew. Finally he went to J. T. Walker, head of Hornblower & Weeks, and said Raytheon could not keep a financial advisor that had no faith in the firm's management or its future. In other words, he fired Hornblower & Weeks. That accomplished, he rejected the Lockheed offer.[83]

The fact was, at the end of May 1955, that Raytheon's annual sales had risen slightly to $182 million, but its net profits had soared to $4.5 million—almost double those of the year before. Personnel remained the same, at seventeen thousand, but the accounts of the firm showed it in a stronger position.[84]

The same could be said of the nation as a whole. Business income was up almost a third from that of 1954, the year before.[85] Washington had announced its nuclear stockpile was four times that of the USSR; Dr. Jonas Salk was hailed for discovering a vaccine effective against the scourge of polio; and a greatly increased number of business mergers took place.

It was galling, in the midst of these breakthroughs, for Raytheon to watch the growth of television and to realize that its well-engineered sets were simply not selling in the marketplace. The hypnosis of television had gripped the land; the previous autumn had seen the first televised Cabinet meeting; people flocked to buy sets. The reasons for Belmont's difficulties, on examination, could be traced to the intense, well-funded, and well-established market position of the giant manufacturers such as RCA and others. Charlie Adams began to look toward the exit on that particular venture, but Dave Schultz remained hopeful.

Belmont, however, was clearly lagging. The Raytheon Distributing Company—the marketing arm for Belmont-Raytheon television—had to be liquidated. Adams' comments over the cadaver were bitter. "It lost money for every month of its existence except for the first few," he said, "and these losses far exceeded its capital investment. It didn't even pay for the overhead of its offices; it did not extend its license into other electrical appliances; couldn't even pay for the sets it received; its accounts receivable situation was bad." [86] Youthful attorney Charlie Resnick, who had been pulled into the Belmont situation at the same time as Argento, and who was familiar with it, thought Adams was impressive. He was sure other moves would follow.

Meanwhile the new Missile & Radar Division evoked an entirely different reaction from Adams and the military. In the spring of 1955 the navy asked Raytheon to demonstrate the Sparrow as a surface-to-air missile, the surface being the U.S.S. *Norton Sound.*

To test the effectiveness of the Sparrow, the Navy flew drone planes at altitudes of 500 to 15,000 feet. The twelve-foot-long Sparrows, each carrying a sixty-five-pound warhead and weighing 376 pounds, were fired from a Terrier launcher, and proceeded faster than sound straight to their targets.

In the meantime, the McDonnell F-3H aircraft was now equipped to carry Sparrow III operationally and production was started at Lowell, Massachusetts, at the rate of one hundred a month. The sales of Raytheon overall took a spurt as abrupt as the missile itself. Men in other parts of the company suddenly became aware of the names of Coffin, Wisenbaker, Phillips, and their associates.

The world does not upend however; it turns. Wallace Gifford, the Submarine Signal executive who had served under Mr. Fay years before and had supervised the integration of his group into Raytheon, passed away, leaving a vacancy on the board. Charlie Adams made

Percy Spencer a director. That pleased many inside the firm. Other changes took place. Vice Admiral E. L. Cochrane, a director for many years, retired to become chairman of the Maritime Commission and was replaced by Robert Cutler, a Boston banker who had served as an assistant to President Eisenhower on the National Security Council.

The Raytheon board consisted, after these changes, of ten men in mid-1955. They were an interesting mix. The senior director was Billy Gammell, who had backed and helped guide the firm from its inception. Carl Gilbert, another director, had known the firm since the thirties. Other directors included Robert H. I. Goddard, a financier; Stanley P. Lovell of World War II OSS fame; William Raye; George Langreth, a New York investment banker; and Robert Cutler. Only Adams himself, Dave Schultz, and Percy Spencer represented operating management.

It all looked very solid, very permanent, and so it was. But it was not so solid that change could not enter to alter its climate and its pattern—no company ever gets that solid. As usual, the change came in an unexpected form.

"I suppose," Dave Schultz once told Norman Krim, "that if you put every vice president on a psychiatrist's couch, he would confess that his secret desire is to become a president." Whether that is true or not is debatable; what was true was that Dave Schultz harbored such a desire.

Nobody had suspected, for no man was more loyal to Laurence Marshall in his days as president of Raytheon, or to Charlie Adams, than Dave Schultz. Quiet and able, he commanded everyone's respect and never betrayed, by the slightest tremor, further or higher ambitions than to be Raytheon's senior financial man.

Some believe that a part of the reason for Schultz's dissatisfaction was in the Belmont situation. He had a deep interest and great faith in the television venture, and its failure to succeed had been a serious disappointment to him. He had, after all, managed to extend its life beyond its rightful span because he had believed in it so deeply. Now it was obvious that Adams was going to get rid of Belmont. While Adams looked in these directions, Schultz received a tempting offer.

It came from the Allan B. DuMont Company and offered Dave Schultz the post of president. In such a post he could prove what he believed, that a small entry could win in the television sweepstakes.

He went to Adams and asked his opinion, and Adams refused to give it. He said simply, "Dave, that's a very fine offer. I would be the last man in the world to stand in your way. You'll have to make up your own mind." [87]

Schultz hesitated for weeks, and Adams put no pressure on him whatever. That would have conflicted with his sense of fair play.

Finally, two days before Christmas—that inevitable season of corporate shifts—Schultz sent Adams a letter of resignation. It was very simply written; the tone was of one old friend to another:

> I want you to know [he said in part] that the most pleasant memories of my many years with the Company will be the recent ones of my close association with you. I am happy that I am leaving the Company in the greatly improved conditions which have taken place in its affairs since you took over the leadership of the business, under very trying circumstances. I appreciate the opportunity you gave me to be associated with you in the success of the Company.
>
> Please convey to my friends on the Board of Directors my deepest respect and thanks for their confidence in me.
>
> I sincerely look forward to seeing you often in the future and to our continued personal friendship. With all best wishes. . . .
>
> DAVE.[88]

The announcement of Schultz's departure from Raytheon appeared in the financial pages shortly after New Year's Day 1956. Among those who perused it with interest was a short, bright-eyed man who was just completing a course in advanced management at Harvard's Graduate School of Business Administration, in Cambridge.

He picked up the phone, dialed Raytheon, and Lillian Ottenheimer, Charlie Adams' secretary answered. She had received very specific instructions and thought she knew how to follow them.[89]

"We will be deluged," Adams had warned. "Have them send in their résumés. I don't want to see any of them, or talk to them on the phone."

She told the caller to mail in his résumé, but his response came before she concluded. "I don't want to do that," he said, "I want to find out if there's a job open, and if there's a job open, the sort of job it is."

Lillian couldn't answer that, and he continued before she could cut him off. "I think it's unfair to expect anyone to send in a résumé without even knowing if there's an opening. And," he concluded, "if there is an opening, it's unfair to conceal it. That means it's not open to everyone qualified."

In the space of a couple of minutes he had turned her around, made her feel their procedure was incorrect. That upset her. She took his name and number, said she would try to find the answers and call him back. Then she walked in to Mr. Adams and described her experience. He listened with interest. He respected Lillian, knew she had considerable experience in dealing with all sorts of callers. Anyone who could so swiftly penetrate her defenses must be extraordinary. He arranged to have Percy Spencer talk to the man. Gratified, Lillian returned to her desk, made her promised call, and was very courteously thanked. She put the receiver down with a smile, stared at the man's name to fix it in her memory: Harold S. Geneen.[90]


He started late and was slow maturing. His first regular job was as a page on the floor of the New York Stock Exchange. From there he went to NYU nights for eight years, working his way as a salesman and finally a bookkeeper. In 1935 he received his degree, applied to Mr. Lehnard, a senior partner with Lybrand, Ross Bros. & Co. for a job, setting his figure at $20 a week.

"We can't pay that," Mr. Lehnard said, and Geneen's heart sank. *I can't get by on less,* he thought. "We'll start you as an extra—at $30 a week," Lehnard concluded. "That's our minimum." [91]

He lived out of New York for the next seven years—out of a suitcase, going wherever Lybrand, Ross sent him. In those days employees did not express their preferences. When the war reached the United States, he volunteered for the navy, having heard they wanted CPA's. "They were delighted," he says, "until I put my glasses on to sign the papers. Then they stopped me. If I was unfit for sea duty, I was unacceptable to the navy." He went back to Lybrand, Ross.

On the American Can account, learning they had the task of making naval torpedoes from drawings only, he worked up a financial and production plan. American Can, delighted, offered him a job, and he found himself linked with Bill Cameron, an American Can vice president. He spent nights in lower berths, traveling between St. Louis, Chicago, and Washington, toiling with unions, learning about production and ad hoc wartime regulations. "It was fast and complex," he says, "but we did a good job for the navy." That was when he grew up.

Afterward there was a letdown. Geneen produced plans for diversification, but at American Can "they only wanted to go back to making cans." He moved on.

He lasted a while at Bell & Howell, but that grew confining. Then he landed at Jones & Laughlin, the steelmaker, as controller. They were a new breed to him: steel men. "I noticed they had stupendous cigar bills," he says. He was astonished. Investigating, "I learned that whenever a new record was set, cigars were handed out—and there were all sorts of records. Records for each machine output, for long tons, for drawn wire, for pig iron, for each type of steel—and so on."

He had not spotted the item by accident; he had learned what many numbers experts never seem to grasp: that there are realities behind the figures. "A controller," he says, "is in a position to control inside finances. He may not be operations, but he can analyze what operations are successful and where weaknesses exist. If he is good, he can find new tools for managers, new ways to improve certain areas."

Casting about to improve Jones & Laughlin, his eye fell on General Motors. He persuaded the management of that giant to let him study their methods for three weeks. He visited GM factories and traced the production flow, department by department. Near the end of the line, "I looked at a small casting department. The man in charge of cutting holes had a budget that showed the cost of cutting, plus time."

Back at Jones & Laughlin he introduced these long lines of budgets and controls to a strip mill, had the satisfaction of seeing savings begin to appear. Raised to vice president, he began to change the internal climate of the firm. Calling in the Psychological Testing Service of Pittsburgh, he had the controller's group evaluated, while denying the obvious purpose involved. "Tests are only indicators," he says, "they are not conclusions."

Simultaneously he argued the firm should diversify, improve its investment image, expand beyond the steel industry. Again, he ran into a frosty reception and soon found himself in trouble with the chief executive of Jones & Laughlin. "He found me hard to endure," Geneen recalls. "By the time I went to Harvard to take that course in Advanced Management, I knew I wasn't going back to Jones & Laughlin—and they knew it, too."

He had dinner with Percy Spencer at the Ritz in downtown Boston, and the older man saw a flinty quality he liked. Then Adams talked to him. Adams himself was overburdened. The firm's government business was growing to immense proportions, requiring frequent trips to Washington. NATO was knocking on the Raytheon door, and this multinational organization required attention on a near-diplomatic level. Internally the Schultz financial systems had been stretched to their limits; better controls were needed. Adams needed an operations man, someone to mind the store. Geneen, eager and experienced, might be the man. Adams listened to him, turned possibilities around in his mind. They were the same age: that helps in a working relationship.

While he thought it through, Adams sent Geneen around to other men and checked their reactions. Roger Damon, who had risen to high levels at the First National Bank of Boston, was enthusiastic.[92] Dr. Edward Bowles, sitting in his consultant's office at Raytheon, was converted from judge to advocate when Geneen turned to him and said, "Do you really think I ought to take this job?" [93]

Once decided, Adams did not stint. He created the post of executive vice president for Geneen, started him at $50,000 a year, and set aside a handsome stock option.[94]

"I knew he would need a lot of room," he said later, "and I determined to give him time to run—and all the room he needed." [95] He did not realize that after years of frustration, there would never be as much room as Harold Geneen needed.

Change was in the air, and not only at Raytheon. Changes in Egypt were at the center of new formations in the Middle East. The Sudan broke free; an Arab League was created. The United States and Britain, alarmed, issued a statement that they stood together regarding that area, and the USSR piously warned that the dispatch of western troops would be a violation of the UN charter.

In Moscow, at the Twentieth Communist Party Congress, Nikita

Khrushchev, emerging as a new strong man, detailed the crimes of Stalin.[96] His speech, hours long, was marked by emotional outbursts from the delegates, sent waves of confusion coursing through not only the Soviet Communist Party but the satellites as well.

In the United States waves of dissension, violence, and argument erupted in the wake of Supreme Court decisions outlawing racial segregation in schools, interstate transportation, and other areas. Yet statistics showed bulging prosperity. Stock prices rose on a wave of new investors, automobile production reached new highs, crops broke all records. Evidences of large sums were apparent on all sides, were reflected in the opulent entertainments: *The King and I*, converted to film by Hollywood, cost $7 million; *Ten Commandments*, $13.5 million; *War and Peace*, $6.5 million.[97]

The government spent huge sums, but not all the channels into which they flowed were visible to the ordinary citizen except in their effect. Electronic weapons, for instance, extended far beyond former categories. The War of the Wizards had never stopped; it had simply been shrouded from average view by security regulations.

One evidence of this was the protest of the USSR against the U.S. practice of floating balloons, equipped with cameras, through Soviet skies. Other, far more advanced vehicles, were also being built. Hamilton Hauck, rising rapidly in the U.S. Navy, had been assigned to oversee the progress of many such efforts, termed "countermeasures."

The systems used to stairstep Raytheon toward the Sparrow and Hawk missiles had, as separate components, a variety of other uses. For instance, a microwave altimeter measured clearances between an aircraft and the ground or water. In zero visibility situations this instrument was invaluable. In its development Raytheon bested RCA and received a large volume contract; the development was tied in to the automatic pilot and other instrumentation.[98]

A larger engineering effort by this time was the Hawk missile. At White Sands, New Mexico, a strip of desert larger than the combined states of Connecticut and Rhode Island closed by the San Andres mountains in the west and the Sacramento mountains in the east, prototype Hawks were tested again and again under the eyes of Ellis Beymer of Raytheon, while Tom Phillips, 2,100 miles away in Massachusetts, waited by the telephone for results.

The tests had proceeded through a rigorous series of flights guided by automatic pilots, controlled only by instruments that first prove the airframe, the rocket motor, and the control system. The goal was to create a missile fully self-guided toward a target.

In June 1956—twenty-three months after the effort had begun—Beymer jubilantly telephoned Phillips that the new Hawk, flying the first fully guided flight with a seeker, had sought, tracked, and scored a direct hit on the target drone, sending it down in flames.

Neither the leader of the team nor its members will ever forget the exultation that lifted them at this news; their long and grueling effort could never seem pale or distant in retrospect.[99]

Against the strain and challenge of their multidimensional effort, the movement in the executive suite of Raytheon seemed far away, relatively unimportant. That indifference was, of course, unreal. The arrival of Geneen would affect them, as it would affect the firm, jar them from their absorption, and force them to take more notice of the corporate structure in which they functioned.

By the end of May 1956, Raytheon was on the edge of a huge upward swing, but the Annual Report figures gave no evidence of this. Sales were $175 million; earnings after taxes a little over $2 million.[100] On the surface, this performance looked less impressive than that of the previous year. If figures alone were the yardstick, Raytheon was sliding backward. In this instance the figures were accurate; their story was misleading.

The company was on the edge of a giant leap. Negotiations were underway to lease a very large plant from Textron at Andover, Massachusetts, for the production of Hawk missiles and Hawk ground equipment. The government plans for Raytheon on Hawk were of sufficient scale that Engine Charley Wilson, Secretary of Defense, himself reviewed the proposed plant, to see if it would meet the expected need. Dr. Martin Schilling recalls that Wilson at first refused to approve the plan because the Andover plant had several stories. "In Detroit we long ago decided on one-floor plants," he growled, "several stories are several bottlenecks." Alternate facilities, however, were scarce. The services wanted the missiles to fill a dangerous defense gap. His aides waited and then presented the plan to Engine Charley again; he reluctantly gave his o.k. "Later," Schilling recalled, "we learned the old man was right." [101]

At the same time Raytheon obtained land near Santa Barbara,

California, and drew plans to create a special new plant to meet
air force needs for electronic countermeasures equipment so secret
they could not be described even to the directors.[102]

A steady drain stopped when Adams found a buyer for Belmont:
the Admiral Corporation. The terms were not entirely to his liking:
private-label contracts with Montgomery Ward and others had to be
filled; accounts receivable had to be straightened and inventories taken.
But Belmont had cost Raytheon another $2 million in loans during fis-
cal 1956 alone, and both the president and the directors of Raytheon
were greatly relieved to be rid of it.[103]

Henry Argento, on the other hand, was bitterly disappointed.
He had worked hard and not succeeded in turning the venture around.
That alone was a bitter draught. In the end, he had sought to protect
some of the executives of Belmont, had assured them that Raytheon
or the new owners would retain them. Adams said, "Admiral refused
to take many employees." With most of his men cast adrift, Argento
came back to Massachusetts but would soon resign to join Philco.
Television was in his blood.

Adams did not, however, stop with pruning; he grafted some new
international branches to the corporate tree. One was a joint venture
called Raytheon Canada, Ltd., which entered the electronics industry
of that country with a contract in hand from the Canadian government to design, produce, and install air-traffic radars in that country.
Another constituted an expansion of Raytheon's Italian activities.

The expansion was based, in large part, upon the considerable
promise then associated with "the Italian miracle"—the economic boom
then in progress in Italy. Dr. Carlo Calosi, who had become a valued
member of Raytheon's management team, had spent three years in
Italy watching and guiding the development of Microlambda, a firm
owned by the Italian government, acting through a larger venture
called Finnmeccanica, which held a Raytheon license and was using
Raytheon technology.

Since Microlambda was doing well with Raytheon products, and
especially since both the Italian government and La Centrale, a large
electric utility in Milan, were prepared to undertake the major share
of capitalization, it seemed logical for Raytheon to accept a 14 percent ownership for its technology in a new venture called L'Ettronica
Sicula S.p.A. Elsi, as it was called, was created to push forward the
long-neglected industrialization of southern Italy. For that reason it

would be located in Palermo, Sicily. Dr. Calosi, who would watch its development and progress in addition to his other activities, was made a Raytheon vice president in recognition of both his added responsibilities and the potential inherent in this expansion. That required another security clearance for Calosi, for he was still an Italian citizen, though he planned to become an American.[104]

Then there was the Datamatic Corporation, the joint venture between Raytheon and Honeywell. More capital had been required, which Raytheon had met, and the new Datamatic 1000—widely touted in advertisements and brochures throughout the business community—was due to appear in September 1956. Adams had been assured its prospects were bright; he certainly hoped so. The computer industry had captured the imagination of the world. Giants were entering the field, which consisted of units that ranged the scale of scientific effort. The Datamatic 1000 was designed for corporate use.

All this was explained by Adams to a group of about ninety Raytheon executives, called for a special and unprecedented meeting. For the first time the Raytheon top management explained the firm's overall position to middle management, produced a five-year projection of what it hoped the future would hold, and introduced Harold Geneen, the new operations boss. The sense of change in the air was almost physical.


Nineteen fifty-six was an election year, but there seemed little intellectual difference in the positions of the major political parties. The nation was well satisfied with President Eisenhower, whose "atoms for peace" program seemed unassailable. It was, during the summer and early autumn, a season for entertainment and relaxation for most.

The movies produced *Around the World in 80 Days;* Broadway mounted *My Fair Lady;* Elvis Presley appeared.[105]

In the middle of summer Nasser of Egypt seized control of the Suez Canal and Britain, the United States, and France took economic reprisals. Secretary of State Dulles announced the United States would no longer pay toward the huge Aswan Dam project.[106] A crisis began to build in the Middle East; British families were airlifted out and maneuvering began. This was trouble for the West, but the USSR had troubles to match. Bloody riots tore through Poland and were as bloodily suppressed. In their train demonstrators arose in Hungary, demanding the removal of Soviet troops from the country, the release of Cardinal Mindszenty, and the return of Imre Nagy to power.[107]

Geneen began by holding meetings and asking questions. In the beginning, these were financial: the controller's office was asked for books, accounts, records, proofs. The meetings and the questions would last for hours, well into the night. First the financial men and then the engineers learned to their amazement that he could read pages of statistics as other men read prose. Then he could, from memory, cite items and the pages upon which they appeared.[108]

His hours threw everyone off balance. Lillian Ottenheimer, whose desk was strategically located between Adams' office and Geneen's, noticed that he arrived late in the morning, started slowly, and gathered steam as he proceeded. By six o'clock in the evening he was in mid-swing, and there would be a group of men waiting to see him in response to his summons. Percy Spencer called him the night superintendent.[109]

Some people regarded him as pure phenomenon, but that estimate was misplaced. Geneen is a product of New York City as definitely as Adams is a product of New England. It was simply that many at Raytheon had never before been exposed face-to-face to the New York style and its disjointed hours, its startling immediacy and indifference to matters beyond the subject at hand.

For Geneen the subject was earnings per share. He harped on that theme. At the same time he began to change the controller's department, the area he considered crucial. He began at the top by moving Al Reed, the former Raytheon controller, to the post of treasurer and hired two new men to be assistant treasurers. Then he persuaded George Ingram, Jr., controller of Riegel Paper Company, to join Raytheon in the spring as controller; hired L. D. Webster, the controller of Boston Woven Hose, to join Raytheon as assistant controller; and transferred one of Raytheon's former assistant controllers to the post of manager of data processing.[110] This was, of course, merely the prelude to full-scale shifts in the corporate orchestra. Flesh peddlers, or management personnel experts, as they prefer to be called, were sent across the landscape to fill other Geneen orders for further changes he had in mind.

\*        \*        \*

The year 1956 came to an untidy close. In late October Israel, acting in concert with France and Britain, invaded Egypt.[111] The following day the Soviet Union invaded Hungary. When Britain and France bombed Egyptian air bases and the British landed paratroops, a wave of angry protest erupted in London, Paris, New York, and Washington. President Eisenhower broke with Britain and France on this issue, and the USSR, while its tanks rumbled through Budapest, threatened a rocket attack against the two western powers.[112]

In this atmosphere the U.S. elections were held and President Eisenhower was returned to office handily, though his party lost and Democrats retained control of both houses of Congress.[113]

When the air cleared in late November 1956, a UN force had been sent to keep the peace in the Middle East. Britain, France, and Israel withdrew with empty hands. A Soviet veto prevented any UN force from coming to the aid of Hungary [114] and thousands fled from that land to the West; more thousands died or were imprisoned by the Soviets.

Other results were mixed. Anthony Eden, the British prime minister, was ruined by the outcome. France was embittered. The Soviets were reinforced in their control over Eastern Europe. The hope of many captive nations that the United States would lead a "crusade" to liberate them was demolished; the rhetoric of Secretary of State Dulles was markedly reduced.


At the very end of the year 1956 Raytheon emerged with a seven-months Annual Report, having decided to change its fiscal year to match the calendar. The change, which measurably regularizes the annals of the company, was taken at the suggestion of Geneen. His eye was turned toward the exchanges, their analysts, and their preference for reports that make industry-wide comparisons easier to draw.

The truncated Annual of December 31, 1956, provides a peephole into the changes at the firm. Sales had reached $111 million; profits were only $655,000—but the backlog of government orders had soared to over $250 million, the highest in the firm's history.[115]

The phenomenon deserves a close look. The Missile & Radar Division, while eyes had been focused on newcomer Geneen, had created an inner company revolution whose effects were felt through all sectors. The microwave and power tube labs had, as a result of working with the missile groups, developed new families of tubes that extended the range, versatility, and power of radars and communications instruments as well as missiles. The same sort of lift, expansion, and extensions were reflected in the equipment division ranks. Their technicians created bombing radars for the new long-range B-52's, the B-58 Hustlers; "countermeasures" had been spun off at Santa Barbara; extensions had been made into air-traffic control and Weather Bureau radars. But the hub of the government business was, of course, the Sparrow III and the Hawk. The Hawk, developed entirely inside the firm at the bargain basement figure of $20 million to that point, had been proven in prototype. At the start of 1957 there was no question that Raytheon had attained a developmental lead in low-altitude missiles comparable to its jump in magnetrons and shipborne radars during World War II.

It was Harold Geneen's great good fortune to appear as the new management star of Raytheon just as the firm had completed a remarkable intellectual and technological effort and was in position to begin reaping its harvest. His appearance, moreover, was enhanced by the extraordinary visibility Adams had provided him, which included election as a director of the firm early in 1957.[116]

Geneen replaced William Raye, who retired. He joined the Raytheon board at the same time as Robert W. Stoddard, president of the Wyman-Gordon Co. of Worcester, who himself had replaced Robert Cutler. Mr. Cutler had been recalled to Washington, to serve President Eisenhower as a Special Assistant.[117]

In one leap, therefore, from the springboard provided by Charlie Adams and Raytheon, Geneen moved from the relative obscurity of a Jones & Laughlin vice president and controller, to the top level of one of New England's largest and most prestigious enterprises. This brought him to the attention of great financial institutions and men of national stature. The truncated Annual Report as of December 31, 1956, added to the impression that he had arrived to bring improvements when it devoted a special section to Geneen's program of "decentralizing the Controller's office and extending controls down through the divisions; developing detailed analytic reports and revising, restaffing many areas."

*     *     *

During the spring of 1957 President Eisenhower worked to over-come the confusion created by the Suez and Hungary incidents. He proposed a new doctrine in which the United States would come to the aid of any Middle Eastern state threatened by attack—provided that aid was requested. He moved to strengthen the resources of NATO, as assurance to the western nations, and especially Britain and France, that the United States would support them militarily against Soviet aggression.[118]

That was not a matter that could be resolved overnight. The British government had been gravely weakened as a result of Suez, and Anthony Eden had resigned.[119] His place as prime minister was taken by Harold Macmillan, who insisted upon a face-to-face meeting before proceeding on any further assumptions of U.S. support. That meeting did not take place until mid-March 1957, and centered around the question of U.S. guided missiles. At its conclusion President Eisenhower agreed that these would be made available to the British and that NATO would be strengthened.

The subject of missiles had also grown very important inside Raytheon. Al Miccioli, who had recently joined the firm, found the climate surprising—"a new world." Unlike many newcomers he could make that sort of judgment from an informed viewpoint, for he had experienced the world of electronics quite fully.

Miccioli, who had a bachelor's degree in electrical engineering from Cooper Union and later earned an M.A. at Columbia, was a World War II veteran, had worked for several small electronic firms, shared in the development of FM radio, and designed instrument testing equipment before going into business for himself in 1954. As one-quarter owner of an enterprise whose four partners each had an equal vote, he had learned something about management as well as business in general. His entry into the design-testing group of Hawk had been in the nature of starting all over again, on a level far below being president of his own venture.

Interviewed by Tom Phillips and then John Farrington, who was a tough examiner, Miccioli started at a modest $8,000 a year, far less than he considered appropriate and certainly less than he had hoped. His misgivings had not been entirely financial; he had always believed he would be "lost" in a large firm. To his surprise, he found the Missile & Radar Division of Raytheon operating like a small, very close-knit firm. He was plunged, at the start, into the new areas of electronic countermeasures—areas unknown to the state of the art—and found himself on new electronic frontiers. "Dig in," Phillips told him, and Miccioli unexpectedly began to enjoy himself.[120]

But if the Missile & Radar Division appeared to have the climate of a small enterprise to Miccioli at that moment, the fact was that it was growing into a huge enterprise and growing fast. On the organization chart the Missile & Radar Division was headed by Dave Coffin. Beneath his name were two boxes. Wisenbaker, as head of the Sparrow program was in one, and Phillips, as head of Hawk in the other. Above Coffin's box was a line leading to Captain David Hull, vice president in charge of the entire equipment division, which consisted of many rows of boxes and titles. In turn, Hull's box led to the new executive vice president, Harold Geneen.

The men of the Missile & Radar Division suspected that the high technology in which they were engaged was a little over Captain Hull's head, but that did not really bother them until the Captain made a decision regarding the future Sparrow III production. It was a decision that clearly limited the potential growth of the Missile & Radar Division; it clapped a ceiling on its production—and an implied judgment upon them.

The situation arose when the navy selected Sparrow III as its operational air-to-air missile. Previously, the navy had awarded Sperry a contract to produce the Sparrow I, and had funded a $40-million production plant at Bristol, Tennessee. When that contract ran out, the navy transferred the Bristol plant to Raytheon for Sparrow III. The Missile & Radar Division, originally exultant at this coup, was dashed to discover Captain Hull believed it already overburdened and overloaded, and decided to give Sperry a license to produce Sparrow III, and to continue its operations at the Bristol plant.

When Coffin indignantly brought that verdict back to Wisenbaker and Phillips, they were dismayed. They decided to appeal to higher authority, and took their case in to Harold Geneen, the new executive vice president. It would have taken a man far less alert than Harold Geneen not to have seen the invisible storm flags flying over their heads. Geneen listened sympathetically and took note of Phillips' relative youth: he was twenty years younger than Wisenbaker and twenty-three years younger than Coffin. After hearing them out, he agreed that, if they said so, the missiles group could handle Sparrow III production in Bristol, and promised to push that arrangement.[121]

Soon afterward Rogers Hamel and Ed Dashefsky, production chiefs at Lowell, assigned a team to go to Bristol, and projected Raytheon production of Sparrows turned toward a quantum increase. These moves marched briskly. When youthful Joe Alibrandi, leading a troop of advance scouts to Bristol, arrived on the scene, he was met by Charles Rockwell, the Sperry plant manager, who was astonished at the announcement the plant was being taken over.

"Over my dead body," Rockwell said grimly, and reached for the phone.[122] He called his headquarters and learned the truth with dismay. A short time later Hamel and Dashefsky's men created what they dubbed the Green Wall concept—a series of wall boards they moved forward, section by section, to convert what Alibrandi jubilantly called a "beautiful modern plant" into another production center for Sparrow III and the Missile & Radar Division.

Meanwhile Adams was busy on other, even larger problems. The Raytheon V loan credits were increased to $35 million, but the firm was still pressed for capital to continue its expansions. One area of special pressure had arisen, moreover, that called for a quick solution: Datamatic.

Honeywell, majority owner of Datamatic, had brought out its computer and made several important sales. That was good. But its entry into the field alerted IBM, the industry leader—and that was bad. IBM produced a competitive machine and sent its extensive sales organization to push Datamatic's head under the water; Honeywell reviewed its program. Its management emerged with a more ambitious plan—one that called upon Raytheon to put up, in addition to the stream of eight chunks of $500,000 it had already put in the pot, an additional $8 million.[123]

"We had little choice," Adams said. "We didn't have that kind of money at the time. The game had grown too large for us; it was obvious we had better sell." [124]

Adams talked to Geneen and showed him the Datamatic agreement. Both men were aware that its terms allowed Honeywell to take Raytheon's interest in proportion to Raytheon's refusal to put up its share of new capital. "That would reduce, in this instance, Raytheon's participation in Datamatic to eight or ten percent," Geneen says, "and make its previous investment a total loss." [125] He was horrified, but Adams, who could easily have made a fortune as a great poker player, appeared calm as a stone.

That calm was lit by inner fires, however, when Geneen returned from a trip to Minneapolis to report that Honeywell's managers, asked to bid on Raytheon's share of Datamatic, had offered $300,000. Adams' anger ran deep, but as usual he kept it mostly to himself, and said little. Geneen, on the other hand, was more vocal, and a number of Raytheon executives—including Paul Hannah—became aware of the problem.

It was a problem that fit as neatly inside Adams' experience as an investment banker as did the operations of the controller's office for Geneen. While the executive vice president toiled with his controls, budgets, forecasts, and estimates, therefore, Adams began to call on his old friends in the financial community. He dropped in at Paine, Webber, who heard him with close attention and deep interest.[126]

Far from being dismayed, they chuckled at the news that Honeywell had turned such a grasping response to Raytheon's candor, and said they'd see if some other, more reasonable purchasers could be found. Since Adams stressed the need for speed, they came back very quickly. No immediate buyer was discovered searching the computer landscape for a large interest in a going venture. But Paine, Webber thought it could put together about $2.5 million toward the proposed Datamatic purchase.

Some men, offered immediate release from great pressure, would have taken this much and felt well ahead—in fact, would have been well ahead. But Charlie Adams had learned enough to know that he had an excellent and marketable commodity in hand. He thought he could do better, so he thanked his friends at Paine, Webber and went to New York, a city he disliked, but one that contained investment groups more expansive in outlook than those in Boston. Once there, he dropped in and talked to Bear, Stearns & Co., an old-line, highly respected firm. He went through the drill again and found them very interested indeed.

All this took time. Searches had to be made, estimates drawn up, people contacted, the computer industry assessed from a new viewpoint. In Minneapolis the Honeywell management, aware that Adams had been angered and was offended by their original offer of $300,000, raised the figure—to $400,000. The chief financial officer of Honeywell, anxious to conclude a matter that created problems in Minneapolis also, kept calling for an appointment to discuss and end the issue.

Finally, Si Lewis, a senior partner at Bear, Stearns, called Adams and said he thought he could put together a group to match the Paine, Webber figure of $2.5 million for Datamatic—but he was not sure. He needed more time. Adams was, therefore, better off than before, but still not out of the woods. At that juncture the chief financial officer of Honeywell called and pressed to come to Massachusetts. Memorial Day was near, and Adams had determined it would not find him in the office, but on the water. He invited Honeywell's man to join him on his boat on Memorial Day, hoping that in the interim the Bear, Stearns effort would succeed.

But when Memorial Day arrived, although it found Adams on his boat, he was still waiting for Bear, Stearns' call. He cast off with his wife aboard and headed toward a rendezvous to pick up Mr. Wilson of Honeywell, his humor by no means as sunny as the day. Finally he veered off course and sailed in to a small pier where he had never before stopped. Striding ashore, he marched up to a farmhouse and talked his way inside and to a telephone.

"After many struggles with a local operator," he said, "I succeeded in putting through a number of complicated calls. Finally I located Lewis, who was himself relaxing at the nineteenth hole of a New Jersey golf and country club." Anxiously he asked Lewis how he was progressing on putting together a group.

"We haven't yet found the right parties," Lewis said, his voice coming faintly over the wire, and Adams' heart sank. "But," Lewis continued, "we'll take another $2.5 million for our own account."

The day brightened magically. Adams put the receiver down with a singing heart, thanked the farm family profusely with many chuckles, and rushed back to his boat. Sailing toward the rendezvous with Wilson, a line on Adams' boat flapped loose and promptly became fouled in the propellor. Adams stripped to his trunks, put a knife in his teeth, and lowered himself over the side into the water; sawed away to part that line while Mrs. Adams leaned over, watching, bursting with laughter.

They finally reached the rendezvous and Al Wilson of Honeywell clambered aboard. Adams watched him, savoring every minute. He saw to it that Wilson was made comfortable and had a drink in his hand, and was completely relaxed. Then Adams waited.

Wilson's patience gave way first. "Well," he said, "have you found a buyer?"

Adams, impassive, said quietly, "We have found a buyer."

Wilson's eyebrows shot up and his eyes widened. "How much?" he snapped.

"Five million."

Wilson almost dropped his glass. "*Who?*" he asked hoarsely.

Adams said, "Bear, Stearns & Co. and Paine, Webber. They'll send me the documents Monday."

Then he leaned forward and said deliberately, "Put up or shut up!" His investment banking background had paid off very handsomely for Raytheon.


On Monday Adams called Geneen to his office and told him about his Memorial Day weekend. Geneen was astonished.

"How do you know the offer's good?" he asked quickly.[127]

Adams looked at him reflectively. *You're very bright*, he thought, *but you don't know everything.* Aloud, he said nothing. In the investment banking business a man's word is his greatest asset. Without it, he cannot negotiate.

Later in the day, when the documents arrived, Geneen had recovered. "I don't think I would have had the nerve," he said admiringly and shook his head.

In due course Honeywell matched the offer—minus 10 percent—and Raytheon as a result is one of the very few firms to have entered the formidable lists of the computer industry against IBM and emerged unscathed.


In general, however, Geneen's flame rose high. In March 1957 he hired E. Douglas Graham, a former Ford executive, to head Raytheon manufacturing. The selection was interesting. Geneen had been smitten, while at Jones & Laughlin, with the systems and controls of the automotive industry. Now he was obviously going to pick them up and plant them in Raytheon. Graham, in fact, arrived trailing a staff of his own and began to study operations and production systems inside the divisions.

In political terms these innovations resembled the movements of an internal revolutionary force that first captured the controller's office. From that bastion a stream of subcontrollers fanned out to seize divisional forts, from which they served as watchers and reporters, as traffic managers over the flow of funds.

The next area was personnel. By early 1957 Raytheon's employees had jumped, in a little over a year, from 17,000 to 22,000 people—and its force was still growing.[128] The firm's labor relations had always been excellent, except at Belmont in Chicago and that was in the past. In 1957 it confronted an array of craft unions with overlapping and conflicting contract expiration dates, and union locals scattered through New England as well as in Oxnard and Santa Barbara, California, and Canada. The company had ongoing and heavy problems of recruitment and evaluation in an increasingly impersonal world. Geneen and his men poured into this area as smoothly and naturally as water.

That particular take-over began with the arrival of William T. Marx, former director of personnel at Celanese Corporation. Marx had already achieved a reputation in New York, and although initially on an equal level with Raytheon's former personnel director, Leslie Woods—who was pushed sideways to industrial relations—proved easily capable of reversing that relationship.[129] Working in extraordinary proximity to Geneen, Marx began to hire and staff the personnel department at a prodigious pace. By autumn 1957 the people inside Raytheon began to realize a new day had dawned in human as well as working relationships inside the firm.


Meanwhile Adams stumbled upon a very large problem outside the firm. Before leaving office Engine Charley Wilson of GM had ordered a speedup on defense production. That started a train of events, led contractors to overtime schedules and increased costs. Unfortunately a business slowdown was reducing tax revenues for the government at the same time this silent snowball began to roll down the mountain. The results were inevitable, but not apparent for a time.

Adams, in Washington and making the rounds, learned of the problem when he was told, by a navy procurement officer, that Raytheon could expect no payments on the Sparrow program for "the next three months." He was appalled and sped immediately to the office of Tom Gates, the Undersecretary of Defense. He was surprised to learn Gates knew the situation but had no immediate answer to it. Adams then wrangled an immediate appointment with Sinclair Weeks, the Secretary of Commerce.

Once inside Weeks's office Adams sat down and talked plainly. "It's now the first of October," he said. "No payments are to be expected from the Pentagon. Raytheon is working on both the Sparrow and the Hawk, and both are multimillion-dollar programs. If payments are not continued as this work proceeds, there is not enough money in the banking system to sustain Raytheon—*and all the other defense companies* that will be affected. Therefore, we will have to close down at the end of the month—and so will everyone else."

Then, as Weeks stared at him in horror, Adams spelled out some of the consequences. "Raytheon," he continued, "employs thirty thousand people. If we accept the usual three-to-one estimate, then their layoff will affect that many more persons, all of whom will have their incomes cut just before Christmas. The same sequence will take place throughout the nation. I think," he concluded, "that the President ought to know about this."

Weeks agreed, and got on the phone. It was not long before the Secretary of Commerce was summoned to the White House, with several other men. The General, folksy on television and the hustings, was in a purple rage and pounded the desk. Orders went out to bring in the Secretary of the Treasury, Mr. Anderson. That gentleman was incautious enough to ask how the money could be raised and Eisenhower's mouth turned down. "That's *your business*," he snapped. They left—were relieved to be gone.

In the end the solution, reached in hurried conferences with Congress, was to raise the legal debt limit and sell Fannie Mae bonds. Within a week Raytheon had its money and so did other defense firms. The nation proceeded unaware of the money crunch it had so narrowly escaped.[130]


Nineteen fifty-seven was an International Geophysical Year, a matter of intense interest to the scientific community and all its tributaries, but beyond the scope and attention of average citizens. In effect, it meant an international scientific effort to explore the oceans, the polar regions north and south, and the cosmos.[131] The average world citizen came to startled attention regarding the subject when the USSR became the first nation to send a satellite—Sputnik I—into space.[132]

Although some hailed the achievement as a great success for humanity, a different reaction arose in many other places. The western world had assumed, almost as a matter of course, that the United States was the world's most advanced scientific power. The thought that the commissars might have superior technology, with all its implications, sent shock waves through the nation and much of the West. Headlines screamed as the 180-pound Sputnik circled the globe in ninety-five minutes. Barely a month later, as if to show the first achievement was no accident, the commissars sent Sputnik II, bearing a doomed Eskimo dog, aloft.

The achievement highlighted the increased prestige and extended activities of the Soviet Union around the world itself. Independent Third World states like Ghana, Indonesia, and India turned visibly toward the Kremlin for intellectual guidance; turbulent internal situations in Asia and Africa continued to reflect its influence.

Evidence of the most significant accomplishment of the year at Raytheon, however, was provided by the cover of the 1957 Annual Report, which showed a color photo of the sixteen-foot Hawk sailing straight up. The entire Missile & Radar Division regarded this proof of high regard with pride.

Their efforts were, in fact, proving spectacular. Dave Coffin was raised to a vice presidency; Wisenbaker, Phillips, and Leiper were given raises and, for the first time, stock options; behind them many men—Fossier, Hamel, Dashefsky, Alibrandi, Miccioli, and others—moved up.

From the Annual Report, it seemed as though the entire firm was bursting its seams. Sales soared to $259 million, a record. Earnings after taxes were $4.8 million—though in part this reflected the Adams coup on Datamatic. A large part, moreover, was due to the missile and missile-related effort; government orders at the end of the year were at a backlog of $260 million.[133]

The string of triumphant statistics, listed in a page subtitled "A Year of Progress," was enough to make Wall Street sit up; the Message to Shareholders helped rivet that attention. In sharp contrast to the Adams style of previous years, this letter was phrased in Wall Street jargon, spoke directly to the financial community. As if this was not enough to prove a new element at work in Raytheon, an organizational chart appeared on the inside front cover. In former years the officers of the firm had been listed in standard form from the president down. This year the format was different. Under the listing of the directors there appeared a large space headlined Office of the President. In it three names appeared: Adams, Geneen, and Spencer. In the lower corners were two smaller names: Edward L. Bowles, general consultant, and Ernest Leathem, assistant to the president.

Then spread across the page appeared a list of names under the heading Functional Management, and below that another list under the description Operating Management Division.

These typographical changes had a curious effect. Adams remained, clearly, president. Geneen was executive vice president and Percy Spencer a senior vice president. But grouping them all inside a space entitled the Office of the President somehow threw them all on the same level, like the troika government the USSR had, for the previous several years, claimed as its own. In Moscow the troika fell apart—or at least two fell apart. In early 1958 Khrushchev would make it clear one driver was enough.

But the new Raytheon description of its management made it seem as though the actual structure of the firm had been changed; Geneen was on a par with Charlie Adams. Adams was not a man to care one whit about that, but the world judges by appearances. Many observers leaped to descry the obvious, and connected that to the reason for the great change in the most important business line of all: the bottom, which showed record, unprecedented profits.


These gleamed brightly against the deepening gloom of the U.S. economic landscape. Unemployment by February 1958 rose to nearly 8 percent; employment dropped to the lowest levels in sixteen years.

Arguments broke out over which political party was responsible for the decline in the economy; world—or rather, western world—scientists protested against the continued testing of nuclear bombs. Nuclear terror had gripped the minds of many. Linus Pauling, noted chemist, predicted tests already made would result in five million

*283*

genetically defective births and create millions of leukemia and cancer cases for the next three hundred generations.[134]

A divide stretched, in other words, between the level of thought and activity on scientific and practical matters, and the level of thought and activity on political and cultural matters. Such a divide has always in fact existed, but by 1958 it was subject to a reversal of influence, in which the average myth, as magnified by the press and television, outshouted the minority fact.

Yet achievements continued to be impressive. The U.S. Air Force, which had silently become the largest single enterprise in the nation with assets of $70 billion the previous year,[135] created squadrons armed with intermediate ballistic missiles. The first few months of 1958 saw the launching of U.S. satellites Explorer I and Vanguard I—both highly sophisticated mechanisms—and impressive strides were made in planning the latest of an array of nuclear-tipped missiles: the Polaris.

Early in March the U.S. nuclear submarine *Nautilus* slid silently beneath the polar icecap, an achievement that proved sea distances could be dramatically shortened. On an instrumental level the United States had one thousand computers in operation, compared with 160 in Europe,[136] and was industrially still far ahead of any nation. Though a recession existed, times were still far better than in previous decades; neither 1948 nor 1938 could approach the prosperity of 1958. Yet President Eisenhower had to make a special address to remind the nation the recession was not permanent.

Curiously enough Raytheon was in somewhat similar condition. Sales were up, profits were up—but so were internal complaints. The atmosphere was not improved, though new faces and new systems appeared in profusion. Geneen's accounting, budget, and billing controls improved Raytheon's situation—on that there was general agreement.

"We had been late with our books," Wisenbaker says, "and Geneen turned that around. The company got its bills to the government quicker, and was paid sooner. That helped." [137]

But not all change is improvement, and changes inside Raytheon were tumbling upon one another. Graham, imported to become head of manufacturing services, sent his men from the automotive industry poking into methods and systems throughout the firm. They reported they were unimpressed by the missile division. That was odd, because missiles had not only been spectacular in its accomplishments, but was also very profitable. What, then, was wrong with missiles? It was operating too informally, did not appear sufficiently orthodox to men trained in the endless repetitions of Detroit's manufacturing complex. Graham determined to introduce changes.

Dave Coffin received the news and returned to Wisenbaker and Phillips shaking his head. Once again they decided to go past the new efficiency experts—Graham & Co.—and go straight to Harold Geneen.

They did; and after their talk, during which they spread a variety of small, intricate missile parts across the top of his desk, Geneen agreed to visit the Andover plant to see for himself the difference between producing missiles and producing ordinary commercial products. Among other details, the experts had questioned whether Andover, under the division's system, could ever produce thirty missiles a month.

Once at the plant Wisenbaker took Geneen by the sleeve and, turning him around, said, "Here, you jerk. Start counting!" and pointed toward rows of gleaming missiles. "There they are!" he said. Phillips was amazed to see that Geneen did not resent the familiarity or the tone, was pleased when the executive vice president concluded a little later, "I'll take the paper men away." [138]

Yet matters did not end there.

Coffin, Wisenbaker, and Phillips were taking on the appearance of rebels—though the division contributed mightily to the expansion of the company, and its leaders really wanted only to work to their full capacity, without uninformed intervention.

Their unease was paralleled in other parts of the corporation. William Marx, who had entered on the respectable but not overpowering level of a personnel director, was elevated to "Director, Employee Relations and Organization Planning." [139] That was a significant new title.

Robert Hennemuth, one of Hannah's bright young lawyers, assigned to industrial relations matters at the time, watched Marx's course with interest. "He filled the personnel department with a hundred and fifty people in a surprisingly brief period of time," he said later.[140] He noticed that the newcomers included a number of staff psychologists.

Operating under the authority and with the backing of the executive vice president, these newcomers proceeded to change the internal style and climate of the firm. Their leader, Geneen, was fond of late meetings that extended from dinners at the Red Coach Grill in Wayland. There were regular attendees, such as Norman Krim, Percy Spencer (whose wife had died, leaving him unoccupied in the evening), DiScipio, a professor from Boston University serving as a marketing consultant, Bill Marx, the personnel expert at Geneen's right hand. Other men came and went. Years later Geneen, to whom this was what strong drink, women, and music might be to other men, recalls, "Interviewing men after work, at dinner; standing on the sidewalk with Marx talking about our impressions late at night, on more than one occasion . . ." [141]

These late dinner sessions had grown from initial lunches, at which the conversation had revolved eternally about Raytheon business problems, systems, people, markets. Krim eventually found them stimulating enough to include his secretary, who took notes. Finally they expanded to the point where Geneen had his assistants bring charts. "Road maps," Krim called them, "stuffed with the names of other companies." One of Geneen's points was that 80 to 90 percent of the business done in the United States was nongovernmental. He was, therefore, talking about fundamental changes in Raytheon. The word had not yet been coined, but he was thinking along conglomerate lines.

Norman Krim, whose professional life had been spent entirely inside Raytheon, was caught up and carried away by the excitement and the inherent drama of these activities, these new personalities and their leader. His admiration was open and unfeigned, even though Geneen and his men had quickly zeroed in on the receiving tube division—Krim's bailiwick—and mercilessly exposed its difficulties. Krim's transistors were losing money. Nevertheless Krim was told he would be sent to Harvard; the implication was that he would be upgraded, improved, placed on new missions.

The same implicit promise attended and softened the impact of Dr. Dora Capwell, a psychologist from Pittsburgh, who suddenly appeared on the Raytheon landscape. Dr. Capwell was the mastermind of psychological assessments and skills evaluation; she had created an IQ and Personality Test of her own that, it was claimed, matched personality traits and mental ability.

Krim, who had once spent a summer at Yale and studied the Pavlovian analog under Dr. Clarke Hall, had long ago rejected such avenues in preference for "the clear logic" of MIT and engineering. Geneen argued him out of this position. "It is really a cultural test," Geneen said, "based on a study of thirty thousand successful executives." He went on to explain that the tests were intended to assess the company overall, in order to rate its competitive ability. "Some divisions are overloaded with brains," Geneen said, and he sought to discover "the upper one-third of the upper one-tenth."

Krim was convinced; became an advocate. Others were skeptical. "Do you mean to say," asked Percy Spencer, "that our chief glassblower, who has been with us thirty years, has to *prove* himself?" The remark went the rounds and was quoted endlessly, but Dr. Spencer's fate was to be forever excluded from the ranks of those accepted as serious intellectuals, despite his achievements.

Yet Spencer would have made an intriguing subject for conventionally trained psychologists. One day, while Spencer was lunching with Dr. Ivan Getting and several other Raytheon scientists, a mathematical question arose. Several men, in a familiar reflex, pulled out their slide rules but before any could complete the equation Spencer gave the answer.

Dr. Getting was astonished. "How did you do that?" he asked.

"The root," said Spencer shortly. "I learned cube roots and squares by using blocks as a boy. Since then, all I have to do is visualize them placed together." [142]

He refused to take the tests, and so did Charlie Adams. With these two exceptions, every person in Raytheon went through the ordeal. T. C. Wisenbaker had no objections. "If they're any good, they'll help us in hiring," he said. Later, he reviewed the results regarding men in his area of responsibility and said, "Some were spectacularly wrong. One fantastically clever man was rated as 'unresourceful.' On the other hand, some estimates were accurate." Wisenbaker decided the results were too random to be reliable and dismissed the entire subject.

Tom Phillips, whose memories of the tests are still fresh, recalls finishing the mathematical section with only a few minutes to spare. He knew he had answered the questions correctly, but his satisfaction would have been greater had he not also known that Fossier had finished twenty minutes earlier and had spent the balance of the time staring—bored—out the window.

The personnel department placed a high value on the results. "Some stars were discovered," Sid Standing says, "but many turned out to be candles."

For a time, however, the tests appeared a surface success and people remained carefully reserved in their comments. Under the surface the results were incalculable. Such mass ordeals are psychological rapes of the personality when conducted under duress, and are so received and regarded. Dr. Spencer and Charlie Adams would not subject themselves to such indignities; others had little choice.

In retrospect, which provides a clear vision of the past, the Dr. Dora Capwell Personality and IQ Tests marked the high point of Harold Geneen's regime at Raytheon. From that moment onward, his rule continued to extend, his prestige outside the firm continued to rise—but internally he became a divisive force.


There is a glacial quality about large corporations; they move slowly but steadily through the waters, and the overwhelming mass of their activities takes place below the tip. At Raytheon the engineers from Submarine Signal, subsumed into the larger organization many years before, unhappily working in the equipment division, began to find new footing. Working at the Wayland Laboratories, they developed advanced subsurface sonar BQQ-1 submarine systems that leaped ahead of the state of the art.

The accomplishment, sparked by Paul Skitzki and Edward Turner, who accumulated over seventy patents in his years with SubSig and Raytheon, brought the group forward to the attention of high authorities once again. "A submarine sonar system by 1958," Turner observes, "cost more than a submarine in World War II." [143]

Success is invigorating. SubSig—as the group continued to call itself—forged into other areas and began to emerge from obscurity.

The missile group, on the other hand, found that even success and eminence can lead to problems. General Medaris, newly appointed missile czar of the army, checked his domain and talked to Dr. Martin Schilling at Redstone Arsenal. Many questions disclosed that Schilling had complete faith in Raytheon and its Hawk. Medaris—jumping quickly—jumped to the wrong conclusion.

"Who's running this show?" Medaris asked. "Raytheon or the U.S. Army?" [144]

Schilling was deeply offended. He had lasted a long time with the army—since 1945. Over the years he had been well aware of the "Christmas list" of contractors who dispensed lures ranging from hospitality to outright gifts, and had remained sternly aloof. "I felt only safe with Raytheon, General Electric, and Western Electric," he says, "they had no Christmas times." With a budget of between $400 million and $500 million a year, Schilling had to be wary.

In addition, times were changing. The economy was still soft in the summer and early autumn of 1958, and the air heavy with political bickering that affected the military and its leaders. Schilling began to look toward the exit.

As the year 1958 progressed, Geneen had continued to staff the firm and to attract some men inside the Raytheon structure toward him in a personal sense. One of these was a remarkably brilliant, financially trained young man named David Margolis, whom Geneen assigned to maintain contacts with the analysts of Wall Street. Years later one observer remarked that it seemed to him that Margolis was always on the phone explaining Mr. Geneen's plans, or Mr. Geneen's accomplishments.

The corridors filled with new faces. Charles D. Manhart, former vice president for sales-government relations at Bendix, was hired as a vice president; John Thompson, former manager of distributor sales for GE, had been hired and placed in charge of distributor products sales; Peter J. Schenk became a new presidential assistant; other names crowded lesser ranks.

Geneen's meetings changed, also. They expanded into full-dress monthly gatherings, where men from all the divisions and the management reviewed their situations. Geneen has a theory about these, which he still holds. "I learned that if I went about asking questions it set up reactions," he said. "Men will say, 'Who told you that?' [145] You learn about men by working with them in an atmosphere where questions are raised."

He liked to raise questions; that was his forte. Hannah, the firm's legal counsel, was struck at how many questions Geneen could ask, and how penetrating they could become. "He kept boring in and boring in," Hannah recalls.[146]

But the monthly meetings expanded beyond anyone's conception of such gatherings. "He made people nervous," recalls Charlie Resnick, then an attorney in Hannah's department. "He struck me as brilliant, but hard. He gave men hell if they made a mistake—and kept silent when they did something well."

Charlie Adams attended Geneen's meetings when he could, and

sat quietly through most of them. He had chosen to give his executive vice president room to run and was not going to change that understanding. But on one occasion Geneen's treatment of one man was, Adams says, "so painful" that Adams was aroused.

In the midst of his remarks, therefore, Geneen was abruptly recalled when Adams turned to him and said, in an iron voice, *"Stop that."* [147]

Geneen flushed and fell silent; it took the meeting several minutes to recover its balance. Later Geneen went to Adams' office. His manner was extremely courteous, and he wondered what had upset the president.

"I served in the navy during the war and was a reserve officer for years," Adams said. "I have known about organizations since childhood, and been exposed to many blunt and forceful men." He did not add, though he could, that his own father had been a formidable figure, capable of searing the air when angry. "In the navy," Adams continued, "we took note of men who misbehaved. Later, they were chewed out—in private. In the future, if you choose to rebuke a man, do it privately. Fire him, if need be. But don't publicly humiliate people. It hurts the team."

The air, in other words, had grown strained, was unhealthy. Yet to outward eyes, Raytheon was moving remarkably. Its sales were up dramatically, its profits were increasing, its number of employees soared to over thirty thousand. On the exchange the Raytheon stock, low in the postwar years, had moved—by the autumn of 1958—to 40, and was continuing straight up.

The Street had discovered Geneen; he was good copy and excellent in interviews. Analysts praised the firm and its management; it attracted much attention. Bank credit had been increased to $75 million; a stock issue of 379,954 shares of common sold very quickly. In this immense and now highly sophisticated establishment, one learns almost with shock that Dr. C. G. Smith, the inventor of the rectifier tube and one of the quartet of Marshall, Bush, Gammell, and Smith, who launched the firm back in 1922, only now chose to retire.[148]

Charlie Adams brought the subject of Dr. Smith to the attention of the directors, and suggested that his pension—quite modest—be improved. They immediately agreed.

Dr. Smith departed as plans were underway to erect, on 130 acres purchased in Lexington, Massachusetts, a new executive office building with a dining room and cafeteria. Geneen and his enlarged staff, the great numbers of new managers, had grown increasingly cramped in the old executive offices and dining space, tucked into a corner of the microwave and power tube division.

Geneen felt cramped in other areas as well. He had established excellent relations with Captain Hull, the vice president in charge of the equipment division. But the executive vice president was well aware that some groups inside that division had, somehow, managed consistently to evade the tight controls he preferred. His solution was to reach far outside the company and bring in Homer R. Oldfield, Jr., and place him in charge of government equipment. That step, taken in December 1958, meant that the missile division, among others, would have a new chief.

None of this showed in the 1958 Annual Report, whose statistics showed Raytheon sales of $375 million and profits of $9.4 million.[149] The number of employees had soared to 38,000; the firm was booming.

The year 1959 opened with the triumph of Fidel Castro and the flight of Cuban president Batista into exile.[150] The U.S. press, which long featured eulogistic articles about the bearded revolutionary and his followers, was jubilant. Cuba, richest island in the Caribbean, with the largest middle class and greatest number of millionaires, the highest standard of living in Latin America, hoped for the best.

Elsewhere, de Gaulle rose to power in France after a long Socialist-dominated hiatus; Laos appealed to the United States for arbitration in disputes with North Vietnam; the United States launched the first atomic-powered passenger-cargo ship [151] and first Mercury space capsule.

Domestically the nation was growing disheveled. Arguments over school desegregation persisted, unemployment remained high though improved over early 1958; Alaska joined the union and the City Council of New York studied plans to secede from the state and become a state in itself. The political scene heated in the Democratic Party; contenders lined up in a long file: Kennedy, Stevenson, Johnson, Humphrey, Symington, Edmund Brown, Robert Meyner, G. Mennen Williams, and others.[152] The Republicans would choose between Richard Nixon and Nelson Rockefeller; bitter backstage arguments broke out in the ranks of the Administration.

Raytheon mirrored, in an uncanny and entirely unplanned way, the larger situation. On the surface all looked serene, but internally the atmosphere had lost its old unity; cliques had formed and maneuvers were conducted whose goals were cloudy, purposes unclear.

Dr. Martin Schilling resigned from the government and joined Raytheon late in 1958. He was welcomed by the missile group eagerly; no man knew the general situation better. His role and responsibilities, however, were unclear—particularly since Geneen was continuing to shift men around.

The fact was that government contracts, increasing by the month and carrying Raytheon upward, constituted 85 percent of the firm's business. Its commercial efforts simply could not get off the ground, and that baffled and balked Geneen. The men at Raytheon, including Charlie Adams, were also astonished to discover that the executive vice president had a habit of disappearing. He would simply not arrive one morning; he would be unreachable or not at home at all—would drop out of sight without a word.[153]

"A week or ten days later," Adams says, "he would reappear, smiling and tanned, and say he had taken a rest. When he returned he would be in an excellent humor, and matters would run quite smoothly for a time."

When the game did not proceed according to plan, Geneen's system was to change the game—not the plan. Charlie Adams, who by this time was beginning to comprehend his executive vice president's approaches, put it with characteristic succinctness. "He is like a man whose idea of winning a ball game," Adams says, "is to add some more bases. By doing that, it doesn't matter if you are tagged out at first or second; you can add four more bases and keep the inning going forever." [154]

At Raytheon he had sought to add bases—in this case, companies— but Adams was not to be stampeded into a headlong expansion program: he had entered the company on the heels of one. Geneen was able to pick up Apelco—Applied Electronics—maker of marine telephones, in early 1958. But in the main he had been blocked, he said later, "by Adams' caution." [155] That caution was not so firm, however, that Adams would not approve any purchases at all. He approved of the acquisition of Machlett Laboratories, the nation's largest manufacturer of X-ray tubes and high-power tubes, for $18.9 million in early 1959.[156]

Still the executive vice president chafed, and he dropped out of sight, for a week or so at a time, more frequently. Although he was as diligent as ever upon his return, Adams began to wonder if Geneen was looking for another job.

Events later proved he was; Adams' instincts were accurate. But the heavy staffing of new people proceeded: one was on a very high level indeed. Geneen produced Richard E. Krafve from Ford, where Krafve had been a vice president. Ford is a very large firm, and was so in 1959; it did not have many vice presidents.

Krafve, however, had been cast into a most unusual situation: he had been the vice president in charge of the Edsel. Later Adams thought it best to check this out and called the fabled Mr. Ernest Breech—the executive who put the postwar Ford Motor Company together and onto the heights. Questioned, Mr. Breech said, "The decision to go ahead on the Edsel was Henry's—and mine. Not Dick Krafve's. He did a very creditable job in creating dealers for the Edsel and promoting the car. The failure was one of concept, in which we were all associated.

"After the Edsel was halted," Mr. Breech continued, "we looked around for a new post for Krafve. We already had a head of Lincoln-Mercury, so we sent him to Canada." [157]

At the time this conversation was held, however, Krafve was already inside Raytheon, had been brought in by Harold Geneen. Geneen described Krafve as a man capable of steering them all into successful waters in commercial areas. He introduced Krafve even to the directors, and persuaded Adams to give the newcomer the resounding title of "Group Vice President," a salary of $50,000, and a top policy assignment.[158]

After Krafve had been installed for a month or so, Geneen disappeared. He was gone, according to Charlie Adams, about ten days. As was his custom, he reappeared without any more notice than he had disappeared and entered the president's office.

"After some amenities," Adams said, "Geneen said, 'Charlie, I've been offered a job and I'd like to talk to you about it.'" Then he told Adams he had been offered the post of chief executive of ITT.[159]

Adams, a hard man to impress, was sincerely struck. ITT! Memories of Colonel Sosthenes Behn came flooding back to him; he blinked and looked at Geneen. "Well!" he said. "That's certainly better than being Number Two here!"

"Well," Geneen said, after a pause, "I really haven't made up my mind about ITT; really—I haven't. I'm intrigued—but I want to be sure."

Leaning back, Adams began to reminisce about ITT and the personalities and composition of the men on the board. He and Geneen were almost exactly the same age, but Adams, with his baldness and long, stern face, looked the elder. He gave Geneen, whom in many ways he liked, some brotherly advice, as one man to another.

"Make sure you get a foolproof contract," he said, "and that you get the authority to run the job properly." He went on that way for a time, and Geneen, nodding, said, "That makes sense; that's good advice."

Finally, talked out, the two men looked at one another and Geneen left the office. The subject was left in the air. But on Monday he returned, and said, "I have a foolproof deal with ITT."

Adams stood up, greatly moved, put out his hand and said, "God bless you; I wish you luck." [160]

The news hit Wall Street early on the morning of May 19, 1959, when Geneen sold his Raytheon stock. Arch Catapono of Merrill Lynch, Pierce, Fenner & Bean immediately took the company off its preferred list. Other brokers followed suit. It was as though Raytheon had suffered a calamitous accident, one that ruined its prospects. Adams was deeply shocked. "I had not realized," he said later, "that he had created a *constituency*." The phrase was apt.

Like any constituency, its allegiance was based on cloudy, somewhat emotional assumptions. Geneen's ideas regarding management, psychological testing, intense group meetings conducted along lines of sensitivity sessions, abstruse accounting concepts and acquisitions as a way of life, were all part of an emerging business ideological movement. He was one of the first of its exponents, and was to prove the fastest and most adroit. In the sixties, the decade ahead, he would soar higher than anyone else and retain his following longer. Eventually he would be intellectually deflated by the same forces that fueled his inflation, but that—in 1959—was unforeseeable. At that moment he was Man of the Hour.

At Raytheon he left behind shock and consternation in some, and a deep sense of relief in others. Within weeks an exodus of his closest followers began. David Margolis, assistant treasurer, resigned, together with George Streichman, to join ITT. William Marx, the personnel director who doubled as an expert on organizational planning and had become widely feared as a hatchet man, followed his leader to New York. Marx wrote an interesting letter to Charlie Adams, which said, in part, ". . . I want you to know how much I appreciate the opportunity you personally gave me to broaden my general management experience by enabling me to play an influential part in the development of the corporate organization." [161]

Not all the Geneen followers were summoned by their leader, however. Norman Krim, an outstanding convert to the Geneen management theories, was among those left behind. Removed as a line executive heading the receiving tube division, he had been sent to the Harvard School of Business, taken the Management Course at Andover, and been active in the search for possible acquisitions. In this he had not been unsuccessful: Machlett had been one of the deals he uncovered.[162] He had also been sent to Asia to explore possibilities in Japan. When the tides turned in the Raytheon organization, Krim was still busy on that project. But he awaited longer-range events with some understandable concern.

Charlie Adams was left with many problems with which to contend. The firm was planning a new issue of common stock, and the fact that it had been maligned in the marketplace was not helpful. In addition, he was knee-deep in negotiations with NATO.

That organization, created in the administration of Harry Truman, had not proceeded as rapidly or as far as common sense dictated during the Eisenhower years. The entire subject of western ability to resist the Soviet expansions had, during those years, undergone considerable pressure and shrinkage.

Eisenhower had reduced conventional U.S. Army and Navy forces, strengthened the Air Force, and pushed programs to develop long-range missiles and nuclear submarines. These constituted final weapons for the defense of the United States. In the meantime, NATO had not strengthened its own forces, developed its own weapons systems, or created a western European military force of great consequence.

Obviously these nations could not exist forever under the U.S.

umbrella of nuclear power, because the Soviets were drawing closer to parity with each passing year. NATO, in the opinion of Washington, would have to build its own weapons.

When its needs were examined, the geopolitical nature of Europe shaped the direction of the answers. Europe's diversity gives a misleading impression of its size. In reality, that multicolored tapestry is tightly packed, its geographical range limited—especially the truncated Europe that remains since the occupation of its eastern portion by the Soviets. Low-altitude missiles are, obviously, especially useful in such crowded areas. The Hawk, all agreed, was ideal.

When Raytheon was approached, however, Adams made it clear that the firm had no intention of handing over its hard-won technology simply because the planners in Washington, London, Paris, and Benelux thought such information would smooth troubled diplomatic waters. Raytheon's know-how was the basis of its commercial existence. It was not to be given away for nothing. Some of the Europeans didn't like that—but Adams is difficult to outface.

He began to make a series of trips to NATO in Paris, and as these trips increased and time extended, the difficulties began to alter into the eternal question of How Much. The Europeans argued among themselves and with the Americans, about who would make what. NATO finally agreed to put up $500 million for the Hawk effort overall, and a multitude of cross-agreements were drawn.[163]

Each of the European NATO member countries wanted to produce everything for itself, though in the beginning there was some thought one nation would build all the defensive radar systems, another the Hawk, and so on. The negotiations were tangled, complicated, difficult, wearisome, and irritating.

Adams plunged into these sessions with zest. He carried Paul Hannah, the firm's legal counsel, with him through virtually all his meetings; on several occasions took T. C. Wisenbaker, and on others Dr. Schilling to field technical questions. The men found the experience impressive.[164]

Adams is a man with a considerable sense of humor whose background helped place him at the top, but who has remained there through ability. A direct descendant of the fabled John Adams, architect of the Constitution and second President of the United States and of John Quincy Adams, whom Charlie Adams greatly resembles in appearance, he bears his historic weight modestly.

Adams' life has been lived in the present and he is no stranger to military or political personalities. His father—who was also named Charles Francis Adams—was Secretary of the Navy under Hoover, and Charlie Adams saw many personages come and go. A man of considerable dignity, his father was sometimes confused with another Charles Francis Adams—no relation—who was president of the Boston Bruins, a hockey team, and a vice president of the Boston Braves, a baseball team.

The elder Adams was often called to the phone late at night to answer questions about athletes who had escaped their keepers or to settle some sporting argument. Charlie Adams was never known to make any comment about that situation, which extended for years and convulsed many. Charlie Adams knew very well that any quip of his would be undying, and therefore kept his lips sealed. For a man with his sense of the comic, this was not the least of his accomplishments.

This innate sense of underlying realities served him in good stead with the Europeans. Dr. Schilling, who watched the interplay and manner of Raytheon's president with the fresh eyes of a newcomer to the company, found the performance noteworthy.

One day in particular stands out in his memory. "One day in Paris we traveled," says Schilling, "by taxi—not a limousine—first to a representative of the U.S. Department of Defense near the Crillon, then to the U.S. Embassy, then to a NATO Progress Meeting, and then back to our hotel to touch base with some Raytheon men. Each conversation was on an entirely different level, and Mr. Adams switched without any visible effort."

The conversations were far-reaching. Among others, the subject of antisubmarine defense in the Atlantic arose. After all, this was the Atlantic Pact. NATO had not yet earmarked funds for such an effort, but Raytheon and its SubSig groups were available, and selected by U.S. Admiral Gerauld Wright, Supreme Allied Commander in the Atlantic. U.S. Secretary of Defense McElroy agreed to furnish interim funds, and Raytheon organized and established, through a nonprofit firm called Sirimar, a research center at La Spezia, Italy. The center, designed to provide antisubmarine information and to develop instrumentations of defense, was established as an informational rather than hardware center. The fact that Raytheon was chosen to organize and manage this center was enormously to its credit, though the project bristled with difficulties.

A glimpse of these is provided by Schilling. NATO had appointed the retired Dutch General Raynierse to push the Hawk arrangements. "He was an expert at pushing," Schilling says appreciatively. But at one stage in the negotiations the lawyers took over. "They were imbedding details into concrete," says Schilling, when General Raynierse suddenly rose to his feet.

To Schilling's everlasting joy, the project director then said, in three different languages, one after the other, "This is crap."

The lawyers, aghast, fell silent and Adams stepped forward. "He and the General stepped into another room," Schilling says, "and returned in ten minutes with everything settled." [165]


Toward the end of July 1959, Adams had the pleasure of presiding over impressive ceremonies that hailed the opening of a new company microwave power tube laboratory at Burlington, Massachusetts. The attendance was evidence, if any was needed, of Raytheon's high rank with the nation's military and scientific establishment. Dr. James Killian, Jr., chairman of MIT, made the main address; James Bridges, director of electronics for the Department of Defense, appeared; so did Lieutenant General Bernard Schriever, R&D chief for the U.S. Air Force; Rear Admiral Masterson, assistant Chief of Naval Operations; Lieutenant General Trudeau, U.S. Army chief of R&D; and the governor of Massachusetts, among others.

The day was sparkling, the ceremonies impressive, and the occasion memorable. A plaque was unveiled that read:

THE SPENCER LABORATORY

NAMED IN HONOR OF PERCY L. SPENCER, MANAGER, MICROWAVE AND POWER TUBE DIVISION, SENIOR VICE PRESIDENT, AND A DIRECTOR OF RAYTHEON. COMBINING THE APTITUDES OF SCIENTIST, ENGINEER, MANAGER AND PIONEER IN SUBTLE PROPORTIONS, CONSPICUOUS FOR HIS INVENTIVE GENIUS, HIGHLY RESPECTED FOR HIS VERSATILITY AND FOR HIS OUTSTANDING CONTRIBUTIONS TO THE VACUUM TUBE ART, BELOVED FOR HIS HUMAN QUALITIES, DR. SPENCER HAS CONTRIBUTED

IMMEASURABLY TO THE GROWTH AND CHARACTER OF RAYTHEON
SINCE ITS EARLIEST DAYS.

DEDICATED   JULY 27,   1959.

Everybody was greatly pleased. The company was beginning to come back together; wounds were healing.

There were, however, many adjustments to be made. Adams, delving into the details of areas he had delegated, became acquainted with facts he had not previously realized. Profit margins were dropping rapidly; projections had been drawn on the basis of missile sales and presented to give the impression that the entire company had been moved forward. Somewhat glumly Adams set about apprising the financial community of the actual situation, made it clear the firm would not, in the near future, continue to move straight up as in the recent past.[166] These disclosures seemed to verify the analysts who had predicted Raytheon would sag without Geneen; Adams gritted his teeth and bit that bullet.

He turned to this task at a time when the firm was far larger than it had been when Geneen entered, and more complex internally than before. His own time had been seriously invaded by the responsibilities and demands that accompanied this growth, and his presence simultaneously needed in Paris with the NATO groups, in Washington with the Pentagon people, on various international fronts as well as inside the company. He was, in a way, beset.

At this juncture the new Raytheon group vice president, Richard E. Krafve, brought in during the spring with great fanfare by Geneen, appeared with a proposition that Raytheon merge with General Instrument.[167]

Krafve could not be faulted for that; it was precisely the top-level sort of business for which he had been hired. As he explained it to the directors and to Charlie Adams, it was not without attractions. A friend of Krafve's was on the board of General Instrument, which then had sales of between $300 and $400 million. If Raytheon combined—and the Krafve probe indicated their product lines did not overlap and therefore no problems existed so far as the Department of Justice was concerned—then the combined firm would be close to sales of $1 billion.

The directors looked at this package, which seemed heavier the longer they regarded it, with considerable reserve. Questions disclosed the fact that George Bunker, the legendary mastermind of Martin-Marietta, owned 17 percent of General Instrument. If Mr. Bunker had made the proposal, there is little doubt the Raytheon chief executive and the board might have been highly interested. But the possibility of a fight with George Bunker was not a prospect to attract anyone in his right mind. Krafve thought Bunker wouldn't fight, would back down against the preponderant majority, if General Instrument's managers and the balance of its board, together with Raytheon, wanted to go ahead.

The Raytheon directors decided otherwise. Nevertheless, the proposition was evidence of energy, courage, and imagination, and brought Krafve quite favorably to the forefront of attention at a very opportune time.

While weighing Krafve as a possible president, Adams made some preliminary organizational changes as the result of the new information he had discovered. Captain Hull, long in charge of the huge equipment division, was moved to one side and removed from line responsibility. At first Adams had planned to appoint Charles D. Manhart, the former Bendix executive Geneen had brought in to head government market areas, group vice president over a reorganized equipment division, now named Government Equipment & Systems. Unfortunately he had hardly come to this choice before he learned Manhart was resented and the promotion would cause dissension.

Adams instead appointed Dave Coffin to the post, with the title of group vice president. At the same time he made T. C. Wisenbaker a vice president. The missile groups cheered both actions; their sense of neglect was, to some extent, assuaged, and they hoped for better relations with management in the future.

The other large part of Raytheon operations—tube operations—was also regrouped and retitled Electronic Components & Devices, and Homer R. Oldfield made group vice president over them.

Then Adams turned toward the question of a new operating manager for the firm overall. Krafve had arrived from the heights of the Ford Motor Company and made an excellent impression. Adams discussed the wisdom of appointing Krafve executive vice president with the directors and the consensus was favorable. Mindful that the world had accused him of holding back Harold Geneen, Adams also promised Krafve that he would, in a reasonable period, make him president of Raytheon if all worked well.[168]

The news of these shifts and changes created little stir inside or outside the company—and that was a relief.

As the year wound toward its close, President Eisenhower made a three-week tour of various nations in Europe, Africa, and Asia. His progress was triumphal; great crowds hailed his appearance. For a brief moment the United States and the marvelous role it had played in history during World War II and in assisting other nations in the years since seemed to emerge into clear view.

At Raytheon the climate of internationalism had expanded during the year as talks between Charlie Adams with officials from West Germany, France, Belgium, Holland, and Italy regarding Hawk grew increasingly constructive. It was now certain Raytheon would collect a substantial sum for its know-how from NATO during the coming year.

Innumerable talks were held between Adams and Dr. Carlo Calosi regarding prospects in Italy. Krafve, whose mother was Italian, had joined in some of these, but Adams made it clear that Krafve's role in international matters was to keep informed, not to formulate policy.

Toward the very end of 1959, however, Adams, Calosi, and Krafve discussed with the directors the outlines of an interesting venture in Italy.[169] The details were complex and subject to change. The initial proposition called for Raytheon to become a 40 percent owner in a new, as yet unnamed, venture, together with Finnmeccanica, a firm in Italy owned by the government, which would also become a 40 percent owner, and the Edison Group of Milan, which would join as 20 percent owners.

Such a firm, according to preliminary understandings, would not only receive the Italian Hawk production contract, but enable Raytheon to establish itself in Europe with a healthy, functioning base of operations. Capital would be required, but this could be resolved by transferring some of the expected NATO payment to the venture.

Intellectually speaking, it was a brilliant stroke, since Adams was, by dint of sheer logic, prevailing with NATO. The expected windfall could be applied to construct an international Raytheon network.

*301*

Japan was being investigated, a central European structure created in Switzerland.

The directors were properly impressed. The question was raised, and recorded, as to whether or not Raytheon's entry into Italy in such a significant fashion might not injure its market possibilities in other parts of Europe. Dr. Calosi said it would not.[170] The board then approved the plan.

The year 1959, therefore, ended on a note of rising optimism. Raytheon sales had risen by more than $100 million for the second year in a row, to reach $494 million. Profits, which included a special tax adjustment of $3 million, had soared to $13.4 million. Subtracting the special credit, however, profits had risen by only $1 million from the previous year, despite the tremendous increase in sales. This could be attributed to losses in receiving tubes. The government business, which constituted 88 percent of Raytheon's volume, remained profitable. Raytheon's backlog of government orders was over $300 million, its employees had increased to more than forty thousand people, and all its statistics represented new company records.[171] For a firm that had been subjected to such a severe attack in the rumor mills of Wall Street, it had done amazingly well. Like the nation, it turned toward the sixties with hope.

# Chapter 8 THE SIXTIES

T H E R E are times when an almost visible turn takes place, when men of one generation suddenly seem to dwindle in both numbers and influence and younger men emerge on all sides. Nineteen sixty was such a year. It was not only the closing year of the Eisenhower administration, but the senescence of the Eisenhower generation. It had been a generation that walked so closely on the heels of men who had matured before or during World War I—such as Franklin Roosevelt, Vannevar Bush, and Harry Truman—that they had all seemed part of the same parade. All of them could share similar memories of an earlier and more bucolic America, isolationist in its attitudes and instinctively hostile to pomp and power alike.

In contrast, both the front runners for their party's presidential nomination in 1960 were men who had matured just before or during World War II. Their recollections represented urban America and did not extend back before the thirties. They came of age at a time when the United States had awesome power around the world.

John Kennedy, reared to enormous wealth, had accompanied his ambassador father to the Court of St. James in London, and watched, with little sympathy, the decline and fall of the British Empire. Richard Nixon, more modestly situated, grew up in rootless, commercialized California. He entered the political hustings as a spokesman for those fervently opposed to a communism they could not always define. Vice President under Eisenhower, Nixon had worked diligently to establish himself as the General's political heir.

Both men were well educated along lines of conventional schooling, skilled in campaigning, and youthful in appearance. Yet neither

*303*

expressed, or seemed to hold, any special political philosophy in a classic sense. A foreign observer might well have wondered why either was his party's favorite for the highest political office at a time when international issues had grown complex and forbidding, and when domestic arguments were rising. In previous periods of tension America had turned toward men of originality or extraordinary stature, not toward men who so conspicuously displayed the polished skills of ordinary times.

But by early 1960 not only a new generation but new attitudes seemed suddenly widespread in America. To some extent these were the unplanned results of years of Cold War and its proliferating security programs. A system originally designed to guard the details of nuclear bombs had spread, subtly but extensively, to place a considerable part of the government's operations, plans, and policies beyond the purview of press and public alike.

Extended over a period of years, the system had created the Strategic Air Command; placed a secret number of U.S. bombers equipped with nuclear weapons in the air at all times, controlled from a red and amber button on the President's desk in the Oval Office at the White House.

Its tentacles had converted, long before, Vannevar Bush's brilliant, improvised Office of Scientific Research & Development into a permanent system that poured $8 billion into R&D throughout the United States in 1960 alone.

Yet a new generation of younger Americans was conspicuously indifferent to international events or their significance, turned instead toward the civil rights movement. The press, curbed in its discussions of overarching realities, turned toward highlighting personalities and searching the nation for inequities.

Everyone knew immense efforts had long been underway in the defense establishment, but nobody seemed able to discuss the burgeoning military establishment of the Soviet Union and the relative strength of the United States without running headlong into the walls of secrecy that had been created around the entire subject. As a result, political debates took on an air of unreality. It is no wonder the front runners of both parties, when they appeared on television—that instrument of popular entertainment—exuded a distinct aura of theatricality.

It was as though the people of the United States were living inside an immense new kind of split-level tower, in which the persons in one section were kept unaware of the activities of persons in another. Only the elite were allowed upstairs, given a peek at the castle plans, or allowed to look outside the tower windows at the surrounding landscape.

In such a structure Raytheon was only one of many organizations whose activities extended across both levels, which was active in both the private and the governmental sectors. Its reports and the activities of its groups reflected this divide wherever and whenever examined.

In this divided world, the managers were constantly confronted with crossroads decisions, with problems of whether to apply certain areas of development toward military or commercial customers. One area that arose as a special problem in 1959–60 was semiconductors. These products, whose discovery had brought a Nobel Prize to Dr. William Shockley and two of his associates, bobbed up time and again for resolution.

Shockley had, after leaving Bell Labs, approached Raytheon and suggested he work for the firm. His terms were $1 million. Raytheon offered to equip a lab for Shockley and guarantee him royalty payments on whatever he developed. But to hand over a cool million was too much. After a month of inconclusive dickering, the genius departed for the West Coast, where he presided over a notable series of changes in the semiconductor industry.[1] Raytheon, still holding its lead in the hearing-aid industry with germanium semiconductors, was not too happy about that.

During Geneen's period, McKinsey & Co. had been asked to investigate the semiconductor situation and make recommendations; so had Arthur D. Little. Various engineering brains inside the firm joined in the discussions.

The consensus was that Raytheon should enter the commercial semiconductor field in a big way.

Krafve, new to the situation, was placed in the position of listening to advice, for he himself knew the subject in only a general sense. The engineers, called in to help him decide, pumped for commercial transistors.[2] Plans were made, therefore, to enter into volume production; scouts located a small Maine town—Lewiston—whose leaders offered inducements to a new employer, and plant construction was begun.

Unfortunately other firms were looking at the same set of facts and arriving at the same conclusion: a peril that arises in all areas of shared, conventional wisdom. While Raytheon was making plans to create a large new factory and make volume transistors for commercial assemblies, scouts from their competitors were locating plant sites, engineers were drawing manufacturing flow charts and going through the same drill.

In other instances the decisions were automatic, and work followed a more direct course. Dr. Charles Stark Draper of MIT was called by the government to work on the design and development of a guidance system for the awesome Polaris missile. The government's suggestion, according to Dr. Draper, was that he work with IBM in developing a miniature computer to direct that missile—designed to be launched from underwater—toward its target. Draper, however, preferred to develop his own computer. Needing industrial support, he and the navy chose Raytheon. Raytheon would then produce the MIT-developed Polaris Mark I Guidance System.

The Polaris effort involved what engineers call "high density packaging"—which means what it seems to mean. Applications ranged through the entire spectrum of electronics and carry one into a field as dense as the packages themselves.

While the men of Raytheon worked in laboratories and plants in early 1960 evidences of other scientific efforts increased not only around them but overhead as well. The United States launched its third space vehicle—Pioneer V—into orbit around the sun, and soon afterward sent aloft a weather satellite that sent photographs of the earth's cloud cover back to earthbound inhabitants.[3] These efforts so intrigued Harold Rosen, who worked at Point Mugu with Fossier on the mathematical analyses of Lark and Sparrow tests, that he left for Hughes Aircraft, where he later became famous for work on communications satellites.[4]

Early in May 1960, however, the world learned that other kinds of vehicles were aloft when the USSR announced, with great fanfare, that it had downed an unarmed American U-2 that had been flying through its skies, taking photographs. Khrushchev called its pilot, Gary Powers, a spy,[5] and promised he would be publicly tried—an experience not always granted Soviet citizens.

The incident marked one of the most protracted and successful propaganda barrages ever launched from the USSR; it was picked up and featured in the western and world press for weeks. The Soviet used it as an excuse to cancel an invitation for President Eisenhower to visit their land, to hector the President and walk out of a Paris Summit Conference, to cancel and walk out of a Geneva Disarmament Conference of several months standing.[6] Few persons realized that the Soviets had known about the U.S. overflights all along; that both great powers had developed an immense array of electronic surveillance instruments to watch one another as a guard against sudden nuclear attack.

President Eisenhower, who had made an extended goodwill tour of Latin America immediately before the U-2 incident, found his attempt to rally hemispheric support against the violently anti-American Castro considerably diminished and soon had to cancel a projected trip to Japan because rioting students protested his arrival.

Yet while riots against the U.S. President were underway, Raytheon's men visited Japan and found its officials cordial, helpful, and interested in joint ventures with U.S. businesses.[7]

Meanwhile Adams, whose attention was largely centered on the overseas network, moved Richard Krafve forward to president of Raytheon, and himself became chairman of the board.[8] The minutes record that Adams also transferred the authority and responsibility of chief executive officer to the chairman's office, so that the situation remained essentially unchanged—but unfortunately he did not choose to make that fact public. Perhaps he took it for granted, which would have been typical. But by not making it plain that he remained the chief executive, he left an area of misunderstanding open both inside and outside the firm[9] that was deepened when Krafve began to behave as though he had complete authority.

The title of president gave Krafve new prestige, of course. Men learned, by degrees, that this was very important to him. In some respects this had its appealing aspect. At Ford Krafve had been one of twenty vice presidents, had a private plane available, and was furnished a new company car every three months. He missed these perquisites at Raytheon and made plans to introduce some special comforts into the new executive headquarters building at Lexington when it was completed.

In other respects Krafve's theories on authority were harsh. Detroit is a hard school; its executives are notoriously tough. In that city, which Krafve describes as being "industrially parochial," power struggles are almost a way of life: General Motors and Ford have endured streams of them. Krafve has vivid memories of one winner of such strains: Robert McNamara, whom he describes as "something like Geneen. He can read and memorize numbers"; he says he refused to report to him—considered him too ruthless.

Krafve likes to tell a story to illustrate how a new boss should behave. "A lumber camp boss picked out the biggest man on the first day and knocked him down. Then he looked around and said, 'Is there anyone else who wants to dispute who's boss?' *That's what must be done.*"

He put his theory into practice at Raytheon. "I had two division managers who arrived late to an appointment with me," he recalls. To one of them Krafve said, "Do you like it here?"

"I don't understand," the man said.

"Answer the question," Krafve snapped.

"Well, yes," the man said.

"The next time we have an appointment and you are going to be late, call and let me know. Then come prepared to discuss the subjects we have agreed to discuss—*or you'll be out on your butt.*" [10]

That was harsh, but Krafve had come up in a hard school, starting from humble beginnings. He once told Dr. Edward Bowles, with whom he held—at least at first—long talks, that "when I was a kid I worked as a repair man for a time. And when I entered some of those luxurious homes, I looked around and said to myself, 'This is what I'm going to get.'" [11]

He climbed well in the competitive thirties, by 1941 was general sales manager in northern Wisconsin for Ebasco. In the army during World War II, he became a management engineer in the organizational group effort headed by General Somervell, "spent four years between Washington, Baltimore, and finally, Germany. I was a troubleshooter."

Mustered out in 1946, he turned down his prewar job. "I had to do it quick; otherwise I might not have had the nerve." He was married and had two children, no job—and no special skill. He joined a management consulting firm in Chicago and was placed on the Ford account. In those years young Henry Ford II was bringing in consultants and working to overcome the incredible regime of Harry Bennett, a task finally achieved by Ernest Breech, universally known as Mr. Breech.

Krafve watched when the Quiz Kids (so named because they asked so many questions) arrived at Ford. "There were ten of them, including McNamara and Tex Thornton, among others. Mr. Breech put them down a level when he arrived," he recalls. But McNamara became Ford controller; "he was the leader of the Quizzers." [12]

Krafve had, for a period, worked on the Ford defense business; he recalls examining Raytheon's defense contracts and noting, with surprise, that the firm received a high percent of its proposals. "Too high a percentage to maintain," he said. "These revenues will drop—unless there's another war."

Krafve was a successful automotive executive who had been a successful management consultant. His assumption that managing is a movable art was, at the time, both fashionable and widespread: it is still widespread. The theory that management is a separate function, applicable to all sorts of situations, is what sells books on management and keeps schools of management packed with aspirants. In 1960 the theory had become a valuable tool in American business language, a prime argument in the hands of conglomerateurs, who argued that professional managers could create a strong commercial organism out of a welter of weak and disparate parts.

To some extent Krafve was a representative—even spokesman—for the movement Geneen expressed so well in action. Like Geneen he was an advocate of psychological testing, and unlike him was quite candid about his reasons. "I want to find the weaknesses," he said. "I want to know if a man's a drunk or a psychotic. It's nice to know that he has a high I.Q., but before a man is placed in a position of power he should be given a psychological run-through."

Once seated at Raytheon he looked about with satisfaction, but he didn't like all he saw. "Missiles were controlled by a tight little group, and they were ignoring the air force," he said.[13] Before he stepped into that situation, however, he decided that Tom Phillips should be made a vice president.

In all, a sure and even brave man, placed by destiny in the wrong place for the second time running.

The departure of an older generation from the national scene was mirrored inside Raytheon. Ray Ellis, head of the radio and radar division of the War Production Board, assistant director of the guided missiles program at Johns Hopkins University, and afterward Raytheon's international head, retired. Captain David R. Hull, chief of the electronic design division of the navy and assistant chief of the Bureau of Ships during World War II, retired as a group vice president of the government engineering division, which included missiles and radar, and was succeeded by Dave Coffin. Ernest Leathem, another navy veteran and longtime assistant to Charlie Adams, retired. The board of directors composed statements of appreciation to all three; all three deserved it.[14]

Fritz Gross, whose contributions had been huge and who had been a leader in the inner circles of the equipment division through the years, was raised to corporate vice president. Dr. Ivan Getting, vice president of Raytheon's engineering-research group, however, was invited, by the Secretary of the Air Force, to become president of the Aerospace Corporation—a nonprofit air force venture. With large national efforts becoming concentrated on space, this was a signal honor and Getting departed; his Raytheon responsibilities were assumed by Dr. Martin Schilling.

Adams' bargaining with the NATO group regarding Hawk culminated in an agreement by the Europeans to pay Raytheon $7 million for its know-how. This handsome sum, which would bring $5 million to the corporation after taxes, was a credit to the chairman's patient skill in negotiation and was a notable achievement.

Adams had already planned how some of this payment would be applied, and had mapped out a somewhat complex program to expand in Europe that would require some $2.8 million. The steps culminated in Raytheon's owning 40 percent of a new Italian venture called Selenia, with Finnmeccanica owning another 40 percent and Italian Edison the remaining 20 percent. The directors, informed at each stage, approved. Selenia would receive a large share of the Italian Hawk contract; it had manufacturing facilities at Rome and Naples, and was already engaged in making Raytheon's radars. In addition, Raytheon had increased its ownership, in lieu of royalties, to 30 percent in Elsi, in Palermo, Sicily.

Dr. Carlo Calosi was to supervise operations in Europe and watch over Elsi, a firm in which Raytheon's interest had grown quite important. Calosi and his wife, who had become well-known and popular figures in Cambridge, moved back to Italy. It was a triumphal return in many respects and contrasted sharply with the time when Calosi had been a fugitive from the Gestapo, and had been plucked from Italian shores by the OSS, wearing an Italian priest's cassock.[15]

International hugger-mugger had not relaxed since that wartime period, however. In midsummer 1960 Bernon Mitchell and William H. Masten, both of the top-level, highly secret U.S. National Security Agency defected to the USSR and revealed all they knew, which was plenty. The event caused the United States to change all its security codes and systems throughout the western world—a tremendous overhaul.[16]

Other dishevelments occurred. The Belgian Congo was a seething mass. Belgium dispatched troops, but Patrice Lumumba, leader of a dissident, Communist-oriented group, appealed to the UN. France was enduring terrorist outbreaks in Algeria.[17] Cuba expropriated U.S. property and mounted shrill diatribes.

In the last year of President Eisenhower's administration, the USSR revealed it had made enormous strides in presenting itself as the supporter of Third World nations against the West and the United States. In September Khrushchev addressed the UN National Assembly on the subject of nonwhite races and world disarmament.[18] He and Castro hugged one another in New York with attendant outbursts of publicity, and the U.S. election campaign—featuring Kennedy and Nixon—proceeded along lines of another world.

Wars, revolutions, elections, and entertainments notwithstanding, the work of the world must continue. Only a philosopher can place work properly. William James, quoted appreciatively in *The Hap-*

*hazard Years* by co-authors George C. Reinhardt and William R. Kintner, described its value in 1960 in accurate terms.

"Every up-to-date dictionary," said Dr. James, "should say peace and war mean the same thing now in *posse*, now in *actu*. It may even be reasonably said that intensely sharp competitive preparation for war of the nation is the real war, permanent, unceasing; and that battles are only a sort of public verification of mastery gained during the peace intervals."

In that competition during 1960, Raytheon's SubSig group, now proudly regrouped, established Raytheon's AntiSubmarine Warfare Center at Portsmouth, Rhode Island. This constituted the first integrated industrial antisubmarine warfare and sonar center in the nation. Raytheon, at the same time, had established and was managing a NATO antisubmarine warfare research center at La Spezia, Italy.[19]

Hawk had become operational with both the U.S. Army and the Marine Corps during the year; a new Sparrow III-A had been designed for the Phantom II, a carrier-based interceptor planned for long service.

All this activity in the defense sector contrasted oddly with the closing days of the election campaign, watched by Americans over the estimated 85 million television sets in operation.[20] Kennedy had charged the Eisenhower Administration with allowing the Soviets to achieve superiority in weapons of war: the missile gap became an issue. His other strong charge, which stung all America to some extent, was that the Administration had been flaccid in allowing the rise of Castro and the establishment of a pro-Soviet, anti-American bastion in Cuba.

Yet the election seemed to swing more on the appearance of the candidates in their televised series of debates than in the content of their remarks. Few could recall what they said; all could describe how they looked.

The results were razor thin. Kennedy's margin was a little over 100,000 out of 68.3 million votes.

A week after the elections, Percy Spencer married Charlie Adams' secretary, Lillian Ottenheimer. She soon found herself being instructed in how to fish; learned that Percy always cleaned the fish he brought home and never shot game unless it was for his table.[21] She was also to learn that Charlie Adams, better known for sailing, was also an ardent hunter and that he and Spencer used to exchange trophies.

New England is like that still: an area where private lives are led by men even when they are part of huge corporations. Adams was a believer in a balanced life. So, the new Mrs. Spencer discovered, was her husband.

Raytheon ended 1960, however, on a slightly bleak note. Sales were at record highs, had reached $539.9 million. But profits had dropped from $3.89 a share the previous year to $3.01. Subtracting the cost of the Adams-NATO coup, and an unexpected tax bill for $1.6 million, earnings per share had plummeted to $2.09. On the surface the final after-tax earnings still looked formidable—they had reached $11.5 million. The fact was that the firm's sales had increased by $45 million—half the amount of the increase of the two preceding years—which had been predicted, but profits had fallen by $2 million.[22] That had not been predicted.

Early in January 1961, William Gammell, Jr.—Billy Gammell—retired as a director of Raytheon. In the end he had traveled with the venture longer and farther than Laurence Marshall, who had sought his support to get started; longer than Dr. C. G. Smith or Vannevar Bush. It could not have been launched without his help, would several times have died prematurely without his support. As the board said in its official encomium, he stepped in "several times in the long and frequently difficult history of the Company at great personal risk to make the difference between success and failure" [23]—a difficult role easily overlooked because it resides in the background, and one seldom appreciated. Lending money, according to Ambrose Bierce, is a way to make enemies.

Yet Billy Gammell made and retained friends; he continued to be a friend to Laurence Marshall. He was keenly interested in events on a continuing and contemporary basis, was invited to attend meetings as a director emeritus and, to nobody's surprise, continues to appear quite often.

Departures from center stage are not always achieved so gracefully. President Eisenhower, now a lame duck, smarted from the tide of criticism attendant upon changes in national mood. General Medaris, retired as the army missile czar, issued a book titled *Countdown for*

*313*

*Decision* criticizing Eisenhower's lack of faith in the space program and accusing him of holding outdated military opinions.[24] Throughout the long and difficult election campaign the previous year, Eisenhower had grown increasingly irritated at the Kennedy charge the United States had fallen behind in the missile race and in overall military strength. The retiring President was aware many high-ranking members of the army and navy held his policies in low esteem,[25] and that he had been accused of too close a personal association with leading industrialists.

In his farewell address to the nation, the retiring President turned upon his critics in a characteristically oblique fashion, saying in part that the nation "should guard against the acquisition of unwarranted influence, whether sought or unsought, by the military-industrial complex. The potential for the disastrous rise of misplaced power exists and will persist. . . . We must also be alert to . . . the danger that public policy itself become the captive of a scientific-technological elite." [26]

Though he quickly followed that by a warning that the Communist nations presented a clear danger, the press paid little attention to that: communism was fading as a bogey. Instead the commentators leaped upon two phrases: "the military-industrial complex" and "the scientific-technological elite" and repeated them endlessly. These eight words spawned books, articles, and attitudes; entered the language and thought of the nation and the world. They became weapons against immense sectors of American industry, science, and the military.

In early January 1961, however, the Eisenhower farewell speech seemed a matter of only a passing moment at Raytheon. The year started in an atmosphere of bad news followed by more of the same. January results were not impressive. The board—still consisting of ten men—was not too pleased.

The directors consisted of Carl Gilbert, George Langreth, Stanley Lovell, Robert Stoddard, William Hogan (of American Airlines: he replaced Billy Gammell), Dean Edmonds of New York, and Roger Damon, now president of the First National Bank of Boston. They were the outside directors; insiders consisted of Adams, Krafve, and Percy Spencer.

They regarded, among other matters, the first of a series of changes that Krafve suggested. The first was the creation of a chief financial officer, a concept new to Raytheon but one that Krafve had brought along in his kit from Detroit.

*314*

"I'm not a real figures man," he says, "but at Ford I was well served, and I wanted the same kind of service. Ingram, as chief financial officer, hired some former Ford men and put in the sort of controls I liked." [27]

Ingram's installation, or upgrading, set chairs in motion. A director of financial analysis and control was hired, as well as a director of systems and procedures and a director of financial audit. Meanwhile Al Reed, who had served with Dave Schultz and Harold Geneen and had been Raytheon's treasurer—or number-one man on finance for years—remained the same in title but would henceforth report to Ingram. Arthur Schene was made controller.[28]

Roger Damon, a tart New England observer, watched these gavottes with an ironic eye. Damon was of the opinion that Krafve could sell well: "Could sell ten out of every twelve men he talked to. But I couldn't follow him. Had an involved spiel." [29]

More innovations followed. The group vice president of Electronic Components & Devices, Homer R. Oldfield, Jr., who was, inevitably, called Barney, proposed that Raytheon purchase a small New Jersey firm called Trans-Sil. He accompanied the recommendation with a discussion of the great potential of the silicon rectifier market. Trans-Sil made these products, and would cost $1.25 million. Someone curiously wondered what firms dominated the silicon rectifier industry. "Westinghouse and General Electric," came the reply, "have seventy percent of the market." Further questioning elicited the information that Trans-Sil had 1.3 percent of that same market. Nevertheless Oldfield was optimistic.[30]

Late in February, at another board meeting, more changes appeared—this time in the semiconductor operations. A vice president of commercial marketing and product planning and a corporate commercial product planner were appointed; comparison studies between Raytheon and other electronic firms were underway.

It was obvious Krafve was staffing to conduct a campaign of some sort to check the Raytheon decline in commercial markets. The directors and Adams waited, with varying degrees of patience, for it to be finished and unveiled. Among these watchful waiters could be counted the missile groups. Their former indifference to moves and personalities in the executive suite had vanished; they had learned better during the Geneen era. Now, well aware their sector was contributing hugely to the firm and was continuing to grow, they awaited the Krafve prescription warily.


On April 17, 1961, less than three months after President Kennedy's inauguration, the Administration launched the Bay of Pigs invasion of Cuba.[31] Originally planned as a rebellion against Castro staged by Cuban refugees with covert U.S. support, it turned into a disaster militarily and a fiasco in terms of both Latin American relations and U.S. world prestige.

Although the President immediately assumed full responsibility, the press chose, to the delight of the Soviets, to blame the Central Intelligence Agency.[32] Within days the initials CIA were made world famous; in the weeks, months, and years ahead, the CIA would become the target of accusations whenever disorders occurred outside the United States.

Such disorders were frequent and increasingly difficult to analyze. They ranged from turbulence in the Belgian Congo, where the UN was assisting the creation of a new state, to terrorism in Algeria. The Algerian situation was put to referendum.[33] When it became clear de Gaulle would release France's hold on that colony, the French Army in Algiers rebelled. The rebellion was an ominous indication of deep-seated western divisions.

President Kennedy discovered how far some U.S. sectors had moved from sympathy with the government when he held a special meeting with seven of the nation's top publishers at the White House. In the wake of accusations that the Cuban invasion had been mishandled by both the government and the press, President Kennedy suggested the presidential office keep the top seven publishers informed of all top security moves—providing they agreed not to publish information they were told was sensitive. They refused. He was astounded; ". . . publishers," he said, "have to understand that we're never more than a miscalculation away from war . . ." [34] He could not understand that they did not believe that; their sense of safety had grown—like a child's—too strong to be shattered by anything short of actual catastrophe.

\*     \*     \*

By midsummer 1961 Adams was able to report a series of international steps to the directors. Raytheon had a one-third participation in the New Japan Radio Company in Tokyo and was in post position to buy A. C. Cossor of Great Britain.[35]

The Cossor acquisition was most interesting. Cossor, a well-known and firmly established British manufacturer of communications equipment, cables, and components, had a subsidiary that made traffic controls and transponder beacons, had a second subsidiary called Cossor Communications that made high-frequency communications equipment and mobile radios. Cossor was not into microwaves, but Raytheon could carry it there.

That was cheering news, though Cossor's sales had recently dropped. Its technical abilities were high and it was centrally situated in the heart of the still-extensive British market with all its connections and influence. Adams received the approval of the board to continue these negotiations to a conclusion and immediately left for London. His travels and international negotiations took a good deal of his time.

Such international matters had grown complex, especially in Italy, a land where a straight line is often regarded as an optical illusion. La Centrale, the majority owner of Elsi, the tube and components firm in Sicily, had suggested that Raytheon purchase an additional 19 percent interest for $337,000, bringing its participation to 49 percent. Elsi planned to enter the production of television tubes and other new market areas and would soon need a transfusion of $1.5 million to make such expansions. But Krafve doubted this sum would be needed before the end of 1962. All that was required for the moment was $220,000. Overall, that meant $557,000. If that sum were supplied, a marketing firm called Raytheon-Elsi would be created, in which Raytheon would own 51 percent, to market Elsi products in Italy and, presumably, elsewhere in Europe.[36]

This was all very complicated but seemed a reasonable result of the promise inherent in Italy so often before discussed. The Vitro Corporation of America had formed a partnership with Selenia, 40 percent owned by Raytheon, to construct a missile test range, for $15 million. Simultaneously Raytheon-Elsi would be created to penetrate the Italian components market. Dr. Calosi, who would supervise everything —Raytheon-Elsi, the Raytheon interests in Selenia and Vitro-Selenia, Cossor (when it was acquired), Raytheon in Switzerland, et al.—was very positive about developments. So was Richard Krafve.

The new president had not been expected to enter, in any deep sense, into international negotiations. Adams had created the international network, was building it carefully, and had retained it under his personal supervision. But Krafve rushed to foreign shores and dove into the details of all transactions. After the Cossor acquisition was assured and Adams had carefully told the English banking community that Cossor's financial connections would remain, more or less, intact in the City, Krafve appeared to give the Cossor executives an opposite understanding.[37] That led Adams into some sharp comments.

Krafve also appeared—quite conspicuously—in Italy,[38] where he toured the area and engaged in long discussions with Dr. Calosi, whom he assured of his support.

Krafve was equally busy at home. While his new marketing executives were conducting surveys and making plans, he decided the missile group was poorly organized. That judgment was surprising because missiles were responsible—and had been responsible even during the Geneen years—for Raytheon's remarkable resurgence.

"Missiles need tighter controls," Krafve announced and told Coffin to split the missile group into two divisions. One would be production, headed by T. C. Wisenbaker; the other development, headed by Tom Phillips.[39] Coffin, as group vice president, would supervise both parts; both vice presidents Wisenbaker and Phillips would report to him.

When Coffin relayed this command to Wisenbaker and Phillips, they protested to Coffin that overall efficiency was at stake—that missiles did not have enough men to create two divisions of first rank. He sympathized, but reminded them that was an order.

Glumly, they set about the organization—divided their resources and set up two shops. Once launched, they made the effort conscientiously. Phillips concentrated on development, Wisenbaker on production.


Krafve's Great Market Plan was unveiled in appropriate detail by group vice president Oldfield in September 1961. The directors were shown charts and slides and subjected to a long, complex, and detailed exposition.[40] It began with the explanation that operations at the Raytheon semiconductor plant in Lewiston, Maine, were proving quite successful; that semiconductors of high quality were being produced at low unit costs. Then Oldfield explained that the marketing groups wanted to tie the operations of the Lewiston plant into a plant owned by CBS at Lowell, Massachusetts, which produced silicon devices and circuit modules.

The purpose, the directors learned, was to "achieve product leadership in areas of importance to both the semiconductor divisions and the corporation as a whole." The plant at Lowell was new; Raytheon had already purchased a CBS inventory of receiving tubes from that installation; the plant purchase would enable all the Raytheon semiconductor activities in the area to be centralized. Why was it available? CBS was abandoning the semiconductor industry.

Next, Oldfield explained, Raytheon should "establish a semiconductor base in the important West Coast region in order to share in its expanding equipment manufacturer's market"; especially near the burgeoning Palo Alto area.

Obviously Raytheon could not acquire the CBS Lowell plant nor establish itself near Palo Alto overnight, unless it bought existing facilities. Since the "semiconductor business was shifting so rapidly, it might be necessary to take such steps even before the next board meeting."

While assistants placed and replaced charts, Oldfield explained the general state of the semiconductor industry and its fast pace, and concluded that the purchase of the Rheem Semiconductor Corporation, a subsidiary of Rheem Manufacturing, appeared most attractive. Its acquisition, said the group vice president, would give Raytheon "an effective and rapid entry into West Coast semiconductors." Its assets were worth $5.4 million, but it was available for $2 million; maybe $2.5 million.

A director wondered if the Rheem staff would transfer to Raytheon and Krafve thought that the leaders would, providing he could promise them stock options.[41]

But that was not all. Krafve believed in large steps, and his men had been very diligent. CBS was abandoning the semiconductor industry and its Danvers, Massachusetts, plant was also available. It was a plant only eight years old, situated on sixty acres on Route 128, containing 160,000 square feet. That also looked very good. It was, really, a bargain, because Machlett, Raytheon's existing subsidiary, needed a satellite plant. The CBS installation at Danvers was really too good for a mere satellite, but it was immediately available; it had cost CBS $4 million to build. Krafve, Oldfield, & Co. thought they might offer CBS

$2 million—and obtain building, land, equipment, raw stock, the work in progress. It might be that the inventory and orders in hand alone would return the purchase price. Perhaps they would go to $2.2 million.

This was a lot to swallow in one gulp, but meanwhile other men and departments were waiting to report and both Oldfield and Krafve appeared very confident. They had uncovered, it seemed, several extraordinary bargains. The directors approved these expansions and Oldfield left, to be replaced as speaker by Glenn Lord, the vice president of government business, who was assisted by David Sullivan, director of market planning in the Office of Government Planning. He had slides to show and discussed the Brobdingnagian budgets of the Department of Defense. That seemed to reduce the proposed new expenditures somewhat.

After that, it was something of a letdown to learn, from chief financial officer Ingram, that the firm's earnings were still dropping and that its existing semiconductor business was in trouble.[42]

Still, there was no gainsaying the huge size and impressive scale of the enterprise. The number of employees hovered around 43,000; the new executive headquarters at Lexington were simple but very modern—most impressive. Krafve, who disliked driving all the way downtown to the Ritz Carlton, talked to one of its best barbers, Fiore Gigliotti—Gig—and asked him how he would like to barber in a special establishment at Raytheon. Gig liked the idea and Raytheon executives were soon astonished to discover they had their own shop.

Gig was somewhat surprised in his own turn. The topflight scientists and engineers of the firm complained that his haircuts were never short enough. Most had never had a New York massage and didn't know what lotions they preferred, had never heard of the extras he suggested.[43]

The Raytheon men, for their part, had barely become used to Geneen's platoons when Krafve's inundated them and they had to adjust to marketing men. Marketing, in the early 1960's, had assumed many of the characteristics of a movement. It was spawning its own trade journals and jargon, and then—as now—seemed heavily populated with fast-talking, high-living types. Tom Phillips, who by chance found himself on a trip with one of the marketing executives, was stunned at this new life style.

"It seemed to me that every time I turned around there was another waiter rushing into the suite with either a cart or a heavy tray of delicacies," Phillips recalled later. "That man never ate alone at company expense; he liked to have as many guests as possible crowded around a groaning board."

Phillips, inclined toward austerity, disapproved.[44]

Norman Krim, on the other hand, encountered a different sort of shock. When all the executives from their various and previously scattered locations moved to the new headquarters building at Lexington, Krim was left behind "with the night watchman." He was not included in anyone's plans and had no particular responsibilities. Miserably he trotted over to Lexington and submitted his resignation; after twenty-six years he was through with Raytheon.

He was not, however, forgotten—though of course he felt he was. Roger Damon, a Raytheon director and president of Boston's First National Bank, called to say that Radio Shack, an electrical appliance firm, was in trouble. Krim looked into the matter and became president of that venture—in many ways a better post than he had had before. Nevertheless he was depressed by the manner of his departure from Raytheon.[45]

Krafve's plans were approved by the directors, but the directors were neither engineers nor close to the semiconductor industry. The fact was that Raytheon's new marketing experts had studied the semiconductor industry on the eve of great changes. Since market studies are based on statistics and statistics are, by nature, historic before they can be collected, they had unwittingly recommended an entry into an altered situation.

Before Krafve had become president, Raytheon had already decided to enter the semiconductor industry and to locate a new plant in Maine. That decision did not, at the time, meet with any dissenting voices.

But at the time of Krafve's marketing plan, the semiconductor industry situation had changed dramatically. Inspired by the great success of Texas Instruments Company, many firms had created new facilities and entered the field. The results were soon to become a classic of overcapacity, accompanied by rapidly falling prices in a fiercely competitive market. It was immediately prior to this stage that the electronic experts inside CBS and the Rheem Manufacturing Company longed to abandon the race—and that Raytheon appeared as a purchaser. The experts had led Krafve toward two horses already slated to be scratched, though the reasons of their owners had not yet become generally discernible.

Meanwhile Raytheon's technical ranks continued to perform at a high level and its backlog of government work, already at record levels, continued to grow.


In Washington President John Kennedy had hit upon the Moon Project as a means of arousing the growing lethargy of the American people. It was, in a way, a brilliant way to outflank the growing numbers who were against any strengthening of the U.S. military. The nation that conquered space had to develop the technology and the means that support military strength. Kennedy's appeal worked; he aroused an enthusiasm that had been sagging in recent years. For a shimmering period he lifted the nation's pride and its spirits, pushed it along the path of competition it had to travel, whether it knew it or not.


Raytheon's semiconductor ventures ran into trouble. The Danvers plant, purchased from CBS with the idea that it would make a fine new location for Machlett, proved completely unsuitable. Machlett's machines were huge; they would cost millions to move—and the managers of Machlett did not want to move. Great pileups indicating other marketing mistakes increased. Although the missiles division was making more money than ever, the firm's overall profits were dropping.

When matters begin to go awry, some men change their plans, others place the blame elsewhere. Paul Hannah, who liked Krafve, said, "He was conscientious and began to work increasingly longer hours. But he showed signs of strain. He grew tired, and a tired man makes mistakes."

Among these mistakes was an increasing impatience with subordinates. That is always a mistake, for it hurts morale and diminishes spontaneity. It was noted that Krafve treated Percy Spencer with scant respect. It was true that Spencer, after herculean efforts sustained for years, was showing signs of age, was faltering. Nevertheless the mistreatment shocked many. Meanwhile Percy not only endured his psychic demotion patiently but recommended Ed Dashefsky to become head of the microwave and power tube division. The selection was a good one, and a contribution to the firm.

Not content with reducing his associates, Krafve came to believe his troubles arose because his managerial hand was impeded by Charlie Adams, the chairman and chief executive. To some extent such a belief is almost a concomitant of being the number-two man in any organization, but it is usually contained within limits. For Krafve it became an unlimited conviction.

His dissatisfaction and the increasing problems of the firm's commercial efforts permeated the executive suite, trickled through the corridors, and—in the mysterious way in which human beings sense and alert one another—became an open company secret. Krafve, his men whispered, was going to push Charlie Adams to one side and consolidate all authority into his own hands.

Eventually these plans and attitudes reached the ears of Dr. Edward L. Bowles, consultant to the firm for many years. Few men have had as extraordinary a career as Dr. Bowles. He had been associated with Raytheon in one way or another since the days of Dr. C. G. Smith. In the years since then Bowles had worked with Dr. Bush at MIT; had been a mover in the radar efforts in the United States during World War II and advisor to Secretary of War Stimson; had served as scientific advisor to General Hap Arnold, to the Truman Administration, to Secretary of the Army Frank Pace; knew the mighty and those in between.

It was something of a surprise for Bowles to learn, via the grapevine, that Krafve was moving toward a showdown with Adams—and was sure that he would win such a confrontation. Bowles talked to some of the directors—men like Roger Damon, Carl Gilbert, and others—and discovered they were also surprised. Bowles discovered the directors were by no means as impressed by the Krafve performance as Krafve assumed.[46]

This was, of course, all behind the scenes and on a very high level.

Tom Phillips, vice president of the missile division, was one of the many outside the developing situation. He had, in fact, changes of his own to contemplate. He had received an offer to head a research and development effort in the Department of Defense.

That department, in the early New Frontier days of the Kennedy Administration, was enjoying a renascence of public approval. Bright young men from all sectors were again being attracted to Washington, where the youthful new President had brought an invigorating air of high national purpose and clearly progressive social ideals. Phillips had every reason to believe the offer would help his career and be an exciting new challenge.

That was important. The long period of effort inside the missile group had been rewarding, but the successive movements in the executive suite were reducing the sense of accomplishment. Geneen had ushered a revolution into the firm that altered its internal climate. Yet Geneen was coherent, clear, and shrewd. His innovations were based on a considerable commercial acumen and impressive financial ability. Krafve, on the other hand, seemed less able and his programs had cost millions of dollars. It was time for a change, and Phillips looked forward to making one.

Dr. Bowles, however, was disturbed. He thought it would be a great loss to Raytheon if Phillips departed. Krafve felt otherwise. He suspected that Phillips was using the Washington offer as a lever for a higher post inside the company, and described it as a "power play." Meanwhile he proceeded with plans to ask the board to make him chief executive of the firm—and to set Charlie Adams aside.[47]

Adams, away in Japan, was kept informed by telephone. At first he was of the opinion matters could be amicably resolved. He could not credit Krafve with such reckless purposes. But the end of the year was approaching, and with it the curious tendency of Americans to wrap matters together for resolution during the Christmas season. Dr. Bowles, directors Gilbert, Damon, and others, were now of the opinion that Krafve had planned a confrontation that would have to be resolved.

Adams returned from Japan to be met at the New York airport by Carl Gilbert. They traveled to Boston together and were in turn met by Dr. Bowles. Bowles drove Adams downtown and dropped him off at the First National Bank where director Roger Damon was waiting. By that time the chairman had decided that Krafve needed high-level technological assistance. The president, he thought, had been misled by the marketing men he had relied upon. The Adams plan, therefore, was to calm Krafve and to try to retain Phillips, and place him near the president.

Unfortunately Krafve was not in the humor to recognize his own errors; he was instead intent upon replacing Adams. He demanded the issue be resolved by the board. The directors would have to choose between Charlie Adams and Richard Krafve. That meeting was held during Christmas week, on December 27, 1961. Later Krafve said, "It was a heavy session."

It was also definitive. The directors voted overwhelmingly to support Adams as chief executive. Krafve's resignation was offered and accepted. Tom Phillips, virtually unknown to the general community, was elected executive vice president and operations manager of Raytheon.

The news created dismay among Krafve supporters but pleasure in the technical ranks. Nobody knows what Adams felt at that point: probably a sense of great weariness. He had brought in two men in succession, both with outstanding gifts and impressive records, who had not worked out as he had hoped. But whatever he thought, he did not forget another matter he had in mind.

A day or so later Norman Krim, seated in his office as president of Radio Shack, looked up with pleasure to see Charlie Adams coming toward him with outstretched hand.[48]


"I was discovered, or pulled out of the woodwork, twice in a twelve-year span," says Tom Phillips. "The first time by T. C. Wisenbaker; the second time by Charlie Adams." [49]

That had been true until early 1962. From that time forward Adams assisted Phillips toward becoming a chief executive, capable of taking an overall view of the company. It began with an assessment of Raytheon's position in February 1962. Phillips' survey is interesting from the start because of some private conclusions he had already reached regarding the proper evaluation of men at work.

"Since 1956, when Geneen brought in his own people," Phillips says, "the air of intrigue had grown thick. First Geneen and then, hard on the heels of his departure, Krafve had created palace guards. One result was that men emerged on the basis of personal relationships.

"The ability to say just the right sort of thing at the precise moment when it could alter the tone and feel of a situation enabled some men to exert great influence."

A feeling rose in Phillips that he had to get rid of that courtierlike atmosphere, clean the air inside the company. "Men," he says, "should be judged on the level of their competence, like engineers—not on the basis of their relationships to other men." [50]

Statistically there was little to discover, much to analyze. Figures from 1961 revealed record sales of $561.9 million, after-tax earnings of $6.8 million. With 3.8 million shares of common stock outstanding, 28,817 shareholders were not pleased to learn that earnings per share had dropped from $3.01 the year before to $1.69 in 1961.[51]

The company's 43,713 employees were organized into twelve divisions, eight of which operated under the direction of two group vice presidents. Its expenditure for research and development was almost $20 million, in addition to government-funded research and development work at the rate of $100 million a year. That was a very high order of technology indeed.

A peek behind the scenes reveals that the final quarter of 1961 had been up, and Ingram, the firm's financial officer, declared its balance sheet was the "strongest in its history." Debt had shifted from short- to long-term loans; government backlog had increased to $360 million. That provided the real base for progress.

Early in February 1962 the directors read and filed a notably calm and civil letter of resignation from Krafve, who departed to become a management consultant on a very high level, thereupon vanishing as far as Raytheon was concerned. Then the board approved of Adams' resumption of the title of president instead of chairman and seated Tom Phillips as a director. "A firm comes of age," Carl Gilbert said, "when it has trained its own leaders." [52] He, as well as the balance of the board, settled back to see how Adams' third candidate would fare.

Phillips himself huddled with Ingram, Raytheon's top financial officer. Ingram, a graduate engineer with an unusual grasp of finance, proved calm, logical, and disarmingly informal. Phillips found the situation tangled in detail but clear in outline.

Raytheon's government business and its microwave and power tube division were making money. But its commercial efforts were losing money, and the decisions of the previous two years had opened hydrants that significantly worsened those losses.

"We stayed," Phillips said later, "with germanium semiconductors too long. On the other hand, silicon was becoming an important material in planar technology." In time this would lead to integrated circuits—i.e., putting many components into a single chip.

It was clear, said Phillips, the plants, equipment, and product lines acquired "during a market convulsion" would have to be withdrawn. He made this recommendation to Adams and the directors in February 1962, at a time when one of the plants had just been occupied by Raytheon and the engineers had not yet moved into the second.[53]

Semiconductors were not the only Raytheon soft spot. The firm had retained an expensive receiving tube product line that had been based, originally, on its television set business. But by 1962 Raytheon was out of the home television and radio set market, and could sell only replacement components in an industry dominated by GE, RCA, and Sylvania. All three had their own captive share of the home set market. Phillips thought it best to retrench, to get out of the commercial receiving tube business altogether.

These were technical decisions, however, that could be made from an evaluation of abstract facts and circumstances. Both Ingram and Art Schene, the former controller of the Missile & Radar Division whom Phillips relied upon, pointed to another area that demanded special attention: "an oversized corporate headquarters staff; a burden on the divisions."

Altogether it was a situation that called for surgical remedies; deadwood in both technical and personal terms would have to be amputated. Yet Phillips and Adams both realized that a firm cannot advance through economies alone. Its income would have to improve, and it was essential that Raytheon diversify into commercial markets. It was their hope that the government defense business, headed by Coffin and Wisenbaker, with new groups and projects expanding under other men, would continue to thrive until the surgery was complete and profitable commercial ventures could be launched.

In Washington another young man, though not as young as Tom Phillips, was coming to similar conclusions about both his countrymen and the world at large. In December 1961 President Kennedy had observed that the United States "was becoming a nation of spectators" and urged more physical activity. Along the same lines, he established, or at least approved of, a new military command in South Vietnam, to be known as the Military Assistance Command. In response to questions from the press, he said these forces "would fire back if attacked, but were not combat troops in the generally understood sense of the word." [54]

Kennedy worked hard to awaken the nation. Colonel John Glenn orbited three times around the world to suitable fanfare, and huge sums were earmarked for the space program. Engineers from all over the nation were recruited for what was, loosely, called the Moon Program. Incredibly complex, spanning all the areas of hard science, it would spawn technology still being unraveled, developed, explored, and applied.

The nation was also experiencing a cultural lift in many directions. In February 1962 Mrs. John F. Kennedy, accompanied by television cameras, displayed the White House in a tour that was watched by an estimated 46 million viewers; shortly thereafter Mrs. Kennedy went on a goodwill tour of Italy and India that constituted a personal and political triumph. A sort of national relaxation was underway, in which Joseph Heller prepared to release his hilarious *Catch 22;* Vaughn Meader, Alan Sherman, and others mimicked the Boston accents and numerous personalities of the Kennedys; a beauty appeared frontally nude in an advertisement in *Harper's;* and sports events of every sort attracted increasing attention.[55]

The atmosphere changed inside Raytheon as well. The directors, who had been inundated by Geneen's financial jargon in the past and then by Krafve's marketing language, were treated, by the new executive vice president, to descriptions of technology. One involved lasers—an area so new the word itself aroused awe.

Dr. Martin Schilling, flanked by physicist Dr. Herman Statz and engineer Stanley Kass, explained that lasers are coherent light rays with great potential in broadband communications, optical radar, and even as weapons—and that Raytheon was active in their development.

In March 1962 Fritz Gross appeared before the directors to describe the equipment division, surface radars, SubSig, and data processing; in May Ed Dashefsky outlined power tube and microwave operations. Phillips was bringing operations to life in the boardroom.[56]

Meanwhile Raytheon's prospects in Italy reappeared. As usual, they assumed a new and glittering form, fascinatingly depicted by Dr. Carlo Calosi. The details were tangled. Elsi, the electronics firm located in Palermo, Sicily, in which Raytheon had become a minority owner by eschewing its royalties, had fallen behind in its payments again. The reasons, as explained to the directors, were flatteringly presented by La Centrale, the majority owner. La Centrale claimed its managers could not efficiently track or guide the production of semiconductors, klystrons, X-ray tubes, and magnetrons—all products produced by Elsi. Raytheon, said La Centrale, with its proven abilities in these abstruse fields, could do a much better job. Therefore it suggested that Raytheon should waive the $1.6 million in royalties due from Elsi and accept more stock in the venture; enough stock to make it majority owner and enable its managers to direct the operation more efficiently. If Raytheon agreed to that suggestion, it was also asked to assume responsibility for a $2-million La Centrale loan to Elsi. Some additional money might be needed for that purpose, but arrangements had already been made for Elsi to raise the sum through a low-interest loan from several Italian banks and IRFIS, an agency of the Italian government. Raytheon would not be asked to guarantee that new injection of capital, because Raytheon could help Elsi on another level.

That level would consist of advancing $1.2 million for the purchase of SELIT. Who was SELIT? SELIT was a small picture tube manufacturer, located next door, by coincidence, to the Elsi factory at Palermo. SELIT was also owned by La Centrale (by this time nothing seems surprising), together with Thomas Company of New Jersey.[57]

The acquisition of SELIT would allow Elsi to enter the manufacture of black-and-white television picture tubes in Italy. Italy was just becoming inflamed by television. With this new market at its fingertips and the improved systems that Raytheon's engineers could bring to Elsi, its chances of success would be immeasurably enhanced.

In the end it came to an additional $1.4 million and brought Raytheon's investment in Elsi to $5 million. The proceedings flowed smoothly from one stage to another, like a meal in an elegant restaurant. It was only the bill that shocked. Phillips, peeking, decided Elsi was worth a longer look.

In midsummer 1962 a new organization chart appeared. The names were fewer and the office of group vice president had vanished. Like Geneen, Phillips preferred to deal with the operating divisions personally. Homer Oldfield, one of the two former group vice presidents, was named Manager, Operations, Europe; Dr. Calosi, by this change, would have help. Dave Coffin, now a senior vice president, would coordinate activities between the government divisions. The equipment division was headed by Fritz Gross. The missile divisions, together again, would be headed by T. C. Wisenbaker.

The directors received news of these reorganizations without surprise; Phillips was expected to make changes. The shifts differed from those made by Phillips' immediate predecessors in one important basic. Both Geneen and Krafve had brought men in from outside, added men and titles, and produced a more crowded, complex organizational chart. Phillips simplified.

The streamlining extended throughout the entire pyramid. A cold wave washed through the marketing groups and swept men, charts, slides, surveys, field trips, and presentations over the side. Robert Hennemuth was given responsibility over personnel as well as industrial relations and told to reduce unnecessary reviewers, evaluators, and interviewers. Banks of cubicles were abruptly vacated.[58]

Even Gig the barber wondered if he would last; it seemed to him that Phillips regarded his row of lotions with a cold and unfriendly eye. His instincts were accurate, but not because the rather stark little shop with its one chair seemed luxurious to Phillips—it was the attitude behind this symbol that the new executive vice president wanted to exorcise. He had gone over accounts with Art Schene and had discovered expensive country club memberships, expense accounts loaded with costly extras. The trend would have to be reversed if the proper example was to be set.

Nevertheless changes in men, plants, plans, and policies is a wrenching and even traumatic experience. Phillips was convinced that Raytheon's commercial groups had to be pruned of unprofitable men and ventures and then set on a new, expanded course.

But the firm's government market sectors were also in need of organizing. Experiments in new radar assemblies were part of a creative shuffle at Bedford Labs that, in the words of Al Miccioli, "made the structure groan." New projects were being devised of considerable interest and potential, but managerial problems arose. It was necessary, because of the complexity of the technology involved, to appoint managers from engineering ranks, because nonengineers could not "track the effort." Yet all engineers are not managers; choices sometimes had to be reconsidered.[59]

The equipment division under Fritz Gross and Harold Hart was spawning progeny, and that was fruitful. Ralph Martin and others were consolidating the Polaris program at Sudbury; SubSig, now under Rogers Hamel, was moving forward. Yet, as Hart said later, "each new spin-off weakened the hive." It takes away valuable and creative men and makes it necessary for the parent to discover, upgrade, and develop a stream of younger men to repair the loss and maintain the forward growth of the division.[60]

Phillips was also greatly worried about the missile division. One of his first acts had been to put it back together—to close the divide Krafve had created between development and production when he and Wisenbaker had directed these branches. But Wisenbaker was unhappy in New England and decided to take early retirement. He had answered the bugle call of duty several times and had played a hero's role in carrying the missile effort forward for years. Without him, there is reason to believe Raytheon would never have succeeded in that effort. His desire to return to the warmth of Miami was understandable, but posed a new problem for Phillips—who could not, in conscience, stand in his way.

All of this meant that Phillips could not relax regarding the government market sector and devote his undivided attention to pruning unprofitable commercial marketing efforts. He had to find a new manager—or managers—for the defense programs. In late August 1962 he told the board about one such selection: former Lieutenant General Donald N. Yates, West Point '31, a Cal Tech graduate, onetime commander of the First Air Force test center at Cape Canaveral, former deputy director of research and engineering at the Defense Department. Yates, together with Dr. Martin Schilling, was given the responsibility over the missile and space programs. Then Phillips settled down, together with Adams and the directors, to take a look at the Raytheon international effort.

By the middle of September 1962 that scene had grown panoramic. Raytheon had operations in Italy, England, France, and Switzerland that employed six thousand people. It included Raytheon A. G. in Switzerland, which made semiconductors, and participation in Selenia, in Italy, which manufactured marine and weather radars, air-traffic controls and telecommunications systems, and was moving into

Hawk missiles. Selenia's backlog of orders had reached $40 million. In addition Raytheon was majority owner of A. C. Cossor of England, which it planned to divide into Sterling Cable and Cossor Electronics; of Sorensen-Ard A. G. and Sorensen, France, which made industrial equipment and instruments; and of Elsi, in Sicily.[61] All were thriving except the last.

Elsi had grown into a Raytheon investment of $5.1 million, with another $850,000 in guarantees for some of its debts; it had sales that amounted to $6 million, assets listed as worth $12.5 million, a plant of 200,000 square feet, and—according to Phillips—too many people.

"Too many people and too much space," he said. In part this conclusion was based on analysis and in part on reports. Elsi engineer Profumo, on the spot, reported that few Italian engineers wanted to move south of Rome under any circumstances; even fewer would consider Palermo, the capital of Sicily.

Phillips had other news for the board, closer to home: both T. C. Wisenbaker and Dave Coffin had decided to retire. Both men were eulogized; Coffin had been with the firm twenty-eight and Wisenbaker almost twenty years. Phillips was sorry about Wisenbaker, but his relations with Coffin had been injured by the events surrounding the company reorganization. Wisenbaker became a consultant to Raytheon, but Coffin soon joined Royden Sanders at Sanders Associates.

Both men were pioneers in one of Raytheon's most important efforts and had made deep and significant contributions. Wisenbaker had served as a technical leader and Coffin had actually held the missile group together by his calm, tactful presence in the days after Royden Sanders had stalked out. "He was," said Phillips later, "our father image at that time." Neither could be, or ever has been, forgotten; their departure left many regrets, and it was widely agreed the firm owed both men an enduring debt of gratitude.[62]


President John Kennedy had made the rise of a Soviet puppet regime in Cuba a central issue in his campaign for the White House. In 1961, shortly after taking office, President Kennedy had suffered a major setback in the Bay of Pigs incident. Early in 1962 he placed Cuba under a virtual U.S. trade embargo; in the spring the President attempted to rally the nation against Castro when the dictator proposed to release 1,100 prisoners from the Bay of Pigs for a ransom of

$62 million. Kennedy appealed to the nation to raise that sum, but only $2.5 million appeared in response. That sum, handed over to Cuba, obtained the release of sixty sick and wounded prisoners, who were accepted into the United States.[63]

Throughout the year 1962 American U-2's flew over Cuba, keeping a wary eye on that anti-U.S. bastion. Meanwhile the intelligence arms of the government received information from Cuban refugees who claimed the Soviets were building special military establishments on the island and importing ballistic missiles equipped with nuclear warheads. These reports were discounted; the refugees were labeled "biased and unreliable." [64]

The rumors persisted, however, and the White House asked for an assessment of the likelihood of events such as the refugees described. In response a National Intelligence Estimate was prepared that declared the Soviet Union was "not likely to apply a policy of such enormous risks as placing nuclear-tipped missiles in Cuba." [65]

Despite this memorandum, evidence began to appear that the Soviet Union was, in fact, in the midst of just such a venture. Aerial photographs made it unmistakable by October 14, 1962, that silos had been created and missiles landed on the island; though it is not clear from later accounts whether or not they were in place, the assumption is they were not.

President Kennedy called in the Soviet ambassador, asked some questions, and was told a number of lies. President Kennedy then asked the intelligence agencies for their estimate of the Soviet reaction to a demand they stop shipping missiles into Cuba and remove those already landed. A second National Intelligence Estimate was prepared saying it was now believed "the USSR would risk war rather than give in to a demand that the missiles be removed."

President Kennedy then chose his own course. On October 22, 1962, he appeared on television, told the people the situation, declared a naval blockade of Cuba, and took defensive measures.[66] The nation held its breath. In some quarters the reaction was curious. New York's Greenwich Village, a noisy arena for numerous and highly vocal groups, suddenly appeared deserted except for regular inhabitants.

A general military alert sounded; carriers with Phantom squadrons equipped with Sparrow III's headed toward the area; Hawk defensive batteries wheeled into place along the Florida shores.[67] A memorable photograph was taken of the President, who visited the scene. He is shown hatless, seated in the rear seat of an open car, his hair tousled by the wind. In the background, sticking upright into the air, looking like a row of giant's teeth, is a launcher with ready Hawks.

At that moment of high national peril the efforts of Phillips, Wisenbaker, Leiper, Coffin, Fossier, Margolskee, Miccioli, and all the other men of the missile group, as well as the firm that supported them through the hard years of the early fifties on through, took on its real meaning. The Sparrow and Hawk missiles they had developed were important weapons capable of intercepting and destroying low-flying aircraft before they could reach their targets.

The moment has since been called the Cuban missile crisis. In reality it was the U.S.-Soviet missile crisis. It passed. Many arguments have arisen since about the manner of its passage and the agreements by which it was concluded. Oddly, there has been far less speculation about Soviet intentions then, or the nature of Soviet demands had its movements not been detected midway. But that is the way of crises once safely overcome: they become subjects of retrospective and often partisan review. At the time it was as though clouds of rhetoric parted to show a gun in the sky. Then the moment passed; talk again rose to drown the memory and to obscure its significance. Meanwhile the Soviet satellite Cosmos began to overfly and photograph the United States.[68]

Nevertheless the atmosphere of crisis faded as quickly as it had appeared. The nation's attention returned to more mundane matters; a young fighter, twenty years old, defeated old Archie Moore, and Cassius Clay was discovered; the nation was saddened by the death of Marilyn Monroe; Billy Sol Estes was sent to prison; military aid was sent to assist India against incursions from China; the U.S. Communist Party was fined for refusing to register as a USSR agency; Cuba began releasing Bay of Pigs prisoners after it was assured of over $50 million in food and medical supplies gathered from private U.S. sources; *Who's Afraid of Virginia Woolf* appeared on Broadway, and *My Fair Lady* finally closed.[69]

At Raytheon, Adams was pleased with Phillips. The two men conferred often and easily; there was none of the subtle tension in the air that had marked the situation with former executive vice presidents.

Raytheon purchased the Autometric Corporation of New York,

*334*

an enterprise engaged in photo reconnaissance, mapping, and data reduction work for the government—activities the Cuban matter made quite relevant and understandable. Phillips told the directors that although the Autometric group would cost less than $1 million, he considered it very important because it consisted "of a talented group of people." [70] It was clear the yardsticks of the company were changing.

By the end of the year 1962 the results of change appeared. Sales had risen, though less than in previous years, to reach $580.7 million; earnings had stopped falling and risen by almost 40 percent to reach $9.5 million. In per share terms, this meant an increase from $1.69 a share to $2.31 a share.[71]

Below these record figures was another line that showed the number of employees, however, and that provided a surprise. Raytheon employment had risen steadily, year by year, since 1950. During 1962 for the first time, that figure was reduced by more than three thousand people.[72] Phillips' ship not only ran faster but with a smaller crew.

Throughout the nation the year 1963 opened to a decidedly mixed scene difficult to define. With the clear backing of the Administration, a nationwide campaign to achieve full civil rights for all citizens continued unabated, but not without resistance in some sections. Pop art— a new pictorial phenomenon featuring soup cans and other once-scorned, homely objects—appeared; so did a new wave of folk singing and group concerts called hootenannies. Joan Baez and Bob Dylan were among those who captured the attention of youth, and the national budget was set at a record level of $98.8 billion.

Internationally the situation was equally mixed. Despite tensions with Cuba, the Soviets in Berlin, and Communists in Vietnam, a treaty banning nuclear tests in the air, in space, and underwater was signed by the United States, the United Kingdom, and the USSR. That was a notable achievement for peace. President Kennedy made it clear he had equally high hopes for the improvement of the nation by sending to Congress—all virtually at the same time—an expanded civil rights bill, a program of medical care for the aged, a proposal to help the mentally retarded, and a tax cut. Despite difficulties, it was clear the new President was working hard to turn the nation toward new constructive avenues.

\*     \*     \*

By early 1963 the Raytheon government groups had been reorganized into four divisions. General Yates headed Space & Information, Dr. Martin Schilling was in charge of Missiles, Fritz Gross headed Government Equipment, and Rogers Hamel led SubSig.[73]

Such a large-scale reorganization contains inherent problems. Corporate divisions and subdivisions, like military organizations, are composed of more than tables of organization; they need time to blend into effective entities. It was also true that Raytheon's backlog of military orders was an impressive $390 million, but managers of a large firm—or any firm—cannot afford to relax in the present: they must organize the future.

In this respect the firm confronted problems. Raytheon's competitors, now abreast of the state of the art, were free to bid on the next generation of missiles. Phillips was concerned over the ability of the government groups to obtain such new contracts, which were needed. His working day was occupied by the commercial sectors, but he began to hold after-hours meetings in his office to review government operations, programs and planning.

Adams, meanwhile, was occupied with international matters, and was away much of the time. He was pleased to report that Cossor, in England, was improving and Raytheon's international sector was expanding with a new office created in South Africa. Elsi, however, needed new loans. Its former majority owner, La Centrale, which once handled Elsi's financial needs, had withdrawn from that task; it would be necessary for Raytheon to come forward with guarantees.[74] Otherwise international was doing well.

The president understood, as do few Americans, that business in Europe is conducted on a personal level. Europeans do not believe that matters of importance can be handled as abstractions without injury. He also knew that Europe is closely knit, cobwebbed with deep interpersonal relationships, and incredibly diverse. He worked hard to keep Raytheon's ventures from developing the weaknesses inherent in absentee ownership.

Both men found their tasks complicated by changes taking place in both the nation and the world.

The new Secretary of Defense, Robert McNamara, introduced a planning-budgeting-programming program that swept aside the for-

*336*

merly independent purchasing systems of the service branches and brought advanced computer techniques to the fore. This change, immense in scope and influence, had in its favor a sophisticated series of techniques that had some unexpected side effects. One was to reduce the influence and authority of the service branches and to introduce a new layer of civilian expertise into defense considerations. Firms like Raytheon who had established relations with particular branches of the services had to learn new contract rules and requirements.

On an international level, the postwar alliance between the United States and western Europe, based on the idea of a combined restraint against the expansion of the Soviets, weakened. France barred Britain's entry into the Common Market, spurned U.S. Polaris missiles, and launched upon a more independent course of its own under General de Gaulle. To bolster the alliance and to encourage West Germany, President Kennedy traveled to Berlin and pledged that "the United States will risk its cities to defend yours." [75]

At the same time the President spurred the U.S. space program, increased U.S. nuclear arms, and renewed economic sanctions against Cuba. None of these moves met with universal approval. The Administration, in mid-term, began to encounter an increasingly critical press, a phenomenon which all U.S. administrations endure. For the first time since the aftermaths of the Spanish-American and World Wars, however, the press began to express some open skepticism about the validity of governmental explanations regarding international matters. This was, in part, a reaction from the Cuban missile crisis, which the media had finally decided was "managed" from the White House.[76]

Yet much of the nation paid little attention to these top-level problems. "Happenings"—an ultra-avant-garde theatrical form performed outside theaters and emphasizing absurd or comic combinations of painting, music, modern dancing, and outré costumes—began to arise. They jostled curiously against long lines of people waiting to see the Mona Lisa, on loan from the Louvre and exhibited throughout the nation. Scientific achievements once considered fantastic appeared in such profusion they barely attracted attention; the fact was the nation was moving toward a living standard more crowded and profuse than any in history.

Raytheon, therefore, was changing in the midst of change, engrossed at a time when the landscape was crowded and incredibly busy. Paul Hannah, the firm's general counsel, took an early retirement for a most unusual reason. He wanted to resume the private practice of law before he grew too old to launch a new career successfully. Hannah left to become a partner in Gadsby, Colson & Morin in Boston (now Gadsby & Hannah). During his tenure at Raytheon he had created an outstanding legal department, and many of his protégés had moved on to high posts elsewhere. He had also, with typical foresight and conscientiousness, trained a successor: Charlie Resnick.[77]

With semiconductors and receiving tube operations being phased out, changes underway in the Department of Defense, and changes pouring over the transom from international quarters, one would have expected the Raytheon managers to show signs of strain. Yet they drew closer together. Adams pulled Phillips into international matters with him; they together agreed—after consultation with La Centrale in Milan—that Dr. Carlo Calosi should concentrate on improving the operations of Elsi, in Palermo.

They also agreed on another and most interesting decision. Phillips, still concerned about the firm's government groups, had elevated Rogers Hamel to vice president; controller Arthur Schene was elevated from vice president Missile Division, to corporate controller, and John Stobo to manager of the Components Division. It was obvious he was still regrouping, reorganizing, and in large measure directing these groups. One would have expected that Adams and Phillips, moving into a working partnership on international as well as domestic Raytheon operations, would have agreed to go outside and hire an executive experienced in commercial marketing. Phillips, after all, was experienced only in government business. Instead Phillips shopped for his own replacement in government programs.

Asked his reasons later, Phillips said, "I knew Raytheon. I knew its past efforts and failures. I didn't want to see a newcomer entering to learn them all over again." Adams agreed.[78]

That basic decision reached, they launched a discreet search which, eventually, carried them into conversations with Dyer Brainerd Holmes, director of Manned Space for NASA.

Holmes, forty-two at the time, was a phenomenon whose face had appeared on the cover of *Time* as the man in the moon barely a year before.[79] Born in New York, raised in New Jersey, he received his degree in electrical engineering from Cornell in 1943, when World

War II was at its peak, was sent to radar school, and served at Pearl Harbor.

After the war Holmes went to work for Western Electric, the manufacturing arm of Bell Labs, and rotated between the two for eight years. "A fine postgraduate exposure," he says. "Western Electric and Bell Labs had the only gray-haired men in the field at that time. That's not true anymore." [80]

Most men—Geneen, Krafve, Phillips himself—have to search about before they find their proper place, but Holmes's career was like the Talos antiaircraft missile he worked on later. Components installed, he was put in place—and soared. After eight years at Western Electric, he moved on to RCA and Talos, which hit its first target on its first try. Holmes had also achieved a memorable success with BMEWS— ballistic missile early warning system—that stretched across Alaska, Greenland, and the United Kingdom.

BMEWS, which cost $1 billion, was launched in 1957. "We surveyed the top of the earth," said Holmes later, "and selected three sites. They were Thule, Greenland, in the center; Clear, Alaska in the west; and Fylingsdale Moors in the east, in England. All three sites were geographically unique and presented formidable problems."

Holmes recalls Thule vividly. "Glaciers were visible," he says. "The landscape was one of an eternal dull twilight; the impression was desolate." The Thule installation however, was built within thirty months on top of the permafrost. When complete, its installations were able to withstand winds of 160 knots. "It pulled together," Holmes recalls, "every technique then available according to the state of the art at the time. RCA," he concludes with quiet pride, "was able to return unexpended money back to the government. We met every schedule— right on the button." Three thousand subcontractors were involved.

BMEWS was an RCA prime contract, and Holmes was the man who put together the overall plan, won the award for the firm and ran it for four years with outstanding efficiency.

Tapped to become the first Director of Manned Space Flight to put men physically on the moon while NASA Director James Webb handled the thorny political problems attendant on the giant program, Holmes took a voluntary salary cut from $50,000 to $21,000. No single project mounted by the United States has ever been more complex or—in the long range—more significant to mankind. Holmes found himself dealing with von Braun on rocket matters and with men from every facet of the hard sciences on the resources, talents, materials, schedules, costs, and risks involved.

Situated in a central coordinating office in Washington, Holmes began with a center at Langley Field, Virginia, where the astronauts for the Mercury flights were trained, and a rocket installation at Huntsville, Alabama, where von Braun and his experts toiled. In time the Langley installation was transferred to Houston, Texas. For Holmes the task began with the Mercury program, then extended into Gemini, and later, Apollo.

The tasks involved were more than complex: they were unprecedented. They drew, as a natural concomitant, formidable personalities in their wake. Holmes toiled on top levels with huge problems and discovered that the complexities of engineering pale beside those of personalities in politics. He recalls the reservations of Jerome Wiesner, who occupied the high and important post of chief of science and technology for the New Frontier: Wiesner had reservations about the entire project. Holmes also learned about the important personages of Congress, the need to acquire their support, and the importance of answering their doubts, questions, and suggestions without murmur.

Holmes met President Kennedy, who remained personally on top of the space program. Kennedy called him to the Oval Office several times to discuss various aspects of the great adventure and to probe its difficulties or accomplishments. Holmes was surprised and pleased when the President quoted, verbatim, from a *Time* article about him; he still wonders why he received such an "extraordinarily good press."

Once the pioneering stage was past, however, Holmes realized the Washington pay scales did not meet the pressing needs of the Holmes family. He began to drop hints that he felt he had done enough; the news that he was available went through technological ranks throughout the nation with lightning speed. Many very large and important firms made flattering overtures.

Adams and Phillips, therefore, reached for a man with extraordinary qualifications. That was understandable on their part, but why did Holmes choose Raytheon instead of one of the giants?

His first thought, he said later, was, *They are clean men.* He knew them, of course, and he also knew Raytheon's situation; knew the Sparrow and Hawk programs had peaked. His second thought, therefore, was, *They need me.*

That meant a lot. "A big company," Holmes says, "is—immense.

*Antennas for the Raytheon-built Tartar fire-control system. (Photograph: 1960)*

*Attending the 1960 dedication of the Portsmouth, Rhode Island, plant were (FROM LEFT) W. Rogers Hamel, then general manager of Submarine Signal Division; Rhode Island Governor Christopher Del Sesto; Mr. Adams; Adm. Chester Nimitz; and President Richard E. Krafve.*

*Harold M. Hart (RIGHT) and James R. Merrill with radar model in 1960. Then manager of the company's Surfac and Radar Navigation Operation, Mr. Hart later became a Raytheon vice president.*

*In 1962, Raytheon's newly installed radar bright-display presentations enabled Indianapolis air-traffic controllers to track aircraft in a normally lighted room.*

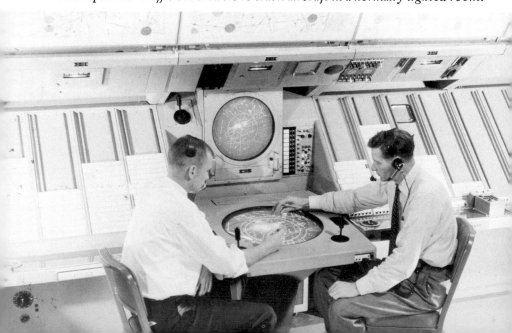

Mr. Adams (LEFT) became Raytheon's president in 1947 and chairman in 1964. With him is Thomas L. Phillips, who became executive vice president in 1961 and president in 1964. (From an annual-report photograph of 1966.)

At the height of the 1962 Cuban crisis, President John F. Kennedy (wearing sunglasses) inspected a Hawk battery deployed in Florida.

*Mr. Holmes, the first director of manned space flight for the United States, appeared on the cover of* Time *in 1962, the year before he joined Raytheon.*

*Finger points to Raytheon-built display keyboard in Apollo lunar spacecraft control panel.*

*Astronaut William A. Anders visited Raytheon in 1964, when the company was producing on-board guidance computers for the Apollo lunar spacecraft.*

*On a Raytheon production line of the sixties, employees inspect guidance computers for Polaris submarine-launched ballistic missiles.*

*963, Mr. Adams (LEFT) President John F. nedy (CENTER) took part 'remonies recognizing theon's participation in 'Tools for Freedom'' 'ram (for the benefit of ents in the Philippines).*

*The Rampart radar, which included this antenna with a sixty-foot diameter, was designed to follow ballistic missiles in their re-entry phase. (Photograph: 1963)*

*Participants in this 1964 planning session include (FROM LEFT) Senior Vice Preside D. Brainerd Holmes; Vice President T.C. Wisenbaker, general manager of Missile Systems Division; newly elected President Thomas L. Phillips; and Vice President Fritz A. Gross, general manager of Equipment Division.*

In 1965, Raytheon received the "employer-of-the-year" award from the President's Committee on Employment of the Handicapped. Sen. Edward M. Kennedy (LEFT) of Massachusetts made the presentation to Mr. Adams (RIGHT) while Harold Russell, chairman of the committee, looked on.

BELOW LEFT   In this 1965 photo, President Phillips holds an early Raytheon tube while company cofounder Vannevar Bush (LEFT) and Senior Vice President Percy L. Spencer look on.   BELOW RIGHT   In 1963, President Adams (LEFT) and Lyndon B. Johnson were principals at the annual dinner of the National Security Industrial Association. Mr. Johnson was vice president of the United States at the time.

*Photographed together in 1954 were (FROM LEFT) Howard Hall, president of Iowa Manufacturing Company; George C. Foerstner, president of Amana Refrigeration; and President Dwight D. Eisenhower.*

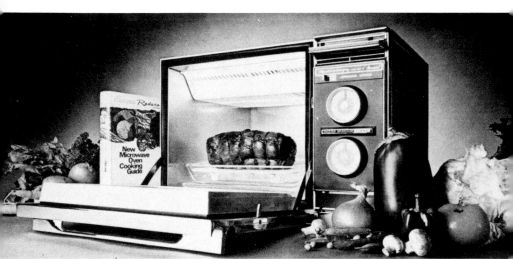

## Raytheon helps housewives cook four times faster on half the electricity.

*A 1974 corporate advertisement showing the Amana Radarange, which was developed from Raytheon's microwave technology of the fifties and is now marketed by Amana worldwide.*

*In 1963, a "product-of-the-year" award from* Missile and Rockets *magazine was accepted for Raytheon by Vice President Edward L. Dashefsky* (LEFT). *Mr. Dashefsky was elected a senior vice president in 1969.*

*Corporate staff heads meeting here include* (FROM LEFT) *Vice Presidents Charles H. Resnick, secretary and general counsel; Arthur V. Schene, controller; and Robert G. Hennemuth, who is in charge of industrial relations.*

Lt. Gen. William B. Bunker, commanding general, Army Materiel Command, visits Raytheon in 1968 to review army missile programs. Prominent in this picture are (FROM LEFT) Eric M. Levi of the Hawk program, General Bunker, Executive Vice President D. Brainerd Holmes, and Vice President Joseph F. Alibrandi, general manager of Missile Systems Division.

Mr. Holmes in his Lexington headquarters office when he became executive vice president in 1969.

*In 1967, the company began testing this phased-array radar for the U.S. Army's Nike-X program.*

*Saudi Arabia's King Faisal consults an aide during 1965 meeting with Vice President Joseph F. Alibrandi (LEFT) and Chairman Adams.*

*A 1966
Business Week
cover story
described
Raytheon's
diversification
moves.*

*Seismograph Service Corporation crew lays recording cable from
Hovercraft during 1968 shallow-water search for oil.*

Roger C. Damon, Raytheon director since 1959, talks with George Ingram, Jr., senior vice president, at a 1966 director's meeting.

Seismograph Service Corporation's former president and chairman, Gerald H. Westby (RIGHT) and Mr. Westby's successor as president, E. D. Wilson. (Photograph: 1966)

Vice President Francis S. Fox, resident of D. C. Heath.

*Mr. Holmes* (LEFT) *makes a point about ground equipment for the Hawk missile system to Saudi Arabia's minister of defense and aviation, Prince Sultan Bin Abdul Aziz Al-Saud* (RIGHT). *Looking on is Ibrahim Al-Sowayel, Saudi ambassador to the United States.*

*Top administrators of Missile Systems Division include* (FROM LEFT) *Vice Presidents Justin M. Margolskee, Mike W. Fossier, Aldo R. Miccioli and Floyd T. Wimberly. Mr. Miccioli, a senior vice president, is division general manager. Models of SAM-D equipment are in the foreground.*

At the 1971 Paris Air Show, Raytheon introduced the computer display channel equipment the company built for the Federal Aviation Agency. Sharing the spotlight at a press briefing were Senior Vice President Joseph F. Shea (LEFT) and FAA administrator Gen. Gustav E. Lundquist.

In this 1971 photo, Vice President Ralph A. Martin (RIGHT) looks at models of sonar equipment with John Chafee, then U.S. secretary of the navy.

Three officials who help direct Raytheon's European operations examine a new type of power cable made by Sterling Cable Company. From left are K. C. J. Hutton, managing director of Sterling; John D. Clare, president of Raytheon Europe International Company; and Lord Sherfield, chairman of A. C. Cossor Ltd.

*With refinery model are Badger's Chairman Adrian J. Broggini* (LEFT) *and President Robert E. Siegfried.*

*Visiting a construction site are United Engineers' Chairman Henry M. Chance II* (LEFT) *and President Thomas M. Dahl.*

I wanted to join a company that was not so large, though certainly I did not want to become a part of a speculating group. I wanted a medium-sized firm where I could make a solid contribution—*and in which I could have a shaping hand.*" [81]

Holmes joined Raytheon as a senior vice president. Adams and Phillips had, in preparation, made some other, corresponding arrangements. George Ingram, Jr., the firm's chief financial officer and a man of fine analytical ability, was also made a senior vice president; both men were also made directors.

As do all newcomers, Holmes looked about with fresh eyes. He surveyed the Raytheon establishment very quickly and saw much at which he frowned. "The labs," he concluded, "were being run as separate enterprises. The commercial divisions were in poor shape." Phillips had told him that, but there's nothing like seeing for yourself.

From the start Holmes appreciated Phillips, who did not stand on ceremony. "He would come to my office, sit down and level," Holmes recalls, "and discuss every difficulty." Holmes's quick eyes noted that Phillips, far from playing "all-seeing Boss," worked hard, long hours and was visibly tired."

He also took note that Phillips was still listening to the missile group. "He met with these men on Saturdays, and would go to the blackboard, draw circuit diagrams, and discuss their situation for hours." Holmes disapproved of that; he thought the executive vice president could be better occupied—but that, of course, was why he had been hired. On the other hand, he was impressed by Phillips' grasp of technological detail and his ability to assess this area: that was important.

Holmes was pleased to learn that Adams had a droll sense of humor and a subtle facility for easing the atmosphere. The older man's mastery of nuance and grasp of political realities impressed the new senior vice president. Washington experience had convinced Holmes of the immense importance of what, with defense-industry jargon, he calls "the political interface."

Added together, this meant the new man found his associates congenial and individually able. That was the most important of all beginnings, and was to carry the three of them forward.

*       *       *

On November 22, 1963, President Kennedy—as all Americans know and at least two generations will never forget—was shot to death from the window of a Dallas building as he was riding in a motorcade through the city.[82] His assassin was a renegade American who had renounced his country, sought Soviet citizenship, lived and married in the USSR, been allowed to leave that land and to return to his own. A Communist though not formally affiliated with the U.S. Communist Party, Lee Harvey Oswald asked for the party attorney upon arrest; was himself assassinated by a nightclub operator named Jack Ruby in full view of television cameras.[83]

The event was interpreted by some as evidence of the intransigent and dangerous nature of right-wing extremism in Dallas. When that theory could not be sustained by facts, even stranger explanations were created that were not dispelled even by the conclusion of an eminent commission headed by the Chief Justice of the United States that the assassin operated on his own.

Not since the assassination of Lincoln had the death of a President so depressed the mood of the country. President Lyndon Johnson moved to carry out the Kennedy program as he understood it. But in the confusion resulting from the assassination the nation suffered grave injury in the eyes of the world. The year 1963 did not so much wind down as shout its way toward extinction.

At Raytheon, in the brief period between the end of November and the end of December 1963, only a few items remain worthy of mention. One was an award to create a missile site radar—an important step forward and the end result of efforts extended over several years by Al Miccioli and based in large part on patents Miccioli and Don Archer had earlier received. Originally the latest effort had not been seriously regarded, because it was launched—or relaunched—as part of a larger missile site radar project required for a Bell Labs proposal. In the period before Holmes arrived, Miccioli had gone to Phillips over the matter, and received permission to go ahead, plus $100,000 with which to work.[84]

The contract came through, which was a real coup for Miccioli, but he was in no condition to rejoice. Congratulations reached him as he was convalescing in the hospital from a heart attack. Nevertheless he had set a train of events in motion that would continue to be important.

The other noteworthy happening was a decision of the Italian government, operating under one of its corporation names as Finnmeccanica, to buy the Italian Edison's share of Selenia, the firm that manufactured Hawks. That shift left Raytheon owning 45 percent of Selenia, with the Italian government—as Finnmeccanica—owning another 45 percent, and Fiat 10 percent. Meanwhile Phillips told the Raytheon directors that Elsi's accounting system was being "reformed." [85]

The year 1963, however, ended on a note of austerity for Raytheon. Sales had slipped almost $100 million to $488.9 million, earnings from $9.5 million the previous year to $6.3 million. The reasons were not mysterious: sales of missiles—the vehicles that had carried the firm upward—had peaked and their volume was declining; the commercial efforts of the firm were not strong enough to take up the slack.

Per share, the results showed earnings of $1.46 compared to the previous year's $2.31. The Lewiston plant was being closed; the management was consolidating receiving tubes. The number of employees had been cut back by over seven thousand. Christmas in New England was not good for many of these that year. Inside the firm no bonuses were issued, and Adams chose to reduce his own salary.[86]


In his first message to Congress in early 1964 President Lyndon Johnson launched his Great Society, which combined economy in government with a determination to forward programs of social betterment. His initial budget pared foreign aid back to 1948 levels, had a $1.1 billion cut in defense spending but a $5.1 billion sum for the space program, and prepared bills to provide Medicare, federal housing and urban renewal, transportation improvements and special assistance to Appalachia. The business sector was heartened, however, by income and other tax reductions of over $11 billion.[87]

Nevertheless there was a clear divide between the optimism and grace of the Kennedy years and the new Administration, which seemed less personally appealing. The aftermath of assassination was reflected in an argumentative mood in the nation, and the media reflected incidents of growing exacerbation.

No part of any society can escape its trends and pressures—and no part is more subject to such pressures than a large public corporation. Raytheon's management learned, during the spring of 1964, that though increased sales and earnings, added numbers of workers, and diligent efforts in the community may not bring a firm much attention, its decline in any respect is considered near-headline news. Its 1963 Annual Report with its lowered sales and earnings, and particularly its cutback in semiconductor operations with the dismissal of thousands of workers, attracted more attention than its successes a few years earlier. Like the United States as a whole, the firm was criticized for having the difficulties it struggled to overcome.

Yet, like the nation, it was actually moving forward quite briskly. In March 1964, it voted, for the first time, a cash dividend to its patient shareholders.

Phillips proposed the purchase of Micro State Electronic Corporation, a leader in certain solid-state devices, and the Penta Laboratories, producers of communication and broadcast equipment. Together, these purchases came to almost $4 million.[88]

Phillips now had the time to turn toward the improvement of Raytheon's activities in nongovernmental areas and to take more interest in international Raytheon activities. This was possible mainly because Brainerd Holmes was taking hold of the governmental divisions.

Holmes has firm theories about organization and little respect for lack of systems. He uses his intuitions as a base from which to operate, but to him "a gut feeling is only a place from which to start."

He began with the space division, while General Yates moved sideways to assist Phillips in corporate planning. Holmes was interested, in the beginning, in the division's activities on the Apollo guidance computer and the Polaris guidance system and other work it was then performing in conjunction with Dr. Charles Stark Draper and his associates at the MIT Instrumentation Laboratory.

Once he had regrouped that effort to his satisfaction for the time being, Holmes turned toward the Missile Division's performance in a major competition to obtain the army's Advanced Air Defense System —the AAD S-70. The army's General Zierdt, like Colonel Eiffler some years before in an earlier missile effort, had established a number of initial tasks. The firms that could best perform these tasks would then be in post position to proceed to the next stage. They involved, of course, many phases of technology and placed considerable emphasis on the abilities of the competitive group managers. As before, Raytheon was in the lists against formidable competitors, including General Electric, Westinghouse, RCA, and Hughes.

Holmes had barely begun to organize the Missile Division for this larger task, however, when it lost a smaller competition within the

*344*

area of its own specialty: air defense. The loss made it clear that Raytheon was behind its competition. Deeply concerned, Holmes talked to General Zierdt and wondered if Raytheon could reenter the AAD S-70 competition later if the requirements for the system changed and if Raytheon meanwhile improved its own abilities at its own expense. The General agreed, but made it clear the requirement would have to change to allow a new competition.

Then Holmes, with the backing of Adams and Phillips, turned to the difficult task of organizing groups that had lost ground and suffered a defeat into efforts that could carry them forward from behind. No greater leadership task exists.

News of the Missile Division disaster was still shimmering in the air when Holmes attended a conference in Huntsville, Alabama. At the session he met, watched, and listened to T. C. Wisenbaker, who was present in his capacity as a Raytheon consultant. *Small, southern, and sensible*, he thought. On the heels of that thought came another: *We must have him.*[89]

That conclusion reveals much about Holmes. Wisenbaker was, after all, not only an older man, but a predecessor. Holmes was a new man in charge; it was obvious that he thought in terms of reaching goals. Returned to Lexington, he went in and told Phillips he wanted Wisenbaker back to head Missiles and Phillips was taken aback.

"He doesn't want to come back," Phillips said, and explained Wisenbaker's dislike of New England. Privately he was somewhat embarrassed. He was well aware of how many times Wisenbaker had answered Raytheon's fire alarms; wondered "how we could have the nerve" to press him yet again for still another emergency. Holmes insisted, and suggested that Wisenbaker be invited to Lexington "for a visit." Phillips agreed and the invitation was sent: both men hoped it would work.

On the other end Wisenbaker, who had learned the missile group had now fallen behind in its own area, was understandably concerned. On receiving an invitation to Lexington he called Phillips, learned it was Holmes's idea, but that the Welcome sign was out.

The rest was automatic—or as nearly so as possible in capturing so elusive a man as T. C. Wisenbaker. His old associates crowded about and told him their troubles; before the visit was over he had agreed to return, but only until the emergency was ended—a year or so. During that time, Wisenbaker said, he would find and train a successor.

One can almost see the heads nodding and hear the voices saying "Fine, fine," while everyone wondered where he'd find a successor in a year. No matter; he was back and both Holmes and Phillips were pleased. Altogether a tactful and well-played move that, under the circumstances, only Holmes could have initiated.

Some other moves, however, were growing tangled. In Palermo, Elsi needed more money. The exact sum expanded over several months as the subject was discussed with the directors, growing from $3.2 million to $5 million. Broken down, this amounted in the end to $3.2 million in cash and another $2.4 million in loan guarantees. Hopefully the enterprise would be able to pay these loans and the guarantees would never be called upon.[90]

Phillips listened, disenchanted. He was well aware Calosi was proud of the Elsi enterprise and often praised its modern facilities, its abilities. But he had also learned that although Italian engineers are competent technically, they are not noted for organization. It seemed to him, as he listened to Dr. Calosi, that more emphasis was being placed "on the social, or rather the societal importance of operations in Sicily" than on their need to return profits to their investors.[91] In addition Phillips had inner doubts about Calosi's insistence that operations in Italy could be understood only by nationals of that country.

Adams was aware of these opinions: he had drawn Phillips into international matters to have such assistance. One result was that, when the earnings of Cossor in England had started to slip, Phillips had made a special trip to that country to recruit John Clare. Clare, whom Phillips had grown to know during the fifties, had been with the British Ministry of Supply and been one of that nation's experts in guided missiles. Phillips recruited him to head Cossor from a post as technical director for ITT Europe, made him deputy manager of Raytheon Europe, in charge of all Raytheon's non-Italian enterprises.

Now the directors were told that Clare would head Cossor in the United Kingdom, that regular quarterly meetings would be held with the international Raytheon managers, that Selenia, busy turning out Hawks in Italy, was still profitable—and that Elsi should receive the funds it needed to allow time for a turnaround. But it did not require extraordinary powers of prophecy to see that if Elsi did not improve, there would be changes on the Italian scene as there had already been changes on the British.

Around them the United States assumed an almost surrealistic aspect under the pressures of an election year and divisions that ran deeper than at any time since the Civil War.

In the South a populist movement bobbed in the wake of Alabama's Governor George Wallace; in the West a conservative movement arose to capture the Republican Party nomination for Arizona Senator Barry Goldwater. From Washington President Johnson directed a campaign that recalled the ideas of the New Deal, updated by the addition of the civil rights movement.

The movie *Dr. Strangelove, or: How I Learned to Stop Worrying and Love the Bomb* appeared, featuring an air force general as a villain. So did *Seven Days in May*, portraying an attempted coup d'etat by the U.S. Air Force. These and other offerings were billed as satires but showed more cynicism than irony; they represented a sharp break with the long patriotic tone of the American theater, but accurately represented the national mood.[92]

By October 1964 the U.S. presence in South Vietnam was under severe criticism from growing numbers of Americans. The tenor of the criticism showed that the acceptance of communism as a form of democracy had not only taken root, but extended to the idea that opposition to communism is antidemocratic. Like Gresham's Law, in which counterfeit coins drive sound currency from the marketplace, the new definition was driving the older underground.

Yet while much of the nation moved toward pacifism, the government moved toward the creation of a more effective defensive network. The progression was confusing both because the descriptions of the nation's defenses were, necessarily, held secret and also because they were wrapped in a jungle of new technical terms difficult for nonexperts to fathom. Intercontinental ballistic missiles, for example, became known by new names as various models appeared in dizzying succession: Atlas, Titan, Minuteman. At the same time the supportive systems to protect these missiles from being destroyed in the event of hostilities were first called Nike-Zeus, then Nike X (to be located near cities), then Sentinel, then Safeguard, and finally, Anti-Ballistic Missiles, or ABM's. All these incarnations confused the public.

*347*

Nevertheless the missile area—mysterious and held secret by government regulations—had moved forward intellectually into new and promising ground. Al Miccioli, who had been increasingly bored as a troubleshooter at Andover once the Hawk was in production, became part of a new effort devoted to new radar instrumentation. This led Miccioli and his associates into the designs of new, unique pulse compression radars, fancy antennas, multiple receivers. This was an area beyond theory, an entry into avenues never fully analyzed that nevertheless can be used—somewhat as electrical force has been used for generations—without being fully understood. "It had a good feel," says Miccioli—but it was far more important than that.

Miccioli designed one assembly—a "phased array," as it was called —which included a steerable antenna on a steady mount with a switch for observation that reacted in the order of a millionth of a second. This particular array had to be placed in a mobile vehicle; it was part of an effort for the U.S. Army. The device helped carry Raytheon back into the competition for AAD S-70, now known as the surface-to-air missiles system: SAM-D.

The "phased array" represented a blend of many disciplines: digital computer, microelectronics, software controls among others. In effect it replaced many radars with a single radar capable of many functions and operating with almost incredibly greater efficiency and speed than its forerunners. Its potential was immense, but few outside the experts could track their progress: the missile groups were charting new pathways of technology.

In 1964, Holmes was pushing the Raytheon missile systems divisions to develop phased array radars as part of the Safeguard ABM system, for which Bell Labs had overall responsibility. The push was as strenuous as any the firm had ever undertaken. One million dollars of its own development money was poured into the effort. That was what the technologists called a big splash, but it was far from being the only one of such efforts.

Under Wisenbaker the missile groups were also working to improve the Hawk; to field an "improved Hawk." At the same time the Polaris groups, now under Ralph Martin, achieved a new contract for guidance equipment. Phillips, watching Holmes and his results, was impressed. The entire governmental sector was revitalized, was moving to new ground and providing the earnings that enabled the executive vice president to turn, at last, toward the quest for commercial growth.

*348*

There was no thought, however, of approaching the commercial sector piecemeal. Adams, Phillips, and Holmes first discussed the big picture. Then Phillips sat down with Holmes, who headed all governmental operations, and Ingram, the firm's financial officer, and with General Yates, who had proven able in forward planning. The men began to draw together the elements of a Five-Year Plan, though the year 1964 was not yet ended and full figures not yet available.

It was obvious that Raytheon's business was, overwhelmingly, in defense. It would be necessary to retain and increase that business if the firm was to maintain and improve its position. But it was also necessary to establish what Phillips called "a significant" commercial business both through acquisitions and internal developments.

These avenues were narrowed because Raytheon had already tried to travel several that were logical for an electronics firm, and had failed. "In the past, we tried both television and large computer manufacturing," Phillips said, "and had to retreat from both." [93]

Nevertheless the plan began to take shape. Phillips himself, still executive vice president, then received encouragement at an opportune moment when Charlie Adams called him aside "for a brief discussion."

It was clear to Adams that Phillips' plans for the company were long range and constructive. He and the executive vice president had established the sort of relationship he himself had once sought with Laurence Marshall and had not been able to achieve. He told the younger man he intended to propose him to the board as president.

Leaning back, he speculated aloud on what that post could mean. "If you become chief executive," he said, looking ahead, "I would expect you to hold that post till you retire. That would give you about twenty years—which is probably more than enough." [94]

In other words, if all went well with Phillips as president, the younger man could expect to achieve the top job toward the end of the sixties. That would be about the time when the results of the evolving Five-Year Plan would be evident. That was not as far away as it seemed: it was already 1964 and Phillips was forty.

To Phillips that ultimate prospect was not the most important point of the conversation. To him the immediate impact was that, as president, he would have the proper credentials to implement the Five-Year Plan. That meant its possibilities were enhanced and his chances of success improved. Meanwhile he was, of course, pleased and encouraged.

A week or so later they were at a SubSig luncheon together and Adams, who had prepared for the moment, rose and made a public announcement that Phillips was the new president of Raytheon.

A month later, on August 3, 1964, three North Vietnamese PT boats attacked the U.S. destroyer *Maddox* in international waters in the Gulf of Tonkin. They were driven away by carrier planes from the U.S. carrier *Ticonderoga*. Three days later, U.S. planes bombed North Vietnamese installations and naval craft, and President Johnson received authority from Congress to use all necessary measures to repel armed attack and provide assistance to any SEATO nation defending its freedom.[95]

The nation, unheeding, swept on to its elections and carried Johnson and Humphrey into office by an overwhelming majority: the Democrats carried forty-four states out of fifty. Since the Republican candidate had been associated with an increased effort in Vietnam, peace groups throughout the nation were jubilant at the outcome, but international events actually remained turbulent. Two weeks after the elections, the United States airlifted Belgian troops into a rebellious Congo; events in Indonesia under Sukarno remained disordered; England had difficulties with Rhodesia.

Yet many constructive signs of an improved society appeared. Dr. Martin Luther King received the Nobel Peace Prize; the Ford Foundation extended $7.7 million to the improvement of ballet in America; the black civil rights movement, assisted by new legislation outlawing discrimination, moved forward and enlisted the sympathy of millions; and the Supreme Court ruled against imbedded inequities in state legislatures.

At Raytheon the directors were pleased to learn the missile group, revitalized by Holmes and working well under Wisenbaker, had not only received a new Sparrow contract but also a production order to produce the navy's heat-seeking air-to-air missile, the Sidewinder.

That Sidewinder, though new to Raytheon, was not new to the navy or Washington; it had been developed by a naval laboratory and produced by Philco and General Electric. Raytheon's achievement, therefore, constituted a coup, since it meant overtaking competitors.

Raytheon was becoming better disciplined, a more tightly organized company. In large measure this tightening was due to the Holmes approach. For Holmes a manager is what a controller is to Harold Geneen: a man who can discern the strong and weak points of an organization and knows how to strengthen or streamline them into more effective form. Like most managers, Holmes can talk on the subject. To him it is important that a manager can inspire loyalty and enthusiasm; it is equally important that he be specific and hold men personally accountable. There was little doubt that he entered at a critical time and made a crucial difference. As usual, when large and important areas of the firm began to improve, other sectors, as though encouraged, also moved upward. Ed Dashefsky, heading, among other areas, the Machlett subsidiary, reported an important government "night vision" contract.

Phillips was also pleased over a possible acquisition that he and George Ingram had come upon. Before it could be discussed, however, the year 1964 came to an end. Sales had dropped again, from $510 million to $454 million. But profits had risen from $6.3 million to $8.2 million. Per-share earnings had increased from $1.46 to $1.96. For the first time dividends—forty-five cents a share—had been paid, at a cost to the company of $1.8 million.[96]

With the 1964 figures in hand, Phillips, Holmes, Ingram, and Yates now completed the Five-Year Plan. They projected a sales increase to $1 billion by 1970, a tripling of earnings to $25 million; double per share earnings to $4. The figures sounded very optimistic, but the four were confident they were realistic.

In discussing the qualifications for a chief executive Adams once said, "He must be lucky." Asked his definition, he said, "One of Tom Phillips' abilities is that he could walk down a dark street lined with open manholes without falling into any of them. It's a sort of ESP."[97]

Adams himself has that quality; his calm course during the successive squeaks and corners of Raytheon is one proof. During the winter of 1964–65 Phillips proved the point, for he unearthed a prospect that fit Raytheon's needs as precisely as a tailored glove a hand. Its name was Amana Refrigeration, and it was headed by George Foerstner.

Behind George Foerstner is one of the strangest and most symbolic sagas in the building of the United States: the Amana colony. The members of the colony belong to the Community of the True Inspiration, an offshoot from the Pietist movement of the seventeenth century, which itself was an offshoot of Lutheranism in the heady days of the early Reformation. More attention has been paid to the Puritans and their efforts; they arrived sooner. The Amana colony (the name is taken from the Bible and means faithful) was very similar. Invigorated by the leadership of a young German carpenter named Christian Metz, they came to the United States in 1842 about eight hundred strong, and settled first near Buffalo, New York. Twelve years later they fled farther from civilization and settled in Iowa on what became 25,000 acres; constructed seven villages with as many churches; built a canal forty feet wide and seven miles long to the Iowa River; and became self-sufficient.[98]

The colony's churches are bare of ornaments and symbols. Their faith is intense and centers around revelation; their services last for hours and messages believed to be divinely inspired are written down. From its inception the colony held all its goods in common. It lasted, as a theocracy, until the early thirties. Foerstner is blunt about the reasons for failure. "Not everybody worked," he says. "Some worked too hard; many more did not work hard enough." [99]

There were other reasons. People wanted possessions of their own as abundance about them mounted in the outside world. Technically the colony almost went bankrupt: it owed $500,000 in 1931. The colony was reorganized, religious authority contracted to matters of faith, a cooperative established in which shares were distributed, church meetings cut from eleven times a week to long Sunday hours.

Amana has flourished as a cooperative; its shares are valuable. It has moved, in a business sense, from communism to socialism, to a mixed economy.

When the colony was passing through its depression transition, George Foerstner's father, a member of the colony, started an auto accessory business. Young George, branching modestly on his own, assembled a refrigerator from spare parts, sold it, and assembled some more. That effort began in 1934. By 1936 he was doing so well the managers of the colony bought his business from him, expanded, but kept him as manager. By 1949 the Amana Refrigeration Company colony managers wanted to sell out for $1 million—if they could find a purchaser. Foerstner went to Cedar Rapids, Iowa, and talked to Howard Hall, head of the Iowa Manufacturing Company, the big man of Cedar Rapids. Hall formed a syndicate that included Foerstner and bought Amana Refrigeration for $1.5 million, an outcome that pleased all concerned. Like his predecessors, Hall retained George Foerstner as manager.

By 1964, Hall, Foerstner, and their associates had carried Amana straight up: sales were almost $25 million. Many of the original investors were wealthy, at least on paper, when time intervened. The factory manager died of cancer; the treasurer had an unexpected heart attack. Estate problems arose; intimations of mortality and its attendant implications clouded Amana's future.

Meanwhile Phillips had George Ingram, Raytheon's financial man, out talking to banks and searching for possible acquisitions. Amana's Foerstner and his associates were discussing the possibility of going public or simply selling out when they received a call from their Chicago bank, and the name Raytheon arose.

The name was not unknown to Amana: Belmont Radio had once had a production plant in Iowa. Foerstner and his associates knew Raytheon as a firm with excellent engineering abilities but not, so far as they knew, any expertise in retail marketing. In Foerstner's opinion, that was a plus: he didn't want outside experts in an area where he considered Amana already competent.

The response to Raytheon, therefore, was favorable. Phillips and Ingram made the trip to the Roosevelt Hotel, in Cedar Rapids, Iowa, to meet Howard Hall, Foerstner, and Beahl Perrine. Hall was chairman of Amana, Foerstner president, Perrine counsel and secretary. The conversations went well—very well. After a return visit and time for mutual examination, the merger brought Amana Refrigeration, with assets of over $17 million, a net worth of $11 million, "no debt and $1.5 million in the bank," into Raytheon in exchange for 447,328 shares of Raytheon common.[100]

Even in ordinary terms the acquisition looked good. Howard Hall was an astute chairman, Foerstner a unique manager of proven ability. Internally the Amana Refrigeration, Inc. was heavy with people from the Amana colony who continued to practice the thrifty ways and diligent pattern that had made the colony famous.

Later it was the microwave ovens that made the merger extraordinarily apt from Raytheon's viewpoint. Through the years the Radarange oven had been the subject of continual efforts and, in early 1965,

*353*

was still being sold, mainly to restaurants. Phillips had assigned teams, and work was underway to design and develop smaller microwave ovens. That step seemed logical; devices of such utility should be designed for a wider market. But Phillips was well aware Raytheon lacked both the distribution and the expertise for a general marketing effort.

The acquisition of Amana provided a vehicle for relooking at the Radarange oven. Foerstner, when shown the microwave oven, was impressed and optimistic. He brimmed with suggestions and observations; in short order, Amana engineers familiar with home appliances joined the Raytheon design teams.

The combination, coming on the heels of Raytheon's corporate decision to expand through acquisition, certainly pointed toward the sort of serendipity to which Adams referred. To Phillips, it was the first big blow in the Five-Year Plan.

Around them the United States reverberated to civil rights marches and demonstrations in the South, while Malcolm X was murdered by Black Muslims in the North.[101] President Lyndon Johnson appeared before a joint session of Congress to ask for a removal of racial barriers to full voting rights for all citizens. Organizations to repair the neglect of decades began to mushroom about the country. Raytheon, and especially Adams, had long been active in such efforts through the Urban Coalition and several other cooperative projects.[102]

At the same time, however, the President stepped up U.S. action in South Vietnam, sending in more than 3,500 marines to swell the American presence in that nation to 25,000 U.S. advisors. Secretary of Defense McNamara estimated, by April 1965, that Vietnam was costing the United States $1.5 billion annually: its forces there, $800 million; its military assistance, $330 million.[103] Simultaneously the President sent thirteen thousand soldiers and seven thousand marines to the Dominican Republic to restore order.

The Johnson Administration drove Gemini I with two astronauts into orbit around the earth; flew the world's first commercial communications satellite—Early Bird; and rolled a mountainous mass of monumental legislation through Congress so hastily some of the bills were not even printed when passed. These included a basic change in immigration laws to eliminate the quota system based on the existing American mix, the creation of a Cabinet-level Department of Housing

and Urban Development, a huge aid-to-education appropriation, Medicare, $1.1 billion to assist Appalachia, and other measures too numerous
to enumerate.[104]

In all it was as though President Johnson was determined to do
everything that could be done, everywhere, for every reason—all at
the same time. One result was to push the stock exchange into the beginning of the most feverish forward thrust in its history; another was
to send huge sums of dollars rolling around the United States and the
rest of the world. The overall result was to excite, agitate, arouse, and
create an almost manic mood in the nation.

Raytheon was affected by the temper of the times, in common
with all other groups, companies, and individuals in the United States.
The learning industry was very much in the limelight. School and
college budgets were growing. Talks were initiated with a textbook
publisher; discussions of teaching machines arose. Both of these were
very hot—very fashionable subjects.

In terms of the overall corporation, prospects appeared promising.
Adams and Phillips, however, did not stop with telling that to the
board. At the annual stockholders' meeting in May 1965, they chose
to unveil and make public their corporate Five-Year Plan, which projected sales of $1 billion and earnings of $25 million—triple the results
of 1964—by the end of 1970.[105]

Virtually every firm makes plans and projections of future earnings, though sometimes they are more hopeful than realistic. But Wall
Street has a long memory and corporate officers are held to their predictions. Raytheon's prediction was, in business terms, something like
Babe Ruth's pointing toward left field during the World Series when
he was at bat: a challenge that would be remembered and whose outcome would be watched.

Like the nation, Raytheon was entering new waters. A man who
had gone away for a couple of years and returned to Raytheon in
1965 would have been astonished at the extent of the changes. They
were more intensive than appearances, facts, and statistics alone could
show. The highly vaunted psychological tests had vanished. "Neither
Adams, Phillips, nor Brainerd Holmes paid the slightest attention to
these evaluations," observes Robert Hennemuth. "After a time it

seemed sensible to wrap them up." [106] The psychologists disappeared as if through trapdoors.

Older figures long familiar and respected became fewer. Percy Spencer, though still a director, finally retired. His retirement was—like all his actions—highly individual. Through all the years of the war and afterward, he had opened the plant, entering before the janitor, leaving after the night shift. In 1965 he retained an office and did not appear until the belated hour of 7 or 7:15 A.M. He left at a quarter to four in the afternoon. These, to Spencer, were retirement hours.[107]

Robert Quimby, the man who had hid his encomium from the Secretary of War for his work on the trigger mechanism of the A-bomb, also retired in early 1965. He was sent to Europe to teach NATO technicians how to build transformers. When that project was over, he was in the first retirement class that Raytheon established, in which people headed for a life of leisure after a long life of work were encouraged and inspired along lines of new interest.[108]

Dr. Edward Bowles also retired from Raytheon. Like Spencer, his retirement was unique. Dr. Bowles, with his myriad interests, his inquisitiveness, his professorial love of talk, and his political instincts, could never really retire. He remains busy today, a consultant to important and far-flung interests.

"I think Tom Phillips had enough of kingmakers," he says and, as usual, sums up the matter with scientific accuracy.[109]

T. C. Wisenbaker left the Missile Division at Bedford to handle operations on the West Coast. In the year he had spent back in New England, he had found and trained another bright young man as a successor: Joe Alibrandi, the production engineer who had headed the task force that took over the Bristol plant from Sperry. Alibrandi was highly regarded and had been rapidly promoted before T. C. Wisenbaker returned for one more year, but it took Wisenbaker, working in his own fashion—side by side—so to develop and exhibit Alibrandi that by the time T. C. left, the qualities he had sensed had become clear to all.

Yet all these changes did not imply any fixity to the living organism the firm represented. It operated in a fast, fluid, complex ambient; it continued to undergo changes, stress, and alterations as it both maintained and extended its efforts.

\* \* \*

Brainerd Holmes, tightening his systems through the government divisions of Raytheon, had one of the most difficult of all areas. In Santa Barbara, years later and seated as chief executive of Infra-Red Industries, Hamilton Hauck looked back at that period and shook his head.

"When Admiral Raborn headed the Polaris project it rolled as though living," Hauck says. "But when he retired from the navy, he had an exit interview with Secretary McNamara, and told the Secretary of Defense he was killing the initiative of the troops. That he had drawn all power into a tight little circle sitting inside the Pentagon.

"More and more people asked questions," Hauck recalls, "and fewer people were allowed to give any answers." [110]

Nevertheless the Polaris team at Raytheon was closely knit and worked well. Its efforts had extended from 1963 when, as an extension of work done at MIT's Instrumentation Lab (later renamed the Charles Stark Draper Laboratory), Raytheon had built a computer and the electronic components of the inertial guidance system. By early autumn 1965, the Polaris program was extended into Poseidon. Ralph Martin moved to SubSig as assistant general manager under Rogers Hamel and soon found himself in the sonar business on an ever-increasing scale. Martin's job was to get the BQQ nuclear submarine sonar on the track.

Like other managers in the huge defense business, however, Brainerd Holmes found his responsibilities increasing and becoming increasingly complicated. The McNamara approach—applauded though seldom grasped—did not make Holmes's tasks any easier. The fact was the "human computer" from Detroit did not streamline the U.S. defense establishment so much as elaborate and complicate its systems.

"He introduced a pre-study system," Holmes said later. "He emphasized paper systems studies at the expense of developing hardware. A tremendous flood of paperwork descended upon us." Behind the scenes at the Pentagon senior men from the army, navy, marine and air forces found themselves reporting to junior men on McNamara's staff.

To Holmes, who had set up the Manned Space Program on the basis of support from a President confident and sure of his countrymen's sincerity, with permission to move swiftly and informally toward national goals, the McNamara system was a disturbing interference with efficiency. "Had it been introduced into the Space Program in the beginning," he says, "that program would have taken twice as long to mount—and might perhaps never have succeeded at all." But that assessment was, to a large extent, retrospective. In 1965 the McNamara systems were still being created and directives were pouring forth; it was too soon to assess their value but was instead the period of inundation, of new rules and new patterns.

The nation, of which Raytheon was only one slivered section, was also moving forward, but into new areas that for the first time in history mixed prosperity with anger, progress with violence. Watts exploded and sent images difficult to forget into the mind of America.[111] The war in Vietnam escalated; more troops were sent, more battles fought. Television coverage brought scenes of death and despair, destruction, the confused faces of U.S. soldiers, fleeing Vietnamese, and inquisitive on-the-scene reporters into the peaceful homes of America in a great confused and confusing jumble. Internationally the world seemed astonished that the United States was so caught and so visibly being drawn into an Asian maelstrom. Nevertheless other trouble spots existed, and Raytheon was reminded of this in unmistakable fashion when it received official word that Saudi Arabia, a land rich in oil, sparse in people, and rimmed on all sides by envious eyes, wanted to purchase the Hawk to improve its air defenses.[112]

On that note of expanded horizons the year 1965 ended. It had been crowded and busy, had contained many surprises. Sales had increased to $487.8 million from the previous year's $454 million, but that was not the most important statistic. It was in terms of results that the improved balance of Raytheon's operations became more evident. Earnings had increased from $8.2 million to $11 million—a jump per share from $1.96 to $2.25.[113]

The year 1966 opened with a host of huge problems jostling for attention but with the nation's business booming. The Gross National Product had soared from $628 billion to $675 billion during the previous year and was still rising; personal incomes as well as corporate profits had increased. The stock exchanges as well as many other industries were setting new records, but inflation undercut the gains for many individuals. Many huge and highly mixed events and problems jostled for attention in the nation; one of those once considered peripheral that moved to the foreground was education.

*358*

A final breakthrough enabling federal aid to education had resulted in a vast wave of funds, special programs, projects, and efforts across the nation's schools. These burgeoned with pupils; enrollments spurted forward on secondary and college levels and set off an accumulating wave of activity in textbook publishing, teacher training, and all the subsidiaries of a vast movement. Education and all its offshoots—training in special skills and subjects—all received enormous impetus from the new "knowledge industry," as it was called.

Raytheon, operating under this influence, bought EDEX, the manufacturer of driver-training equipment in Indianapolis, for $2 million in 1965, and Dage-Bell television camera systems for education at the same time. In early 1966, still impelled toward the knowledge industry, Adams and Phillips bought D. C. Heath, an eighty-eight-year-old publisher of textbooks. Heath was a fairly large purchase, though its sales of $18.4 million were less than Amana's. Its earnings the preceding year had been around $1.7 million.[114] Its acquisition provided Raytheon with software—a new jargon word for curriculum content.

Other firms with heavy electronic interests took similar steps. RCA and CBS, whose communications sectors featured the educational explosion, bought publishing firms, plunged into textbooks, teaching aids, filmstrips, televised classrooms, special programing efforts, and the like.

The government was similarly enthused. The President, educated to be a schoolteacher, issued a stream of statements supporting aid to education, HEW expanded its efforts, Congress voted increasingly huge sums. Nobody—neither industry, nor government, nor the social scientists, and certainly neither teachers nor students—had yet realized that a River of Babble cannot carry, let alone sustain, any idea very long.

Internationally events appeared similarly tangled, surrounded by rhetoric and difficult to keep in clear focus. The year opened with the election of Indira Gandhi, daughter of India's late premier Nehru, to lead her nation. Disorders in Africa and Asia continued, and President Johnson combined the Great Society and the war in Vietnam. The combination of popular domestic programs and an unpopular foreign war made a tense political situation in the United States, but other tense areas lacked the American prosperity, the expansion of leisure activities, and the diversity of its entertainments.

At Raytheon, as in Washington, international conditions created a mixture of advantages and problems.

Alibrandi, now head of the Missile Division, found the Saudi Arabia Hawk development fitting, remarkably well, into his own skills. Flying out to that desolate landscape, Alibrandi discovered that ten Hawk installations would have to be created literally from the sand up.[115] That meant bringing in rock drills and crushers to make cement on the spot and the construction not only of military installations but of homes for technicians and their families. Plans were drawn to build houses, hospitals, schools, and theaters and to train Arabian technicians to take the place of Raytheon men in the final establishment. Accommodations had to be built for 1,600 soldiers; water supplies had to be arranged. Alibrandi found it exhilarating.

Elsi, on the other hand, developed serious troubles. Adams, searching for the causes, found the Italian responses mysterious. "Their attitude toward business is completely different," he says. "They suggest a course of action, and you ask, 'Is it profitable?' They smile and say, 'No.' 'Will it be profitable soon?' A shrug, a pause, and they say, 'No.' " [116]

Even Calosi's eloquence, in other words, was wearing thin. Elsi's continuing problems made it clear the Dottore needed top-level—and far more detailed—supervision. Adams told Calosi he would have to report directly to Phillips.

Informed of this decision, Calosi chose indignation. "Shall I take orders from a *boy?*" he asked indignantly. The answer was, "Yes."


Phillips, meanwhile, followed a lead first tracked and discovered by Adams' old firm, Paine, Webber, Jackson & Curtis. It led him, together with George Ingram, to the Tulsa, Oklahoma, offices of Seismograph Services Corporation, makers of geophysical exploration devices and service providers for the petroleum industry.

Seismograph, created by Gerald H. Westby and two other men in 1931, was well known in the petroleum-exploration industry. It had survived the hard years of the depression, expanded during World War II, and by 1966—still headed by Westby—served an industry increasingly interested in geophysical exploration offshore.

That alone made it attractive to Raytheon, which was already in the marine field and highly advanced in the technology of sonars, data processing, and underwater transducers. At SubSig, where Ralph Martin had ascended to the top, these efforts had resulted in an expansion from 800 to 2,500 people who worked on large sonar control programs for the new navy nuclear submarines. SubSig was swinging toward commercial areas and had, in fact, already created a seismograph transducer.

Phillips and Ingram appeared to talk to Westby and his treasurer, E. D. (Dee) Wilson. Both Raytheon men gave the impression of youthful competence. Wilson, listening, was impressed; so was Westby.

None of the men was in a great hurry: Phillips and Ingram made several trips to Tulsa; Mr. Westby and Dee Wilson visited Lexington. Wilson found his trip a surprise.[117]

"We dress colorfully in Tulsa," he says. "I walked into the Lexington executive dining room wearing an electric blue suit and a loud sport shirt. Every head turned to follow me as I sat down. I felt like some sort of peacock in the middle of all those subdued dark suits and white shirts."

But he was highly pleased by another atmosphere he had not expected, though till it struck him he had not realized he had been harboring reservations. "I was struck," he said, "by how patriotic they are at Raytheon. Somehow I had lumped New England with New York City." He was immensely pleased to discover the difference.

The Seismograph deal was agreed in August 1966. Raytheon would pay 792,023 shares of cumulative convertible preferred and 237,607 shares of common—a good price.[118] Mr. Westby was a shrewd bargainer. In return, Raytheon obtained one of the world's three leading firms in the field of seismic exploration for petroleum and natural gas. No propaganda was needed to underline the significance of this acquisition: Dee Wilson was very clear on that point. "Oil is a part of our national economy," he said. "Without oil we cannot move."

The year 1966 was more than half over by then, and the world had—as usual—seen surprises. Sukarno of Indonesia was unexpectedly toppled and his authority taken by a prowestern group of generals; France detonated its first atomic bomb; and the forces of Mao Tse-tung in China launched a cultural revolution difficult to follow, horrendous in detail.

Yet U.S. technology continued to advance and the American business boom maintained its thrust. Business mergers increased to unprecedented levels; the land overflowed with goods and production rose. During 1966 five successful manned space flights were achieved.[119]

Inside Raytheon efforts to expand and improve defense technology burgeoned at a pace and volume that paralleled the commercial expansion of the firm. Holmes's teams, which shortly after his arrival had lost their place in the competition to complete General Zierdt's tasks, had continued their efforts. Regrouped, revitalized, and reinvigorated, they made such progress from their triumph in the phased array guidance system that they reentered the SAM-D race. Their progress from a seemingly lost position to one of a top competitor was a notable achievement.

Not even a six-weeks' strike by the IBEW—the first in the firm's history—created any serious obstacle. Launched after the retirement of Mr. Moore, a calm labor leader, due to a misunderstanding by a successor initially suspicious of management, it ended on reasonable terms.[120]

By year's end 1966 Adams, Phillips, and Holmes had reason to be pleased with the firm's progress. It had advanced in all sectors—governmental as well as in acquisitions and commercial operations. Sales had soared to over $700 million; earnings per share had risen from $2.25 to $2.96, to reach $18.4 million.[121] A giant leap forward.


Late in January 1967, a fire, made fiercer by an atmosphere of pure oxygen, flared inside an Apollo spacecraft being tested on its launch pad at Cape Kennedy and took the lives of astronauts Virgil Grissom, Edward White, and Roger Chaffee. The effects of the tragedy extended far beyond the event itself.

The NASA organization was shuffled; searching inquiries sent investigators probing through the contracting companies of the space industry—and the critics of the U.S. space effort emerged in full cry. Before they were through, Congress lopped a half-billion dollars from the U.S. space program, and President Kennedy's careful plan to create both an effort and a symbol to pull the nation together was dealt a heavy blow.[122]

Space was not the only area of U.S. difficulties in the new year. Racial violence increased and the presence of almost 400,000 U.S. troops in Vietnam was fiercely protested and debated. Yet a boom of unprecedented proportions picked up added speed and momentum. Well over twenty million Americans were listed as owners of stocks, Wall Street used high-speed tickers and computer-linked desk-top quote machines, and trading in the exchanges soared to almost four times the volume of a decade before.[123] Not since the fabled twenties had business as such attracted so much attention and so many participants.

At Raytheon, as in virtually all other business firms in the nation, this quickened tempo was reflected in many ways. The firm's bank credit rose to $100 million; changes were made as men retired from the board and others stepped forward; new faces appeared in the company. Percy Spencer retired as a director; his place was taken by Gerald Westby of Seismograph. The composition of the board, now expanded to twelve, still showed a majority of its members to be from outside the firm. They included, in early 1967, Charles F. Avila, president of Boston Edison; Roger Damon, now chairman of the First National Bank of Boston; Carl Gilbert, who had also moved up to become chairman of Gillette; Eli Goldston, president of Eastern Gas & Fuel; William Hogan of American Airlines; Robert Stoddard, chairman of Wyman-Gordon; Harvey Brooks, dean of Harvard School of Engineering and Applied Physics; and insiders Adams, Phillips, Brainerd Holmes, George Ingram, and now Westby.[124]

Broader horizons were reflected in all sectors. Phillips and Ingram negotiated to acquire the Caloric Corporation of Topton, Pennsylvania, maker of gas ranges and home appliances—an acquisition that received a green light from the Justice Department early in 1967. Alibrandi flew back and forth from Saudi Arabia where teams—later organized into the Raytheon Service Co.—continued to create Hawk installations. Word came that Japan, a country whose military establishment was limited to purely defensive installations, was also interested in the Hawk.

In the midst of these and other promising activities, only the situation of Elsi, in Palermo, Italy, continued to vex and perplex. In February 1967 the Raytheon directors were told Elsi needed another

*363*

$4 million. In March Phillips flew to Italy, surveyed the situation, and came to the conclusion that Elsi needed new on-the-scene management, and Raytheon's Italian investment as a whole better overall supervision.

The decision reflected a growing dissatisfaction with Dr. Carlo Calosi's managerial performance. Dr. Calosi, who was managing director of Selenia, which was still profitably producing Hawks, as well as managing director of Elsi, lived in Rome. Like most Italians he preferred the civilized surroundings of that glittering city to the oxcarts and donkey carts of Sicily. At a dinner party one night, convivially moved, he parroted Louis XIV's identification of himself with France by lifting his glass and saying, "Raytheon Europe—*c'est moi!*" [125] Phillips was not amused.

As long as Raytheon was a minority owner in Selenia with only 45 percent, there was nothing much that could be done about Dr. Calosi's management of that operation. But by putting another $4 million into Elsi, Raytheon would replace La Centrale as majority owner—and Phillips lost no time in making follow-up changes.

With the approval of Adams and Holmes, the company transferred John Stobo from the missile group to Elsi to manage on-the-scene operations. At the same time John Clare, deputy manager of Raytheon Europe, was asked to take additional responsibility for Raytheon's investments in Italy.

These moves were clear as glass. In effect, they removed Calosi from a dominating position regarding Raytheon's investments in Italy, with the exception of his post at Selenia. However, they also increased the size of Raytheon's investment in Elsi; it was obvious that Raytheon still had hopes of its eventual success.

Analysis of Elsi's situation, however, revealed more deep-seated problems than were previously realized. Its venture into the manufacture of television components was handicapped by the need to import glass from the north, which made its tubes an average 10 percent more costly to make than its competitors'.

The discovery was one of a number indicating that the location of Elsi, as well as its general approach toward business, had been based more on socioeconomic factors than industrial realities. Elsi was highly regarded in Italy because it brought at least the appearance of industrialization to Sicily, was a demonstration that progress could be achieved in the retrograde Italian south. One result was that Calosi

*364*

was a hero in the eyes of many of his countrymen. But Raytheon's managers, delving into the details of Elsi's operations, did not regard waste as progress, did not believe industrial efforts should be based on appearance instead of realities.

Their discoveries led them down avenues of new speculation. Dr. Calosi could never be charged with lack of intelligence; it was inconceivable that he did not know the basic facts they learned. They began to wonder at his motivation, his scale of values. Perhaps, they reasoned, his zeal to improve the southern Italian condition had clouded his vision regarding his responsibilities to Raytheon. Perhaps he had, by a series of rationalizations, reversed his order of priorities. Adams decided that was the case, for he wrote a letter to Calosi in which he discussed the facts of the matter. It was, as one would expect, a very candid letter; he did not make its contents public. But he did, many years later, read aloud some excerpts. "Carlo," Adams wrote in part, ". . . you have made a terrible mess of things." [126]

Shortly afterward Calosi was removed as general manager of Raytheon's European operations. Adams went to Italy where he, John Clare, and other Raytheon executives rotated visiting Italian official officers, ministries, banks—a host of dignitaries and institutions requesting investment and contracts to provide employment. They were courteously received, and their explanations of Elsi's difficulties sympathetically heard. Italian government officials expressed surprise at the extent of the problem, and promised to invest more money into Elsi, to channel orders to that enterprise so it could become a prosperous, ongoing part of Italy's new industrialized south.

The promises were, of course, promising—but Raytheon's executive office was adamant that its own position be understood. Elsi was an investment into which Raytheon had poured large sums. It was not a charitable experiment in any sense; losses could not forever be supported. The Italian reaction was soothing.

Kendall Square in downtown Cambridge is an excellent location, and the managers of The Badger Company, an engineering firm devoted to the construction of petroleum and petrochemical plants and allied projects, were very proud of the new building the company was planning there for itself in mid-1967.[127]

They had every right to this pride: Badger was a firm that had once almost vanished and was, in 1967, enjoying a remarkable resurrection. The company, as such, was very old; it was launched in the mid-nineteenth century and its history is studded with famous New England names. In World War II it held patents on the Houdry Process, a petroleum production process for gasoline famous to everyone in that industry.

After several generations, however, Badger had discovered that it was competing against such firms as Lummus and Kellogg at a time when these competitors had grown huge. Its founding family, Badger, wanted to sell. The firm was purchased by Stone & Webster. Stone & Webster had looked their acquisition over carefully and decided they wanted only Badger's plant-design groups. Badger's manufacturing groups, Stone & Webster ruled, would be redundant to its own; it didn't want them.

Early in 1949 the orphans of the merger created the Badger Manufacturing Company on a modest scale. Ade Broggini and Robert Siegfried, two of Badger's executives, left for Stone & Webster, together with most of the rest. Once inside the maw of Stone & Webster, however, Broggini, Siegfried, and many of their old Badger associates found themselves being absorbed in a digestive process. They disliked the sensation and began to trickle back to the truncated, modest Badger Manufacturing Company. In time Stone & Webster completed digesting its purchase and dropped the Badger name even as a division. That left Broggini, Siegfried, and their companions operating the only Badger enterprise visible on the landscape.

Nurturing their seedling, they prospered swiftly. As time passed, they became especially active building refineries in other nations and created a string of offices around the world. By 1967 their success had grown to the point where they undertook to plan an impressive headquarters at Kendall Square, Cambridge, to house a core of two thousand specialists. This number was subject to expansion on special projects, would swell to as many as ten thousand, including construction labor, according to the number and size of its projects.

By 1967 Badger had grown so considerably that Broggini, the president, and his associates began to wonder whether it should become a public corporation. Their investment counsel—White, Weld & Co.—thought the time was propitious and efforts toward such a step were started.

In preparation for the move, Badger expanded its board of directors and elected several new, prominent men. One was an official of the First National Bank of Boston. Learning the details of Badger's planned expansion into the public sector, he wondered if Badger could be financed and enabled to expand simply by merging with Raytheon.

The men who had once been swallowed and had, like Jonah, emerged from the Stone & Webster leviathan, did not initially regard that with any great favor. Nevertheless, a director is entitled to courtesies and they agreed that it would not be amiss at least to discuss the matter.

Raytheon's Tom Phillips, apprised of this, was pleased. The suggestion had not, of course, been casual. Raytheon had already expanded into petroleum and geophysical exploration by the acquisition of Seismograph. To continue its advance into the construction of refineries and chemical-processing plants was logical, if the proper vehicle could be discovered.

Phillips greeted Badger's president and treasurer Broggini and engineering vice president Bob Siegfried in his office at Lexington one Saturday, therefore, with pleasure. The conversation went well. Siegfried, an engineer like most of the Badger managers, thought Raytheon's president was youthful and direct: he made no claim at being an expert in Badger's field and was blunt about Raytheon's lack of interest in sick companies. Phillips wanted to improve Raytheon by adding healthy, prosperous, and growing ventures to its organization.

Broggini also thought the merger was logical. Boston's financial community is, like that of most cities, relatively small: Raytheon was neither a mystery nor without its admirers. Badger's managers, therefore, decided to drop the elaborate and expensive—as well as uncertain —program of becoming a public corporation and instead to ally the firm with Raytheon. Though such an alliance seemed—and still seems —logical and obvious, mergers are not always logical results.

The Badger executives had undergone a traumatic experience when the original Badger firm had been acquired by Stone & Webster. It took unusual qualities to assure them that a new merger between the success they themselves had built and still another large corporation was the proper course.

Once convinced, Broggini, Siegfried, and their associates joined in an announcement in October 1967 that The Badger Company would merge with Raytheon. The actual marriage was not consum-

*367*

mated for a number of months, but it was clear Phillips had been persuasive.

Another persuasive man—George Foerstner—was also busy. Raytheon and Amana engineers had together designed, developed, and laid out the manufacturing systems for a new Radarange oven for the home market. The new ranges were then tested around the nation. Foerstner believes in field tests. "The engineers themselves used some at home," Foerstner says, "and others were placed in homes in all parts of the nation." Foerstner listened to all the results, heard every opinion with close attention. Some families used Radarange ovens for months.[128]

Foerstner introduced the new range at a Chicago press conference in August 1967. The show—for that is what it was—used between twenty and thirty girls as demonstrators, who showed everyone the incredible speed of the appliances, which cook in seconds. Then he took the girls and the Radarange ovens on a tour in a special railroad car.

His market was the appliance distributors themselves. "Distributors," Foerstner says, "are the first line of defense. The secret in obtaining and keeping good distributors," he continues, "is to appeal to their selfishness. A distributor has to be selfish. He must be able to make enough money handling your appliances to abandon everyone else's line, and switch to yours. Any other appeal is a waste of time."

Foerstner is similarly clear about advertising in the consumer marketplace. "Advertising is the engine of sales," he says. "Without it, sales inevitably drop off. And though half of all advertising money is wasted, nobody knows which half."

The results of his Chicago opening were such a success that Foerstner told Tom Phillips he believed they could sell fifty thousand Radarange ovens a year. Events were to prove that, if anything, he understated his case and the prospects. The possibilities were there to make merchandising history and to change the home cooking industry permanently.

While the company was expanding in commercial areas, the government groups won a missile site radar contract from Bell Labs. The award was part of the Safeguard program and a direct result of the phased array patent obtained by Miccioli and his associates: a notable coup.

Three years before, Raytheon had devised a Five-Year Plan projecting sales of $1 billion and per-share earnings in the area of $4. By the end of 1967 that Five-Year Plan had been achieved two years ahead of schedule. Sales had soared to $100 million over $1 billion, net income to $28 million, per share earnings to $3.95. That was a jump of almost $400 million in sales over the year as previously reported, a figure in itself almost equal to the Raytheon sales in the year Adams, Phillips, and Holmes had projected the Five-Year Plan. Per-share earnings had increased by more than $1.[129]

Closer examination of these results disclosed that overseas activities—one of the two areas Raytheon had considered promising in terms of expansion—had indeed expanded: had risen from $30 million in 1965 to $166 million in 1967. But overall the most important change had taken place in the balance between governmental and commercial activities. Holmes had increased Raytheon's government activities, and done so against heavy competition. Phillips had raised commercial operations from 17 percent of the total business in 1964 to 45 percent in 1967.[130] That meant the firm was no longer precariously poised on one leg; it could walk firmly on two, with only a slight remaining limp.


The year 1968 opened to discover America entangled in world affairs. President Johnson, whose policies of massive expenditures in Vietnam and huge domestic welfare programs at home had released a serious inflation and exacerbated large sections of the nation, started 1968 with the announcement that henceforth U.S. private investments overseas would be sharply curtailed.[131] Ostensibly the purpose of the measure was to retain capital at home, force business into domestic expansions, and increase tax revenues. The President and the Treasury admitted such a policy, if long continued, would amount to a diminution of the U.S. commercial presence in the world, promised it was only temporary. Five years and another President later, it was still in effect.

Raytheon's Adams and Tom Phillips, however, could have been forgiven had they wished the Johnson move, at sharp historic variance with the U.S. belief in free trade, had been made five years sooner: it might have kept them out of Italy—or at least Sicily.

In mid-January 1968, that unhappy island was stricken by an earthquake that made ten thousand people homeless. This calamity, as far as Raytheon was concerned, was paralleled by economic tremors affecting Elsi. In sum, despite an Italian government ruling that the depressed south should receive at least 30 percent of all official industrial orders, Elsi was actually treated if not as an orphan, at least as a child of foreign parents in Sicily.

Despite repeated assurances, the enterprise did not receive Italian government orders, nor did the government fulfill any of numerous promises to shore the sagging enterprise with additional capital.

John Clare, who spent months on Elsi's problems, became, in Phillips' words, "drawn and worried." A stream of discouraging reports flowed from Palermo to Lexington, and Phillips, drawn into the vortex, was constantly on the transatlantic telephone discussing the situation with Clare.

Phillips decided that Elsi would have to retrench, and hoped that would inspire the Italian government to make good on some of its assurances. The decision to lay off some of Elsi's 1,400 workers had the effect of uncapping an economic earthquake in Palermo. Between January and February 1968 the union staged twenty-four wildcat strikes at the plant. Instead of increased efficiency, production was interrupted, stalled, and made even more unprofitable.[132]

To Phillips, who began to feel like a headquarters commander receiving battlefield reports, the situation seemed increasingly depressing. Having visited the scene himself several times, he felt sympathy for the people of Sicily. "They are hardworking and sincere," he observed. "But the plant lacked trained engineers, who would not move south; its production of black and white television tubes was unprofitable; so were its other operations. Clearly the drain could not continue forever." Beyond these points Phillips had come to believe that the promises of the Italian government constituted "so much empty rhetoric."

By March 1968 Phillips told the Raytheon directors about the massive efforts to make Elsi profitable undertaken "by teams of men since 1967." All these efforts, he explained, had been resisted by Italian labor, first by strikes and slowdowns, later by threats of occupation. The situation having grown out of hand, Elsi laid off the remaining nine hundred workers and made plans to close the plant. The Italian

*370*

government was told the plant would not reopen unless the official promises were realized.

At that news, tempers in Palermo rose to fever pitch. Despite union demands, the government did not take any positive steps, and the Elsi management refused to reopen the plant or rescind an order laying off a final nine hundred workers, issued in March 1968. Demonstrations and sympathy walkouts in other, unrelated firms created a crisis for the mayor of Palermo, who then decided to prove that his heart, if not his reason, was in the right place by seizing the Elsi plant under an 1865 law used only once before, "to prevent further disorder."

With the plant now in the possession of the Sicilian government, neither Adams nor Phillips could see any constructive resolution of the Italian problem. The mayor of Palermo, basking in the sardonic applause of the island's trade union leaders, was astonished in his own turn when Elsi was declared bankrupt.

That was almost like setting Etna off again.

Italy is a nation whose government and businesses are intertwined to a bewildering degree. The government owns banks and commercial ventures and has shares in many it does not own outright. It lends money on one hand and capitalizes ventures to compete with its borrowers on the other. In all, it is a highly individual system subject to many pressures, opinions, and emotions, which the Italian temperament finds endurable but which often baffles, exasperates, and defeats outsiders.

Throughout the long saga of Raytheon's difficulties with Elsi, the Italian government played a curious role. It lent the venture money through some of its banks. But Professor Petrilli, head of *IRI* and a towering governmental figure, later said he did not regard Elsi's electronic potential in Palermo as promising.[133] The contradiction between that opinion and his earlier statements did not strike either the professor or his newspaper interviewers as significant.

At any rate Adams and Phillips were shocked by the seizure of the Elsi plant. They pointed out that such a confiscation prevented an orderly liquidation of assets. At the time of the plant seizure, Elsi had three types of loans. Eight million dollars of these had been guaranteed by Raytheon—and Raytheon would pay them. About $6.8 million was secured by the assets of Elsi's plant, equipment, and inventory. Approximately $6 million more was in the form of unsecured loans. Raytheon could hardly be expected, said Adams and Phillips, to pay loans secured by equipment and a plant that had been confiscated. Nor, they added, would it pay the unsecured loans, since there was no legal reason, in their view, why it should.

That sent the Italian bankers up the wall. They had, all along, taken it for granted that Raytheon would happily pay all Elsi obligations. Americans always paid. Behind the scenes great arguments began that at first did not emerge into public view. Elsi had to go to a Palermo court to have its declaration of bankruptcy approved. Discussions were held *in camera* while this last step in the minuet was underway.

Raytheon was very active, and had been for many years, in the Boston community. In 1968 its charitable contribution as a corporation, long ago set at 1 percent of corporate earnings before taxes, reached $600,000.[134] That figure did not include, of course, the contributions from Raytheon individuals. In addition to donations, the executives at Raytheon were personally active in a great many community efforts and projects. Adams had headed the United Fund campaign. In 1968 one project of special interest was an offshoot of the Raytheon equal opportunity employment program, which had been long and deeply established.

This program carried Raytheon into a joint effort for the creation of a special training center to teach the unskilled the basics of drafting, clerical work, or electronic assembly. It included courses in English and mathematics. It was to operate buses to and from the inner city and was very hopefully regarded. That hope, incidentally, was not in vain: a high percentage of those who attended were able to obtain jobs and to keep them successfully.[135] The percentage reflected, though, a somewhat shrewd selection process, although Raytheon had nothing to do with that. The clients, or students, were channeled through a larger Boston committee.

Early in 1968, while the center was being built in Waltham, Tom Phillips dropped in on Percy Spencer and asked him if—from his retirement—he would serve as a consultant to the effort.

Percy was taken aback and found several reasons to be reluctant.

*372*

He had spent his life seeking the company and respect of the brightest men in the community; he was not sure he wanted to work with those who might have to be persuaded into intellectual interest. The center was a distance away and involved driving—which Percy disliked.[136]

But after he returned from Florida in the spring of 1968, Percy decided to give the center a reluctant try. He went there, and discovered they had hopefully furnished and set aside an office for him. He sat there, somewhat grumpily, and the students—who were of all ages and many different ethnic backgrounds, with a heavy preponderance of blacks—began to drop in on him with equal hesitation. He grew interested, and so did they. To Tom Phillips' pleasure, Percy soon became enthusiastically involved. He instructed all over the place and even gave women tips on typing. Then he began to create draftsmen and mechanics, to teach genuine skills; he became a familiar, helpful presence.

On May 21, 1968, he was in his office at the center when one of the black supervisors, walking past, saw him stricken and vainly reaching for the phone. He was rushed to the Peter Bent Brigham Hospital. He later emerged greatly diminished physically, the victim of a debilitating stroke, but alive and able to return home.

A few weeks later, Lillian Spencer opened the door and saw, to her pleasure, Adams in hunting clothes, carrying his latest trophy to her husband. She ushered him in; the two men chatted. Spencer was not left alone; Tom Phillips called frequently. Laurence Marshall, his old boss, showed up with a film his son John had made in Africa and showed it in its entirety. Spencer was amazed—it was an excellent film; the Marshalls had become experts in their new venture in anthropology. Marshall's trips are still held in high esteem; he is still hale, keen as ever. His mother lived to be 102; Laurence Marshall may well equal her record.

Even Henry Argento appeared from Philco to call upon Percy, who had been like a father to him years before. Percy was still rich in friends.[137]

In October 1968, Adams reported to the board, "with pleasure," that Tom Phillips had been the firm's president and chief operating officer for the past four years, and successfully so. He recommended that Phillips be made chief executive, and that the powers from his office as chairman be transferred to Phillips' office as president. Then he added a typical Adams touch: he reversed their salaries, so the younger man's was higher than his own.[188]

His action in stepping aside as chief executive for Phillips was dominated by the intention to see the firm continued. In conversation later, he compared this sense of continuity—though he did not put it that way—with the giant paper pyramids being hastily thrown together by the conglomerateurs. "Will they last?" he wondered, "or will they come down as fast as they went up? I believe we have men here in New England as capable as in New York, and without the distractions or the hysteria of that city, able to build very sound and stable enterprises." [139]

Sound and stable enterprises did not seem so possible to others at the time. The United States went toward its elections with the searing fear that it might not be able to maintain its political system after horrendous riots surged around the Democratic nominating convention in Chicago. The press blamed the police and the mayor of the city for too stern an attitude originally and too violent a reaction later in the unruly demonstrations that erupted. Democratic candidate Humphrey emerged in the polls trailing behind Richard M. Nixon. But in November when the votes were counted, they proved amazingly close; Nixon won by a very slim majority.

At year's end the election appeared not to have created any cessation of argument. Unlike previous periods, the nation showed no inclination to forget its campaign arguments and unite; not even the presence of 500,000 troops overseas and bitter war seemed able to bring the people together.

The situation was, like the year before, burning with bitterness, no matter who said what. The administrators of the Johnson regime had, for the most part, departed: Secretary of Defense McNamara went to the World Bank; his successor—Clark Clifford—said the defense establishment would work on societal problems.[140] Yet business boomed; Wall Street distributed bonuses and brokering seemed the easiest of all the ways to make money, almost as easy as in 1928.

But beneath the surface the pace of actual business slowed. Production was down, in terms of real wealth being created. Inflation was up. Raytheon counted its results for 1968 and was, unsurprisingly, in step with the nation. Sales had risen, though slightly, to reach $1.157 billion. Net earnings were up to $29.5 million: per-share earnings, before a two-for-one stock split, were $4.18.[141]

It looked as though the great leap days were over, but Raytheon was now very large. Its backlog of government orders had risen to $429 million, an increase of almost $50 million over the year before. The coming year would provide its own surprises for many, and Adams' assessment of the value of building soundly would find its contrasts in Wall Street.

When D. Brainerd Holmes was elected executive vice president of Raytheon early in 1969, Tom Phillips was keenly aware that "the antimilitary atmosphere made it hard to even talk about what could be talked about." That sounded paradoxical, but was not. The antimilitary climate of the press and much of the public dialogue had reached a point where not only military secrets but even military-connected accomplishments could hardly be mentioned without provoking sarcastic and openly hostile reactions.

Holmes—and not only Holmes, but the thousands of Raytheon men and the teams he inspired—were working at peak levels under the strains of unpopularity and forced silence. It was true, of course, that much of Raytheon's defense work and many of its installations were held behind heavy curtains of official secrecy.

"I sometimes get the idea the entire firm is classified," Adams says wrily. "We have very impressive installations that not even our directors have seen." [142]

As the man in charge of overall operations in these installations, Holmes, says Phillips, "stimulated their developmental efforts; made them more creative." That is a considerable accomplishment. While Phillips turned toward commercial developments, Holmes not only introduced what he himself calls "systems discipline," but had created controls that protected the firm from the cost overrun problems that had injured some of its competitors: he had managed to estimate in advance of unpredicted inflation and carry Raytheon to the front line of technology.

That is an impressive accomplishment in the best of times, but Holmes was not working in the best of times.

*       *       *

375

General Yates retired, and so did T. C. Wisenbaker, for the third or fourth time—nobody could quite remember. Wisenbaker, who remained a consultant, returned to the sun of Florida, but he left Missiles in good shape. Holmes, who kept turning from one of his burners to another, watched developments in the equipment division closely. He had, the preceding year, brought in Dr. Joseph Shea, who had worked for him in Washington, D.C., in the early days of the Manned Space Program.

Shea was, to an extent, a casualty of the holocaust at Houston when three astronauts had burned to death. As Houston manager, he had been in charge of the Apollo Command Module and the Lunar Excursion Module, and he had enjoyed a remarkably good relationship with the journalists who covered the space center. Faced with their subsequent shift of attitude toward the U.S. space efforts after the tragedy, Shea had looked toward the exit, went briefly with Polaroid, and then switched to Raytheon.[143]

He found the equipment division doing over $100 million a year but with thin profit margins. It was a difficult division to manage because it had, unlike Missiles or SubSig, a less clear charter. It created radars and displays, worked in communications and computers; it dealt with governmental agencies in all sorts of different sectors and interests. Shea's task was not made any lighter when Holmes subsequently shifted the former space division of Raytheon into the equipment division also, for good measure. Shea settled down to explore his new province.

Fortunately he had Vice President Harold Hart, who had been an equipment division leader for years and had served as assistant manager under Gross, at hand as a guide. Hart's knowledge of the strengths, weaknesses, and personalities of the division was unexcelled, his own abilities long proven. Shea's arrival enabled Fritz Gross, who had told Holmes he was tiring of heavy line responsibilities, to move sideways to head corporate engineering. Holmes has a high regard for Gross, whom he terms "superb. And he runs flat out." [144]

Gross had run flat out, however, for almost thirty years. In that long period he had been one of the prime movers in the development of the SG radar that played so important a role during World War II, in the computer developments that culminated in the Datamatic venture, and in an incredibly wide array of other efforts. A cheerful man, Gross has the added talent—invaluable in any organization—of being able to work amicably with almost everybody. His new duties were designed to capitalize on his vast experience and knowledge and that special overriding talent as vice president of corporate engineering.

News that Holmes himself had moved up occasioned no surprise. The troika of Adams, Phillips, and Holmes had been well established for years. But a subtle shift took place. Phillips had become chief executive; Holmes was now executive vice president, and Adams moved back. The chairman became the elder statesman to whom both the younger men could turn. An ideal situation. Adams was very pleased. "A great stillness," he calls it. "A calming of the waters. You may say that it all took too long, and you would be right. I think it took too long myself. But it was done." [145]

Frank Fox, who had been president of Time Inc.'s Silver Burdette and before that a senior vice president of McGraw-Hill, was hired by Tom Phillips in 1968 to coordinate the educational acquisitions of Raytheon. Fox, steeped in publishing with emphasis on the social sciences, went through the Raytheon establishment with growing amazement. "I walked past rows of people staring into microscopes and reviewed banks of computers," he says, "and wondered how these people could work with beasts that couldn't be seen." [146]

Fox was deeply impressed to discover that Raytheon scientists and engineers "may have been responsible, all told, for five hundred books, and countless articles and monographs in the literature of infrascience."

Nevertheless Fox arrived after the widely touted "educational revolution" had collapsed in its own rhetoric. *Fortune* magazine and other publications, which only a few years earlier had featured breakthroughs in education, had moved on to other, more exciting and less embarrassing subjects. Raytheon discovered, after the tides of fashion shifted, that the "education industry" could not use the hardware of high technology.

After sifting through several minor acquisitions based on the hopes of that tide when it first appeared, Raytheon found itself in a changed market holding only D. C. Heath, the publishing firm, as a

*377*

basis for continued effort. "You are, really, in the publishing business," Fox said. Phillips agreed, and later put Fox in charge of Heath.


Meanwhile Raytheon remained a partner in Selenia, in Italy, with 45 percent ownership. Finnmeccanica, operating as an agency of the Italian government, held another 45 percent, and Fiat 10 percent. In Lexington both Phillips and Adams watched Selenia's course under Managing Director Dr. Carlo Calosi. Dr. Calosi, who was still a Raytheon vice president, was presiding over an effort that began to turn in a familiar direction.

Selenia, which made Hawks, radars, air-traffic controls, and an array of sophisticated electronic components and devices based on Raytheon-developed technology, was having difficulties in the Italian marketplace. The response of its managers was to cut prices in order to win new contract awards. The results were an increase in sales but a decrease in profits.

"Actually," says Phillips, "Calosi had two half-bosses—and neither could control his decisions." [147] But Phillips and Adams, steeped by now in the intricate minuets of Italy, could certainly control Raytheon's choices. They decided that the firm's $3.2 million investment in Selenia would remain static—they would not add to it. When they were informed—as they had expected—that Selenia would need more capital, up to $10 to $11 million more, they were not surprised. Their answer was a firm No.

Finnmeccanica's executives were surprised. Dr. Calosi—an eloquent man—had convinced them that Selenia was a jewel, with a glittering future. The Finnmeccanica's managing director, visiting Lexington to discuss that future, seemed firmly convinced of its reality. When Phillips indicated Finnmeccanica could increase its share of Selenia by putting up the entire new capital, the Italian director looked "like the cat that swallowed the canary."

The outcome was that Raytheon curtailed its ownership in Selenia; Finnmeccanica's ownership rose to 72 percent. At that point, Adams wrote Calosi and explained the Raytheon view of Selenia in detail.

"Its pattern," said Adams of Selenia, "is no longer compatible. Its profits are negligible; it no longer makes sense." He made it clear that his personal regard for Dr. Calosi remained high and that he would

*378*

enjoy future contacts of a social nature. But Dr. Calosi was no longer a vice president of Raytheon: his new bosses were the new controlling owners of Selenia.

Neither Adams nor Tom Phillips will ever forget their Italian experience. "All Raytheon's know-how went to Selenia," Phillips mourns. "The wrong country at the wrong time."

Nevertheless Raytheon could balance that disappointment with successes. Adams had believed in free trade all his life; his NATO experience had been a great triumph. He had carried Raytheon abroad and been successful overall; Phillips and he still watch the expansion of Raytheon around the world.

Around them the United States watched the same sort of emerging international pattern, in which success and disappointment were intermingled. The war in Vietnam, widely unpopular, continued to cost huge sums and many casualties. The new administration, handicapped in part by an inability to attract topflight men, moved cautiously—for many, too cautiously.

Early in March 1969 hundreds of college professors, researchers, and students suspended class activities for a day to protest the role of scientists in military-related research. The demonstration was part of a growing antimilitary and antitechnological movement reflected in other nations as well. In France de Gaulle lost a referendum, decided his day was done, and stepped down. In Sweden the voters swung to the left; Italy's political situation remained disordered.

For a brief moment in midsummer 1969 the clouds over the United States parted, however, to show the blue skies and great vistas John Kennedy had hoped to make permanent. On July 10 Apollo 11, sent aloft by a Saturn booster rocket, made a successful trip to the moon. Neil Armstrong and Colonel Edwin Aldrin walked around on that surface to the awe and wonder of the world, rejoined Michael Collins in the command module, and safely returned to earth.

It was probably the greatest engineering feat in mankind's long history, into which the American nation had poured immense manhours, scientific explorations, engineering talent, and money spread over nearly a decade.

The men of Raytheon watched with special interest, for many had been part of the effort. Brainerd Holmes and Dr. Joseph Shea had

*379*

helped organize it on the highest levels. Ron Greenslade had guided the design and manufacture of computers for the space vehicles—which were outgrowths of efforts in support of the Draper Lab. Throughout all the technological ranks of Raytheon were scattered other men who had contributed to that mighty victory of mankind against the empyrean; over endless space and its vast reaches.

On earth President Nixon began the gradual withdrawal of U.S. forces from Vietnam and ordered a 10 percent reduction of the U.S. military presence in other areas. In Congress a debate began regarding the ABM system as originally projected by the Johnson Administration, and a cutback was ordered. Some senators and congressmen, adding their voices to many in the national community, questioned the enormous size of defense efforts and the continuation of new weapons development.

The President, who had previously declared his intention to negotiate new agreements with the Soviets if possible, proclaimed his Administration would pursue such efforts. Foreign policy advisor Henry Kissinger and Secretary of State Rogers declared U.S. defense efforts would not impede a conference newly arranged to limit strategic arms and slow the race between the United States and the Soviet Union.

Added together, the debate and response, as well as a number of polls, indicated the nation was weary of international military efforts and that great changes in mood and approach had overtaken the climate of Washington.

In all areas, change is the only constant. Raytheon had changed, had grown into a complex organization of many divisions and subsidiaries; its people were numerous and its activities increasingly diverse. To maintain coherence and to keep himself informed, Phillips had continued the monthly meetings instituted by Harold Geneen, maintained by Krafve, and still in existence when he himself arrived in the executive suite. "Moment of truth meetings," Hennemuth calls them. These are serious, but by no means the subject of whispers; the corridors do not echo any fears. Men are not embarrassed. The intent is to keep track and to learn what soft or trouble spots are developing, where new efforts should be made or old ones dropped.

In October 1969, three men were moved up to become senior vice presidents: Joe Alibrandi, Ed Dashefsky, and Joe Shea. The same month, as though fate was determined to illustrate the fluidity of corporate life, Alibrandi received another telephone call from Harry Derbyshire, a former controller of the missile division. Derbyshire had, several times, tried to entice Alibrandi to the Whittaker Corporation—a Los Angeles-based electronics firm—but Alibrandi had not been interested.[148]

In October 1969, Alibrandi was told that Whittaker's chairman was coming to Boston for a visit and would like to have dinner with him. That was an invitation discourteous to decline, and an appointment was arranged. The men met, Alibrandi was charmed and began to weaken. The lures were glittering.

By 1969 Ade Broggini, chairman of Badger, was so pleased with the results of his firm's merger with Raytheon that he suggested a further expansion in the engineering industry. Talking to Phillips, Broggini dwelt on the growing need for nuclear energy. In turn that topic led to evaluating firms active in that field. Steve Brodie, a Badger executive, knew Henry Chance II, the president of United Engineers & Constructors in Philadelphia. In due course, Brodie placed a call to Chance and said he would like to pay him a visit—and perhaps bring some friends. Chance, slightly surprised, agreed: it is hardly the sort of call one can refuse.

In due course Brodie appeared in United Engineers' office flanked by Bob Siegfried, who had become president of Badger, and by Tom Phillips. Both Brodie and Siegfried glowed about Raytheon—stressed its high technology, its affinities with MIT and other advanced groups—and urged Chance to join United Engineers to the enterprise.[149]

"I don't know," Chance said. "At this moment I only have to take orders from my wife. If we join Raytheon I'll have new bosses." But he called Tom Dahl, then executive vice president of United Engineers, to join the conversation. That was a clear sign of interest.

United Engineers was created out of four older engineering

groups in 1928. Its parts included subway builders, skyscraper experts, engineers experienced in power construction, and electrification projects. In 1938 it came into the control of Colonel Edwin M. Chance, father of Henry Chance II.

By 1969 United Engineers was a very large firm, far larger than most engineering firms, which are fragmented—much like attorneys or physicians—into small professional partnerships throughout the country. For generations these operated without advertising and offered their services, discreetly, "to help you design" projects. That pattern was broken by Bechtel, which shook professional engineering groups by heavy advertising and open efforts to obtain contracts.

United Engineers was initially shocked by this but, deciding modesty was slim consolation for extinction, updated its own approach to advertising and the search for business. By the time Tom Phillips, Siegfried, and Steve Brodie called on Henry Chance, United Engineers had achieved third place in its industry—a ranking that sounds somewhat better than it was, since both Bechtel and Stone & Webster were far larger.

Phillips had arrived at an opportune moment. For a considerable time, United Engineers had obtained most of its contracts from the steel industry and had specialized in projects ranging from $2 million to $5 million each. But engineering work changes as society shifts its priorities; by 1969 the demand for more energy sources in all forms—petroleum, coal, gas, nuclear power—had become urgent. One unforgettable, almost ominous indication of that had appeared with the blackout over New York.

In order to expand into this new area and share in its great potential, United Engineers was in the process of shifting more of its resources into energy. Merger with Raytheon would bring greater resources to United Engineers and, what was equally important, comprehension. The talks moved forward well and extended to visits back and forth.

With international Raytheon on the move under John Clare in Europe, and assisted by the enlarged contacts and activities of Mr. Adams, with the government sector under Holmes expanded to well over $700 million a year, with commercial markets expanding and an excellent new acquisition drawing near, Phillips had every reason to be pleased as 1969 drew toward its close.

In common with all other corporations, Raytheon's management was concerned, however, by the sharp decline of stock values in the exchanges by year's end. Some of the nation's most famous and widely touted conglomerates were more than concerned: they were deeply worried. But Raytheon had not enjoyed the fickle favoritism of the exchange and therefore its worries in that respect were not extensive. Sales in 1969 were $1.2 billion, earnings $35.3 million—a clear improvement over the preceding year. Broken down, that came to $2.34 per share of common—an increase of 25 cents over the 1968 figure.[150]

Henry Chance, majority stockholder and president, signed the sale of United Engineers to Raytheon just as the year ended, for 500,-000 shares of Raytheon preferred, Series A. That step marked a significant advance in Phillips' program.

Around them all—Phillips, Holmes, Adams, and their associates—the climate of the nation and the world was highly mixed. The decade had started with the rise of a new generation of Americans reaching toward control of events; to the campaign oratory of John Kennedy denouncing the Soviet advance into Cuba and calling for America to move forward again. It ended with clear signs that America was withdrawing in anger—but not so much in anger at the world as at itself.

# Chapter 9 THE SEVENTIES

THE eighth decade of the twentieth century opened to a United States reflecting a revolution of manners, style, and attitude that had taken place during the preceding decade in such subtle stages that none could mark its beginning nor foresee its end.

The theater, which reflected these changes, had moved from a heavily commercial to an increasingly art-oriented medium. Films like *Easy Rider, Midnight Cowboy*, and *M\*A\*S\*H* marked a departure from the traditional stage of manners; Henry Hewes, the reviewer for the *Saturday Review*, wrote about "the revolt against decorous language."

Yet the nation was not moving away from reality, for it was deep in discussions of problems once considered the special province of experts. One of these subjects was pollution of the air, land, and water through the unrestricted use of pesticides and chemicals, of unchecked industrial growth and community sprawl. That concern led President Nixon, early in 1970, to sign a bill passed swiftly by Congress called the National Environmental Policy Act. Its passage was more than symbolic: it was evidence that the nation's attention was turning from the seemingly abstract challenge of space to the everyday challenges of life on earth.

Pollution, however, was not the only large and serious subject on the landscape. The expensive mixture of heavy federal aid to education, the communities, welfare, and social reform combined with the huge costs of the Vietnam war to create the most serious inflation since the Korean war twenty years earlier. In an effort to brake this spiral, the Administration applied, deliberately, "brakes," and the Federal Reserve applied a tight money policy.

*384*

One result was a slowdown of the economy in late 1969. Another was a stock market slide. Many observers had expected Wall Street to encounter troubles, but even the most knowledgeable had underestimated the extent to which these troubles would escalate.

"By May," wrote John Brooks, "a portfolio consisting of one share of every stock listed on the Big Board was worth scarcely half what it had been worth at the start of 1969." [1]

A generation before such signs of economic decline had sent waves of panic through the land and helped launch a wide-scale depression. It is to the credit of the U.S. press that it did not contribute toward such a calamity in 1970, but the reasons were not based on reportorial or editorial restraint so much as on the fact that many other issues competed for attention.

The Vietnam war was high among these. The President was gradually diminishing the American combat presence in this arena, but far more gradually than the critics of the conflict demanded. With the U.S. military presence being reduced in other areas as well, the entire defense establishment diminished. Government defense contracts were "extended"—which meant that delivery dates were postponed and the pace of their costs stretched out.

With both the government markets and the commercial marketplace in decline, it speaks well for Raytheon that its position remained remarkably steady although the price of its stock dropped together with that of other firms. The management decided its stock had dropped below its real value and began some cautious but public purchases. Holmes, faced with stretched-out contracts, cut back on his payrolls; layoff notices went out.[2]

Yet, so mixed were conditions that Amana was able to continue its growth in microwave oven sales to consumers and the firm's overall performance remained strong. Overseas Raytheon continued to expand, and the acquisition of United Engineers sent that firm after larger contracts. Frank Fox, head of D. C. Heath, received permission from Phillips and the directors to purchase Caedmon Records, a firm specializing in the spoken word, for $2 million.

Even the departure of Joe Alibrandi to become, shortly, the president of Whittaker did not cause more than regret;[3] Holmes had the government groups well organized and had a replacement ready. The firm had grown in management depth.

A discordant note, however, was sounded after the sale of Raytheon Learning Systems, an Indianapolis-based manufacturer of equipment for use in driver training. At first the sale of a losing property seemed a stroke of luck. But the purchaser—Visual Electronics—turned out to be more visual than electronic. It had claimed to be worth $8 million but actually negotiated the purchase of Raytheon's subsidiary mainly as a desperate means to enlarge, impress, and keep itself afloat. The expedient did not help, and Visual Electronics soon filed for bankruptcy, carrying the assets of Raytheon's Learning Systems down the drain in the debacle.[4] That caused an embarrassing after-tax loss of $3.5 million—a sum that was not immense, but not inconsiderable either.

Some estimate of Raytheon's growth, however, could be gained from the fact that it could now absorb such a loss. Commercial business by 1970 accounted for almost half of all Raytheon's activities, government business the other half. Its legs were nearly even, and it walked easily.

That was the condition of Raytheon on September 7, 1970, when Percy Spencer died, aged seventy-six.

It is not possible for a man to spend so much of his life with an enterprise without developing strong attitudes toward its destiny: Percy was very pleased to have been associated with so notable a success. But he was also a success himself. Featured in *Reader's Digest* in August 1958, he had achieved fame beyond the measure of most men; in terms of real accomplishment, a great deal more than many better-known men.

In terms of Raytheon, Percy Spencer ranked alongside the four original founders in importance. His funeral was attended by an overflow crowd and brought Laurence K. Marshall, Charlie Adams, Tom Phillips, and Brainerd Holmes together as pallbearers. Obituaries appeared across this nation and Canada. A truly remarkable saga; an incredible journey.


Nineteen seventy was a year in which, from a business viewpoint, firms were fortunate to hold their position. It was a year that held few great or stirring international events beyond the new neutrality of West Germany and what appeared to be a cessation of disorder inside China. It was a year in which the Administration had hoped to improve its congressional strength in the November elections, and did not.

Yet, from a business viewpoint, a year that is bad for business is a good year in which to cull the sound from unsound enterprises. It ended for Raytheon with sales of $1.2 billion, earnings $34.3 million. Per share that broke down to $2.32. Overall, this was a drop of $1 million in earnings. Two cents a share.[5]

*The Wall Street Journal,* no stranger to the business scene, arrived to ask Raytheon why it had done so well compared to so many casualties. In his article, staff reporter David Gumpert expressed surprise that Raytheon was able to prosper in its "transfer technology," citing the success of Radarange ovens when General Dynamics had lost $7 million in microfilm in the first half of 1970; was equally surprised that Raytheon could turn a profit on defense contracts when giant Lockheed had lost $200 million on U.S. cargo plane contracts.[6]

Its fiscal results marked Raytheon and its position. Its management and name began to emerge again on a scale commensurate with its abilities.

By early 1971 the Gross National Product of the United States—an abstraction upon which economists dote—crossed the $1 trillion mark for the first time.[7] The New Year dawned not only on continuing demonstrations against the U.S. presence in Vietnam, but on a nation whose citizens had, during the previous decade, mostly moved to residences within fifty miles of either the East, West, Lakes, or Gulf coasts. There had been a slow and persistent trickle of people out of such inland states as West Virginia and the Dakotas. The result was that 54 percent of the people in 1971 lived along the coasts and 46 percent inland in the United States. That was a historic reversal of a long tide—though few remarked upon it.[8]

Another tide reversal, however, that received more attention was President Nixon's plan for a $16 billion revenue-sharing between Washington and the states. The suggestion was made at the same time the federal budget was set at a record $229.2 billion.[9] Realities had begun to obtrude: the responsibilities of Washington had grown so far-flung they threatened to dwarf the activities of states and localities. The President searched for some means to reverse this apparently inexorable tide. Unfortunately the issue, bound in economic details, was difficult to simplify or popularize and failed to strike many responsive sparks from the public.

More heat was generated in the press by the supersonic transport plane program. Instituted by President Johnson and equally supported by President Nixon and the Pentagon, competitive to a similar program long underway by the Soviet Union, Britain, and France, the SST was opposed by environmental groups. In the end the American program was canceled.

Yet in reality the world remained eager for industrialization. Badger, now headed by Bob Siegfried, found new contracts and clients in places as far apart as Brazil and Turkey. And despite the publicized protests against technology, United Engineers under Henry Chance continued to find heavy demands for nuclear and fossil-fuel power plants throughout the United States.

Both firms helped swell the Raytheon backlog of orders and to change its mix. That was a significant development. In the past the Raytheon backlog meant defense contracts; by early 1970 an increasing percentage came from the private sector, and of that percentage, a significant part from outside the United States.

Perhaps it was this diversity and balance that made it possible for Raytheon successfully to issue $50 million in debentures in 1970. At any rate the financial community was sufficiently impressed to buy the entire issue rapidly, and the list of underwriters, headed by Morgan, Stanley & Co., read like a blue book.[10]


An enterprise, like its managers, must have some of the luck that Adams once said was essential to a chief executive. One of Raytheon's more fortunate circumstances, especially during the sixties, was that it was never selected as a target by antiwar demonstrators. Such luck could not last forever, nor did it.

In 1970 anti-Raytheon handbills appeared in the Lexington area and it was learned that a demonstration would be mounted outside headquarters. Hennemuth, the personnel director, and Jack Campbell, the public relations director, conferred with Phillips about possibilities and learned he expected to receive and talk to the demonstrators when they appeared.

They did appear, and all of them were admitted to the building and conducted to a conference room. Phillips appeared, and Hennemuth was an interested—almost absorbed—spectator.

"He answered their accusations, questions, and arguments calmly," Hennemuth said later, "but they rambled, shouted, cursed. Phillips was taken aback: he had expected the idealistic youths so often described.

"Finally," Hennemuth concluded, "they left in disorderly fashion.

In their progress toward the door they noticed the Raytheon office workers had left their desks and were watching them, and they shouted curses at them." [11]

That cost the demonstrators sympathy. There is a vast difference between demonstrating—or seeing a demonstration—and being the target of a demonstration.

Such incidents, however, were winding down in the nation. In Washington, D.C., a widely publicized effort to halt U.S. governmental proceedings for one day was mounted by an estimated twelve thousand demonstrators, to attendant publicity. The attempt failed when hundreds of demonstrators were arrested. Some sections of the media, which had regarded the projected restraint of the government with equanimity, were indignant that the demonstrators were restrained instead. An argument was mounted that such mass arrests were unconstitutional and the clamor this created tacitly masked at least some of the failure of the demonstration. The organizers, however, were disheartened and antiwar demonstrations visibly diminished in the land. Subtle changes were taking place.

Some other indications of these changes were reflected inside Raytheon when special projects were launched to apply some of the firm's high technology to societal areas such as highway traffic congestion, waterways pollution, and the like.

Both Holmes and Phillips are of the opinion that "it takes no pair of geniuses to extrapolate the decline of government-funded R&D efforts and the need for a technology transfer." But though they agree on the major outlines, they differ—as partners often do—on the pace of these developments.

Holmes, a realist, points out that the application of high technology to community and regional problems will not be easy or rapid. "The sums available to individual communities are not large," he observes. "The grasp of technology on the part of smaller communities or, for that matter, even metropolitan governments, is not advanced. A technological approach is, therefore, limited, hindered, and in some instance delayed by political and financial considerations."

Phillips, however, takes a long-range view. "There is no doubt the technology exists," he says, "and equally no doubt it will be applied."

Meanwhile both men have pushed a number of such projects in

several communities, and plan more. Their reaction to the environmental movement, therefore, has been not only sympathetic but constructive. Like leaders of other sectors of U.S. industry, they discovered that the environmental concern of the nation had carried industry beyond the point of debate.

The same observation was made in Badger, where Bob Siegfried and his engineers obtained some contracts to design and equip existing petroleum and chemical plants with antipollution systems, install desulphurization units in others.

The environment became a key consideration in United Engineers' business. "Environmentalists rank as equals to those who design and build," said Tom Dahl, somewhat hyperbolically. "We have to consider new factors such as the effect of a power plant on cloud patterns and salt drift. Once, in the design of a nuclear power plant, someone asked what would happen if an airplane, flying overhead, plummeted onto the plant. That sent us back to our drawing boards and estimates, to draw a plan to reinforce the roof—at an added cost of fifty million dollars." [12]

Taking a longer view, though, Chance and Dahl wonder if there is enough money in the United States—or the world—to build the plants that will be needed to meet the projected energy needs of the nation. To that wonder they add others: Will there be enough uranium? Enough available oil?

These somber philosophical questions, however, did not prevent United Engineers from undertaking the studies and reviews necessary, designing and making arrangements to construct plants that are mind-boggling in terms of cost, literally beyond individual comprehension in detail. The rules of the seventies, an accumulation of all that existed plus all that had been added, forced United Engineers into the printing business as a part of its overall effort: turned it into one of the largest commercial printers in Philadelphia. One project alone, for the Carolina Light & Power Company—to create a Brunswick Steam Electric Plant—required 350 sets of twelve volumes each (4,200 books in all) to be produced and distributed. To reproduce these plans, UE employs one hundred people in reproduction alone, who work an average seventy hours a week each, send out rivers of details regarding each step of such a project to the crafts and subcontractors involved; send sets of the overall to more than thirty governmental agencies—each armed with awesome powers to delay, halt, examine, probe, approve, or reject.

"The cost of everything pushed up," Dahl says, "paper, ink, people, goods, services. Nobody mentions it, but engineers now have to have lawyers at their sides at every step—and legal costs are a very heavy part of construction efforts."

It is, in some ways, a forbidding world—a maze within a maze—and yet one of the basic mazes that support the rest of us.

In mid-1971 President Nixon took two steps he had often vowed he would never take. They were, surprisingly, steps he had campaigned against throughout his long political career.

The first was the announcement, in July 1971, that he would visit Red China and confer with its leaders. The recognition of Red China was an admission that, for the first time in a century and a half, China had regained its status as a great world power. Few persons can bear to examine the means by which its Communist leaders organized the nation and led it to this peak, but all can agree it is a historic achievement.

President Nixon's recognition of the permanent nature of Asian changes deepened his determination to remove the U.S. military forces from Vietnam. He conducted that operation gradually, while seeking a formal peace agreement.

In August 1971 the President acknowledged further realities—this time on the domestic front—by suddenly imposing a wage and price freeze on the United States and slapping an extra 10 percent tax on all imports. The move was made in an attempt to break the spiral of serious inflation and to improve the badly unbalanced fiscal situation of the nation. It set off great international reverberations and the dollar was sharply devaluated in the exchanges. At home the freeze captured the marketplace in midstride and congealed many inequities, but was widely hailed for its temporary relief.

Nineteen seventy-one proved a good year for Raytheon. The figures of the Annual Report showed sales of $1.3 billion—an increase—and earnings of $35.1 million. That was a jump of over $4 million. Per-share earnings were up 11 cents to $2.43.[18]

The firm had gone through the long business decline of the nation dating from the latter half of 1969 and extending all through 1970 and only beginning to turn upward in 1971 with barely a bobble; had lost less and improved more than its competitors. Comparisons make horse races; Raytheon had reason to be pleased. Phillips and Adams, in fact, were so confident they predicted, in the Message to Stockholders, that by 1975 Raytheon would have $1.8 billion in sales and earnings per share of $3.50.[14]

Actually this second Five-Year Plan had been formulated in 1970, but at the time the firm was in registration with a new issue and regulations forbid optimistic forecasts at such a moment. Even so, its inclusion in the Annual Report of 1971 was a bold step in the mixed economic situation of the time.

By early 1972 the United States learned it had, the previous year, developed an international trade deficit for the first time since 1888. The total came to $2 billion. Almost 6 percent of the people were unemployed, but 82 million were employed; inflation was still influencing prices, but conditions were good and the standard of living in the United States was still on a level far beyond the most hopeful expectations of people in other lands.

Internationally the landscape showed a world moving, in the main, to the left. The postwar U.S. dream of containing communism had burst at the seams. The western alliance was no longer very firm. NATO was reduced. Britain was having trouble with terrorists in Northern Ireland; France was pursuing its own course. West Germany had grown independent, Scandinavia unfriendly. In the Middle East only Israel, a client state, was a firm ally. In the UN American influence was no longer dominant.

The war in Vietnam was winding down. Protests still rose against U.S. air strikes that covered the steady withdrawal of its troops and their departure from that land; but their fervor had diminished. In that atmosphere President Nixon made his heralded trip to China and there promised the United States would remove its troops from Taiwan and Indo-China. The United States would, in other words, alter its Asian policy.

In addition the President announced plans to go to the USSR— for the first such visit by a U.S. President in history—to conclude a series of trade and commercial agreements. It was hoped that improved

U.S.-Soviet commercial ties would help give the commissars an equity
in peace that would lead to a more stable world situation.

It was a season, in other words, for new moves. Raytheon, which
had announced an agreement in principle in the previous December,
now made public its acquisition of the Iowa Manufacturing Company,
makers of aggregate-producing and asphalt-mixing plants. Wall Street
was surprised; the analysts regarded the new acquisition as a step outside Raytheon's historic pattern and even outside the expansions it had
taken in recent years. The analysts were accurate enough, but Phillips
and his associates had reason on their end as well.

Iowa Manufacturing had been a profitable venture for many years
and was headed, since its founding, by the redoubtable Howard Hall
of Cedar Rapids, from whom Raytheon had purchased Amana. Howard Hall had died the previous year at age seventy-four. His brother-
in-law, Beahl Perrine, was now managing his estate. Iowa Manufacturing, therefore, was a known entity to Raytheon, and when Perrine
brought the subject forward, Raytheon was interested.

The acquisition was announced in March 1972 and marked a step
toward heavy equipment that the Raytheon managers considered well
worth taking.

That step forward was balanced, however, by a misstep whose
consequences did not emerge until 1972. Late in 1969 Raytheon had
received an order for $19 million in special communications and data-
gathering equipment for use in hospitals from a small firm called National Data Communications, Inc., in Texas.[15]

Unfortunately National Data Communications could not sell the
systems, and deliveries began to mount. Raytheon halted deliveries and
looked into the situation. In the process it concluded that NDC had
an excellent business concept but could not succeed because it lacked
resources. Meanwhile Raytheon was stuck with a heavy inventory of
display equipment on hand—and no customer. It decided to sell the
displays to hospitals directly.

In response NDC sued Raytheon. Charlie Resnick, Raytheon's
general counsel, and Holmes both flew to Texas to assess the situation.
Resnick looked into the legal side and concluded that Raytheon's

*393*

chances in court were not the best. Holmes talked to the leaders of NDC and concluded they had good cause for their suit. The result was an out-of-court settlement that proved quite expensive. Special charges totaled more than $6 million, and Resnick regards it as the worst problem of his professional career.

In some ways the experience was ironic. Years earlier, Laurence Marshall, who would probably have liked the Texas entrepreneurs, forced an equally harsh settlement on the managers of the Q.R.S. company in Chicago. In fact, it was a similar settlement that saved an earlier and far smaller Raytheon from expiring in 1928, and sent it on to higher and larger efforts. Obviously the wheel never stops turning.[16]

In the summer of 1972 the President ordered heavy air strikes against North Vietnam, not to achieve its destruction but to force it to the peace table. These were underway when he visited Moscow and were still underway when the Soviet Union and the United States reached highly promising agreements at the SALT talks.

Among other matters, the SALT talks limited the U.S. ABM system, in which Raytheon had originally contracted to supply the missile site radar, the heart of the system. Originally the United States planned seventeen ABM sites, then twelve, then four and finally, two. One was deployed.

A series of highly publicized debates both in and out of Washington had prepared Raytheon for this cutback, however. Its defense sector had long since scattered its projects into many baskets. Raytheon had, in addition to its missiles production—which had expanded into improved Hawks and Sparrows—a huge $558 million defense order based on the complex SAM-D air-defense system. This program, upon which it had been working on advanced development since 1967, and which several times had been slowed by the uncertainties of Washington, was now extended.

By autumn the United States and the USSR had concluded a number of trade agreements of considerable importance, including thirty joint environmental projects to improve cities, farms, rivers and lakes, and the air of both countries; they had laid plans for cooperative efforts in space and announced more efforts would take place.

Despite the now settled habit of the U.S. press of feeding the nation a diet of bad news, there was much good news to report. The rate of inflation had slowed; statements from the White House and news of troop withdrawals made it clear that the war in Vietnam would soon end as far as the United States was concerned.

Like the rest of the nation the firm received the 1972 election results with surprise. The President's chances had appeared excellent, but nobody really expected such a huge, mountainous landslide. On the heels of these results the Vietnam peace talks began, at last, to turn toward resolution.

Phillips, Holmes, and their associates were pleased, but the days flow like water and each carries its own cargo. The new year, 1973, was upon them and their eyes were fixed upon the future. Adams, however, who has a deep sense of continuity, wondered if it might not be an appropriate time to take a backward look—just for the record, mind you—at the road Raytheon had traveled. It might, he thought, be helpful to some of the younger men, to recall—while they were still available and before they were forgotten—predecessors Laurence Marshall, Vannevar Bush, Billy Gammel, and others. For the response of Tom Phillips, Brainerd Holmes, and the rest to that suggestion, please turn back to the beginning.

# NOTES

## NOTES TO CHAPTER TWO

1. Vannevar Bush, *Pieces of the Action* (New York: William Morrow and Company, Inc., 1970), p. 163.
2. Ibid.
3. Interview, Laurence K. Marshall, 1973.
4. Ibid.
5. Mark Sullivan, *Our Times*, vol. 6, *The Twenties* (New York: Charles Scribner's Sons, 1935), p. 13.
6. Ibid.
7. Bush, *Pieces of the Action*, p. 164.
8. Ibid.
9. Portland (Me.) *Sunday Telegram*, Jan. 13, 1957.
10. Bush, *Pieces of the Action*, p. 164.
11. Ibid., p. 155.
12. Ibid., p. 154.
13. Interview, Billy Gammell, 1973.
14. Interview, Herbert Marshall, 1973.
15. C. G. Smith, "Helium in the Prehistory of Raytheon." Oct. 5, 1957, Ratheyon Communications Dept.
16. Vannevar Bush and C. G. Smith, "A New Rectifier." Paper presented to Boston Section of the Institute of Radio Engineers, April 8, 1921; presented in New York, Oct. 5, 1921.
17. Bush and Smith, "Control of Gaseous Conduction." Paper presented to Annual Convention of the A.I.E.E., Niagara Falls, Ont., June 26–30, 1922.
18. Lindley H. Clark, Jr., "Speaking of Business," *Wall Street Journal*, July 6, 1973.
19. Bush, *Pieces of the Action*, p. 165.
20. Ibid.
21. Interview, Laurence K. Marshall, 1967.
22. C. G. Smith, "Early Days of Raytheon." July 18, 1951. Unpublished ms., Raytheon Communications Dept.

23. Bush, *Pieces of the Action,* p. 166.
24. Smith, "Early Days of Raytheon."
25. Ibid.
26. Raytheon Directors' Minutes, 1922.
27. Smith, "Early Days of Raytheon."
28. Ibid.
29. *The Encyclopedia of American Facts and Dates,* 4th ed. (New York: Thomas Y. Crowell Company, 1966), p. 464.
30. Ibid., pp. 463 and 465.
31. Raytheon Directors' Minutes, 1967.
32. Interview, Laurence K. Marshall, 1967.
33. Interview, Laurence K. Marshall, 1973.

## NOTES TO CHAPTER THREE

1. *The Encyclopedia of American Facts and Dates,* 4th ed. (New York: Thomas Y. Crowell Company, 1966), p. 467.
2. Interview, Laurence K. Marshall, 1967.
3. C. G. Smith, "Early Days of Raytheon." Unpublished ms., Raytheon Communications Dept., July 18, 1951.
4. Raytheon Directors' Minutes, 1925.
5. Vannevar Bush, *Pieces of the Action* (New York: William Morrow and Company, Inc., 1970), p. 198.
6. Interview, Mrs. Percy Spencer, 1973.
7. Interview, Dr. Edward L. Bowles, 1973.
8. Percy L. Spencer, "Raytheon—1925 to 1959." Unpublished ms., Raytheon Communications Dept., 1960.
9. Raytheon Director's Minutes, 1925.
10. Percy L. Spencer, unpublished ms., Raytheon Communications Dept. 1951.
11. Interview, Laurence K. Marshall, 1973.
12. Richard M. Watt, *The Kings Depart* (New York: Simon and Schuster, 1968), p. 517.
13. George C. Reinhardt and William R. Kintner, *The Haphazard Years* (Garden City, N.Y.: Doubleday & Company, 1960), pp. 123, 141.
14. Interview, Laurence K. Marshall, 1967.
15. Smith, "Early Days of Raytheon."
16. Interview, Laurence K. Marshall, 1967.
17. Ibid.
18. Smith, "Early Days of Raytheon."
19. Interview, Mrs. Lorna Marshall, 1973.
20. Bush, *Pieces of the Action,* p. 199.
21. Ibid., pp. 176–77.

22. Frederick Lewis Allen, *Only Yesterday* (New York: Harper & Brothers, 1931), p. 662.
23. Interview, Laurence K. Marshall, 1973.
24. Ibid.
25. Smith, "Early Days of Raytheon."
26. Raytheon Directors' Minutes, 1928.
27. *Tele-Tech*, Jan. 1952, Caldwell-Clements, Inc., New York.
28. Raytheon Directors' Minutes, 1928.
29. Smith, "Early Days of Raytheon."
30. *Time Capsule/1929.*


## NOTES TO CHAPTER FOUR

1. Interview, Ruth Babb, 1973.
2. Raytheon Annual Report, 1929.
3. Raytheon Directors' Minutes, 1930.
4. Raytheon Annual Report, 1930.
5. Ibid.
6. Neville Williams, *Chronology of the Modern World: 1763 to the Present Time* (New York: David McKay Company, Inc., 1967), p. 526.
7. *The Encyclopedia of American Facts and Dates*, 4th ed. (New York: Thomas Y. Crowell Company, 1966), p. 488.
8. Interview, Laurence K. Marshall, 1967.
9. Raytheon Directors' Minutes, 1931.
10. Williams, *Chronology of the Modern World*, p. 528.
11. Ibid., p. 529.
12. Ibid., p. 530.
13. *Encyclopedia of American Facts and Dates*, p. 490.
14. Vannevar Bush, *Pieces of the Action* (New York: William Morrow and Company, Inc., 1970), p. 271.
15. Raytheon Annual Report, 1932.
16. Interview, Laurence K. Marshall, 1967.
17. Interview, Henry Argento, 1973.
18. Interview, Sid Standing, 1973.
19. Ibid.
20. George C. Reinhardt and William R. Kintner, *The Haphazard Years* (Garden City, N.Y.: Doubleday & Company, 1960), p. 157.
21. Interview, Laurence K. Marshall, 1967.
22. Percy L. Spencer, unpublished ms., Raytheon Communications Dept., 1960.
23. Ernest F. Leathem, "A History of Raytheon Manufacturing Company." Unpublished ms., Raytheon Communications Dept., n.d.
24. Spencer, unpublished ms., 1960.
25. Williams, *Chronology of the Modern World*, p. 535.

26. Ibid., p. 532.
27. Ibid.
28. This was the last presidential inauguration in March; the Twentieth Amendment to the Constitution changed the date to January 20.
29. Raytheon Directors' Minutes, 1933.
30. *Encyclopedia of American Facts and Dates*, p. 496.
31. Ibid., p. 498.
32. Ibid.
33. Interview, Laurence K. Marshall, 1973.
34. Raytheon Directors' Minutes, 1933.
35. Ibid.
36. Interview, Henry Argento, 1973.
37. Williams, *Chronology of the Modern World*, p. 538.
38. Ibid., p. 538.
39. Ibid.
40. Reinhardt and Kintner, *The Haphazard Years*, pp. 168–69.
41. Spencer, unpublished ms., 1960.
42. Raytheon Directors' Minutes, 1933.
43. Private correspondence, Dr. Edward L. Bowles, 1973.
44. Interview, Robert Quimby, 1973.
45. Ibid.
46. Interview, Carl Gilbert, 1973.
47. Reinhardt and Kintner, *The Haphazard Years*, pp. 125, 126.
48. Ibid., p. 188.
49. Williams, *Chronology of the Modern World*, p. 542.
50. Reinhardt and Kintner, *The Haphazard Years*, pp. 179, 180.
51. A. P. Rowe, *One Story of Radar* (Cambridge: Cambridge University Press, 1948), pp. 4–6.
52. Private correspondence, Henry Bernstein, Captain, USN (Ret.), 1973.
53. Spencer, unpublished ms., 1960.
54. Interview, Fritz Gross, 1973.
55. Raytheon Directors' Minutes, 1934.
56. Interview, Laurence K. Marshall, 1967.
57. *Encyclopedia of American Facts and Dates*, pp. 504–7.
58. Interview, Norman Krim, 1973.
59. *Encyclopedia of American Facts and Dates*, pp. 504–5.
60. Williams, *Chronology of the Modern World*, p. 546.
61. Eugene Lyons, *The Red Decade* (New York: Bobbs-Merrill Company, 1941), pp. 9–19.
62. Williams, *Chronology of the Modern World*, p. 546.
63. Interview, Sid Standing.
64. Rowe, *One Story of Radar*, pp. 6–7.
65. Reinhardt and Kintner, *The Haphazard Years*, pp. 157–58.
66. *Encyclopedia of American Facts and Dates*, p. 498.
67. Williams, *Chronology of the Modern World*, p. 552.

68. *Encyclopedia of American Facts and Dates*, pp. 508–10.
69. Spencer, unpublished ms., and Leathem, "A History of Raytheon Manufacturing Co."
70. Interview, Carl Gilbert, 1973.
71. Raytheon Annual Report, 1936.
72. Williams, *Chronology of the Modern World*, p. 544.
73. Ibid., p. 556.
74. Raytheon Directors' Minutes, 1937.
75. *Encyclopedia of American Facts and Dates*, pp. 512–13.
76. Raytheon Annual Report, 1937.
77. Rowe, *One Story of Radar*, p. 23.
78. Bush, *Pieces of the Action*, p. 32.
79. Interview, Norman Krim, 1973.
80. Interview, Laurence K. Marshall, 1967.
81. Interview, Ruth Babb, 1973.
82. Interview, Laurence K. Marshall, 1973.
83. Frederick Lewis Allen, *Since Yesterday* (New York: Harper & Row, 1940), pp. 244–49.
84. Williams, *Chronology of the Modern World*, p. 560.
85. *Encyclopedia of American Facts and Dates*, pp. 514–16.
86. Reinhardt and Kintner, *The Haphazard Years*, p. 162.
87. *Encyclopedia of American Facts and Dates*, p. 520.
88. J. A. Stratton, *Research Laboratory of Electronics—The Beginning of an Idea*, MIT, address, 1966.
89. Release, MIT, June 30, 1963.
90. Interview, Norman Krim, 1973.
91. Raytheon Directors' Minutes, 1938.
92. Ibid.
93. Williams, *Chronology of the Modern World*, p. 566.
94. Ibid., p. 564.
95. Raytheon Annual Report, 1938.
96. Raytheon Directors' Minutes, 1938.
97. Interview, Charles Francis Adams, 1973.
98. *Encyclopedia of American Facts and Dates*, p. 520.
99. Williams, *Chronology of the Modern World*, p. 566.
100. Rowe, *One Story of Radar*, p. 26.
101. *Encyclopedia of American Facts and Dates*, pp. 521–22.
102. Interview, Roger Damon, 1973.
103. *Encyclopedia of American Facts and Dates*, p. 520.
104. Bush, *Pieces of the Action*, pp. 56–57.
105. Interview, Laurence K. Marshall, 1967.
106. Interview, Henry Argento, 1973.
107. Interview, Norman Krim, 1973.
108. Interview, Henry Argento, 1973.
109. Interview, David Schultz, 1973.
110. *Encyclopedia of American Facts and Dates*, pp. 520–21.

*401*

111. Williams, *Chronology of the Modern World*, p. 568.
112. Raytheon Annual Report, 1939.
113. Sir Robert Watson-Watt, *Three Steps to Victory, A Personal Account* (Long Acre, London: Odhams Press Limited), p. 284.
114. Ibid.
115. *Encyclopedia of American Facts and Dates*, p. 521.
116. Williams, *Chronology of the Modern World*, p. 568.
117. Ibid.
118. Martha Byrd Hoyle, *A World in Flames* (New York: Atheneum Publishers, 1970), p. 15.
119. Williams, *Chronology of the Modern World*, p. 570.
120. *Encyclopedia of American Facts and Dates*, p. 521.
121. Hoyle, *A World in Flames*, pp. 25–26.
122. Williams, *Chronology of the Modern World*, p. 570.
123. Jose Ortega y Gasset, *The Revolt of the Masses* (New York: New American Library, 1950). The theme, long famous, is based on the "vertical barbarian," who rises from within society.

NOTES TO CHAPTER FIVE

1. Martha Byrd Hoyle, *A World in Flames* (New York: Atheneum Publishers, 1970), p. 64.
2. Ibid., p. 26.
3. Ibid., pp. 27–28.
4. Ibid., pp. 29–30.
5. George C. Reinhardt and William R. Kintner, *The Haphazard Years* (Garden City, N.Y.: Doubleday & Co., Inc., 1960), p. 164.
6. Vannevar Bush, *Pieces of the Action* (New York: William Morrow & Company, Inc., 1970), p. 31.
7. Interview, Dr. Edward L. Bowles, 1973.
8. A. P. Rowe, *One Story of Radar* (Cambridge: Cambridge University Press, 1948), p. 57.
9. Interview, Dr. Edward L. Bowles, 1973.
10. Neville Williams, *Chronology of the Modern World: 1763 to the Present Time* (New York: David McKay Company, Inc., 1967), p. 572.
11. Ibid.
12. Hoyle, *A World in Flames*, pp. 39–45.
13. Bush, *Pieces of the Action*, p. 36.
14. Ibid., p. 37-40.
15. Raytheon Annual Report, 1940.
16. Raytheon Directors' Minutes, 1940.
17. Interview, Fritz Gross, 1973.
18. Interview, Laurence K. Marshall, 1967.
19. Interview, Dr. Vannevar Bush, 1973.

20. *The Encyclopedia of American Facts and Dates,* 4th ed. (New York: Thomas Y. Crowell Company, 1966), p. 528.

21. Williams, *Chronology of the Modern World,* p. 574.

22. Hoyle, *A World in Flames,* p. 53.

23. Ibid., pp. 56–57.

24. Ibid., pp. 56–58.

25. Interview with Carl Gilbert, who quoted Sir John Cockcroft, 1973.

26. Sir Robert Watson-Watt, *Three Steps to Victory, A Personal Account* (Long Acre, London: Odhams Press Limited), p. 295.

27. Interview, Dr. Edward L. Bowles, 1973.

28. Watson-Watt, *Three Steps to Victory,* p. 295.

29. Release MIT, July 30, 1963.

30. Interview, Laurence K. Marshall, 1967.

31. Interview, Dr. Edward L. Bowles, 1973.

32. Percy L. Spencer, unpublished ms., Raytheon Communications Dept., 1960.

33. Interview, Carl Gilbert, 1973.

34. Interview, Mrs. Percy Spencer, 1973.

35. Spencer, unpublished ms., 1960.

36. Interview, Norman Krim, 1973.

37. Interview, Henry Argento, 1973.

38. Interview, Laurence K. Marshall, 1967.

39. Ibid.

40. Spencer, unpublished ms., 1960.

41. Interview, Fritz Gross, 1974.

42. Hoyle, *A World in Flames,* p. 57.

43. *Encyclopedia of American Facts and Dates,* p. 524.

44. Hoyle, *A World in Flames,* pp. 59, 60.

45. Ibid., pp. 60, 61.

46. *History, Organization and Products,* Raytheon Management Training Program, Section 1-A, p. 15.

47. Ibid.

48. *"G" Whizz,* Raytheon house organ, Vol. 3, No. 16, Aug. 24, 1945, p. 1.

49. Ibid.

50. Raytheon Technical Writing Dept., "Of Microwaves and Men," unpublished ms., 1967.

51. Interview, Laurence K. Marshall, 1967.

52. Interview, Henry Argento, 1973.

53. *Encyclopedia of American Facts and Dates,* pp. 528–31.

54. Reinhardt and Kintner, *The Haphazard Years,* p. 158.

55. Raytheon Directors' Minutes, 1941.

56. Raytheon Annual Report, 1941.

57. Raytheon Directors' Minutes, 1942.

58. Hoyle, *A World in Flames,* p. 83.

59. Private correspondence, Commander I. L. McNally, 1973.

60. Interview, Henry Argento, 1973.
61. Williams, *Chronology of the Modern World*, p. 578.
62. *Encyclopedia of American Facts and Dates*, pp. 528–29.
63. Hoyle, *A World in Flames*, pp. 72–74.
64. Private correspondence, Commander McNally, 1973.
65. Hoyle, *A World in Flames*, pp. 101–2.
66. Otto J. Scott, "The Division of Rubber Chemistry," New York: *Rubber World* magazine, Part III, 1966, pp. 22–23.
67. Harry Howe Ransom, *The Intelligence Establishment* (Cambridge, Mass.: Harvard University Press, 1970), p. 53.
68. Walter Lord, *Day of Infamy* (New York: Henry Holt and Company, 1957), pp. 44–48.
69. Interview, Mrs. Lorna Marshall, 1973.
70. Interview, Mrs. Robert Quimby, 1973.
71. Interview, Clark Rodiman, 1973.
72. Ransom, *The Intelligence Establishment*, p. 43.
73. Hoyle, *A World in Flames*, pp. 108–23.
74. Interview, Clark Rodiman, 1973.
75. Spencer, unpublished ms., Raytheon Communications Dept., 1960.
76. Interview, Laurence K. Marshall, 1967.
77. Hoyle, *A World in Flames*, p. 127.
78. Bush, *Pieces of the Action*, p. 197.
79. E. B. Potter and Adm. Chester W. Nimitz, *The Great Sea War* (New York: Bramhall House, 1960), pp. 220–21.
80. Hoyle, *A World in Flames*, p. 120.
81. *The Great Sea War*, pp. 221–46.
82. Release, MIT, June 30, 1963.
83. Ibid.
84. Private correspondence, Henry Bernstein, 1973.
85. Ibid.
86. *Encyclopedia of American Facts and Dates*, pp. 517, 533.
87. Hoyle, *A World in Flames*, p. 148.
88. George Baker, *Location of Submarines by Sonar*, Raytheon, 1945.
89. Ibid.
90. *Time Capsule/1942*.
91. Interview, John Collier, 1966.
92. Otto J. Scott, "The Division of Rubber Chemistry," New York: *Rubber World* magazine, 1967, pp. 24–27.
93. Private correspondence, Henry Bernstein, 1973.
94. Hoyle, *A World in Flames*, p. 150.
95. Ibid., pp. 129–33.
96. Potter and Nimitz, *The Great Sea War*, pp. 275–76.
97. Ibid., p. 262.
98. Samuel Eliot Morison, *The Struggle for Guadalcanal* (Boston: Little, Brown and Company, 1949), p. 170.
99. Potter and Nimitz, *The Great Sea War*, p. 269.

100. Interview, Milton W. Mix, 1973.
101. Potter and Nimitz, *The Great Sea War*, p. 277.
102. Baker, *Location of Submarines by Sonar.*
103. Ibid.
104. Hoyle, *A World in Flames*, p. 154.
105. Private correspondence, Henry Bernstein, 1973.
106. Raytheon corporate files, 1943.
107. Raytheon Directors' Minutes, 1943.
108. Private correspondence, Henry Bernstein, 1973.
109. Interview, Clark Rodiman, 1973.
110. *Encyclopedia of American Facts and Dates*, pp. 536–40.
111. Ibid., p. 513.
112. Williams, *Chronology of the Modern World*, p. 586.
113. Ibid., p. 586.
114. Raytheon corporate files, 1943.
115. Raytheon Annual Report, 1943.
116. Baker, *Location of Submarines by Sonar.*
117. Bush, *Pieces of the Action*, p. 93.
118. Ibid., p. 81.
119. Baker, *Location of Submarines by Sonar.*
120. Bush, *Pieces of the Action*, pp. 97–98.
121. Hoyle, *A World in Flames*, p. 177.
122. Project McGregor, Subversion Work Among Flag Officers of the Royal Italian Navy, by OSS, Nov. 1, 1943. (Declassified, Sept. 15, 1945)
123. Interview, Fritz Gross, 1973.
124. Interview, T. C. Wisenbaker, 1973.
125. Interview, Mrs. Lorna Marshall, 1973.
126. Potter and Nimitz, *The Great Sea War*, p. 278.
127. Ibid., p. 284–89.
128. Ibid., pp. 282–84.
129. Ibid., pp. 287–88.
130. David Irving, *The German Atomic Bomb* (New York: Simon and Schuster, 1967), p. 150.
131. Reinhardt and Kintner, *The Haphazard Years*, p. 202.
132. Hoyle, *A World in Flames*, pp. 208–10.
133. Williams, *Chronology of the Modern World*, p. 588.
134. Project McGregor, OSS.
135. Interview, Dr. Edward L. Bowles, 1973.
136. Interview, Mr. & Mrs. Laurence K. Marshall, 1973.
137. Interview, T. C. Wisenbaker, 1973.
138. Interview, Dr. Edward L. Bowles, 1973.
139. Interview, Fritz Gross, 1973.
140. *Encyclopedia of American Facts and Dates*, p. 543.
141. Ibid.
142. Hoyle, *A World in Flames*, p. 316.
143. Bush, *Pieces of the Action*, p. 8.

144. Hoyle, *A World in Flames,* pp. 228–33.
145. Williams, *Chronology of the Modern World,* p. 590.
146. Hoyle, *A World in Flames,* p. 232.
147. Ibid., p. 217.
148. Raytheon Annual Report, 1944.
149. Raytheon Directors' Minutes, 1944.
150. Spencer, unpublished ms., 1960.
151. Interview, Robert Quimby, 1973.
152. Williams, *Chronology of the Modern World,* p. 590.
153. Hoyle, *A World in Flames,* p. 238.
154. Ibid., p. 217.
155. Ibid., pp. 217–19.
156. Ibid., pp. 219–21.
157. Ibid., p. 232.
158. Release, MIT, June 30, 1963.
159. Hoyle, *A World in Flames,* pp. 265–66.
160. Ibid., p. 266.
161. Williams, *Chronology of the Modern World,* p. 592.
162. Hoyle, *A World in Flames,* pp. 251–52.
163. Ibid., p. 261.
164. *"G" Whizz,* Vol. 3, No. 16, Aug. 24, 1945, p. 2.
165. Interview, Clark Rodiman, 1973.
166. Raytheon corporate files, 1944.
167. Raytheon Directors' Minutes, 1944.
168. Hoyle, *A World in Flames,* pp. 277–82.
169. Ibid., pp. 283–85.
170. Ibid., p. 270.
171. Ibid., pp. 267–68.
172. Ibid., pp. 272–73.
173. Interview, Norman Krim, 1973.
174. "The Rise of Raytheon," *Fortune,* Oct. 1946, p. 137.
175. Raytheon corporate files, 1945.
176. Raytheon Directors' Minutes, 1945.
177. Ibid.
178. Ibid.
179. Interview, Henry Argento, 1973.
180. Hoyle, *A World in Flames,* pp. 295–96.
181. Ibid., pp. 300–2.
182. Bush, *Pieces of the Action,* p. 291.
183. Williams, *Chronology of the Modern World,* p. 594.
184. Hoyle, *A World in Flames,* pp. 307–13.
185. Potter and Nimitz, *The Great Sea War,* pp. 441–47.
186. Hoyle, *A World in Flames,* p. 316.
187. Ibid., pp. 318–19.

## NOTES TO CHAPTER SIX

1. Interview, Robert S. Quimby, 1973.
2. Raytheon Technical Writing Dept., "Of Microwaves and Men," unpublished ms., 1967, p. 14.
3. Since, according to *Time* magazine's issue of Dec. 15, 1941, "nearly 1 million European Jews fled Germany between 1933 and 1940. Principal havens: 330,000 to Russia, 150,000 to England and the Benelux countries, 135,000 to the U.S.," it seems unlikely to improbable that none of those admitted to the USSR would have been physicists; that none of these physicists would have known about the nuclear experiments.
4. Vannevar Bush, *Pieces of the Action* (New York: William Morrow and Company, 1970), p. 282.
5. Martha Byrd Hoyle, *A World in Flames* (New York: Atheneum Publishers, 1970), p. 297.
6. David Irving, *The German Atomic Bomb* (New York: Simon and Schuster, 1967), Chapter 11.
7. Bush, *Pieces of the Action*, p. 109.
8. Irving, *The German Atomic Bomb*, Chapter 1.
9. Robin Higham, *Air Power* (New York: St. Martin's Press, 1972), p. 135.
10. Hoyle, *A World in Flames*, p. 323.
11. A. P. Rowe, *One Story of Radar* (Cambridge: Cambridge University Press, 1948), pp. 179–80.
12. Raytheon Annual Report, 1945.
13. Raytheon Directors' Minutes, 1945.
14. Bush, *Pieces of the Action*, pp. 83, 84.
15. "G" *Whizz*, Raytheon house organ, Vol. 3, No. 16, August 24, 1945, p. 5.
16. Interview, Dr. Vannevar Bush, 1973.
17. Ibid.
18. Bush, *Pieces of the Action*, pp. 281–85.
19. Interview, Dr. Vannevar Bush, 1973.
20. Interview, T. C. Wisenbaker, 1973.
21. Ibid.
22. Interview, Charles Francis Adams.
23. *The Encyclopedia of American Facts and Dates*, 4th ed. (New York: Thomas Y. Crowell Company, 1966), pp. 552–53.
24. Neville Williams, *Chronology of the Modern World: 1763 to the Present Time* (New York: David McKay Company, Inc., 1967), p. 602.
25. Raytheon Directors' Minutes, 1946.
26. Interview, Paul Hannah, 1973.
27. *Missile Messenger*, Raytheon house organ, Vol. 4, No. 4, p. 2.
28. Interview, Herbert Marshall, 1973.
29. Raytheon corporate records, 1946

30. Raytheon Annual Report, 1946.
31. Interview, Paul Skitzki and Dr. Edward Turner, 1973.
32. H. J. W. Fay, *Submarine Signal Company: A Created Industry*, Raytheon, 1963.
33. Ibid.
34. Interview, Paul Skitzki and Dr. Edward Turner, 1973.
35. Interview, Fritz Gross, 1974.
36. Ibid.
37. Interview, Henry Argento, 1973.
38. Interview, Billy Gammell, 1973.
39. Private correspondence, Captain Henry Bernstein, USN (Ret.).
40. Interview, Henry Argento, 1973.
41. Raytheon Directors' Minutes, 1946.
42. Interview, Henry Argento, 1973.
43. Finance Committee Report, Raytheon Directors' Minutes, Feb. 1947.
44. Raytheon Directors' Minutes.
45. Ibid.
46. Interview, T. C. Wisenbaker, 1973.
47. Interview, Rear Admiral Hamilton Hauck, USN (Ret.), 1973.
48. Interview, Charles Francis Adams, 1973.
49. *Encyclopedia of American Facts and Dates*, p. 554.
50. R. W. Pethybridge, *A History of Postwar Russia* (London: George Allen, Ltd., 1966), pp. 69–71.
51. *Encyclopedia of American Facts and Dates*, p. 556.
52. Ibid., p. 560.
53. Raytheon Annual Report, 1947.
54. Raytheon Directors' Minutes, 1947.
55. Interview, Charles Francis Adams, 1973.
56. Interview, T. C. Wisenbaker, 1973.
57. Interview, Clark Rodiman, 1973.
58. Interview, Norman Krim, 1973.
59. Interview, Henry Argento, 1973.
60. Raytheon Directors' Minutes, 1948.
61. Ibid.
62. Interview, Billy Gammell, 1973.
63. Interview, Charles Francis Adams, 1973.
64. Raytheon Directors' Minutes, 1948.
65. *Encyclopedia of American Facts and Dates*, pp. 558–59.
66. Ibid., p. 560.
67. Williams, *Chronology of the Modern World*, p. 610.
68. George C. Reinhardt and William R. Kintner, *The Haphazard Years* (Garden City, N.Y.: Doubleday & Co., Inc., 1960), p. 199.
69. *Encyclopedia of American Facts and Dates*, pp. 558–61.
70. Williams, *Chronology of the Modern World*, p. 610.
71. Interview, Laurence K. Marshall, 1973.
72. Ibid.

73. Raytheon corporate records, 1948.
74. Interview, Hamilton Hauck, 1973.
75. Interview, T. C. Wisenbaker, 1973.
76. Interview, Tom Phillips, 1973.
77. Williams, *Chronology of the Modern World*, p. 610.
78. Raytheon corporate records, 1948.
79. Raytheon Annual Report, 1948.
80. Williams, *Chronology of the Modern World*, p. 611.
81. Interview, Norman Krim, 1973.
82. Raytheon Directors' Minutes, 1948.
83. Ibid.
84. Interview, Carl Gilbert, 1973.
85. Interview, Norman Krim, 1973.
86. Interview, Paul Hannah, 1973.
87. Interview, Carl Gilbert, 1973.
88. Raytheon Directors' Minutes, 1948.
89. Interview, Dr. Edward Bowles, 1973.
90. Raytheon Directors' Minutes, 1948.
91. Ibid., 1949.
92. Ibid.
93. *Encyclopedia of American Facts and Dates*, p. 564.
94. Williams, *Chronology of the Modern World*, p. 614.
95. *Encyclopedia of American Facts and Dates*, p. 564.
96. Williams, *Chronology of the Modern World*, p. 614.
97. Raytheon Directors' Minutes, 1949.
98. Ibid.
99. Raytheon Annual Report, 1949.
100. *Encyclopedia of American Facts and Dates*, pp. 564–67.
101. Raytheon corporate records, 1949.

## NOTES TO CHAPTER SEVEN

1. *The Encyclopedia of American Facts and Dates*, 4th ed. (New York: Thomas Y. Crowell Company, 1966), p. 575.
2. Raytheon Directors' Minutes, 1952.
3. Ibid.
4. Interview, Ruth Babb, 1973.
5. Interview, Charles Francis Adams, 1973.
6. *Time Capsule/1950.*
7. Ibid.
8. Author of *The Human Use of Human Beings* and numerous articles stressing perils of a computerized society.
9. *Encyclopedia of American Facts and Dates*, p. 568.
10. Laurence K. Marshall, letter to *Criterion*, Jan. 1973.

*Notes*

11. Quoted inside Raytheon by an executive who heard and remembered the remark.
12. Raytheon Table of Organization, 1950.
13. Raytheon Annual Report, 1950.
14. Neville Williams, *Chronology of the Modern World: 1763 to the Present Time* (New York: David McKay Company, Inc., 1967), p. 620.
15. *Encyclopedia of American Facts and Dates*, p. 570.
16. Francis Bello, "The Year of the Transistor," *Fortune*, March 1953.
17. Raytheon Directors' Minutes, 1950.
18. *Time Capsule/1950*.
19. Williams, *Chronology of the Modern World*, p. 622.
20. Raytheon Directors' Minutes.
21. Interview, Robert Hennemuth, 1973.
22. Interview, Mike Fossier, 1973.
23. Interview, Fritz Gross, 1974.
24. Interview, Tom Phillips, 1974.
25. Interview, Paul Hannah, 1973.
26. Raytheon corporate records, 1950.
27. Often reviewed: culled here from *Time Capsule/1950*.
28. Raytheon corporate records, 1950.
29. Raytheon Directors' Minutes, 1950.
30. Interview, Charles Francis Adams, 1974.
31. Raytheon Annual Report, 1951.
32. Interview, Charles Francis Adams, 1974.
33. Raytheon Directors' Minutes, 1950.
34. Interview, Ed Dashefsky, 1973.
35. Interview, T. C. Wisenbaker, 1973.
36. Williams, *Chronology of the Modern World*, p. 624.
37. *Encyclopedia of American Facts and Dates*, p. 574.
38. David Reisman, *The Lonely Crowd: A Study of the Changing America* (New Haven: Yale University Press, 1951).
39. Raytheon Annual Report, 1951.
40. Raytheon Directors' Minutes, 1951.
41. Interview, Hamilton Hauck, 1951.
42. Interview, T. C. Wisenbaker, 1973.
43. Interview, Hamilton Hauck, 1973.
44. Interview, Ruth Babb, 1973.
45. Interview, Mrs. Percy Spencer, 1973.
46. Bello, "The Year of the Transistor."
47. Interview, Norman Krim, 1973.
48. George Freedman, "C. G. Smith," unpublished ms., Raytheon Communications Dept., n.d.
49. Interview, Norman Krim, 1973.
50. Bello, "The Year of the Transistor."
51. Williams, *Chronology of the Modern World*, p. 629.
52. Raytheon Directors' Minutes, 1951.

53. Interview, Charles Resnick, 1973.
54. Interview, Tom Phillips, 1974.
55. Interview, T. C. Wisenbaker, 1973.
56. *Encyclopedia of American Facts and Dates*, p. 576.
57. Raytheon Annual Report, 1952.
58. Ibid.
59. Interview, Joe Alibrandi, 1973.
60. Interview, Tom Phillips, 1973.
61. Williams, *Chronology of the Modern World*, p. 631.
62. Interview, Dr. Martin Schilling, 1973.
63. *Encyclopedia of American Facts and Dates*, p. 581.
64. Ibid., p. 582.
65. Raytheon Directors' Minutes, 1953.
66. Interview, Henry Argento, 1973.
67. Williams, *Chronology of the Modern World*, p. 632.
68. *Encyclopedia of American Facts and Dates*, p. 582.
69. Raytheon Annual Report, 1953.
70. Interview, Tom Phillips, 1973.
71. Interview, Sid Standing, 1973.
72. *Encyclopedia of American Facts and Dates*, p. 581.
73. Ibid., p. 584.
74. Interview, T. C. Wisenbaker, 1973.
75. Interview, Dr. Martin Schilling, 1973.
76. Interview, Tom Phillips, 1973.
77. Raytheon Annual Report, 1954.
78. Interview, Mike Fossier, 1973.
79. Ibid.
80. Williams, *Chronology of the Modern World*, p. 636.
81. *Encyclopedia of American Facts and Dates*, p. 588.
82. Raytheon Directors' Minutes, 1955.
83. Interview, Charles Francis Adams, 1974.
84. Raytheon Annual Report, 1954.
85. *Encyclopedia of American Facts and Dates*, p. 589
86. Raytheon Directors' Minutes, 1955.
87. Quoted by Dr. Edward L. Bowles, interview, 1973.
88. Raytheon Directors' Minutes, 1955.
89. Interview, Mrs. Percy Spencer, 1973.
90. Ibid.
91. Interview, Harold S. Geneen, 1973.
92. Interview, Roger Damon, 1973.
93. Interview, Dr. Edward L. Bowles, 1973.
94. Raytheon Directors' Minutes, 1956.
95. Interview, Charles Francis Adams, 1973.
96. Williams, *Chronology of the Modern World*, p. 648.
97. *Encyclopedia of American Facts and Dates*, p. 595.
98. Raytheon briefing paper, 1958.

99. Interview, Tom Phillips, 1973.
100. Raytheon Annual Report as of May 31, 1956.
101. Interview, Dr. Martin Schilling, 1973.
102. Raytheon Directors' Minutes, 1956.
103. Ibid.
104. Ibid.
105. *Encyclopedia of American Facts and Dates*, p. 595.
106. Williams, *Chronology of the Modern World*, p. 650.
107. Ibid., p. 652.
108. Observed by Norman Krim, Sid Standing, many others.
109. Interview, Mrs. Percy Spencer, 1973.
110. Raytheon Table of Organization, 1956.
111. Williams, *Chronology of the Modern World*, p. 652.
112. Ibid.
113. *Encyclopedia of American Facts and Dates*, p. 598.
114. Williams, *Chronology of the Modern World*, p. 652.
115. Raytheon Annual Report, Dec. 31, 1956.
116. Raytheon Directors' Minutes, 1957.
117. Ibid.
118. *Encyclopedia of American Facts and Dates*, p. 598.
119. Williams, *Chronology of the Modern World*, p. 654.
120. Interview, Al Miccioli, 1973.
121. Interview, T. C. Wisenbaker, 1973.
122. Interview, Joe Alibrandi, 1973.
123. Raytheon Directors' Minutes, 1957.
124. Interview, Charles Francis Adams, 1974.
125. Interview, Harold S. Geneen, 1973.
126. Interview, Charles Francis Adams, 1973.
127. Ibid.
128. Raytheon corporate records, 1957.
129. Interview, Robert Hennemuth, 1973.
130. Interview, Charles Francis Adams, 1973.
131. Williams, *Chronology of the Modern World*, p. 661.
132. *Encyclopedia of American Facts and Dates*, p. 655.
133. Raytheon Annual Report, Dec. 31, 1957.
134. *Encyclopedia of American Facts and Dates*, p. 607.
135. Ibid., p. 600.
136. Williams, *Chronology of the Modern World*, p. 665.
137. Interview, T. C. Wisenbaker, 1973.
138. Interview, Tom Phillips, 1973.
139. Raytheon Table of Organization, 1958.
140. Interview, Robert Hennemuth, 1973.
141. Interview, Harold S. Geneen, 1973.
142. Interview, Mrs. Percy Spencer, 1973.
143. Interview, Dr. Edward Turner, 1973.
144. Interview, Dr. Martin Schilling, 1973.

145. Interview, Harold S. Geneen, 1973.
146. Interview, Paul Hannah, 1973.
147. Interview, Charles Francis Adams, 1973.
148. Raytheon Directors' Minutes, 1958.
149. Raytheon Annual Report, 1958.
150. Williams, *Chronology of the Modern World*, p. 666.
151. Ibid., p. 667.
152. *Encyclopedia of American Facts and Dates*, p. 610.
153. Interview, Charles Francis Adams, 1973.
154. Ibid.
155. Interview, Harold S. Geneen, 1973.
156. Raytheon Directors' Minutes, 1959.
157. Interview, Charles Francis Adams, 1973.
158. Raytheon Directors' Minutes, 1973.
159. Interview, Charles Francis Adams, 1973.
160. Ibid.
161. Raytheon Directors' Minutes, 1959.
162. Interview, Norman Krim, 1973.
163. Raytheon Directors' Minutes, 1959.
164. Their opinions are unanimous.
165. Interview, Dr. Martin Schilling, 1973.
166. Interview, Charles Francis Adams, 1973.
167. Interview, Richard E. Krafve, 1973.
168. Interview, Charles Francis Adams, 1973.
169. Raytheon Directors' Minutes, 1959.
170. Ibid.
171. Raytheon Annual Report, 1959.


NOTES TO CHAPTER EIGHT

1. Interview, Norman Krim, 1973.
2. Interviews, Richard E. Krafve and Tom Phillips, 1973.
3. *The Encyclopedia of American Facts and Dates*, 4th ed., (New York: Thomas Y. Crowell Company, 1966), p. 618.
4. Interview, Mike Fossier, 1973.
5. Neville Williams, *Chronology of the Modern World: 1793 to the Present Time* (New York: David McKay Company, Inc., 1967), p. 674.
6. *Encyclopedia of American Facts and Dates*, p. 618.
7. Raytheon Directors' Minutes, 1960.
8. Ibid.
9. Interview, Richard E. Krafve, 1973.
10. Ibid.
11. Interview, Dr. Edward L. Bowles, 1973.
12. Interview, Richard E. Krafve, 1973.

13. Ibid.
14. Raytheon Directors' Minutes, 1960.
15. Interview, John M. Shaheen, 1973.
16. Harry Howe Ransom, *The Intelligence Establishment* (Cambridge, Mass.: Harvard University Press, 1970), pp. 128–29.
17. Williams, *Chronology of the Modern World*, p. 676.
18. Ibid.
19. Raytheon corporate records, 1960.
20. Williams, *Chronology of the Modern World*, p. 677.
21. Interview, Mrs. Percy Spencer, 1973.
22. Raytheon Annual Report, 1960.
23. Raytheon Directors' Minutes, 1961.
24. *Encyclopedia of American Facts and Dates*, p. 626.
25. General Maxwell D. Taylor, U.S. Army Chief of Staff, retired and issued a book *The Uncertain Trumpet*, making the point at considerable length.
26. The phrase is credited to Professor Moos.
27. Interview, Richard E. Krafve, 1973.
28. Raytheon Table of Organization, 1960.
29. Interview, Roger Damon, 1973.
30. Raytheon Directors' Minutes, 1960.
31. Williams, *Chronology of the Modern World*, p. 680.
32. Ransom, *The Intelligence Establishment*, p. 240.
33. Williams, *Chronology of the Modern World*, p. 680.
34. Ransom, *The Intelligence Establishment*, p. 206.
35. Raytheon Directors' Minutes, 1961.
36. Ibid.
37. Interview, Richard E. Krafve, 1973.
38. Ibid.
39. Interview, T. C. Wisenbaker, 1973.
40. Raytheon Directors' Minutes, 1961.
41. Ibid.
42. Ibid.
43. Interview, Fiore Gigliotti, 1973.
44. Interview, Tom Phillips, 1974.
45. Interview, Norman Krim, 1973.
46. Interview, Dr. Edward Bowles, 1973.
47. Interview, Richard E. Krafve, 1973.
48. Interview, Norman Krim. Afterward, Krim left Radio Shack, is now a management consultant, numbers Raytheon among his corporate clients.
49. Interview, Tom Phillips, 1973.
50. Ibid.
51. Raytheon Annual Report, 1961.
52. Interview, Carl Gilbert, 1973.
53. Interview, Tom Phillips, 1974.

54. *Encyclopedia of American Facts and Dates*, pp. 636–38.
55. Ibid., p. 632.
56. Raytheon Directors' Minutes, 1962.
57. Ibid.
58. Interview, Robert Hennemuth, 1973.
59. Interview, Al Miccioli, 1973.
60. Interview, Harold Hart, 1973.
61. Raytheon corporate records, 1962.
62. Interview, Tom Phillips, 1973.
63. *Encyclopedia of American Facts and Dates*, p. 640.
64. Ransom, *The Intelligence Establishment*, p. 97.
65. Ibid., pp. 147–48.
66. *Encyclopedia of American Facts and Dates*, p. 644.
67. Raytheon Annual Report, 1962.
68. Ransom, *The Intelligence Establishment*, p. 23.
69. *Encyclopedia of American Facts and Dates*, pp. 637–49.
70. Raytheon Directors' Minutes, 1962.
71. Raytheon Annual Report, 1962.
72. Raytheon personnel files, 1962.
73. Raytheon Organization Chart, 1963.
74. Raytheon Directors' Minutes, 1963.
75. *Encyclopedia of American Facts and Dates*, p. 650.
76. Ibid., pp. 651–52.
77. Interview, Paul Hannah, 1973.
78. Interview, Tom Phillips, 1973.
79. *Time*, August 10, 1962.
80. Interview, D. Brainerd Holmes, 1973.
81. Ibid.
82. *Encyclopedia of American Facts and Dates*, p. 559.
83. Ibid., p. 660.
84. Interview, Al Miccioli, 1973.
85. Raytheon Directors' Minutes, 1963.
86. Raytheon Annual Report, 1963.
87. *Encyclopedia of American Facts and Dates*, p. 662.
88. Raytheon Directors' Minutes, 1964.
89. Interview, D. Brainerd Holmes, 1973.
90. Raytheon Directors' Minutes, 1964.
91. Interview, Tom Phillips, 1973.
92. *Encyclopedia of American Facts and Dates*, p. 662.
93. Interview, Tom Phillips, 1974.
94. Interview, Charles Francis Adams, 1974.
95. *Encyclopedia of American Facts and Dates*, pp. 668–69.
96. Raytheon Annual Report, 1964.
97. Interview, Charles Francis Adams, 1974.
98. Synopsized from material prepared by the Amana colony.
99. Interview, George Foerstner, 1974.

100. Raytheon Directors' Minutes, 1964.
101. *Encyclopedia of American Facts and Dates*, p. 677.
102. Interview, Robert Hennemuth, 1973.
103. *Encyclopedia of American Facts and Dates*, p. 678.
104. Ibid., 680–87.
105. Raytheon Directors' Minutes, 1964.
106. Interview, Robert Hennemuth, 1973.
107. Interview, Mrs. Percy Spencer, 1973.
108. Interview, Robert Quimby, 1973.
109. Interview, Dr. Edward L. Bowles, 1973.
110. Interview, Hamilton Hauck, 1973.
111. *Encyclopedia of American Facts and Dates*, p. 681.
112. Raytheon corporate records, 1965.
113. Raytheon Annual Report, 1965.
114. Raytheon Corporate Records, 1966.
115. Interview, Joe Alibrandi, 1973.
116. Interview, Charles Francis Adams, 1973.
117. Interview, E. D. Wilson, 1973.
118. Raytheon corporate records, 1966.
119. Grolier *Encyclopedia Year Book*, 1967, p. 75.
120. Interview, Robert Hennemuth, 1973.
121. Raytheon Annual Report, 1966.
122. *World Almanac 1968*, p. 50.
123. Ibid.
124. Raytheon corporate records, 1967.
125. Interview, Tom Phillips, 1973.
126. Interview, Charles Francis Adams, 1973.
127. Interview, Robert Siegfried, 1973.
128. Interview, George Foerstner, 1973.
129. Raytheon Annual Report, 1967.
130. Raytheon corporate records, 1967.
131. *Reader's Digest Almanac, 1969*, p. 10.
132. Raytheon corporate records, 1968.
133. Professor Petrilli, also head of Italian Government IRI, quoted in the *Bulletin of the News Agency of the Chamber of Deputies*, Rome, June 20, 1968.
134. Raytheon corporate records, 1968.
135. Interview, Robert Hennemuth, 1973.
136. Interview, Mrs. Percy Spencer, 1973.
137. Ibid.
138. Raytheon Directors' Minutes, 1968.
139. Interview, Charles Francis Adams, 1973.
140. *Reader's Digest Almanac, 1968*, p. 25.
141. Raytheon Annual Report, 1968.
142. Interview, Charles Francis Adams, 1973.
143. Interview, Dr. Joseph Shea, 1973.

144. Interview, D. Brainerd Holmes, 1973.
145. Interview, Charles Francis Adams, 1973.
146. Interview, Frank Fox, 1973.
147. Interview, Tom Phillips, 1973.
148. Interview, Joe Alibrandi, 1973.
149. Interview, Tom Dahl, 1973.
150. Raytheon Annual Report, 1969.

## NOTES TO CHAPTER NINE

1. John Brooks, "The Go-Go Years," *The New Yorker*, June 23, 1973.
2. Raytheon corporate records, 1970.
3. He became president in three months.
4. Interview, Charles Resnick, 1973.
5. Raytheon Annual Report, 1970.
6. David Gumpert, "Aerospace Crisis," *Wall Street Journal*, March 5, 1971.
7. *The American Almanac*, U.S. Bureau of Census, 1973, p. 313.
8. Ibid., p. 6.
9. *Information Please Almanac, 1973*, p. 383.
10. *Prospectus*, Raytheon, June 30, 1971.
11. Interview, Robert Hennemuth, 1973.
12. A nuclear plant may cost $1 billion.
13. Raytheon Annual Report, 1972.
14. Ibid.
15. Raytheon corporate records, 1972.
16. Interview, Charles Resnick, 1973.

# INDEX

AADS-70, 344–45, 348

ABM system, 347, 348, 380, 394

Acme Delta Manufacturing Company, 62, 67

Adams, Charles Francis, Jr., 91–92, 187–189, 206, 207, 208, 209, 211, 214, 217, 220, 221–22, 223, 224, 228, 229–30, 233, 235, 236, 238, 240–41, 246, 247, 249, 252, 256, 259, 260, 261, 269, 270, 273, 280–81, 283, 287, 288, 289, 290, 292, 293–94, 299, 300–1, 307, 312–13, 314, 315, 323, 324–26, 327, 331, 334, 336, 340, 341, 345, 346, 349, 351, 354, 355, 359, 360, 362, 363, 364, 365, 369, 371–72, 373–74, 375, 377, 378–79, 382, 386, 395; background and early career, 176–77, 295–96; as director, 182; as executive vice president, 189–192; and Harold Geneen, 262–64, 266; and NATO, 295–98, 301, 310, 313; as president, 199, 202–3, 205; as vice president, 194–96, 197, 198

Adenauer, Konrad, 212, 240

A eliminator. See rectifier

Airframe, 197, 203–4, 212

Air power, 71, 72, 78–79, 84. See also Radar

Aldrich, Richard S., 14, 23–24, 25, 27, 80, 108

Alibrandi, Joe, 241–42, 282, 356, 360, 363, 381, 385

Amana Refrigeration Company, Inc., 351–54, 359, 368, 385, 393

American Appliance Company, 23–29, 34, 249

American Appliance Company (Indiana), 34

American Radio and Research Corporation, 34

American Radio Relay League, 123–24

American Research and Development Corporation, 6–7, 11–13, 15–17, 19–20, 25

American Telephone and Telegraph Company, 39, 48, 215, 232

Ames, John S., 24, 26

AMRAD. See American Research and Development Corporation

Amtorg, 41

André, Dr., 38, 44, 206

Antisubmarine defense, 297

Antisubmarine warfare research, 312

Antiwar demonstrations, 388–89

Applied Electronics, 292

Apollo guidance computer, 344

Apsey, Laurence, 205

Archer, Don, 342

Raye, William H., 182, 189, 262, 273
Raytheon A.G., 317, 331
Raytheon Annual Report: 1930, 56;
 1931, 58; 1933, 66; 1934, 73; 1935,
 74; 1936, 90–91; 1939, 97; 1941,
 118–19; 1943, 144; 1944, 154; 1945,
 170–71; 1946, 182; 1947, 194; 1948,
 205; 1949, 211; 1951, 232; 1952
 241; 1953, 249; 1954, 256; 1956, 268,
 272, 273; 1957, 282–83; 1958, 291;
 1960, 313; 1961, 326; 1962, 335;
 1963, 343–44; 1964, 351; 1965, 358;
 1966, 362; 1967, 369; 1968, 374–
 75; 1969, 382–83; 1970, 387; 1971,
 391–92
Raytheon Anti-Submarine Warfare
 Center, 312
Raytheon Canada, Ltd., 269
Raytheon charitable contributions,
 372
Raytheon Charitable Foundation,
 259
Raytheon Distributing Company,
 261
Raytheon dividends, 54, 141, 162,
 344, 351
Raytheon Electronic Components &
 Devices Division, 300
Raytheon Equipment Division, 215,
 248, 376
Raytheon Europe, 346, 364
Raytheon Government Equipment
 and Systems Division, 300, 336
Raytheon Lamp Company, 66
Raytheon Learning Systems, 385–86
Raytheon Manufacturing Company,
 35, 47, 49, 66, 249
Raytheon missile group, 300, 318,
 322, 332, 334, 341, 348, 350
Raytheon Missile and Radar Divi-
 sion, 259, 261, 272, 274–75, 284–
 85, 336, 344–45, 348, 373
Raytheon Operating Management
 Division, 283
Raytheon patents, 32, 66–67, 69, 173–
 74

Raytheon pension plan, 206
Raytheon Power Tube Division, 215,
 273
Raytheon Production Company, 49,
 66
Raytheon profits. *See* Raytheon An-
 nual Reports
Raytheon radar school, Nahant, 142
Raytheon radio tube. *See* S tube
Raytheon Receiving Tube Division,
 286
Raytheon Service Company, 363
Raytheon Space & Information Divi-
 sion, 336, 344
Raytheon special training center,
 372–73
Raytheon stock issue, 66, 83, 89, 154–
 55, 162, 171–72, 290, 295, 388
Raytheon taxes, 206, 232, 233, 241,
 313
RCA, 35, 39, 45–46, 48, 50, 53–54, 61,
 152, 184, 215, 216, 237, 261, 267,
 327, 339, 359; antitrust suit against,
 81, 84, 88–89
Rectifier, 38, 44–45, 68, 95, 255
Reed, Allen, 220, 249, 271, 315
Refrigerator, 21–22, 23–27
Renegotiation of contracts, 179, 186–
 87, 243
Resnick, Charlie, 238, 261, 289, 338,
 393, 394
Rheem Manufacturing Company,
 319, 322
Rheem Semiconductor Corporation,
 319
Riddell, Edward, 67
Ridgway, Gen. Matthew B., 71
Robertson, John, 162
Rodiman, Clark, 123–24, 126, 133,
 153, 174, 197
Roosevelt, Franklin D., 64–65, 67, 69,
 71, 79, 82, 83, 87, 93, 99–101, 104,
 116, 131, 160, 164, 192
Ropes, Grey, Boyden & Perkins, 69,
 81, 92, 206
Rosen, Harold, 225, 238, 245, 306

Russell Electric Company, 171, 188, 194, 205, 215, 233

Safeguard missile program, 348, 368
SAM-D, 348, 362, 394
Sanders Associates, 234, 239, 245, 250, 332
Sanders, Royden C., 152, 174–76, 189–90, 203, 224, 226, 227, 230, 231, 234, 239, 245, 252, 332
Sarnoff, David, 33
Schene, Arthur, 315, 327, 330, 338
Schiff, Col. Jacob, 26
Schenk, Peter J., 289
Schilling, Martin, 244–45, 250, 253, 268, 288–89, 296–98, 310, 328, 331, 336
Shockley, William, 206, 305
Schultz, Dave, 45–48, 59, 81, 85, 96, 127, 141, 154, 164, 187, 188, 191, 194, 197, 205, 206, 217, 220, 224, 243, 247, 249, 261, 262–63, 317
Seeker system, 175–76, 196–97, 212–13, 225–27
Seismograph Services Corporation, 360–61
Selenia, 310, 317, 331–32, 343, 346, 364, 378–79
SELIT, 329
Semiconductors. See Transistors
SG radar, 117, 118, 124, 126, 133–34, 136–40, 146–47, 148, 170, 172, 186
Shaheen, Lieut. John M., 146, 150–51
Shea, Joseph, 376, 379, 381
Sidewinder missile, 350
Siegfried, Robert, 366–67, 381–82, 388, 390
Silicon devices, 315, 319, 327
Sinclair, Harry, 26
Skitzki, Paul, 183, 288
Slepian, Joseph, 23
Smith, Al, 44, 64
Smith, Cap, 171, 187, 204–5, 259
Smith, Charles G., 6, 11, 15–17, 20, 31, 35–37, 50–51, 77–78, 85, 102,

Smith, Charles G. (*continued*) 237, 255, 290, 313; and refrigerator, 21–22, 23–27
Smith, John, 133
SO radar, 133–34, 140
Sorensen-Ard A.G., 332
Sorensen, France, 332
Soviet Union, 40–41, 49, 72, 76–77, 100–1, 103–4, 119, 131, 135, 138, 140, 157, 160, 165–66, 177, 192, 200, 201, 226, 243, 248–49, 260, 266–67, 270, 272, 282, 283, 332–34, 392, 394; and Korean War, 222–23, 227
Space program, 284, 306, 322, 328, 337, 338–40, 354, 362–63, 376, 379
Spanish Civil War, 80, 82–83, 97
Sparrow missile, 245, 251, 252, 253, 257, 258, 261, 267, 273, 275, 280–81, 306, 312, 333, 334, 340, 350, 394
Spencer, John A. (Al), 6, 11–15, 17, 33
Spencer, Lillian. See Ottenheimer, Lillian
Spencer, Percy, 33–34, 35, 36, 50–51, 54, 62–63, 72, 85, 88, 95, 108, 125, 129–30, 155, 167–68, 172, 185, 195, 211, 222, 225, 235–36, 238, 247, 249, 255, 259, 262, 264, 283, 286, 287, 288, 298–99, 314, 323; assistant vice president, 205; honorary degree, 220–21; magnetron, 112–15; marriage, 312–13; mercury rectifier, 68
Spencer Laboratory, Burlington, 298–99
Spencer Thermostat Company, 14, 17, 18, 19, 21, 22, 31, 37, 95
Sperry, 98–99, 175
Standing, Sid, 60, 77, 251, 287
Statz, Herman, 328
Sterling Cable, 332
Stevenson, Adlai E., 243
Stobo, John, 338, 364
Stock market crash, 1929, 52–57
Stoddard, Robert, 273, 314, 369
Stone & Webster, 366–67, 382

Wisenbaker, T.C. (*continued*)
311, 325, 327, 334, 356; head of Lab
16, 233, 234, 238, 239, 242, 245, 251,
252–53, 257, 261; head of missile
divisions, 330, 345–46, 348, 350;
Lab 16 missile projects, 189–90,
196, 203, 212, 225, 231; retirement
of, 331, 332, 376; as vice president,
300
Wood, Earl, 77
World War II, 103–4, 110, 116, 119,
121–22, 132–33, 145–46, 155–58,
159–61, 164–66, 238, 241, 243; air

World War II (*continued*)
raids in, 109–10, 115–16, 119, 143–
44; naval battles of, 127–29, 135–
39; radar in, 136–39, 149; Soviet
Union in, 119, 124; U-Boats in,
119, 125, 131–32, 138–40, 144–45

Yates, Lieut. Gen. Donald A., 331,
336, 344, 349, 351, 376

Zeta Puppis, 15, 32
Zwecker, Ashley, 62